# Modernism and empire

edited by
Howard J. Booth and Nigel Rigby

**Manchester University Press**
Manchester and New York

*distributed exclusively in the USA by St. Martin's Press*

*Published by* Manchester University Press,
Oxford Road, Manchester M13 9NR, UK
*and* Room 400, 175 Fifth Avenue, New York, NY 10010, USA
http://www.man.ac.uk/mup

*Distributed exclusively in the USA by*
St. Martin's Press, Inc., 175 Fifth Avenue, New York,
NY 10010, USA

*Distributed exclusively in Canada by*
UBC Press, University of British Columbia, 6344 Memorial Road,
Vancouver, BC, Canada V6T 1Z2

*British Library Cataloguing-in-Publication Data*
A catalogue record for this book is available from the British Library

*Library of Congress Cataloging-in-Publication Data applied for*

ISBN   0 7190 5306 4  *hardback*
       0 7190 5307 2  *paperback*

First published 2000

07 06 05 04 03 02 01 00        10 9 8 7 6 5 4 3 2 1

Designed and typeset
by Lucy Morton & Robin Gable, Grosmont
Printed in Great Britain
by Bell & Bain Ltd, Glasgow

*To my parents,*
*John and Jean Booth*
(H. J. B.)

*To Eileen*
(N. R.)

# Contents

# List of illustrations

# Notes on contributors

**Bill Ashcroft** is author and joint author of several books and articles on post-colonial theory, including *The Empire Writes Back* (1989), *The Post-Colonial Studies Reader* (1994) and *Key Concepts in Post-Colonial Studies* (1998). He is Associate Professor in the School of English at the University of New South Wales, in Sydney.

**Elleke Boehmer** is the author of *Colonial and Postcolonial Literature* (1995), the novels *Screens Against the Sky* (1990) and *An Immaculate Figure* (1993), as well as of numerous essays and articles on post-colonial writing and theory. She has edited *Empire Writing: An Anthology of Colonial Literature* (1998), and co-edited *Altered State? Writing and South Africa* (1994). In 1997 she was the recipient of an Arts Council of England Writer's Award. She is Professor of Postcolonial Studies at Nottingham Trent University.

**Howard Booth** is currently Lecturer in Nineteenth- and Twentieth-Century Literature and Culture at Birkbeck College, University of London. He has co-edited a special issue of the *D. H. Lawrence Review* on 'D. H. Lawrence and the Psychoanalytic' and is the author of a number of articles on nineteenth- and twentieth-century literature.

**Helen Carr** is a Reader in the Department of English, Goldsmiths College, University of London, and co-editor of *Women: A Cultural Review*. Her publications include *Inventing the American Primitive: Politics,*

*Gender and the Representation of Native American Literary Traditions, 1789–1936* (1996) and *Jean Rhys* (1996). She has written widely on post-colonial and feminist subjects and is at present working on a group biography of the imagist poets, to be published by Jonathan Cape.

**Rod Edmond** was born in New Zealand and educated at Victoria University, Wellington and Merton College, Oxford. He is Senior Lecturer in English and Director of the Centre for Colonial and Postcolonial Research at the University of Kent at Canterbury. His main research interests are in Romantic, Victorian and Modernist writing, colonial discourses and contemporary Pacific and New Zealand writing. Publications include *Affairs of the Hearth: Victorian Poetry and Domestic Narrative* (1988) and *Representing the South Pacific: Colonial Discourse from Cook to Gaugin* (1997).

**Máire ní Fhlathúin** lectures in Nineteenth- and Twentieth-Century Literature at the University of Nottingham; her main interests are in post-colonial theory and fiction. She has published on Rushdie, Kipling and Anglo-Indian history, works on early-twentieth-century Irish literature, and is assistant editor for the *Year's Work in English Studies* (New Literatures Section).

**Abdulrazak Gurnah** was born in Zanzibar, Tanzania. He was educated there and in England and now teaches literature at the University of Kent. He is the author of five novels, *Memory of Departure* (1987), *Pilgrims Way* (1988), *Dottie* (1990), *Paradise* (1994), which was short-listed for the Booker Prize 1994, and *Admiring Silence* (1996). He has edited two collections: *Essays on African Writing: A Re-evaluation* (1993) and *Essays on African Writing: Contemporary Literature* (1995).

**C. L. Innes** was born and educated in Australia, before going on to postgraduate study and teaching in Oregon, Alabama, and Cornell University in New York State. While teaching at the University of Massachusetts in the 1970s she was Associate Editor of *OKIKE* Magazine, an African Journal of Creative Writing edited by Chinua Achebe, with whom she has also co-edited two collections of African short stories. In addition to essays on African, African-American, Australian and Irish authors, her publications include *The Devil's Own Mirror: Irish and Africans in Modern Literature* (1990), *Chinua Achebe*

(1990) and *Woman and Nation in Irish Literature and Society, 1880–1935* (1993). She is currently writing a history of Black and South Asian writing in Britain. Lyn Innes is Professor of Postcolonial Literatures at the University of Kent.

**Janet Montefiore** is Reader in English and American Literature at the University of Kent. She has wide-ranging teaching and research interests in Victorian, modernist and postmodernist literature (both canonical and otherwise), contemporary poetry, women's poetry, and feminist and post-colonial theory. She is the author of *Feminism and Poetry* (1987, second edition 1994), of *Men and Women Writers of the 1930s* (1996), and of numerous critical essays, a selection of which is forthcoming from Manchester University Press.

**John Nash** is Lecturer in English at Trinity College, Dublin, where he teaches in critical theory and modern literature. He has published several essays on Joyce and is the editor of *Joyce's Audiences* for *European Joyce Studies*.

**Nigel Rigby** completed his Ph.D. on European writings on the Pacific at the University of Kent in 1995. He taught English at the University of Newcastle-upon-Tyne and is now Head of Research at the National Maritime Museum, Greenwich, where he recently curated an exhibition on Trade and Empire. He is a Contributing Editor for the post-colonial journal *Wasafiri*.

**John Salter** is Lecturer with the Arts Faculty at the Sunshine Coast University College in Queensland. His main research interests are in literary and cultural theory and Australian literature and cultural studies. His publications focus on post-colonial readings of Australian literary works, comparative literature, and the relationships between writing and regional cultures and societies.

**Mark Williams** is Senior Lecturer in English at the University of Canterbury, Christchurch, New Zealand. He has published widely on New Zealand, post-colonial and modern literature. Books he has authored, edited or co-edited include: *Leaving the Highway: Six Contemporary New Zealand Novelists* (1990); *The Radical Imagination: Lectures and Talks by Wilson Harris*, edited with Alan Riach (1992); *Patrick*

*White* (1993); *Opening the Book: New Essays on New Zealand Writing,* edited with Michele Leggott (1995); *Post-colonial Literatures in English: Southeast Asia, New Zealand and the Pacific, 1970–1992* (1996); and *An Anthology of New Zealand Poetry in English,* edited with Jenny Bornholdt and Gregory O'Brien (1997).

**Patrick Williams** is Reader in Critical and Cultural Theory in the Department of Literature and Languages at Nottingham Trent University. His publications include *Colonial Discourse and Post-Colonial Theory: A Reader,* with Laura Chrisman (1993); *Introduction to Post-Colonial Theory,* with Peter Childs (1998); and *Ngugi wa Thiong'o* (1999), published by Manchester University Press.

# Introduction

## Howard J. Booth and Nigel Rigby

Modernism and post-colonial studies are both seen in ways that have militated against the consideration of 'modernism and empire'. Accounts of literary modernism that crystallised in the decades after the Second World War did not mention the late colonial context, while post-colonial studies has often only sketched in its relation to modernism. Colonial discourse theory tends to end its analyses in the early twentieth century, while work on contemporary post-colonial issues usually begins with the widespread decolonisation that followed the Second World War: the literary texts examined are therefore early and foundational texts and contemporary writing. A few texts, in particular Joseph Conrad's *Heart of Darkness* and E. M. Forster's *A Passage to India*, have been used, especially in the teaching of modernism, to establish a peripheral theme of race and colonialism in the period. *Modernism and Empire*, though, is the first book-length study that seeks to explore the pervasive but complex interrelations between British colonialism and the modern movement.

For key figures in establishing what came to be called post-colonial studies – one thinks, for example, of Chinua Achebe and Edward Said – modernist literature was at once the near-contemporary established great literature of their early maturity and the father to be slain and overcome. Achebe's 1974 lecture on Conrad's *Heart of Darkness*, accusing Conrad of racism, raised a storm. He recorded the mixed reaction in a later essay: 'an elderly English professor had walked up to me and said: "How dare you!" and stalked away. A few days later another English professor said to me: "After hearing you the other night I now realize that I had never really read *Heart of Darkness* although I have taught it for years."'[1] There was clearly much resistance to introducing issues of imperialism and race into debate on this important 'early modernist' text,[2] but there was also force in Cedric Watts's response that pointed to the way that the text's narrative and themes are often anti-colonial.[3] Imperial man is shown in *Heart of Darkness* as dissolving in the new uncertainties and doubts of the period. Strong identifications held by the critics obscured what is remarkable about *Heart of Darkness* and, one wants to add, *many other* texts from the period, namely that colonialist tropes co-existed with the ideas and narratives that questioned, and in time helped to end, formal British imperialism.

The set of themes and issues for debate that cluster under the heading 'modernism', and that began to form after 1945, excluded empire. Major themes in the study of literary modernism throughout the world were Western-orientated and centred. Anglo-American modernism could be seen in terms of the influences from the nineteenth century, the adoption of developments from the Continent, the impact of the First World War, Marxist accounts which stressed the avant-garde attack on centres of power, issues of time – and even, amazingly, the consideration of space and 'Primitivism' – without mentioning colonialism. While no account of contemporary poetry and fiction would leave out writing in English from all over the world, 'modernist writing' from the period 1890–1940 is usually held to be an exclusively European and American phenomenon. In terms of historical understanding, while the synoptic histories on the bookshelf now stress world-wide forces, the understanding of literary history in English remains parochial. To take Eric Hobsbawm's books, the 'Age of Empire' goes down to 1914, thus covering most of the 'early modernist' period, and the account of the 'short' twentieth century is similarly global in its preoccupations.[4] The legacy of the founding period of the study of modernism, when 'international relations' meant relations between great Western powers, needs overturning.

*Modernism and Empire* explores the relation between British colonialism and literature. The years after the First World War saw the land occupied by the British Empire reach its maximum. Dissemination among the various colonising and colonised populations of the discourses that supported colonialism were also at their most extensive: the Empire was bolstered through new media, imperial ideas were stressed in schools, Empire Day was introduced, and millions went to see colonial exhibitions – though such efforts also suggest that the case for colonialism was now having to be made more strongly because of increasing doubts about the project.[5] After The Second World War, though, available literary-critical positions, for all the debate between them, colluded in excluding references to colonialism. The stress within certain forms of modernism itself on an aesthetic world that excluded the contamination by politics contributed to the wish of New Critics to avoid political questions. Among liberal critics the 'Winds of Change' in Africa and wider decolonisation made imperialism seem something from a guilty past, to be located firmly in certain minor authors and the adventure tale in the late Victorian period,[6] and not to be mentioned in respect of modernism. Post-war British identity increasingly disavowed the existence of the Empire, and so references to it in accounts of the literature of the pre-war period were few. Marxist analysis did not focus on the imperial issue, as there is often something inward looking about British Marxism, and many anyway held that the first focus had to be attacking the holders of capitalist power, before other 'marginal' concerns such as race and the colonial legacy could be addressed. The contention here is that colonialism needs to be considered in accounts of modernist writing, and that such a project also has much to offer the analysis of the structures of the following post-modern and post-colonial world.

The writing from the period when colonialism was both at its height and also exhausting its forward movement, coming under question and becoming untenable, was inevitably 'mixed': it is this complex utterance that the articles in *Modernism and Empire* seek to explore. It not just that a number of different political attitudes to empire are voiced in the texts of the period. Issues of whether it was complicit with or opposed to imperialism run deep, into the underpinning structures of thought, literary form, and language. Modernism can be seen as just part of 'modernity', which began (though this is of course debated) with the Renaissance and has only been critiqued, analysed, and perhaps surpassed by postmodernity in the late twentieth century. A major issue in the philosophy of modernity is the relation of self to other, and the power relations involved. The critique of modernity has involved examining how the modern subject was also an inherently 'colonising' subject. Couze Venn has argued that the subject in modernity has a constitutional instability that requires the 'other' to be at once present and subjugated. Seeing much theoretical work as pursuing this critique of modernity, Venn argues,

> The colonized becomes the object through which Western 'man' absolves and resolves himself. The conquest and mastery of otherness binds the one and the other, unites being into humanity. Violence is intrinsic to this project, epistemic (Derrida, Spivak), ontological (Levinas) and psychic (Fanon), adding to the brutality of conquest; together they collude to bend the other to that project. Western imperialism is the expression of this subjugative and subjectifying enterprise. It functions as proof of the power, righteousness and authority of the Western modern subject. Thus violence is not merely a contingent feature of Western civilization. It is, rather, its unspeakable dynamic.[7]

In this account, the modern – with modern*ism* at its end before the inauguration of postmodern critique – is saturated to its core with colonialist attitudes. This analysis, though, is one internal to the West – it also has to be asked how modernism appeared to those situated at the colonial margins, and how it might have been appropriated in the effort to establish national and post-colonial literatures. A number of articles in this volume take up that challenge, and Bill Ashcroft and John Salter, in their consideration of Australian art and writing, argue strongly that, since 'Modernity and modernism are rooted in empire', a total break from the modern movement now needs to be effected as its 'dissemination … consolidated the circulation of Eurocentric cultural power'.

Alternatively, modernism's place near the 'end of modernity' has led some to locate in modernism a questioning of attitudes to the 'other' and to colonialism. The argument is that more than an increasing liberal disquiet over colonialism can be seen in modernism, rather it is the true starting point of post-colonial critique. Michael Bell sees post-colonialism as just the rather intellectually vulgar afterglow of modernist analysis, though his book *Literature, Modernism and Myth: Belief and Responsibility in the Twentieth Century* (1997) shows the influence of recent post-colonial studies in its angle of approach to modernist mythopoeic writing. His argument attacking post-colonial studies can be seen when he reopens the debate on *Heart of Darkness*. He contends that a 'more inward understanding of modernism' than that shown by Achebe and Said in their writing on the text would demonstrate that 'rather than modernism being reluctantly disturbed by an incipient late-colonial conscience, although that is part of it, modernism was itself the means for a diagnostic understanding of the colonial mentality'.[8] Modernism, and its philosophical underpinning, had problematised the relation to the 'other', and found ways of producing texts that allowed for multiple voices and a respectful relation to alterity and difference. While, as a number of articles in this book maintain, a complex relation of the West to its 'others' is found in many modernist texts, there are severe problems with the sweeping nature of Bell's claim. There are many authors and texts from the modern movement that are extreme and violent in their attitudes to race and empire, rather than respectful and hybrid – and whether *any* author found a place wholly outside the dominant discourses of race and empire can be questioned. The politics and writing of a period do not necessarily share in its best thought.

What, though, was modernism's relation to politics? Is it reasonable to expect an artistic movement to change minds and attitudes? In modernist studies, these questions are usually addressed through continental Marxist theory, and debate on how avant-garde art can unsettle, disturb and produce change. Issues around modernist aesthetics, Marxist theory of modernism, and post-colonial studies (itself of course deeply indebted to Marxism) need more analysis than can be provided in a short introduction. Patrick Williams pursues these issues in his chapter on the theoretical issues involved in bringing together 'modernism' and 'empire'. One of the central questions of his chapter is whether or not modernist writing strategies can provide an edge against colonialism; his conclusion is that they can.

It is not only that issues of modernism and empire have been insufficiently addressed, but that the small literature that exists claims that the issues can be readily understood. The main (though short) text in the field is Fredric Jameson's essay 'Modernism and Imperialism'.[8] This article is not just a characteristic 'Jameson Raid' on post-colonial theory: he is the Rhodes of the affair. Jameson does not seek to begin debate but to end it. One of his earliest moves is to pull up the drawbridge on the modernist canon, and to exclude the literature of empire (he cites Kipling, Rider Haggard, Verne and Wells). In this model, writing and colonialism is seen as a minor subtheme: a comfortable and comforting view. With the 'literature of empire' goes the writing *from the Empire*, which is not even mentioned. He sees imperialism as registering not only on the content and themes of modernist writing, but on its very 'style'. The Marxist insight that economic conflict lies behind superstructural change leads Jameson to see the 'First World' subject after the Congress of Berlin in 1884 as feeling her- or himself to be part of a global economic and social system. However, at this time there was a silence where the voice of the different should have been. Modernism at the level of form reflects a sense of a gap between what it can say and what it feels the need to gesture towards. Jameson's main example is what he rightly admits to be a surprising choice, the 'closet modernist' E. M. Forster and his novel *Howards End*. At the end of his article Jameson argues that Ireland's unique status as near to Britain and yet also colony allows James Joyce in *Ulysses* the opportunity both to use modernist form and consciously to interpret issues of empire.

Although this is in many ways a ground-breaking essay, Jameson's argument is highly problematic. Modernism's relation to imperialism is forced into a single linear narrative of cause and effect. The good insights – for example, the relation of literary change to the globalising of historical and economic conditions,[10] or the relation of colonialism to the very form and language of the writing – are vitiated by the knowing, simplifying framework. Other forms of relation between the writing of the modern movement and colonialism are not addressed. Ireland's relation to modernism and empire is crudely oversimplified in this account: for example, Joyce's own consideration of these issues is by no means as straightforward and clear-cut as he suggests.[11] Jameson also fails to address how the colonial 'other' was for ever being spoken about and interpreted for the 'Home' population.

Perhaps most extraordinary of all is this confidence that there is no non-Western writing of note at this time. From within the British Empire, there is – as an initial list – the response to modernism in Australia, New Zealand, South Africa, India, the Caribbean and in writing in English from Arab writers.[12] Efforts to delineate different types of response to modernism could distinguish between settler cultures and those locations where there was another language and written literary tradition that predated colonialism. As a working hypothesis, it could be argued that Black Africa, with the imposition of the English language and a Western education a recent development, was an unlikely location for any writing that could be called modernist in form (which also assumes that African writers wanted to write in this way). But a hypothesis such as this has to be adopted tentatively by the metropolitan critic, and if it is an informed supposition it should be flagged as such, and not maintained easily and dogmatically as the truth about the 'other'. Jameson's intervention does not take the form of a contribution to debate; rather, it is framed as the distinguished theorist handing down the law.

All the chapters in this volume find many other concerns under the heading of 'modernism and empire' than those identified by Jameson, but two (related) issues to do with the psyche and otherness can be profitably identified here. Both late colonialism and modernism share many of the same structuring discourses, particularly concerns over the decline and decay of civilisation. Possible responses to collapsing certainties include working with a changing world, or fighting it with a compensatory extreme resistance. Questions of psychology, modernism and late colonialism are of great importance. Psychoanalysis, indeed, often equated its early development to exploration, discovery and colonialism – one thinks of Freud calling female sexuality a '"dark continent" for psychology'.[13] It is possible to argue that as the world map was coloured in by the occupying colonial powers, the last colonies were found among the new topographies of the psyche. Deleuze and Guattari argued in their *Anti-Oedipus* that 'Oedipus is always colonization pursued by other means, it is the interior colony, and … even here at home, where we Europeans are concerned, it is our intimate colonial relation'.[14] The modernist theme of anxiety and mental torment about the new uncertainties was closely bound up with fears around colonialism. Doubts gathered around the project of empire, whether it could be sustained or was nearing its end. Was the racial and colonial 'other' the barbarian at the door, to be resisted to preserve psychological security and cultural values? Or were they what offered an exhausted and tired West, its people and its literature a way out? Modernist writing often answered 'yes' to both of these questions – with important implications for the complexity of its subject matter, narrative form, symbolism and language.

After Patrick Williams's consideration of the theoretical issues raised by the volume, Rod Edmond examines degeneration theory, perhaps the major discourse that modernism and late colonialism share. Edmond also re-evaluates the relationship between the metropolitan centre and imperial margins in his discussion of Conrad's *Almayer's Folly*, *The Secret Agent* and T. S. Eliot's *The Waste Land*. The questions around the politics of modernism that Edmond addresses towards the end of his chapter are taken up by Helen Carr in her chapter on 'Imagism and empire'. Looking at the inception of high modernism in Britain she reopens debate about 'primitivism' and demonstrates the marked Irish and anti-imperial influences on innovative and radical poetry. While Carr examines the presence of empire in early modernism, Janet Montefiore raises the relation of Rudyard Kipling – supposedly the archetypal 'imperialist' writer – to the modern movement. She examines the representation of pedagogy in writing, moving from how British public school boys are given classical precedents for imperial rule in the short story 'Regulus', through Kim's induction into the mixed systems and values of East and West, to how these attitudes dissolve in the face of a modernity of power and force depicted in Orwell's fiction. Elleke Boehmer examines the potentially unsettling colonialist engagement with otherness in her study of Leonard Woolf, Yeats and Tagore.

A three-article section specifically dealing with Irish writing begins with a chapter by C. L. Innes on Yeats, Joyce and the implied 'double audience' for their writing. Máire ní Fhlathúin examines the writings of Patrick Pearse, the first 'president' of an independent Ireland, killed after the Easter Rising of 1916, in relation to modernism, while John Nash mounts a persuasive rereading of the 'Cyclops' chapter of *Ulysses*, examining Joyce's use of the anti-Parnell and pro-Imperial *Times* newspaper. Howard Booth's chapter examines Lawrence's changing attitudes to other peoples and cultures, particularly the supposed ability of the 'other' to provide a new start for Lawrence and for the West as a whole. In his chapter on the novelist, poet and short story writer Sylvia Townsend Warner, Nigel Rigby looks at her broadly anti-imperialist treatment of a missionary on a Pacific Ireland in *Mr Fortune's Maggot*, focusing on the relation between imperial discourse and sexuality.

Introducing the important theme in the volume of non-Western modernisms, Mark Williams explores New Zealand writing, looking in particular at Mansfield's relation to contemporary efforts to reconsider both the white Pakeha and the Maori traditions. Abdulrazak Gurnah looks at settler discourse in the Kenya of Karen Blixen and Elspeth Huxley. At the end of the volume John Salter and Bill

Ashcroft discuss Australian modernism in the arts in their wide-ranging chapter.

As this account suggests, efforts have been made in *Modernism and Empire* to register recent developments in work on modernism and in post-colonial studies. Authors outside the traditional modernist canon, links between 'high' and 'low' moderns, writing by women and non-Western texts are all examined. The relation of modernism and colonialism to *post*-modernity and the *post*-colonial is also thematised. In order to demonstrate the importance of issues of empire to a wide range of texts, there are no chapters that centre on *Heart of Darkness* or *A Passage to India*, though both texts are often referred to. While *Modernism and Empire* focuses on writing, where other arts had a key role in shaping the literary response – as happened with the visual arts in Australia – an interdisciplinary approach has been taken. The main area where modernism and post-colonial issues have been raised in recent years is Irish writing, and that lively area of debate is reflected here.

As many perspectives on colonialism and non-metropolitan writing from the time of modernism as possible are included – hence the pieces addressing Ireland, India, Ceylon (as it then was), Kenya, Australia and New Zealand. But complete geographical coverage is not possible in one volume. As already stated, British colonial experience alone is addressed – though it would clearly be a fascinating project to compare how the writing of the other European colonial powers related to imperialism. Further, while Anglo-American modernism is considered – hence discussions of Eliot and Pound – the volume does not deal directly with North America. The relation of American modernism to colonialism is a big topic. Houston A. Baker, Jr has questioned the assumption that modernism is essentially a white phenomenon, with the Harlem Renaissance a failed project to realise a fully modernist art. His political strategy is therefore to question and invert embedded cultural hierarchies.[15] Less well explored, though, is the relation of American writing to the global colonial context. At one level the rising stock of American literature in the modernist period adds to its status as the first successful, fully formed post-colonial literature to emerge. But the confidence of American modernist writing also reflects the fact that America – despite, for example, Woodrow Wilson's challenge to colonialism through his emphasis on self-determination – was becoming the powerhouse of a new form of capitalism and imperialism that would hold the old power differentials in place by new means. Colonial relations between rich and poor have been sustained by consumer capitalism and military power.[16] Canada's position in the modernist period as a dominion of the British Empire and a near neighbour of the United States make its literature particularly interesting. However, questions about Canadian modernism need to come with a full sense of that North American context.[14]

Some new work on modernism reaccentuates long established themes – such as the significance of the First World War, the impact of technological advances, or the influence on Anglo-American modernism of French writing. But over the last twenty-five years there have also been efforts to question the very definition of modernism. Work on gender and sexuality in modernist literature has transformed the area. The stress on 'high modernism' over other forms of writing has been questioned because of perceived elitism, and an unwillingness to acknowledge the growing force at the time of popular culture. Clearly focusing on empire's relation to writing can be said to add to those voices that have been calling for the analysis of multiple modernism*s*. There are dangers, though, in simply toying with the old term. The established arguments around modernism remain at the centre, while the new issues cluster on the increasingly crowded periphery. As the spatial metaphors here suggest, the imperial heart of modernist studies is one centre that has, so far, managed to hold.

## Notes

1  Chinua Achebe, *Hopes and Impediments: Selected Essays 1965–87* (London, Heinemann, 1988), pp. ix–x.
2  For the use of the phrase 'early modernism' to designate the period down to 1916, see Christopher Butler, *Early Modernism. Literature, Music and Painting in Europe 1900–1916* (Oxford, Oxford University Press, 1994).
3  Cedric Watts argues that Achebe had presented such a reductive assessment of Conrad's subtle technique, that he had entirely missed the fact that Conrad and Achebe were really on the same side in fighting imperialism. Cedric Watts, '"A Bloody Racist": about Achebe's view of Conrad', *Yearbook of English Studies*, 13 (1983) 196–209.
4  Eric Hobsbawm, *The Age of Empire, 1875–1914* (London, Weidenfeld & Nicolson, 1987); *Age of Extremes: The Short Twentieth Century, 1914–1991*

(London, Michael Joseph, 1994).

5 For empire and education, see the chapter 'Imperialism and the school textbook' in John M. Mackenzie, *Propaganda and Empire. The Manipulation of British Public Opinion, 1880–1960* (Manchester, Manchester University Press, 1984), pp. 173–97. Empire Day was introduced in 1904, and was held on the late Queen's birthday. Museums and exhibitions covering imperial themes have a long history in Britain and can be traced back to the eighteenth-century ethnographic collections built up by gentlemen scientists such as Sir Joseph Banks, and to the East India Company Museum housed in the Company's headquarters in Leadenhall Street in the early nineteenth century. The real beginning, however, is generally acknowledged to be the Great Exhibition of 1851, in which the colonies and dominions had their own exhibition spaces to display their own manufactured goods and products. The success of the Great Exhibition led directly to a series of clones in the second half of the nineteenth century specifically celebrating the Empire and colonies. In the period of modernism, the Empire Exhibition at Wembley in 1924–25 attracted a staggering eleven million visitors, and the dramatic exhibition posters by the famous war artist Gerald Spencer-Pryse were the genesis of the advertising campaign of the Empire Marketing Board (Stephen Constantine, *Buy and Build: The Advertising Posters of the Empire Marketing Board* [London, Public Records Office, 1986]). After independence movements gathered momentum after the Second World War, Empire exhibitions became unfashionable; recent attempts by museums to look again at the history of the British Empire have had a mixed response. A proposed Empire and Commonwealth Museum at Bristol has so far failed to attract sufficient funding, and the Raj Exhibition at the National Portrait Gallery in 1991 was accused, perhaps rather unfairly, of simply replicating Raj nostalgia. The Transatlantic Slavery Galleries at Merseyside Maritime Museum present a sordid aspect of imperial history with care, although the galleries were only made possible through generous private sponsorship. Despite considerable weight now being given to colonial issues in the British education system, institutions still feel ambivalent about displaying Britain's imperial past.

6 Patrick Brantlinger has questioned the way the impact of British colonialism on literature has traditionally been squeezed into the end of the nineteenth century. His study *Rule of Darkness: British Literature and Imperialism, 1830–1914* (Ithaca, N.Y., Cornell University Press, 1988) moves the study back earlier into the nineteenth century. *Modernism and Empire* moves the period investigated forward well into the twentieth century.

7 Couze Venn, 'History lessons: formation of subjects, (post)colonialism, and an Other project', in Bill Schwarz (ed.), *The Expansion of England: Race, Ethnicity and Cultural History* (London, Routledge, 1996), pp. 32–60. The quoted passage comes from pp. 42–3.

8 Michael Bell, *Literature, Modernism and Myth: Belief and Responsibility in the Twentieth Century* (Cambridge, Cambridge University Press, 1997), p. 149.

9 Fredric Jameson, 'Modernism and imperialism', in *Nationalism, Colonialism and Literature* (Derry, Field Day, 1988). Reprinted in Seamus Deane, Terry Eagleton, Fredric Jameson and Edward W. Said, *Nationalism, Colonialism and Literature* (Minneapolis, University of Minnesota Press, 1990), pp. 43–68.

10 For a sensitive consideration of the themes of space in the major post-colonial theorists see Laura Chrisman, 'Imperial space, imperial place: theories of empire and culture in Fredric Jameson, Edward Said and Gayatri Spivak', *New Formations*, 34 (Summer 1998) 53–69.

11 Whereas articles such as David Spurr's 'Writing in the *Wake* of Empire', *MLN*, 111 (1996) 872–88 claim that Joyce is pursuing some kind of pure anti-imperialist agenda, John Nash's chapter in this volume, focusing on the 'Cyclops' chapter in *Ulysses*, shows that the view of Joyce and Bloom as simply totally open-minded internationalists is unsustainable.

12 The last of these is the least well known, but see Geoffery Nash, *The Arab Writer in English: Arab Themes in Metropolitan Language, 1908–1958* (Brighton, Sussex Academic Press, 1998).

13 Sigmund Freud, *The Question of Lay Analysis, The Standard Edition of the Complete Psychological Works*, Vol. 20, ed. James Strachey *et al.* (London, Hogarth Press and the Institute of Psycho-Analysis, 1959), p. 212.

14 Gilles Deleuze and Félix Guattari, *Anti-Oedipus: Capitalism and Schizophrenia*, trans. Robert Hurley, Mark Seem and Helen R. Lane (Minneapolis, University of Minnesota Press, 1973), p. 170.

15 Houston A. Baker, Jr, *Modernism and the Harlem Renaissance* (Chicago, University of Chicago Press, 1987).

16 See Amy Kaplan and Donald E. Pease (eds), *Cultures of United States Imperialism* (Durham, N.C., Duke University Press, 1993). These questions are often addressed in terms of debate on 'Post-Americanist' and 'Post-Nationalist' writing, which is again often inward looking. See, for example, Donald E. Pease (ed.), *National Identities and Post-Americanist Narratives* (Durham, N.C., Duke University Press, 1994).

17 A particularly important writer here is Willa Cather: see Guy Reynolds, *Willa Cather in Context: Progress, Race, Empire* (London, Macmillan, 1996).

# 1

# 'Simultaneous uncontemporaneities': theorising modernism and empire

## Patrick Williams

> Modernism is not a positive slogan.
>
> Adorno, *Aesthetic Theory*

As Mikhail Bakhtin remarks in the closing pages of *The Dialogic Imagination*, 'Every age reaccentuates in its own way the works of its most immediate past',[1] and while all cultural movements or periods are always reaccentuated phenomena, reworked retrospective constructs, there is a paradoxical sense in which that is especially true of modernism, the would-be essence of the Now (rather than the Then). That remains the case even though modernism has obviously been more self-conscious than preceding movements, and hence more concerned with manifestos, programmes, and the like, which in part constitute the process – contemporary, rather than retrospective – of self-definition. As part of the continuing reaccentuation of modernism, the sections of this chapter address in turn certain preliminary questions; representative examples of the post-colonial reaccentuation of modernism; aspects of the mutual impact of modernism and imperialism; more complex models of modernism in the imperial context; and finally the locating of modernism in expanded concepts of modernity and imperialism.

The most significant, and arguably the most problematic, reaccentuation of modernism was the one that occurred after the Second World War, and established its dominant and enduring form. This was above all produced by (and for) modernism's institutionalisation in the Western academy, and is well enough documented not to require further elaboration here. An example of a more positive reaccentuation that addressed one of institutionalised modernism's constitutive absences was the highlighting of its gender politics, which represented a powerful and necessary reinstatement of the role of women writers, scandalously ignored in the original post-Second World War construction of the modernist canon.

At almost the same time as this positively oriented feminist re-working, postmodernism was producing modernism as its (ideo-logically necessary) antithesis, a reaccentuation which is currently perhaps the only rival to the institutionalised academic model for the title of dominant version. For postmodernism, modernism is mono-lithic and totalising (but also simultaneously selective and excluding):

> As an initial counter move, modernism is discarded by some critical postmodernists as a Eurocentric and phallocentric category which involves a systematic preference for certain forms and voices over others. What is recommended in its place is an inversion of the modernist hierarchy – a hierarchy which, since its inception in the eighteenth, nineteenth or early twentieth centuries (depending on your periodisation), consistently places the metropolitan centre over the 'underdeveloped' periphery, Western art forms over Third World ones, men's art over women's art, or alternatively, in less anatomical terms, 'masculine' or 'masculinist' forms, institutions and practices over 'feminine' or 'feminist' ones.[2]

As a preliminary note of caution about this type of formulation, it is perhaps worth asking, if the feminist critics are correct and there was a substantial female presence in modernism, in what way modern-ism as a movement (as opposed to the post-war domesticated and institutionalised construct) could be regarded as excluding women.

The reaccentuation of modernism that concerns us here is that which has taken place in the context of recent work in the field of post-colonialism.[3] This is perhaps the only area where anything like a sustained consideration of the relation of modernism and empire has taken place – empire being another of the constitutive absences of the institutionalised version of modernism. However, before looking at this post-colonial reaccentuation in some detail, it is necessary to address a number of basic questions which relate to this chapter and to the book as a whole. I take it to be the task of this chapter to offer a more or less theorised understanding of the relation between the terms of the book's title – theory being approached not as the master-discourse that will explain everything, but rather in the spirit of Stuart Hall's remark: 'Theory is always a detour on the way to something more important.'[4] In this case, the 'more important' which lies beyond the limits of the detour of this particular chapter is a comprehensive articulation of the intersections of the globalised formations of modernism and imperialism – and it needs to be made clear (despite any ritualistic feel this may have) that a title such as 'Modernism and empire' cannot possibly be taken as referring to singularised or homogenous entities, however they may be represented elsewhere. On the contrary, one of the difficulties of writing about 'Modernism and empire' is coping with the multiplicities involved (which is why some would prefer to homogenise them as much as possible). Even if we wish to retain a term like 'empire' (and problems undoubtedly follow from that, which will be addressed later), it is clear that even within one national variety, the British Empire, there were multiple forms of colonialism at work, as critics such as Nicholas Thomas have pointed out.[5] Modernism, of course, fractures along lines of national location, political affiliation and, above all, the range of movements routinely subsumed within it: Cubism, Expressionism, Dadaism, Futurism, Imagism, and so on. At the same time, it has to be said, modernism effects all kinds of connections across the different lines of division, and the complex relations of continuity and discontinuity it displays are an almost paradigmatic aspect of the broader social and historical processes at work in the modern period. Questions which then arise include: do these different modes of colonialism incite or inhibit different modes of modernism; and would the different forms, processes and practices involved mean that, for example, there would be a specifically white settler modernism?

There is also the problem of how precisely to – as Fredric Jameson would say – 'think together' these two terms, and chronology and periodising provide an obvious starting point, if not an altogether trouble-free one. Modernism has been given very different life spans by different critics: Peter Faulkner, for instance, allows it a mere twenty years (1910–30); while Bradbury and McFarlane in their well-known collection suggest twice as long (1890–1930). Even some of the most recent volumes concerned with rethinking modernism from different perspectives, such as Bonnie Kime Scott's *Refiguring Modernism*, or Alice Gambrell's *Women Intellectuals, Modernism and Difference*, will not grant it a life beyond 1945–46. As we will see later, however, the idea that modernism is finished is not the position of this chapter.

There is also the matter of whether this (longer or shorter) span is to be thought of in terms of radical difference from, or of types of continuity with, what preceded or followed it. Although the self-presentation of modernism (and a certain critical consensus) emphasises its break with the past, various forms of continuity have been argued for, linking backwards to Romanticism or anti-rationalist trends in nineteenth-century culture, or forwards, beyond the notional cut-off point of the re-emergence of realism in the 1930s. The 'end of empire' can be more precisely charted (formal decolonisation is fairly tangible), but exactly when the end began is still hotly disputed. In trying to align modernism and empire, one possible chronological model would, then, stress the final years of the nineteenth century as the moment of the appearance both of modernism and of 'high' imperialism (with the Berlin Conference, the Scramble for Africa, and the intensification of imperial rivalries), and 1945 as a point by which they had both, one way or another, lost credibility and run out of steam. That, however, is only one way of seeing the relationship.

## Post-colonial reaccentuations

If the institutionalised version of modernism has been regarded as a problem by many because it is depoliticised, or rather de-radicalised, modernism for numbers of post-colonial critics is a problem because it is seen as deeply complicit with, or at the very least parasitic upon, the power of empire:

> Modernism and the sudden experimentation with the artistic forms of the dominant bourgeois ideology, such as late nineteenth century realism, are themselves, in part, products of the discovery of cultures whose aesthetic practices and cultural models were radically disruptive of the prevailing European assumptions … It was this material [colonial 'loot' from Africa] which, placed on display in the early decades of the next century, was to inspire the modernists and encourage them in their attempts to create the images of an alternative and radically 'unrealistic' art.[7]

It is worth commenting on this in a little detail, since it both instantiates and informs a particular post-colonial perspective. The first point is whether modernism, even if it is viewed in terms of break rather than continuity, constituted such 'sudden' experimentation, as opposed to a process which had been emerging for some time. The second and more substantial point concerns the extent to which African and other colonial artefacts had a 'radically disruptive' effect on Europe. Part of the power of colonialism had always rested on its ability to absorb elements of 'alien' cultures (or even entire cultures) without thereby being fundamentally disrupted – otherwise it could not have survived. The model of colonialism with which *The Empire Writes Back*, from which this quotation is taken, and numbers of other post-colonial books work is certainly of a formidably incorporative system, assimilating cultural or other elements from around the world. The idea, then, that African carvings and other artefacts somehow managed radically to disrupt Europeans' outlook on cultural difference and their place in the world – rather than simply being absorbed into museum collections, their power nullified – is hard to square with the other assumptions. Arguably, it was only when they were moved from their 'safe' (because largely invisible) ethnographic context into the cultural mainstream – that is, when Western artists began to make them part of Western art – that they became disruptive as a result of their very visible incorporation. The moment of that incorporation also has implications for the model and dating of modernism being proposed. Ashcroft *et al.* suggest that, 'It was this material which, placed on display in the early decades of the next century, was to inspire the modernists.' If this colonial inspiration only began when modernism had, according to standard estimates, already been going for twenty or thirty years, then the idea that colonialism forms the essential ground for the emergence of modernism looks less convincing.

Stephen Slemon makes a similar argument for modernism being 'unthinkable had it not been for the assimilative power of Empire to appropriate the cultural work of a heterogeneous world "out there" and to reproduce it for its own social and discursive ends' – though unfortunately, since his article is principally concerned with postmodernism, he does not elaborate on how this is the case. However, he does go on to suggest that 'the modernist era is coming to be re-read not simply as the manifestation of a period or style but also as the representative marker of a *crisis* within European colonialism – as Edward Said has recently suggested'.[8] This offers a rather different perspective on the relation between modernism and empire, with the former functioning as the sign not of imperial power or confidence, but precisely of the loss of that confidence. However, the passage in Said to which Slemon refers does not necessarily support his contention:

> [Grand narratives] lost their legitimation in large measure as a result of the crisis of modernism, which foundered on or was frozen in contemplative irony for various reasons, of which one was the disturbing appearance in Europe of various Others, whose provenance was the imperial domain. In the works of Eliot, Conrad, Mann, Proust, Woolf, Pound, Lawrence, Joyce, Forster, alterity and difference are systematically associated with strangers who, whether women, natives or sexual eccentrics, erupt into vision, there to challenge and resist settled metropolitan histories, forms, modes of thought.[9]

The 'crisis of modernism' Said discusses can presumably only be seen as a 'crisis within European colonialism' to the extent that it is located within Europe, since Said gives no real indication that the impact on 'metropolitan histories, forms, modes of thought' throws colonialism as a system into crisis in any way.

There is also the question of whether modernism's Others as listed by Said are necessarily imperial Others. Leaving aside those writers such as Proust or Mann who are scarcely concerned with empire, the Other in Forster's work, for instance, is at least as likely to be Italian – and therefore, however belatedly, a member of the colonising elite – as colonised or non-European. (There is the additional problem that the vitality and sensuality of Italy are more disruptive of settled notions of Englishness than the 'muddle' of India.) Said's list of 'women, natives or sexual eccentrics' looks at least as much like the standard range of deviant Others against which societies posit their normative Selves as anything specifically related to imperialism, and of course the use of the threatening or challenging stranger as a means of constituting collective identity goes back a thousand years and more in literature. To make these points is in no sense to disconnect imperialism and modernism, but rather to suggest that influential examples of post-colonial reaccentuation of the relationship may not have found the best way of connecting them.

One of the reasons for post-colonial animosity towards modernism is no doubt the fact that post-colonial critics encounter modernism as already *in situ*, an institutionalised, would-be hegemonic, seemingly reactionary presence, and one which even in its self-reflexive moments appears obsessively concerned with the condition of the West.

However, why so many critics working in the post-colonial field, which, in the tradition of those other 'hermeneutics of suspicion', feminism and Marxism, prides itself precisely on not taking things at face value, have simply accepted that particular perception as the truth of modernism is something of a mystery. The ability of modernism to play a disabling or disempowering role (not least for those already disempowered), in addition to its appropriative one, is argued by Kumkum Sangari:

> As a cultural ensemble, modernism is assembled, in part, through the internalisation of jeopardised geographical territory – which is now incorporated either as 'primitive' image/metaphor or as mobile non-linear structure. Though intended as critique, such incorporation often becomes a means for the renovation of bourgeois ideology, especially with the institutionalisation of modernism. Ironically, the 'liberating' possibilities of an international, oppositional, and 'revolutionary' modernism for early-twentieth century 'Third World' writers and artists came into being at a time when modernism was itself recuperating the cultural products of non-western countries largely within an aesthetic of the fragment.[10]

Overall, this summary is persuasive, though certain aspects of it are problematic, for instance, the idea of modernism as 'the internalisation of jeopardised geographical territory' needs a great deal more explanation, given the widespread perception that the emergence of modernism coincides with the high point of imperial confidence and expansionism. Similarly, the institutionalisation of modernism may indeed have bolstered bourgeois ideology, but that occurred after the Second World War, and scarcely fits the chronology of the rest of the passage. Finally, if modernism was so thoroughly premised on appropriating the cultural products of other societies on the basis of the strength of imperialism, wherein lay its liberatory potential for Third World writers? One possible answer lies in the very terms of Sangari's criticism. The idea of the fragment was obviously important for some modernist authors, though fewer than Sangari suggests. For a critic such as Walter Benjamin, analysing the modern from within the process of its formation, the fragment, rather than constituting the sign of despair-inducing cultural collapse – most famously in terms such as Eliot's in *The Waste Land* ('These fragments I have shored against my ruin') – could, if properly (i.e. dialectically) analysed, offer the scope for revolutionary understanding and activity.

Both modernist writers and post-colonial critics could benefit from
a Benjaminian sense of the fragment: as marker of the discontinuous
nature of modern existence and the refusal to think of the latter in
terms of abstract generalities; as an example of the significant moments and nodal points of history (as opposed to continuist notions
of history as progress) which need to be brought into 'shocking'
juxtaposition with our own time; as a concern for disregarded or
'insignificant' objects and forms in opposition to great cultural mon-
uments and aesthetic canons; as a championing of the fragmentary
nature of memory as against the seamless narratives of dominant
historiography.[11] Importantly also for Benjamin, thinking dialectically
involved constantly developing new methods and insights to cope
with new material – a more politicised and theorised version of
Pound's quintessential modernist injunction to 'Make it new'.

## Reciprocal effects

An important aspect of 'thinking together' modernism and empire
is to consider the possible effects that each had on the other. At the
level of the material impact of empire on modernism, we have already
encountered the argument that the former provided the material
ground for the latter, first through the appropriation of non-Western
artefacts, and second through the presence of the Other in the
colonial metropolis. We have also seen some of the problems with
such an argument. At the level of ideology, we can see both pro- and
anti-colonial effects. Despite the fact that modernism is routinely
considered to be formed by, or complicit with, Enlightenment thinking, with its now unacceptable notions of (ceaseless, unilinear, teleo-
logical) progress, modernists in general have little time for the idea
that 'empire equals progress', which was so central to imperialism's
ideological self-justification. Nevertheless, the idea of cultural superiority, that 'the West is the best', surfaces in very different writers: in
Yeats, for example, in a late poem like 'The Statues', or in E. M.
Forster, in the remarkable short chapter in *A Passage to India* which
narrates Fielding's return to Europe. The fact that in both of these
cases the opposition is between Western form, order and beauty, and
Eastern formlessness as actual or potential threat to the stability of
that order, supports Said's contention regarding the operation of
ideology in a particularly deep-seated and persistent manner. Dis-

cussing what he calls 'latent Orientalism', as 'an almost unconscious (and certainly an untouchable) positivity', Said says: 'Whatever change occurs in knowledge of the Orient is found almost exclusively in manifest Orientalism; the unanimity, stability and durability of latent Orientalism are more or less constant.'[12]

In terms of anti-colonial positions, the awareness of what Terry Eagleton calls the 'performative contradictions' of ideology – the gap between rhetorical assertion and practical action – in the sphere of empire is clear to many modernists. It is also notoriously part of the contradictions of *Heart of Darkness* that the performative contradictions of colonialism are simultaneously highlighted, excoriated and, in so far as they relate to the British, palliated. There is, however, a sense in which a contradictory response to the performative contradictions of ideology is a logical consequence of the beliefs of some modernists:

> A novelist like E. M. Forster is perfectly capable of discerning something of the exploitative conditions on which his own liberal humanism rests, without thereby ceasing to be a liberal humanist. Indeed a guilt-stricken insight into the sources of his own privilege is part of his middle-class liberalism; a true liberal must be liberal enough to suspect his own liberalism.[13]

The impact of so powerful a formation as empire ought also to be visible in both the form and the content of the literary works of modernism. For Fredric Jameson, in one of the rare pieces which specifically connects modernism and imperialism, recognition of the mark left by the latter on the content of literature is on one level obvious, scarcely interesting. Of greater significance is imperialism's impact on the forms and structures of modernism, resulting in particular in a 'spatialising' of form, which is, among other things, an attempt on the text's part to tackle that recurrent Jamesonian task, the project of 'mapping the totality':

> But since representation, and cognitive mapping as such, is governed by an 'intention towards totality', those limits must also be drawn back into the system, which marks them by an image, the image of the Great North Road as infinity: a new spatial language, therefore – modernist 'style' – now becomes the marker and the substitute (the 'tenant-lieu', or place-holding, in Lacanian language) of the unrepresentable totality.[14]

At the same time, Jameson argues that empire hardly ever appears as the content of modernist works – a remarkable assertion indeed from someone who has written so memorably on Conrad. This looks like an inexplicable willed blindness on Jameson's part: the only literature he sees as offering accounts of the colonial process is 'the literature of imperialism ... (Kipling, Rider Haggard, Verne, Wells) [which] is by and large not modernist in any formal sense';[15] otherwise, the colonised Other figures only by its representational absence. Jameson's argument that the nature of the modern imperial system places particular limits on cognitive and representational scope is an attractive one, but does not necessarily work very well in his textual analysis. In discussing the 'closet modernist' E. M. Forster, Jameson concentrates on *Howards End*, rather than on *A Passage to India* (where his idea of a representative absence is clearly in danger), but offers the following comment in a footnote: 'About *A Passage to India*, what needs to be said here is ... that the novel is restricted to British and Muslim characters (Islam being, as Lévi-Strauss instructs us in *Tristes Tropiques*, the last and most advanced of the great Western monotheisms) the Hindus specifically designated as that Other are inaccessible to Western representation.'[16] Unfortunately for Jameson's argument and its rather worrying echoes of standard imperialist ideologies of the essential inscrutability or unknowability (here unrepresentability) of Asians, there is, at the very least the presence of Professor Godbole to disturb its narrative coherence. There is also, and more fundamentally (special pleading on behalf of Islam notwithstanding), the question of how Aziz and the other Muslim characters are not colonised Others – and represented as such – in the view both of the British in the text and of the British ruling the imperial system. Once again, this rather essentialised Hindu/Muslim split appears to repeat British imperial ideologies and government practices.

One critic determined to work against this (apparent) representational absence is Edward Said, his reading of Jane Austen's *Mansfield Park* being a classic affirmation of the determining, if often occluded, presence of the empire in texts whose attention is focused elsewhere. (Averted attention from the political is also of course one of the standard accusations against modernism.) Unlike Jameson, Said sees narrative representation of empire as a significant link between the moments of realism and modernism: 'Conrad, Forster, Malraux, T. E. Lawrence take narrative from the triumphalist experience of imperialism into the extremes of self-consciousness, discontinuity, self-referentiality and corrosive irony, whose formal patterns we have come to recognise as the hallmarks of modernist culture.'[17] One point on which Said joins Jameson is in regarding empire as having an impact on the form of modernist works, including a spatialising effect, though he interprets this very differently from Jameson. Whereas for the latter spatialising figures the attempted mapping of the restructured imperial world system, and is thus to be read as something like the product of Western success, for the former it is almost the reverse:

> When you can no longer assume that Britannia will rule the waves forever, you have to reconceive reality as something that can be held together by you the artist, in history rather than in geography. Spatiality becomes, ironically, the characteristic of an aesthetic rather than of political domination, as more and more regions – from India to Africa to the Caribbean – challenge the classical empires and their cultures.[18]

Whether or not many modernists actually pictured themselves heroically holding reality together through their artistic efforts, the question of metropolitan and imperial confidence, and of challenge or opposition from the colonised, is one to which we shall return.

The possible effects of modernism on empire can be more briefly dealt with. At the level of imperial governance, there is little indication that modernism influenced practices or policies (unsurprisingly, no doubt). At the level of institutions, there is the suggestion that modernism was imposed via the colonial education system, which would imply a high degree of ideological and aesthetic acceptability in the eyes of the governing classes, if not any obvious effect on the nature of the educational establishment. Ian Adam and Helen Tiffin believe that this was a deliberate strategy: 'For if "modernism" was imposed by England through colonial education systems, post-modernism and post-structuralism have followed, less openly perhaps, and therefore more insidiously, in its wake.'[19] At the level of ideology, modernism might be seen as potentially having more of a disturbing effect: imperial ideology speaks Western progress and expansion, modernism highlights multiple forms of dislocation, fragmentation and entropy; imperial ideology proclaims Western superiority, modernism alternately celebrates and mourns the decline of the West. Overall, however, the resistance of a system like imperialism to influence by an aesthetic/cultural movement such as modernism is hardly to be wondered at.

## Widening horizons: voyages in and out

As Raymond Williams importantly argued, part of the problem in analysing modernism is the difficulty – and necessity – of getting beyond the terms in which it defines itself and which routinely constitute the grounds for its examination, and thus anything which helps to break from the simple identification of modernism with the metropolis is to be welcomed. It is an irony which he would no doubt have appreciated that even an analysis as acute and attentive to detail as that of Williams can still be caught within certain ways of seeing modernism, if not within its powerful self-serving ideologies. He says, for instance:

> Thus the key cultural factor of the modernist shift is the character of the metropolis: in these general conditions, but then, even more decisively, in its direct effects on form. The most important general element of the innovations in form is the fact of immigration to the metropolis, and it cannot too often be emphasised how many of the major innovators were, in this precise sense, immigrants.[20]

Modernism is thus still viewed as the product of the Western metropolis and its immigrant intellectuals, rather than a cultural practice which might in fact be widely disseminated by those very imperial processes (social, cultural or economic) that, among other things, brought the immigrants to the metropolitan centre, and included what Said in *Culture and Imperialism* has called the 'Voyage In', where writers and other intellectuals journeyed to the imperial heartland, some never to re-emerge.

   Issues facing modernist writers generally, of affiliation (aesthetic, cultural or ideological), location (geographical, institutional, etc.) and address (audiences – real and ideal), take on a different cast in the context of the Voyage In. There is, for instance, the question of whether making the Voyage In necessarily implies affiliation with Western ideologies in general and those of modernism as elite cultural form in particular. In addition, the process of 'writing back' from the imperial peripheries, which has figured so large in certain kinds of post-colonial thinking, is rendered more complex, first because, rather than a necessary instantiating of colonial resistance, this may be no more than the non-metropolitan regions speaking in their own voices, regardless of the content or the actual oppositional nature of what is said, and second because that 'own voice' may at least be partly ventriloquising the most elite of contemporary Western forms. Whether such ventriloquising necessarily equals co-optation by Western ideologies is another question, and an appropriate answer needs to be based on an examination of the specificities of individual or national conditions.

There are also questions relating to the trajectory of modernism, either into or out from the metropolis. For example, how far are writers like Mansfield or Rhys who make the Voyage In bringing modernism with them, or are they coming to the imperial centre precisely to become involved in it? And to what extent does the empire 'export' modernism, either deliberately or accidentally? Although, as we saw earlier, Adam and Tiffin believe that there was indeed a deliberate attempt to export it, it is difficult to see how this might have been the case, except at the university level, and that involved so few colonial subjects – and arguably so little modernism. There is also the problem of what period we are talking about: with the post-war deradicalising and institutionalising of modernism, it becomes possible for someone like Ngugi in the late 1950s and early 1960s to study English Literature 'from Chaucer to T. S. Eliot with a touch of Graham Greene',[21] but it is hard to see colonial authorities prior to that doing any vigorous promotion of literature that was regarded as variously avant-garde, effete or subversive.

As suggested, one particular problem with all the generations of reaccentuation (including in part the post-colonial) is precisely the insistence on seeing modernism as a metropolitan phenomenon. What, however, the present collection, in common with some post-colonial work, makes clear is the need – in addition to the basic one of considering modernism in relation to empire – to confront the existence of a modernism from the empire. The collection discusses a preponderance of writing not from England but from Australia, New Zealand, India, Kenya and Ireland, among other places – and this is by no means the complete cartography of non-metropolitan modernisms. This type of reconfiguration, if correct, forever alters the map of modernism. However, the radical feel of this needs to be tempered by the recognition that it remains very much a white modernism, and that is one of the principal aspects of its incompleteness. Nevertheless, some critics would see this whiteness as appropriate. Jameson, for example, argues: 'Nor will it, from the point of view of the colonised, be of any interest to register those new realities, which are the private concern of the masters, and which a colonised culture must simply refuse and repudiate.'[22] Here 'the colonised' are the non-white populations, and the form of modernity which modernism instantiates is deemed to be of no relevance to them – though it is not clear why this should be the case. (This appears almost to be a case of – to misuse a contemporary slogan – 'It's a white thing – you wouldn't understand'; which, in view of Jameson's politics, is scarcely comprehensible.) What Jameson is looking for is a national situation which reproduces the appearance of First World social reality and social relationships – perhaps through the coincidence of its language with the imperial language – but whose underlying structure is in fact much closer to that of the Third World or of colonised daily life.[23] And he finds just such a situation in Ireland. Yet again, though Ireland is undeniably closer to the metropolis in so many ways, its difference from other colonies (except in epidermal terms) remains obscure: for example, English is as much the language of colonial imposition in Ireland as in India.

Another reason for the white-faced nature of this modernist configuration is the fact that this modernism from the empire was significantly based on 'the Voyage In', which, though it was not confined to them, was, for a variety of reasons, easier for white writers to undertake, and more generally comprehensible at the level of the hegemonic attraction of aesthetic ideologies and cultural formations. (This again raises the perennial issue of the affiliation of writers, as well as the political implications of their adoption of modernism.) A further reason for the somewhat skewed nature of this particular formation is that it represents modernism from the empire rather more than modernism in the empire.

An indication of the radical difference which changing that preposition might make is given in Iris Zavala's *Colonialism and Culture*, where, focusing on Latin America and the Hispanic Caribbean, she argues for 'the new historical poetics of modernism as sustaining narrative of anti-colonial struggle'.[24] With that sort of perspective, we are clearly a long way from modernism as the handmaid of colonialism. In particular, this suggests an entirely different political role and cultural dynamic for modernism. Instead of modernism as metropolitan imposition or cultural domination by the colonisers, there is the possibility of modernism as the collective resistance of the colonised, anti-colonial insurgency at the level of culture.

Zavala also suggests that 'The "voyeuristic eye" of the modern, which aestheticized every object, captured the icons of contending cultures (European, but particularly French) to introduce the heteroglotic world of the Americas.'[25] This offers a useful way of rethinking the modernism-as-appropriation model which was prominent in the post-colonial critiques examined earlier. If it is simply part of being modern to incorporate elements from other cultures, then potentially no more guilt attaches to European modernism than – in this case – to Latin American modernism, and the former looks rather less like a mere reflex of generalised colonial acquisitiveness. Clearly, different cultures are far from equal in the power they possess to acquire or assimilate elements of other cultures (this, for example, is part of the basis of Said's argument in *Orientalism*), but in Zavala's account it does not appear that the 'weak' cultures of Latin America had any special difficulty in taking from the 'strong' cultures of the West.

The image of a demonised, voraciously appropriative modernism is also challenged from a somewhat different standpoint by Adorno: 'Ever since the beginning of modernism, art has absorbed objects from outside, leaving them as they are without assimilating them (e.g. montage). This indicates a surrender by mimesis to its antagonist, a trend which is caused by the pressure reality exerts on art.'[26] The idea that modernism might possibly adopt something resembling an ethical stance towards 'alien' elements – making use of them but respecting their difference – clearly has not been taken up by post-colonial critics eager to assert the opposite. It remains, however, a suggestive possibility, especially in view of the way in which so many post-colonial critics have wrestled with the question of whether the relation of Self and Other (here figured particularly as the centre and the periphery, the colonisers and the colonised, or the West and the Rest) is ineluctably one of domination and appropriation of the latter by the former, or whether, for example, the ethical attitude towards the Other ('responsibility for the Other, being-for-the-other') proposed by Levinas offers a way out.[27]

## Modernism and imperialism: simultaneous uncontemporaneities

One of the few points of consensus in definitions of modernism is that it is 'the art of modernity', or that it constitutes 'a cultural response to modernity' – however modernity is understood, and whatever the form or content, political or aesthetic ideologies, which such a response might involve. Rather than thinking of empire as actively involved in the exporting or disseminating of modernism (which, as already noted, might be ideologically or politically suspect in the eyes of imperialists), we could see it as exporting (inevitably, if in some instances reluctantly) modernity. To that extent, as modernity becomes internationalised or globalised through the actions of the imperialist system, it would then be reasonable to expect modernism as response to match its spread. However, modernity has also been typically regarded as a Eurocentric or metropolitan-located phenomenon; thus the restricted perceptions of modernism remain hard to shift. Nevertheless, while modernity's Eurocentrism has often formed the grounds for attacks on it, that link is by no means inescapable: 'the association between the Occident and modernity has to be viewed as radically contingent in historical terms. If there is no necessary relation between these terms, then it follows that to oppose either one of them is not necessarily to oppose the other.'[28] This would mean for instance that modernity could be (hypothetically, provisionally) welcomed in the non-Western world, even as the precise form it takes in the West, or the West's way of promoting or exporting it, could be stringently opposed.

There are a number of ways in which modernity – as a state or condition, as a conceptual or temporal category – can be linked with modernism, colonialism and capitalism. One such is the expansionary dynamic which modernity, capitalism and colonialism are seen as possessing. Social theorist Anthony Giddens comments that 'Modernity is inherently globalising';[29] historian Immanuel Wallerstein notes the globalising tendency of capitalism – 'The historical development of capitalism has involved the thrust towards the commodification of everything',[30] a condition he regards as close to being achieved; and Edward Said, focusing just on what Eric Hobsbawm has called 'the long nineteenth century', traces colonialism's spectacular expansion:

> [I]n 1800 Western powers claimed 55 per cent but actually held 35 per cent of the earth's surface; and ... by 1878 the proportion was 67 per cent, a rate of increase of 83,000 square miles per year. By 1914 the annual rate had risen to an astonishing 240,000 square miles, and Europe held a grand total of roughly 85 per cent of the earth as colonies, protectorates, dependencies, dominions and commonwealths.[31]

An obvious question, then, is what relation exists between these expansionary dynamics outlined above. At the very least, there is the contemporaneity mentioned earlier in this chapter: the late nineteenth century, which is the period of such rapid colonial growth, is also one of intensified capitalist development and competition, as well as, for many commentators, the start of modernity (and the modernist response). The connections may, of course, consist of more than that. Jameson, for example, argues: 'That modernism is itself an ideological expression of capitalism, and in particular of the latter's reification of daily life, may be granted a local validity'[32] (though no doubt some literary critics would not want to grant any validity to opinions of that sort). Further, the link between colonialism and capitalism has long been acknowledged in some, predominantly but not exclusively Marxist, circles and rejected in others. One particular problem with the term 'empire' is that it is frequently and too easily taken to be synonymous with the period of colonialism, and the implication then is that the process to which it refers has come to an end. (This is one source of some critics' unhappiness with the term 'post-colonialism'.) Against that, one of the most useful insights to emerge from the nexus of anti-colonial and post-colonial theory is of colonialism as simply one period or stage in the continuing spread of imperialism, a process which did not end with the formal dissolution of the colonial empires, and one which is by and large synonymous with the global spread of capitalism. Straightforward identification of modernity with capitalism and imperialism certainly has its problems, however. In our immediate context, there is the danger of a kind of syllogistic slippage, whereby 'modernism is the art of modernity' becomes 'modernism is the art of capitalism' (as in the Jameson quotation above), and then 'modernism is the art of imperialism', which would return us to the 'colonialism produces modernism' position of *The Empire Writes Back* in an intensified form.

Modernism and modernity exist in complex relations with a third and arguably even more important term: modernisation. Social theorist Johan Fornas attempts to encapsulate this relationship: 'While modernity is the result of modernisation that provokes modernisms, modernity is also the condition in which modernisation appears, and of which modernisms are necessary constituents.'[33] In this, modernisation is an ensemble of economic, technological and political processes premised on change (though not necessarily rapid change); modernity is a state or condition characterised by fundamental ambivalence, and modernism is 'a heterogeneous group of collective ways of relating or reacting'[34] to the other two. These ways of reacting are also fundamentally ambivalent: modernism famously, or notoriously, both celebrates modernity and vigorously opposes it. In addition, in what Marshall Berman has called the first modernist text, *The Communist Manifesto*, Marx long ago poetically described the ambivalent nature of capitalist modernity, and also saw the same combination of lamentable destruction and necessary progress being brought to India by colonialism.

Many elements of this are, of course, well known in discussions of modernism. What is at issue here is the question of the persistence of modernism and modernity. The end of modernity has long been both called for and contested, from Ihab Hassan's cry 'When will the Modern period end? Has a period ever waited so long?',[35] to Habermas's famous assertion that modernity remains 'an incomplete project'.[36] While Habermas was seen as fighting a (losing, probably conservative) rearguard action against the encroachment of the postmodern, taken as signalling the end of modernism, younger social theorists like Fornas, who do not have the same stake in supporting modernity as the older generation, have continued to reject the notion either of a decisive break constituted by postmodernism, or of the demise of modernism and modernity. Fornas discusses various alternatives to postmodernity and concludes:

> Intensified, heightened, super-, reflexive or late modernity is a more relevant label for recent developments. This concept makes it possible to avoid the historical vagueness in an undifferentiated perspective on the whole modern epoch (which blinds us to the differences between the late eighteenth and the late twentieth century) as well as the self-contradictions of a 'post-modernity' (which is after all neither opposite nor subsequent to modernity).[37]

Recent studies of modernism concur, both with the idea of persistence and with that of intensification. Richard Sheppard, for instance, notes: 'The problematics of modernism are still with us, albeit in a more drastic form.'[38] Figure I sets out in tabular form the main dimensions of the modern. This is deceptively simple, given all the complexities involved, but does allow a ready sense of the interconnections.

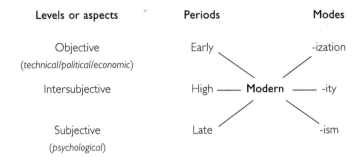

| Levels or aspects | Periods | Modes |
|---|---|---|

Figure 1   The main dimensions of the modern
Taken from Fornas, *Cultural Theory and Late Modernity*

Against the simple versions of linearity and succession which characterise so many accounts of modernism and post-modernity, Fornas argues that 'It is important to delinearise history, and search instead for its overlapping tendencies, forms and logics.'[39] This sense of significant historical overlap recalls Raymond Williams's influential model of the coexistence of dominant, emergent and residual social formations, or elements within a single formation.[40] If we further combine this with Elleke Boehmer's image of an internationally 'efflorescing' modernism,[41] then we have something like a version of the older Marxist notion of 'combined and uneven development' – here at the level of culture, rather than the economy – or, in Ernst Bloch's formulation, 'simultaneous uncontemporaneities'.[42] In this perspective, the related but different temporalities and trajectories of modernism and modernity (and imperialism) would be 'combined and uneven' within the same social formation, but there would also be simultaneous uncontemporaneities, in that while at a particular moment modernism might be fully developed in Europe, it might not yet exist at all in Africa, for example.

Figure 2 offers a speculative diagrammatic version of how the 'combined and uneven development' of modernism and modernity might look in this perspective: the continued trajectory of modernity and modernisation, with no postmodern break, but rather an intensification or upsurge in the second half of the twentieth century, and

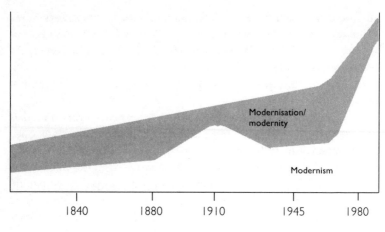

**Figure 2**    Combined and uneven development

the different pattern of modernism, with its later emergence, insti-
tutionally acknowledged peak and trough in the first half of this
century, and re-emergence in the shape of (post)modernism and post-
colonial modernisms. A 'combined and uneven development' perspective on modernism and imperialism would also want to register
the ways in which they display relations of continuity and discontinuity, both internally and, in this instance, between one another.
These would include, for instance, modernism's modes of connection
to and disconnection from imperialism in terms of geographical
location, political positionality, trajectory and temporality, as well as
its internal (dis)continuities: assimilated by or resisting modernity;
enormously assimilative in its turn, or isolationist and defensive. Such
a perspective also makes clear why, in the combined and uneven
context that imperialism offers on a world scale, modernity and
modernist responses to it emerge and subside at very different
moments, and with their own particular rhythms and according to
their own particular agendas – so that one reason for the somewhat
weaker or slower growth of modernism in the Anglophone Caribbean
would be the perceived political and cultural need for realism as a
more appropriate means of responding to the situation at that time.[43]
It is also important to keep in mind the extent to which the adoption
of realism or modernism remains a matter of choice and not simply

an automatic reaction to prevailing circumstances, since discussions of modernity and modernism frequently lose sight of human agency against the backdrop of powerful social and historical forces. As Fornas argues, however, 'People make moves in modernity which determine the direction it will take. Modernity is less a fate than a human product.'[44]

One of modernity's principal exports has been Westernised models of nationalism, national identity, and above all the nation-state; once again, imperialism in the shape of the colonial empires both promoted and resisted that process. For the last century or more, one of the most powerful ways for a particular group of people to constitute themselves as modern has been via the claim to national status (and of course it is not the least among the paradoxes of the nation that such a claim frequently involves the simultaneous claim or invention of millenial traditions and lineages). This assertion of absolute modernness and great ancientness is one instance of, in Bloch's terms, 'simultaneous uncontemporaneities'. It also has suggestive parallels with the way in which the would-be utter newness of modernism so frequently makes use of the ancientness of myth, or indeed the way in which capitalism relies on the (apparent) total novelty of the commodity to mask what Benjamin calls the 'ever-same' relations of capitalist production.

In our immediate context, the national introduces an additional element of tension or contradiction, in terms of modernism's relation to both political nationalism and aesthetic internationalism. One important aspect of that is the articulation of, for example, would-be separate and specific Australian or New Zealand modernisms in opposition to European versions, though that desire to localise, ground, or otherwise fix modernism is complicated by the unfixedness of the very modernists required to participate in pinning it down, epitomised in Katherine Mansfield's Voyage In to the modernist centre and refusal to be the figurehead of New Zealand modernism. There is also the irony that for some modernists – most famously Joyce, perhaps – the national is precisely the cause of their rootlessness, the very thing from which they are in flight.

If the Australian and New Zealand approach is very much grounded in the appropriation of Western forms to use against the West for nationalist purposes, an altogether different strategy of opposition is constituted by modernism in an anti-national or trans-national framework such as the Black Atlantic.[45] Here, for instance, the modernist aesthetics of European-based negritude draw together figures from the Caribbean and Africa, but also connect with the different modernism of the Harlem Renaissance, as well as the vestigial or emergent modernisms present in the Caribbean itself. The internationalism of Black modernism can be seen as the cultural counterpart (though not in any deliberate or instrumental way) of the political internationalism of movements such as the Pan-African Congress, which themselves draw on ideals of the Enlightenment or modernity such as freedom and justice (which are demonstrably not among the aspects of modernity being most enthusiastically exported) as the basis for their opposition to those societies at the heartland of modernity.

The relation of black peoples and cultures to modernity is clearly another area for further research, though it is one which has been waiting, indeed languishing, at least since the 1930s when C. L. R. James in *The Black Jacobins* argued that the slaves on the Caribbean sugar plantations had been living a 'modern' existence before the emergence of the European proletariats in the Industrial Revolution.[46] Extending this, Paul Gilroy has argued that a proper historical emphasis on the slave trade and black culture requires that the notion of modernity be fundamentally rethought. One of the necessary reminders in this narrative of the black dimension of modernity and modernism is the latter's scope for acting as both the ground and the vehicle for opposition, and Gilroy examines the way in which black expressive cultures can form, in Zygmunt Bauman's words, 'a counter-culture of modernity'. One further point to make here is that in the current era of globalisation, the age of the all-powerful nation-state has followed that of the all-powerful colonial empire into decline (though by no means extinction), without the end of imperialism or capitalism (or arguably modernity and modernism) being in sight.

The moves, in Fornas's terms, that people make in modernity include, as already indicated, resistance to modernity and, given the problematic relations of so many non-Western societies to modernity, the fact that modernism as opposition or critique is most alive in post-colonial writing should perhaps come as no surprise. In one of the rare articles to contemplate this kind of survival of modernism, Neil Lazarus discusses contemporary South African writing, following

Adorno in seeing modernism as resistant – above all to modernity. The decision to base such a discussion on Adorno might seem paradoxical or foolhardy, given his explicit rejection of the more overt forms of political or textual radicalism, the very ones which (variously) typify South African writing, but Lazarus uses Adorno to improve on Adorno. He says:

> Our task as cultural theorists today, therefore, becomes that of retrieving modernism from Adorno's evolutionary schema of modernity. This is particularly important for those scholars working on 'Third World' and 'minority' cultures, or on those cultures, like the South African, which find themselves suspended uneasily between centre and periphery.[47]

Against Adorno's grim vision of modernity as the all-encompassing 'administered world' and the culture industry, Lazarus goes on to locate those moments in Adorno where another, more helpful, possibility glimmers – which is in itself an ironic echo of the way that, according to Adorno, no oppressive system can completely extinguish the resistant possibilities of art – and to retrieve a more complex and conflicted version of modernity, like that posited by social theory. Adorno himself remains aware of fragile future possibilities, and in a work which Lazarus does not cite he has this to say:

> Art's Utopia, the counterfactual yet-to-come, is draped in black. It goes on being a recollection of the possible with a critical edge against the real; it is a kind of imaginary restitution of that catastrophe which is world history; it is freedom which did not come to pass under the spell of necessity and which may well not come to pass ever at all.[48]

This is a rich passage, with its strong echoes of Marx and Benjamin. It is also, in spite of its mournful cast, an image of (necessary) hope. The resistant potential of art, not least its negating of the conditions we inhabit, must be utilised: 'Art,' says Adorno, 'is the negative knowledge of the actual world'[49] (and this is one of the ways in which, as indicated by the epigraph to this chapter, 'Modernism is not a positive slogan'). In the context of the catastrophe which is world-wide capitalism, in the yet-to-be-realised realm of freedom which would be the (properly) post-colonial, the need for a critical modernism to provide 'an edge against the real' and resist by whatever means imperialist late modernity is as urgent as ever.

## Notes

1 Mikhail Bakhtin, *The Dialogic Imagination* (Austin, University of Texas Press, 1981), p. 421.

2 Dick Hebdige, 'Postmodernism and "the other side"', in David Morley and Kuan-Hsing Chen (eds), *Stuart Hall: Critical Dialogues in Cultural Studies* (London, Routledge, 1996), pp. 177–8.

3 As many readers will be aware, post-colonialism represents a complex and contested area of current work. For anyone not familiar with the field, the following may be helpful: Bill Ashcroft, Gareth Griffiths and Helen Tiffin, *The Empire Writes Back* (London, Routledge, 1989); Elleke Boehmer, *Colonial and Postcolonial Literature* (Oxford, Oxford University Press, 1994); Peter Childs and Patrick Williams, *Introduction to Post-Colonial Theory* (Hemel Hempstead, Prentice Hall / Harvester Wheatsheaf, 1997); Patrick Williams and Laura Chrisman (eds), *Colonial Discourse and Post-Colonial Theory: A Reader* (Hemel Hempstead, Harvester Wheatsheaf, 1993).

4 Stuart Hall, 'Old and new identities, old and new ethnicities', in Anthony King (ed.), *Culture, Globalisation and the World System* (London, Macmillan, 1991), p. 42.

5 See Nicholas Thomas, *Colonialism's Culture: Anthropology, Travel and Government* (Cambridge, Polity Press, 1994), for a particularly intelligent discussion of this.

6 Peter Faulkner, *Modernism* (London, Methuen, 1977); Malcom Bradbury and James McFarlane (eds), *Modernism* (Harmondsworth, Penguin, 1976); Bonnie Kime Scott, *Refiguring Modernism* (Bloomington, Indiana University Press, 1995); Alice Gambrell, *Women Intellectuals, Modernism and Difference* (Cambridge, Cambridge University Press, 1997).

7 Ashcroft, Griffiths and Tiffin, *The Empire Writes Back*, p. 156.

8 Stephen Slemon, 'Modernism's last post', in Ian Adam and Helen Tiffin (eds), *Past the Last Post* (Hemel Hempstead, Harvester Wheatsheaf, 1991), p. 1.

9 Edward Said, 'Representing the colonised', *Critical Inquiry*, 15 (Winter 1989) 222–3.

10 Kumkum Sangari, 'The Politics of the Possible', *Cultural Critique*, 7 (Fall 1987) 182.

11 See Walter Benjamin, *Illuminations* (London, Fontana, 1973), and *One-Way Street* (London, Verso, 1985).

12 Edward Said, *Orientalism* (New York, Vintage, 1979), p. 206.

13 Terry Eagleton, *Ideology* (London, Verso, 1991), p. 61.

14 Fredric Jameson, 'Modernism and imperialism', in *Nationalism, Colonialism and Literature* (Minneapolis, University of Minnesota Press, 1990), p. 58.

15 *Ibid.*, p. 44.

16 *Ibid.*, pp. 65–6.
17 Edward Said, *Culture and Imperialism* (London, Chatto & Windus, 1992), p. 227.
18 *Ibid.*, p. 229.
19 Adam and Tiffin (eds), *Past the Last Post*, p. ix.
20 Raymond Williams, *The Politics of Modernism: Against the New Conformists*, ed. Tony Pinkney (London, Verso, 1989), p. 45.
21 Ngugi wa Thiong'o, *Decolonising the Mind* (London, James Currey, 1986), p. 12.
22 Jameson, 'Modernism and Imperialism', p. 60.
23 *Ibid.*
24 Iris Zavala, *Colonialism and Culture* (Bloomington, Indiana University Press, 1993), p. 3.
25 *Ibid.*, p. 79.
26 Theodor Adorno, *Aesthetic Theory* (London, Routledge & Kegan Paul, 1984), p. 193.
27 Emmanuel Levinas, *Ethics and Infinity* (Pittsburgh, Duquesne University Press, 1985), p. 52.
28 David Morley, 'EurAm, modernity, reason and alterity', in Morley and Chen (eds), *Stuart Hall*, p. 349.
29 Anthony Giddens, 'The consequences of modernity', in Williams and Chrisman (eds), *Colonial Discourse and Post-Colonial Theory*, p. 181.
30 Immanuel Wallerstein, *Historical Capitalism* (London, Verso, 1983), p. 16.
31 Said, *Culture and Imperialism*, p. 6.
32 Fredric Jameson, *The Political Unconscious* (London, Methuen, 1981), p. 236.
33 Johan Fornas, *Cultural Theory and Late Modernity* (London, Sage, 1995), p. 40.
34 *Ibid.*, p. 38.
35 Ihab Hassan, *Paracriticisims* (Urbana, University of Illinois Press, 1975), p. 15.
36 Jürgen Habermas, 'Modernity: an incomplete project', *New German Critique*, 22 (Winter 1981) 3–15.
37 Fornas, *Cultural Theory and Late Modernity*, p. 36. Whole debates are here, as elsewhere, summarily reduced for want of space.
38 Richard Sheppard, 'The problematics of European modernism', in Steve Giles (ed.), *Theorizing Modernism* (London, Routledge, 1993), p. 42.
39 Fornas, *Cultural Theory and Late Modernity*, p. 33.
40 See Raymond Williams, *Marxism and Literature* (Oxford, Oxford University Press, 1977).
41 Boehmer, *Colonial and Postcolonial Literature*, p. 130.
42 Ernst Bloch, *Heritage of Our Times* (Cambridge, Polity Press, 1991).
43 Significantly, Simon Gikandi's interesting study of modernism and Caribbean literature, *Writing in Limbo* (Ithaca, Cornell Univesity Press, 1992), concerns itself with texts from the 1950s through to the 1980s.

44 Fornas, *Cultural Theory and Late Modernity*, p. 40.

45 See Paul Gilroy, *The Black Atlantic* (London, Verso, 1992).

46 C. L. R. James, *The Black Jacobins* (London, Allison & Busby, 1980).

47 Neil Lazarus, 'Modernism and modernity: T. W. Adorno and contemporary South African literature', *Cultural Critique*, 5 (1987) 153.

48 Adorno, *Aesthetic Theory*, p. 196.

49 T. W. Adorno, 'Reconciliation under duress', in Ernst Bloch *et al.*, *Aesthetics and Politics* (London, Verso, 1977), p. 160.

## 2

# Home and away: degeneration in imperialist and modernist discourse

## Rod Edmond

The subject of this chapter is the shared and mutually reinforcing influence of degenerationist ideas on imperialist and modernist writing at the end of the nineteenth century and the beginning of the twentieth. The importance of degenerationist ideas in imperialist thought is well documented. Their relation to modernism has been less discussed, and how this relation was inflected by imperialism hardly at all. The few attempts to do so have been flawed by a desire to find modernism either innocent or guilty of the charge of involvement with this often unsavoury way of thinking. I shall try and sketch a more nuanced account of the relation, mainly through a discussion of Joseph Conrad and T. S. Eliot. In the final part the chapter will broaden into a critique of Fredric Jameson's attempt to theorise the relation of modernism to imperialism.

In the 'Ithaca' section of Joyce's *Ulysses* the catechetical narrator intones 'the annihilation of the world and consequent extermination of the human species, inevitable but impredictable'.[1] This idea of the inevitable extinction of humanity had acquired particular and urgent meanings during the second half of the nineteenth century, putting new life into the time-honoured idea of historical decline and becoming associated with contemporary scientific theories of degeneration. The entangled relation of these three terms – decline, degeneration, extinction – and the connection they provide between imperial discourse, on the one hand, and modernism, on the other, needs to be outlined.

The idea that empires rose and fell was a commonplace. Macaulay looked back to Gibbon when in 1840 he imagined a future time when 'some traveller from New Zealand shall ... take his stand on a broken arch of London Bridge to sketch the ruins of St. Pauls'[2] (later represented by Doré, see Plate 1). This figure from across the world 'meditating on Time's ruins' is comforting rather than troubling. Macaulay's presumably European New Zealander (Britain had annexed New Zealand in 1840) can take over from where his forebears have left off. It is an imperial vision of cultural continuity underwritten from the colonial margins as much as it is a melancholy tableau of the end of British civilisation.[3] Even the prospect of the rise of black empires could be viewed with equanimity in the 1840s. In Captain Marryat's *Masterman Ready* (1841) young William Seagrave is given a history lesson by his father on the value of colonies, in which he learns that the Moors ('quite as black as the negroes') were once the greatest nation of their time, and that skin colour is no barrier to becoming an imperial power. Mr Seagrave can even foresee a time when Britain's greatness might be eclipsed by an African nation.[4]

Later in the century, however, the inevitable rise and fall of nations came to be regarded with less complacency. Although the parallel with Rome was frequently drawn as the British Empire reached its zenith and Victoria became 'Regina et Imperatrix' (under the 1876 Royal Titles Act), such analogising was double-edged. Seeley's *The Expansion of England* (1883) emphasised the might of Rome, but Froude's *Oceana* (1886) was more struck by the resemblance between English social decay and the late days of the Roman Empire. Racial theory, with its insistence on the purity and supremacy of Aryan races, implied the inevitability of decline as races and cultures mixed and reproduced. Its high priest Gobineau began his *Essai sur L'Inégalité des Races Humaines* (1853) with the sentence: 'The fall of civilisation is the most striking and, at the same time, the most obscure of all phenomena of history.'[5] After Gobineau the fall of empires was often emphasised, even as the British Empire reached its pre-eminence. The growing challenge from the industrial and imperial expansion of Germany and the United States further underlined the disturbing implications of comparisons with Rome.

Extinction follows logically from decline, and there was nothing new in the idea that humanity grew towards death. This truism, however, was bleakly confirmed in the later nineteenth century by

**Plate 1**   Gustave Doré, *The New Zealander*,
from Gustave Doré and Blanchard Jerrold, *London: A Pilgrimage* (1872)

developments in the biological, physical and human sciences. The great fear expressed by Tennyson at the heart of *In Memoriam* (1850) that no species was exempt from the universal law of extinction was confirmed by Charles Darwin. If the 1850s finally saw humanity knocked off its pedestal, the following decade brought fears about the permanence of the universe itself. William Thomson's theory that the earth was dying because the sun was cooling was widely discussed and accepted from the early 1860s until the discovery of radioactivity at the beginning of the twentieth century established a source of energy for the sun.[6] This enervated cooling sun appears frequently in later nineteenth-century French and British writing, in Flaubert and Loti, Stevenson and Wells, for example, and intensified the discourse of decline and extinction.[7] Thermodynamics seemed to offer a vision of universal history, and its second law – that although the energy in closed systems remains the same, these systems become more and more disorganised – an explanation for the apparently growing disorder of human society.[8]

A third ingredient was the widespread belief in the inevitable extinction of many colonised native peoples. Already current in the first half of the nineteenth century, this idea was reinforced by neo-Darwinian theories, which made it a natural law beyond the power of human capacity to prevent. This, of course, was profoundly ideological, substituting a natural process for the human violence of colonisation. It took many forms, from the decadent tragic exoticism of Pierre Loti's *Le Mariage de Loti* (1880) to the indifferent calculus of the chief accountant in Conrad's *Heart of Darkness* (1899). This recurring contemplation of the death of other cultures, however, also raised the prospect of the death of the writer's own. Stevenson pictured the last of the Marquesans huddled around the dying fire of life like 'old Red Indians, deserted on the march … the night round populous with howling wolves', and then elaborated the scene into one of universal extinction: 'I saw their case as ours, death coming in like a tide, and the day already numbered when there should be no more Beretani [Britain] and no more of any race whatever, and … no more literary works and no more readers.'[9] A complex dialectic was at work. This obsession of Western observers with the death of other cultures was, in part, a displaced expression of fear of the extinction of their own. But it was difficult to describe and track this process without being reminded of that very fear. Tennyson had looked at the fossil remains of simple forms of life and panicked. Something analogous happened when the West looked at its primitive others.

In the later Victorian period extinction was no longer just the final and remote destination of all cultures and empires but something more imminent and particular. The idea took on new force as various forms of degeneration – biological, physical, cultural, historical – were postulated and described. The spread of European empires during the nineteenth century was central to this process. One of the most vivid and repeated expressions of the fear of degeneration in colonial settings was the phenomenon of 'going native', of the European becoming decivilised in savage surroundings. Conrad's Kurtz is at the end of a tradition stretching back at least as far as *Robinson Crusoe* (1719). Defoe's hero is put into 'murthering humour' at the sight of the cannibal feast, and dreams of slaughtering the savages. Around this same time he witnesses the wreck of a European ship and mourns the loss of its entire company. The juxtaposition is plain. One 'fellow-Christian' would provide him with civilised companionship and innoculate him against the reversion to savagery, which the sight of it in its most extreme form, cannibalism, threatens.[10] The later rescue of Friday is emphatically a way of underscoring the line between civilisation and barbarity. Friday comes from the direction Crusoe is fearful of travelling in.

In this, as in so much else, *Robinson Crusoe* is a foundation myth. Nineteenth-century missionaries in Africa and the Pacific feared for themselves and particularly for their children. Would civilisation survive the encounter with its other? And if missionaries themselves could succumb to the call of the wild, how much more vulnerable were their offspring, whose only link with civilisation was through their exposed families. Missionary writing, particularly the correspondence, is tense with these anxieties. In Melville's *Typee* (1846) Tommo suffers from an unexplained sore leg, which repeatedly prompts his wish to escape the benevolent captivity of his hosts. This is not the ache of civilisation but the fear of savagery, a physical expression of the horror of losing one's civilised identity, which, as nineteenth-century colonial texts repeatedly demonstrate, was easily misplaced.

Fears of degeneration became medicalised towards the end of the century. Disease and infection were always a hazard for travellers, and home was a place to return to for quarantine and recuperation. This marked another of the borders separating civilisation from its other. But the *raison d'être* of empire was trade, and disease has always followed trade routes. The possibility of a free trade in disease as well as goods was widely discussed in the late nineteenth century. Leprosy was one focus of this concern. No longer a scourge in Europe, its visibility in many of Europe's colonies, combined with ignorance of its causation and transmission, provoked anxiety about its possible return. Books such as Henry Press Wright's *Leprosy: An Imperial Danger* (1889) appeared. Stevenson, who visited the leper colony on Molokai in the Hawaiian islands, saw it as a potentially lethal threat to the health of Europe: 'To our own syphilis we are inured, but the syphilis of eastern Asia slays us; and a new variety of leprosy, cultivated in the virgin soil of Polynesian races, might prove more fatal than we dream.'[11] Several of Jack London's Hawaiian stories express a more extreme version of this fear of a reverse invasion of the coloniser's body, of a bacteriological revenge for the dismemberment of a culture. Empires, it was feared, could bite back, infecting the hand that held the Bible, the gun and the dollar.

The late nineteenth-century city was another fecund site for theories of degeneration with a pronounced medical character. George Gissing's London novels of the 1880s, with their picture of urban life as a jungle in which debased and dangerous forms of life bred and proliferated, are a particular point of reference here. His rediscovery of 'darkest England' differed from the mid-century literature of the city in the emphasis it gave to genetic debasement, social contamination and the Social Darwinist naturalisation of urban life. Biological theories of decline were becoming the dominant form of social critique, and the body was increasingly used as a source of knowledge about society rather than as simply a rhetorical figure for it.[12] Gissing is no less trenchant than Dickens in his exposure of the condition of London, but his insistent translation of the social into the natural leaves him frightened or disgusted. Wherever he looks he discovers degeneration. Evolution has turned back on itself, and everywhere the worse is driving out the better. Much of this anticipates Conrad and Eliot's London.[13]

Correspondences were repeatedly drawn between the pathogenic environments of the modern city and its colonial outposts. Common to both was the increasingly medicalised and problematic imperial body. Daniel Pick has argued that as the whole social process came to be understood in organic terms, the condition of England question was redefined as one of the condition of the English body.[14] And William Greenslade has shown how the health of the masses, imperial strength and the fate of the nation became overlapping and over-riding concerns at the turn of the century. The occasion for this was the discovery of the poor physique of recruits for service in the Boer War, and the intense concern about the fitness of the nation this provoked.[15] It was at this moment that ideas of imperial and metro-politan degeneration came together in a generalised fear about the condition of the national body. This concern, however, was already present in the culture, ever alert to new targets. Degeneration had become, in Pick's term, 'the condition of conditions, the ultimate signifier of pathology',[16] multiform and ubiquitious, forever crossing the boundaries put up to segregate it from the fit. It became the place where metropolitan and imperial spheres met, and where concerns about home and away were most sharply focused.

The writer who bridges these *fin de siècle* anxieties and high modern-ism is Conrad, someone for whom the concepts of home and away were always problematic.[17] *Almayer's Folly* (1895) and *The Secret Agent* (1907), for example, represent both modern imperial centres and their colonial outposts as pathogenic environments, and establish a series of correspondences between these two settings which suggest that degeneration is the universal condition of conditions at the turn of the twentieth century. Oblivious to the boundaries set up to contain it, degeneration undermines both metropolitan and colonial spheres.

In *Almayer's Folly* the apparently optimistic universalism of the 'Author's Note', with its insistence on the common mortality of all people 'in houses or in huts, in the streets under a fog, or in the forests behind the dark line of dismal mangroves that fringe the vast solitude of the sea',[18] is undermined as Almayer's dream of a paradisal life in Europe becomes the nightmare of regression in the jungle. Married to a savage wife who, rather like Mrs Rochester, burns the furniture and destroys the curtains in 'unreasoning hate of those signs of civilisation' (p. 26), by the end of the novel Almayer's closest kinship is with his pet monkey, which 'seemed to have taken complete charge of its master' (p. 203). Involution has taken over, and Almayer has sunk back into 'the seething mass of corruption ... the death and decay' (p. 71) which underlies tropical nature. All those boundaries and categories which formed the basis of his understanding of the world have dissolved. His cherished mixed-race daughter, for whom he has secured 'Christian teaching, social education, and a good glimpse of civilised life' (p. 42) in Singapore, has been drawn back to the world of 'her betel-nut chewing mother, squatting in a dark hut, disorderly, half naked, and sulky' (p. 29); she rejects her father for Dain, 'the ideal Malay chief of her mother's tradition' (p. 64). The thunder has spoken (p. 19) and the jungle reasserted itself. In truth, Almayer and the debased civilisation he represents have nothing to offer her. His world is without foundation, and the 'one life' of the 'Author's Note' is shown to be based on the universal principle of degeneration.

*Almayer's Folly* dramatises a set of fears common to a great deal of colonial discourse in the nineteenth century, namely that civilisation is skin deep, that Europeans cut off from the roots that nurtured them are easily decivilised, and that native populations are ineducable. This prototypical 'heart of darkness' narrative has a long nineteenth-century pedigree. Andrea White places it alongside Benjamin Kidd's *Control of the Tropics* (1898), which argued against European colonisation on the grounds that the European races needed to be protected from contamination, but this is not just a *fin de siècle* fear.[19] It looks back to Robert Knox's influential *The Races of Men* (1850) and can be found in missionary writing in the early nineteenth century.[20] What is different about Conrad is not the idea that civilisation dissolves in the heat, but that it is a sham.

This absurdist view of metropolitan and imperial culture is explored more deeply in *The Secret Agent*, which draws together many of the ideas of decline, degeneration and extinction outlined above. As in *Almayer's Folly*, but viewed from the other end, the novel sets up a series of correspondences between London, the sunless centre of empire, and 'the Empire on which the sun never sets'.[21] These range from a passing but graphic comparison between capitalism and cannibalism which terrifies Stevie (p. 51), to the description of the remains of Stevie's body laid out on a table at Greenwich Hospital as resembling 'an accumulation of raw material for a cannibal feast' (p. 86). It also includes a more developed analogy between the Assistant Commissioner's police work in an unnamed tropical colony and his pursuit of the London anarchists (pp. 99, 150). Such comparisons are reflex to the Assistant Commissioner. The interestingly named Chief Inspector Heat, though impeccably Anglo-Saxon, reminds the Assistant Commissioner physically of a 'certain old fat and wealthy native chief' whose duplicity he once uncovered. This unlikely comparison is supported by an appeal to a similar resemblance recorded in Wallace's 'famous book on the Malay Archipelago' (p. 118), which Conrad much admired. Such comparisons provide an important outer context for the novel's overwhelming preoccupation with social and physical degeneration at the heart of Britain's empire. As the 'Author's Note' has it, London is 'a monstrous town more populous than some continents ... a cruel devourer of the world's light' (p. xxxvi), and therefore with some responsibility for the dark places of the earth.

The concern with degeneration and possible extinction in *The Secret Agent* takes different forms and is represented as coming from both without and within. None of the anarchists is British, and the plan to blow up the first meridian is the work of a foreign (Russian) power, yet London provides the setting in which disease and destruction can flourish. The novel opens and closes with the threat of viral infection. Verloc arrives 'in London (like the influenza) from the Continent' (p. 6), and the final sentence has the Professor passing 'unsuspected and deadly, like a pest in the street full of men' (p. 311). The extent of London's immunity to such infection is left disturbingly open.

The focus throughout is on bodies seen in various states of degeneration or disintegration. The physical oddity of almost every character described is marked. The novel is particularly concerned with obesity, as if the bloated anarchists are, like their bombs, threatening to explode. Characters who are not outsize are preternaturally thin or dimunitive. The Professor's tiny frame contrasts with the swollen anarchists and suggests the perfect detonator he is working to produce. His lamentable 'physical wretchedness' (pp. 62, 94), and implied impotence (the india-rubber ball in his trouser pocket is worked hard), are also set off against 'the vigorous, tenacious vitality of the Chief Inspector' (p. 94). These modes of description, although normally ironised, are also characteristic of the anxieties about population, degeneration, and the threat of the debased in *fin de siècle* writing about London.

This attention to the physical symptoms of degeneracy, and their troubling implications for moral and social health, is both sustained and undercut by Ossipon's Lombrosian discourse. The irony lies in the way in which the text uses an identical discourse to place and type the members of the anarchist group, not least Ossipon himself: 'A bush of crinkly yellow hair topped his red, freckled face, with a flattened nose and prominent mouth cast in the rough mould of the negro type' (p. 44). In this way the narrative simultaneously employs and satirises such modes of description and their cultural and ideological implications.

Late in the novel Ossipon's bush of hair is described as 'Apollo-like in [its] sunniness' (p. 309), the last of many signal appearances and disappearances of the sun at the centre of this Empire on which it is said never to set. In the novel's first set-piece description of London a bloodshot Coleridgean sun hangs low above Hyde Park Corner. Although 'punctual and benign', disturbingly it casts no shadow (p. 11). While it favours the prosperous habituées of the West End it never shows itself to the shady street in which the Verlocs have their shop (p. 258), and for Winnie, distraught over the death of her brother Stevie, it has gone out altogether: 'She kept still as the population of half the globe would keep still in astonishment and despair, were the sun suddenly put out in the summer sky by the perfidy of a trusted providence' (p. 244). This irregular shadowless sun, obscene as Ossipon's hair, offers no heat to London, which is compelled to generate warmth itself from the stuffy rooms in which Verloc lives and the anarchists meet, or from the chafing corrupt vitality of its ubiquitous Chief Inspector. Neither of these sources purveys much light.

This concern with the physical sources of heat, light and life is bound up with the threatened big bang of chaos and extinction which obsesses the Professor and blows Stevie to bits. Initially this takes parodic form in the account of how Stevie exploded fireworks on the staircase of the office where he worked, his quivering compassion having been raised to a frenzy by 'tales of injustice and oppression' told him by the other office boys (p. 9). Stevie shadows the anarchists, as both their dupe and innocent secret sharer. Ossipon's nightmare vision of the 'overlighted' Silenus Restaurant, 'changed into a dreadful black hole … choked with ghastly rubbish of smashed brickwork and mutilated corpses' (p. 67), anticipates Stevie's death on his way to blow up the Greenwich Observatory. This, in turn, is described in vividly disturbing detail. Stevie's body is 'a heap of nameless fragments' (identifiable only by the overlooked name tag) and its cannibalisation is underlined by the macabre but distancing comparison of the Chief Inspector to 'an indigent customer bending over … the by-products of a butcher's shop with a view to an inexpensive Sunday dinner' (p. 88).

A similar double-effect is achieved by the constable's grisly inventory of Stevie's bits and pieces: "'Look at that foot there. I picked up the legs first, one after another. He was that scattered you didn't know where to begin'" (p. 89). The Chief Inspector is soon reminded of such difficulties by the Professor, who is wired up to explode should any attempt be made to arrest him: "'But you may be exposed to the unpleasantness of being buried together with me, though I suppose your friends would make an effort to sort us out as much as possible'" (p. 93). These images of bodily dissolution into what Thomas Hardy, in his poem 'The Levelled Churchyard', termed 'human jam' express a much larger fear of social and natural dissolution that pervades *The Secret Agent*. Fragments of Stevie's body continue to fall in Winnie's vision of the scene in Greenwich Park, 'where after a rainlike fall of mangled limbs the decapitated head of Stevie lingered suspended alone, and fading out slowly like the last star of a pyrotechnic display' (p. 260).

The body in pieces, whether fragmented or mutilated, has often been used as a way of expressing a distinctively modern sense of the loss of wholeness and coherence.[22] This became marked around the turn of the twentieth century when biological theories of decline were increasingly applied to social theory, and the body itself became a source of knowledge about society rather than merely a way of thinking about it. This, in turn, intersected with the physics of Thomson, Maxwell and their popularisers, who had given wide currency in the later nineteenth century to ideas of dissipation, disorder and what was known as 'heat death' from a slowly dying sun. Together, these can be connected to the apocalyptic element which emerged in modernism and which is often seen as one of its defining characteristics.[23]

Conrad, however, is not apocalyptic in Yeats's, Lawrence's or even Eliot's sense, although he is closer to Eliot than to the others. His London will not end apocalyptically. The anarchists are bloated windbags, and the Professor is intermittently aware of the futility of his mission to 'destroy public faith in legality' (p. 81). Alone in the streets of London, the live atoms of his fissive project – its people – 'swarmed numerous like locusts, industrious like ants … pushing on blind and orderly and absorbed, impervious to sentiment, to logic, to terror, too, perhaps' (p. 82). This is not the stuff of revolution.

Yet if dreams of apocalypse are futile, a steady, perhaps irreversible, entropy is at work. The term itself was first proposed by Clausius in the late 1860s, and became entwined with other scientific theories of dissipation and disorder. Clausius argued that the entropy of a system is always increased by any transport of heat within it, and therefore that 'the entropy of the universe tends to a maximum'.[24] It is tempting to read the peregrinations of the Chief Inspector through the streets of London as one of several contributions to its entropic state. Its various agents, secret or otherwise, damage the systems they are there to preserve. The boundaries erected to safeguard its healthy sectors from the diseased are forever being transgressed. The great lady patroness's house is host to the Assistant Commissioner, Vladimir and Michaelis (policeman, foreign power and terrorist). The virus and the system are inseparable.

This is a one-sided account of *The Secret Agent*. The novel's irony resists, to a degree, its otherwise totalising vision. The blindly swarming mass of the streets provides inert resistance to the Professor's theories, and, rather like Pound's 'rabble/ Of the filthy, sturdy, unkillable infants of the very poor', in his poem 'The Garden', promises some kind of survival and inheritance. And Conrad, of course, is using these ideas as metaphors rather than laws. It is certainly not the argument of *The Secret Agent* that history is shaped by the laws of physics rather than by human agents. Jacques Berthoud, for example, has shown how Conrad's hostility to the post-Enlightenment dogma of rationality is expressed in this novel through the narrator's denunciations of science, and through Ossipon and Verloc's 'scientistic' incomprehension of human suffering.[25] Nevertheless, this hostility to the foundational claims of science does not prevent Conrad from using physical theories of entropy and solar decline to diagnose the signs of his times. Michael Whitworth makes the point that literature often scapegoats 'science' as representing mechanistic values hostile to 'imagination' while adopting its more imaginatively stimulating ideas.[26] This is true of *The Secret Agent*, whose meta-irony depends on meta-narratives derived from solar physics and human biology. And like other modernist texts it shares the tendency of its period to conflate the scientific with the social and political.

The threat to the imperial city of London comes from the east, from the Russian diplomat Vladimir, who is described as having 'guttural Central Asian tones' (p. 36), and the members of the anarchist group, who are mainly of Eastern European origin. In this *The Secret Agent* is drawing on a well-established tradition of seeing 'the East' as disorderly and threatening, a zone of racial strife and the clash of empires. Bram Stoker's *Dracula*, published in Queen Victoria's Jubilee year of 1897, vividly expresses this, linking otherness with imperial and urban degeneration through the subject of vampirism.[27] As Van Helsing remarks in the novel, vampires flourished in 'old Rome' and have followed the wake of the Hun and the Saxon,[28] thereby associating them with the fall of empires. Count Dracula comes out of Transylvania, in the Carpathians, a region then notorious for its polyracial character and cultural and imperial violence, and he suggests imperial decay both at home and abroad.

The Count invades London in an act of what Stephen Arata calls 'reverse colonisation', threatening its inhabitants with vampirism and deracination. Arata associates *Dracula* with other invasion-fear novels of the period such as Rider Haggard's *She* (1887), in which Queen Ayesha plans to sack London and depose Queen Victoria, and H. G. Wells's *The War of the Worlds* (1898). Although he distinguishes between invasion novels which focused on the threat from other imperial powers, dynamite novels which emphasised anarchist or nihilist activities, and reverse colonisation narratives which were obsessed with the return of the primitive or the atavistic, these were clearly related and overlapping categories.[29] Stoker's Count and Wells's Martians, for example, are both alien invaders threatening to take over London by targeting the bodies of its inhabitants. As Maud Ellman puts it, bodies in Stoker's novel 'are repeatedly pierced, punctured, and penetrated, generally in all the wrong places'.[30]

Predictably, the threat posed by the other is through sameness as much as difference. Dracula, as Arata says, is the most 'Western' character in the novel. His impersonation of an Englishman is faultless, and his invasion of London repeats and parodies British imperial practice abroad.[31] Lacking a reflection himself, he mirrors perfectly but monstrously the culture he threatens. The degeneration he represents so powerfully also finds its weaker double in the effete and vulnerable society he invades. Imperial and urban gothic feast on each other, becoming mutually parasitic.[32]

Eliot's *The Waste Land* is likewise concerned with the vulnerability of an anaemic culture to the destructive energy of those beyond its borders. The classic texts of high modernism are not usually placed alongside the more popular writing of the period, modernism's revolution in form having tended to camouflage its ideological affinities with very different kinds of writing. One of the few attempts at doing so is David Trotter's 'New Imperialist' reading of *The Waste Land*. Rather than reading Eliot's poem in terms of these 'crisis novels' of the *fin de siècle*, however, Trotter approaches it through a 'New Imperialism' which believed that the heart of empire was clogged and needed to be galvanised from the border where civilisation and barbarism met: 'The Imperialists believed that the vitality of the race could be renewed by journeys to the frontier.'[33]

Positioning *The Waste Land* alongside popular imperialist narratives which culminate in regeneration across the colonial frontier, Trotter argues that the poem's journey from London – 'the dead heart of the system' – to the frontier suggests the possibility of a similar regeneration. Although the landscape of 'What the thunder said' is most often read as dramatising a spiritual quest, much of it is built out of contemporary explorer narratives, Shackleton on South Georgia, Doughty's *Arabia Deserta* (1888), Conrad's *Outcast of the Islands* (1896). It is, therefore, not just a spiritual or psychological landscape but a frontier zone traversed by explorers, a landscape 'in its own right ... dark ... alien and glamorous'.[34] For Trotter, regeneration is implicit in the heroism of such narratives and in the frontier over which 'those hooded hordes' swarm. He neutralises the apparent threat of these invaders by assimilating them to the modernist celebration of apocalypse, via a passage from a letter of Lawrence's, written in 1916, exulting in 'seeing the hordes surge out of Arabia, or over the edge of the Iranian plateau'. Trotter argues that a 'similar excitement informs Eliot's contemplation of hooded hordes swarming over endless plains, down on to the broken towers of Jerusalem, Athens, Alexandria, Vienna, London. It is the frontier rather than the chapel which defines authenticity.'[35]

The more obvious, and plausible, reading of these lines is that the forces from over the border threaten rather than rescue authenticity. The towers are not already broken but 'falling'; this is a consequence of the counter-pilgrimage, or reverse colonisation, of the hordes rather than an invitation to rebuild. Associations with the fall of Rome are unavoidable, particularly given its significance in imperialist discourse of the time. Although Trotter acknowledges that Eliot's note to these lines refers to Hermann Hesse's *Blick ins Chaos* and the idea that the communist masses of the East threaten the cities of the West, this becomes lost in the idea of Eliot's shared excitement in the modernist apocalypse. The Eastern reference of these lines is unmistakable and significant. The 'endless plains' over which the hordes swarm were originally 'Polish plains'.[36] Again, I think, we are meeting the idea of Eastern Europe as a source of political and social contamination.

Of course there was a frequent regenerative use of other, so-called primitive cultures within modernism. Alignments between the high culture of Western modernism and non-European primitivism were, however, more common in European and North American than in Anglo-American modernism, a contrast I shall return to at the end of this chapter. They were most conspicuous in modernist painting and sculpture, where they were a matter of formal liberation and a celebration of 'the natural' over the artifice and redundancy of official bourgeois culture. Eliot sometimes echoed this use, for ironic counterpoint in 'Portrait of a Lady' for example, but not in terms of some Lawrentian cult of the primitive and the apocalyptic as Trotter suggests, and certainly not when contemplating the threat of Russian communism or other Asiatic disorders.

Within Anglo-American modernism, at least, there was always the problem of drawing on that which was felt to be threatening, dying or unassimilable. And Eliot's pessimism about the health of Western culture was a long way from Lawrence's frequent desire to smash it all down. Although the cultural thought of both writers has common roots in anthropology, something they share with other modernists, their relation to ideas of the savage or primitive was very different. As Robert Crawford puts it: 'For Lawrence, the savage world was authentic and admirable. For Eliot … it was horribly inescapable.'[37] Rather than the 'relation between Modernist apocalypse and Imperialist apocalypse' which Trotter proposes, I would argue for the relation between the imperialist and modernist obsession with degeneration at both the centre and margins of empire.

Trotter, in fact, also acknowledges this, and shows Eliot to have been familiar with the language and categories of eugenics which had done so much to formulate anxiety about the degeneration of the imperial race. He reads the contrasting encounters in 'A game of chess' between the upper-class man and woman, and the two working-class women, as an expression of the eugenicist fear that the worst were multiplying while the best were unable or refusing to reproduce.[38] There is ample evidence of this kind of ideological deformation elsewhere in the poem. The 'small' and 'carbuncular' house agent's clerk is a conspicuous example of the fear of genetic contamination by the physically degenerate but sexually active lower orders. This section, even more extreme in the Drafts of the poem, is not just an expression of class prejudice.[39] The poem's attention to the young man's physique is inflected by those concerns with the national body which recruitment for the Boer and First World Wars had prompted. His assault fails to arouse the typist but not the poem, which, for all Tiresias's long-suffering forbearance, reacts to such ill-breeding through the stereotype(ist)s of eugenicist discourse. All this, however, is a long way from either apocalypse or frontier regeneration. The 'hooded hordes' are no more revitalising than the 'young man carbuncular'. In terms of the discourse of degeneration, and the relation it provides between imperialism and modernism, they are different versions of the same fear. For both Conrad and Eliot, the long nineteenth-century fear that the European self dissolved or fell victim to its other the further from the centre it travelled has been compounded by the fear that an analogous degeneration was occurring at the heart of empire. Such fatty tissue, and its accompanying arterial sclerosis, had its counterpart in the moral and physical diseases of colonial outposts. Blood was no longer being successfully pumped to the extremities of the imperial body; infection, thriving at the extremities, threatened to overwhelm its vital organs. Centre and margins were locked together in a mutually reinforcing set of fears.

This would seem to leave me at odds with William Greenslade's excellent study, *Degeneration, Culture and the Novel 1880–1940*, which is intermittently concerned to defend modernism from the kinds of charge I have been making, and to establish its anti-degenerationist credentials. It would also seem to put me in the same camp as John Carey, whose *The Intellectuals and the Masses* Greenslade criticises.

Greenslade's is the more nuanced case. He argues, for example, that although Conrad used degenerationist concepts he did so to question the 'civilised normality' invoked to prove degeneracy; is there, Conrad asks, a defensible civilisation from which to speak?[40]

We have seen this in the case of Ossipon, and the point is more generally true. But we have also seen that Conrad makes serious use of degenerationist ideas to diagnose European civilisation and its discontents. Even when ironised, the language, categories and the anxieties they represent are central to the analysis and the prognosis. Eliot, too, was similarly troubled by the idea that there was no secure footing on which to base a defence of civilisation. Again, however, the problem of degeneration is analysed with its own concepts, becoming in the process self-fulfilling. Eliot's degenerationism, in fact, is far more blatant and less ironised than Conrad's, sharing as it does his period's eugenicist concern with the multiplication of the unfit, the involution of the lower classes, the debilitation of the national and imperial body and the decline of the west.

Like Conrad, Eliot was also influenced by the physical sciences and their analogous theories of decline and disintegration. His interest in Henry Adams's use of thermodynamics to underpin a social theory of growing disorder is well documented; the verbal explosion into 'fractured atoms' at the end of 'Gerontion' is one example of this.[41] 'Burbank with a Baedeker: Bleistein with a Cigar' is a related, compressed and repellent expression of this concatenation of ideas in Eliot's work. In different but related ways both Conrad and Eliot associated the savage with the urban, and the colonial with the metropolitan, in terms of degeneration and atavism. Greenslade, in rebutting Carey's sweeping accusation that modernism was a disdainful attempt to exclude the masses from culture, finally downplays the extent to which it was vitiated by degenerationism.

Carey's argument, on the other hand, has the deceptively seductive appeal of all single-cause explanations. It reduces a diverse and contradictory movement to a single determining position and then represents it as a calculated conspiracy. Carey mentions, but ignores, someone like Joyce who had a very different kind of cultural politics. He also mentions but ignores those criticisms of the dumbing down of mass culture made by European Marxists. The manipulation of ordinary men and women by a powerful and profit-hungry press in the early twentieth century was not the mere fantasy of a few alienated intellectuals with dodgy social ideas. The unfortunate, even repellent forms that some kinds of modernist reaction to early-twentieth-century mass culture took does not mean that there wasn't, and isn't, a problem.

Greenslade also makes the point that modernists themselves were the target of degenerationist discourse, their avant-gardism becoming subject to the kind of medico-pathological hostility we have seen directed at others.[42] Carey might well see this as rough justice. Certainly he provides ample evidence to demonstrate the complicity of many modernist writers in some of the most extreme forms of degenerationist discourse. One quotation from Eliot will suffice: 'the forces of deterioration are a large crawling mass, and the forces of development half a dozen men'.[43] But the point is that such discourse was far more inclusive than Carey realises. It was there, in the culture, waiting to be used by all and sundry. Modernism was tainted by it but not responsible for it. If Greenslade is mistaken, finally, in trying to separate the two, Carey's attempt to pin it on the modernists becomes reductive and obsessive. By concentrating almost exclusively on the high talk of modernists and Nietzscheans, thereby imitating the very practice he charges them with, Carey ignores the ubiquity of these ideas in the culture at large and their long nineteenth-century prehistory, developed through Victorian colonial discourse and science.

It should by now be apparent that any attempt to consider the relation of modernism and empire needs to avoid both a sharp temporal antithesis between the Victorian and modernist periods, and an analogous spatial antithesis between the imperial centre and its colonial outposts. Fredric Jameson's attempt to theorise this relation does neither.[44] Jameson sharply distinguishes the literature of imperialism from modernist texts whose structure and inner forms were marked by it. This, for example, would place Kipling and Eliot in opposed camps, ignoring recent work which has shown the important influence of 'the imperialist' on 'the modernist'.[45] Jameson also argues that imperialism in the late nineteenth and early twentieth centuries meant rivalry between imperial powers rather than the relation of metropolis to colony. In fact it meant both, but this narrowed definition of imperialism, in which the 'overriding ... consciousness of imperialism as being essentially a relationship between First World powers ... tended to repress the more basic axis of otherness, and to raise issues of colonial reality only incidentally' allows Jameson to posit an absolute polarisation of self and other.[46] It also allows him to argue that in the high modernist period the global space of empires became unrepresentable, except in the terms of imperialist adventure literature which, according to Jameson, was modernism's antithesis. Rivalry was substituted for exploitation and the colonised other rendered invisible.

His case rests on a passage from E. M. Forster's *Howards End* (1910) which is scarcely able to carry the weight it is asked to bear. The obvious counter-example of *A Passage to India* (1924) is dismissed in a footnote which assimilates all the Muslim characters to the imperial project and casts the Hindus as the authentic, unrepresentable other. The argument is not always easy to follow, putting me in mind of the 'kangaroo leaps' of Mrs Wix's discourse which so amaze Henry James's Maisie. Certainly, however, it ignores the diverse ways in which the 'unrepresentable' was repeatedly represented, and the different forms this took. It also continues to the very end to insist on an absolute separation between the imperial centre and the colonial margin, which is at odds with the by now extensive body of post-colonial theory Jameson acknowledges at the beginning of his essay.

In looking at degeneration, I have been arguing against this kind of polarisation and for a process of shuttling, displacement and sub-stitution in which the metropolis and the colony were in constant interaction. Jameson's 'master narrative', in which the imperial world system, having rendered national daily life incomplete, demands a compensating totality from which all colonised people are absolutely excluded, might well have been one of the forms this took within modernism.[47] This is no reason, however, to accept Jameson's own totalising account as the only or even the dominant form it took. His insistence that the representational dilemmas of the new imperial world system could only inflect modernism in this way is curious, and at odds with the texts, canvasses, scores and other configurations of modernism.

Jameson's exception to the representational impossibilities posed by the new imperial world system is Joyce's *Ulysses* (1922). This was because of Ireland's unique 'overlap and coexistence between ... two incommensurable realities ... the metropolis and the colony'.[48] In other parts of the Empire, 'the colonial subject will be unable to register the peculiar transformations of First World or metropolitan life which accompany the imperial relationship. Nor will it, from the point of view of the colonised, be of any interest to register those new realities, which are the private concern of the masters, and which a colonised culture must simply refuse and repudiate.'[49] Jameson, himself a sophisticated critic of vulgar Marxism, here stands guilty of vulgar post-colonialism. His assumptions about coloniser–colonised relationships are undertheorised and ahistorical, confirming the criticisms of this aspect of Jameson's work already made by Aijaz Ahmad.[50]

Put simply, Jameson denies that other colonies had cities, or that other colonised writers had experience of metropolitan life. Conrad the Pole was, of course, born a 'colonised subject.' A more flexible and nuanced understanding of the metropolitan–colonial relationship would also read Eliot and Pound as falling within its terms. Mansfield is another modernist who well understood the overlapping, not incommensurable, realities of both colonial and metropolitan city life, as Mark Williams has shown elsewhere in this volume. And this knowledge, experience and interaction was not restricted to the white settler colonies either. Ireland was not the only colonised society in which the otherwise 'incommensurable realities' of metropolis and colony coexisted, and hence the location of the only 'Third World modernism'.[51]

'Commensurability', anyway, is a far more complex term than Jameson allows. As used by Anthony Pagden, for example, it is profoundly ideological, a way of overcoming difference, of appropriating the other through what Pagden terms 'the principle of attachment'.[52] It had certainly not vanished from the mediating repertoire of colonial and imperial discourse in the early twentieth century, but was present and available for modernists to draw upon. The primitivist strain within modernism, found more in visual than written representation, was making good use of it at precisely the moment Jameson argues that the metropolitan/colonial axis of otherness had become unrepresentable. Gauguin is the obvious example.

It is nevertheless the case that Joyce's writing, unlike Conrad's and Eliot's, produces a modernist discourse of empire which resists degenerationism and myths of decline and extinction. Joyce's *Portrait of the Artist as a Young Man* (1916) scorns the rhetoric of eugenics,[53] the narrator of 'Ithaca' sees the end of the world as 'impredictable', and the concern with cultural difference in *Ulysses* has none of the anxiety manifested in Conrad and Eliot. It offers, instead, an inclusive vision expressed through its modernist techniques of multiple, contrasting and incomplete points of view. Eliot, by contrast, uses similar techniques for an exclusive vision of cultural decline and degeneration.

There must be many reasons for this. One would be Joyce's antagonistic relation to the cultural nationalism of the older generation of writers of the Irish Literary Revival. Another would be Jameson's point about the mixed (but not unique) metropolitan and colonial culture of Dublin. Yet a further approach would be by way of a comparative study of the different national forms of modernism. Anglo-American modernism seems to have been particularly concerned with degeneration and decline; indigenous North American modernism much less so. It was not only Joyce but also William Carlos Williams and Wallace Stevens who resisted or were immune to degenerationist ideas. One obvious explanation for this is the different stages of development between British and United States imperialism at the beginning of the twentieth century. Relatively speaking, one was declining, the other confidently expanding; one carried its history of shame with it, the other had most of it still to come.

As an urbanising colony with a vital literary culture of its own, Ireland shared some cultural characteristics with the United States. Lacking independence, however, it was not able to celebrate its indigeneity in the manner of Williams's or Stevens's early poetry. *Ulysses*, of course, is haunted by synthetic and inauthentic versions of this. It is able, nevertheless, to end with a 'Yes', not a whimper. More wholeheartedly, Stevens in 'Ploughing North America' can burst into 'Tum-ti-tum/ Ti-tum-tum-tum!' rather than the self-mockery and '"false note"' of Eliot's 'dull tom-tom'. The language of disintegration, contamination and disease is much less marked in Joyce, Stevens and Williams than in Conrad, Eliot and Pound. 'Yes' is not to be found in Eliot's lexicon; 'Spring and all' moves past the 'contagious hospital' to contemplate the imminent 'stiff curl of wildcarrot leaf'; nobody is exuberantly ploughing Europe; there is only the digging of trenches.

To sum up: I have argued that although modernism was a metropolitan phenomenon, it drew on the outposts of empire. The 'empty cisterns and exhausted wells' of Europe needed replenishment, but what flowed in from outside was unsettling, untreated and possibly contaminating. The disturbing implications of this suspect relief were registered and analysed in representations of the metropolitan city, which came to be seen in terms of the kinds of physical, moral and social collapse typical of the representation of colonial environments. Common to both was the threat to hierarchy, whether from visible forms of ethnic and class-based challenge in colonised territories and the cities of Europe, or the more secret agents of degeneration discussed in this chapter. One of the threatened hierarchies was that of European culture itself, whose terminal condition modernists diagnosed and mourned. In this way the culture of modernism became entwined with the politics of imperialism.

## Notes

I would like to thank Keith Carabine for his comments on the Conrad section of this essay, and for helping to clear a path through the thicket of Conrad scholarship.

1  James Joyce, *Ulysses*, ed. Declan Kiberd (Harmondsworth, Penguin, 1992), p. 794.

2  T. B. Macaulay, 'Von Ranke', *Critical and Historical Essays*, vol. 3 (London, Longman, 1862), p. 101. The specific point Macaulay was making was that the Catholic Church would survive even such general ruin; see Nancy Aycock Metz, '*Little Dorrit*'s London: Babylon revisited', *Victorian Studies*, 33:3 (1990) 481.

3  James Belich, *Making Peoples: A History of the New Zealanders from Polynesian Settlement to the End of the Nineteenth Century* (Auckland, Allen Lane, 1996), pp. 297–8 and n. discusses the recurrence of this trope in British culture. He asserts, on what basis is unclear, that Macaulay thought of his New Zealander as Maori.

4  Captain Marryat, *Masterman Ready, or The Wreck of the Pacific* (London, Macmillan, 1841), p. 117.

5  In Patrick Brantlinger, *Bread and Circuses: Theories of Mass Culture as Social Decay* (Ithaca and London, Cornell University Press, 1983), p. 142; see also Raymond F. Betts, 'The allusion to Rome in British imperialist thought of the late nineteenth and early twentieth centuries', *Victorian Studies*, 15:2 (1971), and William Greenslade, *Degeneration, Culture and the Novel 1880–1940* (Cambridge, Cambridge University Press, 1994), p. 30.

6  See Crosbie Smith and M. Norton Wise, *Energy and Empire: A Biographical Study of Lord Kelvin* (Cambridge, Cambridge University Press, 1989); Gillian Beer, '"The Death of the Sun": Victorian solar physics and solar theory', in *Open Fields: Science in Cultural Encounter* (Oxford, Clarendon Press, 1996).

7  See Daniel Pick, *Faces of Degeneration: A European Disorder, c.1848–c.1918* (Cambridge, Cambridge University Press, 1989), pp. 1, 160, 209; Rod Edmond, *Representing the South Pacific: Colonial Discourse from Cook to Gauguin* (Cambridge, Cambridge University Press, 1997), pp. 165–6, 245–6.

8  See Greg Myers, 'Nineteenth-century popularisations of thermodynamics and the rhetoric of social prophecy', in Patrick Brantlinger (ed.),

*Energy and Entropy: Science and Culture in Victorian Britain* (Bloomington and Indianapolis, Indiana University Press, 1989), pp. 308, 311.

9   Robert Louis Stevenson, *In the South Seas*, in *The Works of Robert Louis Stevenson*, Pentland Edition (London, Cassell, 1907), vol. 17, pp. 34, 42.

10   Daniel Defoe, *The Life and Adventures of Robinson Crusoe* (Harmondsworth, Penguin Books, 1978), pp. 189, 190, 193.

11   A. Grove Day (ed.), *Travels in Hawaii: Robert Louis Stevenson* (Honolulu, University of Hawaii Press, 1973), p. 84.

12   Pick, *Faces of Degeneration*, pp. 5, 180.

13   Gissing's novel *The Unclassed* (1884) has a figure called Slimy, whose 'thick, grizzled hair' obscures 'almost every vestige of feature, with the exception of one dreadful red eye, its fellow being dead and sightless'. Compare this with Eliot's 'Burbank with a Baedeker: Bleistein with a Cigar', in which 'A lustreless protrusive eye/ Stares from the protozoic slime'.

14   Pick, *Faces of Degeneration*, p. 195.

15   Greenslade, *Degeneration, Culture and the Novel*, pp. 182–91, 211; also Pick, *Faces of Degeneration*, pp. 185–6.

16   Pick, *Faces of Degeneration*, pp. 8–9.

17   There is an extensive literature on the influence of contemporary ideas of decline, degeneration and extinction in Conrad's fiction, although the relation between colonial and metropolitan worlds is underexplored. John W. Griffith, *Joseph Conrad and the Anthropological Dilemma* (Oxford, Clarendon Press, 1995) includes a full discussion (see especially chs. 3, 6, 8) but concentrates on colonial settings. Michael Whitworth, 'Inspector Heat inspected: *The Secret Agent* and the meanings of entropy', *The Review of English Studies*, 49:193 (1998), which appeared as this chapter was in the final stage of revision, takes little account of the colonial aspects of the novel. Other works to be noted include Allan Hunter, *Joseph Conrad and the Ethics of Darwinism* (London, Croom Helm, 1983); Robert G. Jacobs, 'Comrade Ossipon's favorite saint: Lombroso and Conrad', *Nineteenth Century Fiction*, 23:1 (1968); Martin Ray, 'Conrad, Nordau, and other degenerates: the psychology of *The Secret Agent*', *Conradiana*, 16:2 (1984).

18   Joseph Conrad, *Almayer's Folly*, ed. Jacques Berthoud (Oxford, Oxford University Press, 1992), p. lxii. Subsequent page numbers in parentheses refer to this edition.

19   Andrea White, 'Conrad and imperialism', in J. H. Stape (ed.), *Joseph Conrad* (Cambridge, Cambridge University Press, 1996), p. 186.

20   See Edmond, *Representing the South Pacific*, ch. 3.

21   Joseph Conrad, *The Secret Agent*, ed. Roger Tennant (Oxford, Oxford University Press, 1996), p. 214. Subsequent page numbers in parentheses refer to this edition.

22   See, for example, Linda Nochlin, *The Body in Pieces: The Fragment as a*

*Metaphor of Modernity* (London, Thames & Hudson, 1992).

23 See, for example, Kenneth Graham, 'Conrad and modernism', in Stape (ed.), *Joseph Conrad*, p. 214; Graham's argument draws heavily on Frank Kermode's *The Sense of an Ending*.

24 *Oxford English Dictionary*.

25 Jacques Berthoud, '*The Secret Agent*', in Stape (ed.), *Joseph Conrad*, pp 117–19.

26 Michael Whitworth, 'Inspector Heat inspected', p. 42.

27 See Alexandra Warwick, 'Vampires and the empire: fears and fictions of the 1890s', in Sally Ledger and Scott McCracken (eds), *Cultural Politics at the Fin De Siècle* (Cambridge, Cambridge University Press, 1995).

28 Bram Stoker, *Dracula*, ed. Maud Ellman (Oxford, Oxford University Press, 1996), p. 239.

29 See Stephen D. Arata, 'The occidental tourist: *Dracula* and the anxiety of reverse colonisation', *Victorian Studies*, 33:4 (1990) 623–4, 627–33.

30 Maud Ellmann, Introduction, Bram Stoker, *Dracula* (Oxford, Oxford University Press, 1996), p. xx.

31 Arata, 'The occidental tourist', pp. 633, 637–40.

32 For the term 'imperial gothic', see Patrick Brantlinger, *Rule of Darkness: British Literature and Imperialism 1830–1914* (Ithaca, Cornell University Press, 1988), pp. 228–9. For the overlap of imperial gothic with fears of urban degeneration, see Kathleen L. Spencer, 'Purity and danger: *Dracula*, the urban gothic, and the late Victorian degeneracy crisis', *English Literary History*, 59:1 (1992) 197–225.

33 David Trotter, 'Modernism and empire: reading *The Waste Land*', *Critical Quarterly*, 28:1 & 2 (1986) 145.

34 *Ibid.*, 147. *Dracula* also begins as a late-nineteenth-century travel narrative, and continues to use many of its conventions; see Arata, 'The occidental tourist', pp. 634–5.

35 *Ibid.*, 148.

36 T. S. Eliot, *The Waste Land: A Facsimile and Transcript of the Original Drafts*, ed. Valerie Eliot (London, Faber & Faber, 1971), p. 75.

37 Robert Crawford, *The Savage and the City in the Work of T. S. Eliot* (Oxford, Clarendon Press, 1987), p. 178. This valuable study of Eliot's knowledge of early twentieth-century anthropology explores the confluence of urban and savage worlds in his poetry, giving a more subtle account of Eliot's changing relation to the primitive than is possible here. Crawford does not, however, connect this interest to other kinds of social theory and imperial discourse.

38 Trotter, 'Modernism and empire', pp. 151, 152.

39 Eliot, *The Waste Land: Original Drafts*, pp. 45–6.

40 Greenslade, *Degeneration, Culture and the Novel*, pp. 75, 107.

41 See Myers, 'Nineteenth-century popularisations', pp. 308–9; Erik Svarny, *'The Men of 1914': T. S. Eliot and Early Modernism* (Milton Keynes and

Philadelphia, Open University Press, 1988), pp. 179–80. Crawford, *The Savage and the City in the Work of T. S. Eliot*, p. 115, gives further evidence of Eliot's acquaintance with the second law of thermodynamics.

42 Greenslade, *Degeneration, Culture and the Novel*, pp. 258–9.

43 John Carey, *The Intellectuals and the Masses: Pride and Prejudice among the Literary Intelligentsia 1880–1939* (London, Faber & Faber, 1992), *passim*.

44 Fredric Jameson, 'Modernism and imperialism', in Seamus Deane, Terry Eagleton, Fredric Jameson and Edward W. Said, *Nationalism, Colonialism and Literature* (Minneapolis, University of Minnesota Press, 1990), pp. 43–68.

45 See in particular Crawford, *The Savage and the City in the Work of T. S. Eliot, passim*. This also shows the influence of the imperialist adventure stories of Mayne Reid on the young Eliot's interest in 'primitive man', a more radical deconstruction of Jameson's polarisation.

46 Jameson, 'Modernism and imperialism', p. 48.

47 *Ibid.*, pp. 58–9.

48 *Ibid.*, p. 59.

49 *Ibid.*, p. 60.

50 Aijaz Ahmad, 'Jameson's rhetoric of otherness and the "National Allegory"', in *In Theory: Classes, Nations, Literatures* (London and New York, Verso, 1992).

51 Jameson, 'Modernism and imperialism', p. 64.

52 Anthony Pagden, *European Encounters with the New World* (New Haven and London, Yale University Press, 1993), pp. 21–34.

53 Greenslade, *Degeneration, Culture and the Novel*, p. 205.

# 3

# Imagism and empire

## Helen Carr

The political allegiances of modernist writers, for a long time effaced in Anglo-American literary criticism, have become in recent years the subject of considerable scrutiny. Where once the deeply dubious views of some high modernists were largely ignored, and the value of the modernist aesthetic unquestioned alike by critics left or right, now modernists are castigated for their elitism, racism, anti-Semitism, fascism, misogyny and even, by some, for their failures as parents. Judgements about modernism tend to veer (like the modernists) to extremes, and there is a danger of claiming too readily that they and/or their works are all good or all bad, when different modernists had very different beliefs, individual modernists frequently held very contradictory views, and modernist works are equally varied and fissured. I want here to look at some aspects of the imagist movement and its relation to racial and imperial politics, and tease out some of the tangled issues involved in its emergence as the opening moment in Anglo-American literary modernism.[1]

I have argued elsewhere that the imagist poets' search for an elemental, pared down, limpidly intense poetry and their turn away from Western modernity to the distant and the archaic, the Japanese, the Chinese, the early Greek, or the ancient Hebrew, came from a similar impulse to the more generally recognised move to the 'primitive' in the visual arts – Picasso's indebtedness to African art and to Cycladic and ancient Iberian sculpture, for example, or Kandinsky and his *Blaue Reiter* group's response to the art of Italian primitives, peasants, Japanese and Tahitians.[2] In reaction to earlier apolitical and formalist accounts, first Marxist and then post-colonial critics have argued that modernist primitivism was all too often complicit with the sins of colonialism. At the most hostile, modernist artists' fascination with 'primitive' art has been read in recent years simply as an extension of empire, the aesthetic equivalent of imperialist pillage, the rifling of subordinated cultures for artefacts and inspiration, for exotica and dreams to bring new vitality to a jaded West. I don't want to dismiss that analogy out of hand, for it certainly has some validity, nor do I want to claim that individual modernists were free from racism, prejudice or ethnocentrism. But to see the cultural change of which modernist primitivism is part as no more than a variant on the same imperial appetite appears increasingly inadequate. Modernist primitivism is complex and ambivalent, inextricable from an anxious loss of faith in the Western imperialist project; indeed, a loss of faith in the Western project as a whole. Nineteenth- and early-twentieth-century imperialism as a political practice was supported by an ideology whose core belief was that the innate superiority of the highly evolved white races made their expansion and dominance both beneficial and inevitable. Imagism, like so much modernist art, registers the weakening, indeed the crumbling, of that ideology.

One of the problems with the purely negative analysis of modernist borrowings from other cultures is that it can produce its own kind of Eurocentrism. For example, one critic argues that in modernist art, 'The assimilation takes place on Western terms. Nothing indigestible is consumed; no ideas or information that would shift or dissolve "our" preconceptions about the makers of those "other" cultures nourish this body.'[3] This, I would argue, is to aggrandise and mythologise the West. Was the West so powerful and so internally coherent that it was unaffected by its contact with other cultures? Surely not. There have been a series of challenges to this view of the impervious, almighty West, largely aimed at the version of this argument put forward in Said's *Orientalism*. In colonial discourse analysis, Homi Bhabha has drawn attention to the ambivalence and angst of the language of colonialism. Critics like Lisa Lowe have pointed out how far from homogeneous the West actually was.[4] In colonial history, it is now being argued, it is essential to study the 'centripetal' effects of colonialism as well as its more obvious 'centrifugal' impact. If one turns to the alternative reading of modernism currently put forward by African-American critics, in many ways following the lead of the Harlem Renaissance writers and artists, one finds a strikingly different 'centripetal' analysis. Modernism, Henry Louis Gates claims, was a 'mulatto' movement. It could not have happened without the impact of African art on the painters who became the leading modernists. 'The Cubist mask of modernism', he writes, 'covers a black Bantu face'.[5] Gates is of course fully aware of the distortions and limitations of negrophilia, but his radical reversal of the terms in which that cultural exchange has been interpreted highlights the way virtuous Western self-flagellation can border on narcissism. Zhaoming Qian in *Orientalism and Modernism* argues that far from 'inventing' Chinese poetry, as Eliot suggests, Pound's poetry was remade by what he learned through translating these texts.[6] Much valuable work has been done in the past few years on Western representations of other cultures – I have worked in that area myself – but that is not all there is to say. Western art did not omnipotently absorb fragments of these cultures and remain unchanged. It was radically transformed by them. To take the impact of the Japanese haiku less seriously than that of the Italian sonnet is to perpetuate Western disdain for other cultures.

Modernism, as Benjamin argued, registered a change in sensibility that followed the material changes of modern life. It was no coincidence that imagism emerged in a metropolis which was the centre, not just of a country, but of an empire, a metropolis where the fruits and consequences of imperialism were inescapable. (This imperialism, it must not be forgotten, was not confined to territorial colonisation, to which post-colonial literary theory, as the descendent of Commonwealth studies, largely restricts itself.) It was no coincidence either that those poets came together, as dissenting groups in a metropolis could, from different places, social classes and cultural backgrounds. I shall take some moments in the imagist story to illustrate the way its poetics come out of a questioning of Western representations and Western superiority, emerging in a climate which took distrust of the British imperialism very much for granted. This questioning might be part either of a democratic and liberatory politics, as it was with the poets F. S. Flint and Joseph Campbell, or entwined with far more disturbing views, as in the case of Ezra Pound. I shall look first at the famous meetings in Soho at the Tour Eiffel Restaurant in 1909,

which may or may not have lasted into early 1910; and then more
briefly at the period when Pound named and launched the movement.

## The Tour Eiffel

The Thursday night meetings in the Tour Eiffel restaurant in Soho
were originally set up in March 1909 by two young men from very
different backgrounds: T. E. Hulme, aged twenty-six, born into the
Staffordshire squirearchy, sent down from Cambridge for unidentified
riot, ex-mathematician, self-taught philosopher and for a brief time
poet; and Frank S. Flint, aged twenty-four, brought up in the extremes
of London poverty, educated at night-school, a post-office clerk,
aspiring poet and critic, and a gifted linguist. Hulme was later to
become a convinced supporter of Charles Maurras's right-wing Action
Française; Flint always remained on the left, an eclectic Nietzschean
and socialist, a follower of William Morris in his belief that beauty
was as important as bread if the life of the poor were to be truly
ameliorated. The Tour Eiffel meetings were a rebellious offshoot of
the more respectable Poets' Club, which met in Mayfair. Flint and
Hulme first discovered each other when Flint published an attack on
the bourgeois stuffiness of the Poets' Club, of which Hulme was
then secretary, suggesting with wild romanticism that poetry could
only be revolutionised in the kind of Bohemian French cafés
frequented by Verlaine. While Hulme mocked this notion (citing
Mallarmé in evening dress), he was clearly attracted by it.[7] A variety
of other poets joined them, most famously Ezra Pound, like Flint
also twenty-four, and only six months in London. The other members
were Edward Storer, whose *Mirrors of Illusion* Flint had warmly praised
the previous year in *The New Age*: F. W. Tancred, whose presence in
the group was intermittent and largely dependent, it appears, on the
fact that he could be relied on to admire both Hulme and Pound;
and two Irish poets Joseph Campbell and Desmond FitzGerald. The
only woman in the group was the actress and occultist Florence Farr,
who wrote several books, though little poetry; she had, however,
worked with Yeats on reciting his poetry to accompaniment of a
psaltery, specially made for her by Arnold Dolmetsch. In his first
letter to Flint about the group, Hulme mentioned that Ernest Rhys
and Ernest Radford, earlier associated with the Rhymers' Club, were
to come, but there is no other reference to their presence; if they

did turn up that first time, it seems unlikely they returned.[8] Hulme, Edward Shorter and Joseph Campbell had all already experimented with *vers libre*, Campbell under the influence of Whitman, but the other two learning from the French *vers libristes*. As is well known, the group was 'brought ... together', as Flint put it in 1915, by 'a dissatisfaction with English poetry as it was then ... being written'.[9] Flint was right to put the group's unity, such as it was, in the negative. They were against the established way of doing things, but what to do instead was another question.

The significance of the Tour Eiffel meetings has been disputed from the time Pound split with the other imagists in 1914, and particularly in later years by admirers of Hulme in battle with the larger band of Pound's followers. Although Pound and Flint put aside earlier contentions to agree the outline of a history in the early 1920s, the dispute has continued, fuelled by the conviction that literary change must be brought about by individual great men, and that a choice must be made between Pound and Hulme as the originator of imagism. Literary change, I would argue, is not brought about by single authors, nor does it come in Lamarckian leaps, though modernists liked to claim that it did, but is the result of manifold shifts in cultural and political life, among a range of writers and thinkers, even if these shifts come to most striking fruition in the work of a few. The work of each of the writers associated with the Tour Eiffel, as well as that of each of the later imagists, was both symptomatic of the changes that were at work and contributed to them. In any case, the Tour Eiffel poets were not the only ones in London concerned about the state of poetry. The reviled Poets' Club had been founded only a year earlier. Edward Thomas, later in 1909, apologised for shocking the aptly named Square Club by giving the *arriviste* Pound's *Personae* a good review, claiming he had been led astray by his 'pure love of praising the *new* poetry' (my emphasis).[10] When the Georgian anthologies were launched in 1912, their aim was precisely to revitalise English poetry. But beyond this, the critique of contemporary poetry mounted by the Tour Eiffel group was only one aspect of the insistent questioning of social, sexual and artistic conventions in pre-war London, and cannot be understood without that context. Hulme, Pound, Flint and FitzGerald all wrote for the journal *The New Age*, a left-wing weekly financed by the Fabians, though often expressing wilder and more maverick views on a variety of areas, from marriage to the arts, than the respectable Fabians had intended. Though its editor, A. R. Orage, at that time a guild socialist himself, did not in any way demand that his writers embraced his politics, they were all part to a greater or lesser extent of the 'advanced', 'free-thinking' milieu in London, 'the proponents of radical new ideas' as Samuel Hynes describes them.[11] As Hynes points out, those various new ideas were by no means necessarily compatible with one another, but the Tour Eiffel poets were one of many intersecting groups who proposed change, liberation, openness, experiment in some sphere or other. Politics, philosophy and the arts were all discussed in terms of hidebound conventions that needed to be shattered and in metaphors of surfaces and depths, in which the superficial and false were to be disrupted by the vitality and authenticity of what lay beneath. The Tour Eiffel meetings only lasted for a comparatively short time, and no coherent literary programme emerged at the time. However, between them the poets who met there brought together approaches which would fuse and bear fruit a little later, working in opposition to the status quo, and either using translations or producing poems that imitated or ventriloquised voices from elsewhere: one can already trace the broad impulse to move away from the traditions of Western high art.

### Flint and the haiku

'We proposed,' Flint wrote in his wry 'History of Imagism' in 1915, 'to replace [traditional English poetry] by pure *vers libre*; by the Japanese *tanka* and *haikai*; we all wrote dozens of the latter as an amusement; by poems in a sacred Hebrew form … ; by rhymeless poems like Hulme's 'Autumn'.[12] It is not surprising that in this list Flint mentions first *vers libre* and Japanese poetry, for him the two most important elements, and forms which he describes later in his history as 'akin in spirit'. (In his review of Storer's French-influenced *vers libre* poems, Flint had described him as 'aiming at a form of expression, like the Japanese, in which an image is a resonant heart of an exquisite moment'.[13]) It seems likely that it was Flint who introduced the haiku to the group, though, as he says, it was quickly taken up by others, at the time particularly by Hulme. In Flint's first article in *The New Age* in 1908 he had praised the haiku form, but criticised the heavy, florid versifications that English translations of Japanese poems usually employed, quoting a couple of examples of more direct translations, which he in turn had translated from the French:

> Alone in a room
> Deserted –
> A peony

and

> A fallen petal
> Flies back to its branch:
> Ah! a butterfly![14]

These haiku could lay claim to be the first published imagist poems, and in that sense their status as translations of translations is entirely fitting. As Flint knew, Japanese forms had already had a considerable impact on French poetry, as they had had on French art. He had found the French versions in some articles sent home from Japan, in the wake of the Russo-Japanese war, by a French doctor and poet, Paul-Louis Couchoud, a friend and medical advisor of Anatole France, to whom Couchoud dedicated the book in which these articles were later collected. Couchoud saw the delicate minimalism of Japanese poetry as the fulfilment of the ideals of '*l'orphisme mallarméen*'.[15] Flint repeats the comparison:

> 'to them in poetry as in painting, the half-said thing is dearest' – the suggestion not the complete picture (one thinks of Stéphane Mallarmé.) ... To the poet who can catch and render, like these Japanese, the brief fragments of his soul's music, the future lies open ... The day of the lengthy poem is over – at least for this troubled age.[17]

Couchoud's account of the Japanese undoubtedly appealed to Flint. Couchoud stresses that they are lovers of nature and of beauty, less materialistic than the West, simpler in lifestyle but richer in aesthetic response. The militarist West is at last beginning to treat them with respect, Couchoud says, because they have defeated Russia and Germany, whilst the respect should have been given sooner for their artistic and cultural life, in which all participate, not just an aristocratic few. In Japan 'tout le monde est poète, musicien et peintre, sans y penser ... L'art est diffus dans le peuple tout entier. Il a saturé le pays. Il imprègne la vie.' It is perhaps less developed than the art of the West, Couchoud comments (not a sentiment Flint echoes) but 'il remplit mieux que le nôtre son rôle social'.[17] These points are just

the ones that American supporters of imagism were to make about
Native American life and poetry a few years later, and, like them,
Flint fears this utopian way of life is endangered by the West: 'The
Japanese are quick to take an artistic hint; in fact even the most lowly
are all poets (or should we say, *were* poets?).'[18]

In Couchoud's account, the supreme gift of Japanese poetry is
that it offers an image which captures an instantaneous response
before its freshness is destroyed by ratiocination; its brevity and
spareness makes it possible to evade the loss of authenticity suffered
once syntax interposes its conventions:

> Du poème japonais surtout le discursif, l'explicatif sont extirpés. La bizarre
> fleur se détache unique sur la neige. Le bouquet est interdit. La poème
> prend à sa source la sensation lyrique jaillissante, instantanée, avant que
> le mouvement de la pensée ou de la passion l'ait orientée et utilisée ...
> Les mots sont l'obstacle. La chaîne des mots introduit un ordre élémentaire
> qui est déjà un artifice.[20]

Couchoud here is clearly influenced by Bergson's contrast between
the *immédiatement donnée* of direct intuition and the deadening language
of intellectualised knowledge. This belief that the brief, momentary
haiku images gave a direct accesss to experiences which words by
their very nature obscured was precisely in keeping with Hulme's
own interest in Bergson's philosophy, which already lay behind his
theory of 'the image', or rather of 'images'. Bergson believed that the
arbitrary divisions of language alienate us from the fluidity of experience, and that (in Hulme's words) 'one must dive back into the flux
... if one wishes to know reality'.[20] One way of achieving direct
intuition is through art. Bergson had written in his *Introduction to
Metaphysics* (translated in 1911 by Hulme and Flint): 'No image can
replace the intuition of duration, but many diverse images, borrowed
from very different orders of things, may, by the convergence of
their action, direct consciousness to the precise point where there is
a certain intuition to be seized.'[21] Hulme had made his own adaptation of this in 'A Lecture on Modern Poetry' (delivered to the
Poets' Club, it appears, before the Tour Eiffel meetings commenced,
in November 1908):

> Say the poet is moved by a certain landscape, he selects from that certain
> images which put in juxtaposition in separate lines serve to suggest and
> to evoke the state he feels. To this piling up of distinct images in different

lines, one can find a fanciful analogy in music ... Two visual images form
what one may call a visual chord. They unite to suggest an image which
is different to both.[23]

The haiku, which consists of two images without syntactical connection, a metaphor which simultaneously offers vehicle and tenor, so
the whole is the tenor transformed by the vehicle, is the perfect
exemplum of this. Simplicity, brevity, fusion, direct and instantaneous
impact were all to be central to later imagism: why the aesthetic
represented by the haiku was so important to literary modernism is
something to which I shall return.

## Pound and the past

Pound himself averred that he remembered little of this discussion,
and his poetry at this stage gives little evidence of having paid attention to this strand of the Tour Eiffel debates. He only recognised
the relevance of these ideas to his own poetry after he had attended
Hulme's lectures on Bergson's philosophy in the autumn of 1911;
Pound's haiku-like poems did not appear until 1913, although Pound's
dramatic lyrics, one might argue, had always aimed to evoke a Paterian
'moment ... a moment of song, self-analysis, or sudden understanding
or revelation', and so, like the haiku, to capture a fleeting intensity.[23]
Pound, however, although on principle against the established way of
doing anything, was, when he joined the Tour Eiffel group – ironically
in terms of his later reputation – not yet censorious of London
literary life. He had, it must be admitted, found his first visit to the
Poets' Club rather dull – perhaps why he turned to the Tour Eiffel
– but in general he was still in such a state of relief at his escape
from Crawfordsville, Indiana, that he accepted London as a cultural
haven, and was even ready to cast a generous eye on its poetic scene.
In early 1909 the enemy remained for him American provincial
philistinism, though already by the end of the year the group had
taught him to find targets for his scorn in England too. Shortly
before he joined the Tour Eiffel poets, he had written to William
Carlos Williams that 'London, deah old London, is the place for
poesy'.[24] His later denunciation of the 'arthritic milieu' of the London
in which he first arrived was the product of future disappointments.[25]
Pound still remained very much a follower of the Pre-Raphaelites,

Pater and the Nineties poets; like them he was a seeker of beauty in the past; his favoured past – medieval Provence and Italy – he had found through them. He was still, as according to Williams he had been as a student, 'completely indifferent' to the present, and 'absorbed, completely absorbed … in the romantic times'.[26] In 1909, Flint reported, Pound 'could not be made to believe there was any French poetry after Ronsard. He was very full of his *troubadours*.'[27] His letters home show him agog with excitement at meeting poets who had belonged to the Rhymers' Club. Significantly, the contemporary English poets whom he most admired when he first arrived were either from the nineties' generation or younger poets whose poetry looked back to earlier forms.[28] His great hero was of course Yeats, but, as James Longenbach has pointed out, it was the earlier Yeats of *The Wind among the Reeds*, rather than the Yeats whose work had gained a new edge under the influence of Synge in the most recent poems included in *In the Seven Woods*.[29]

Pound himself has been one of those responsible for the notion that the tradition those nineteenth-century poets represented was the antithesis of modernism – soggy, sentimental verse which was repudiated by their virile successors, a view echoed in numerous literary histories. Josephine Guy, however, argues convincingly in her book *The British Avant Garde* that the Pre-Raphaelite and Aesthetic movements were modernism's prelude, not its contrary.[30] The harbingers of modernism in France, Baudelaire, Rimbaud and Verlaine, she points out, constructed an aesthetic which set itself in opposition to its society by embracing the bohemian, the scandalous and the urban demi-monde; what Morris, Pater and Wilde did in their work was equally oppositional but, under the pressure of British conservatism, necessarily more oblique. They offered a critique of modernity by constructing their own version of history, one which offered alternative values to the present. Their emphasis on private sensibility constituted a resistance to an increasingly bullish British nationalism (which was, though Guy does not stress this, inseparable from growing imperialism and jingoism). Pound's own version of medieval and early renaissance culture had this same counter-cultural energy, developed in opposition to the belief in progress, the modern and the utilitarian that had surrounded him in Philadelphia. In 1909 Pound had not moved from that 'British' version of the avant-garde, nor was he to do so until 1912. Until then his experimentation with form was limited to his translations and pastiches of earlier poetry. Maintaining an alternative history of cultural tradition was, in any case, to remain central for Pound in his modernist days, as it was for Eliot: *Make It New* was, after all, the title of a book largely concerned with the writers Pound admired from the past, most of them predating the seventeenth century.[31]

## Pound and the Celts

If Pound was not yet ready to admit the need for radical poetic change, nor to look to non-Western countries for poetic forms, another kind of oppositional stance and cultural primitivism within the Tour Eiffel attracted him more: the Irish. It was perhaps from them he first learnt to recognise and criticise the British establishment. The extent of the involvement of the Tour Eiffel poets with the Irish literary movement has been largely unnoticed, as have their close links with the Irish Literary Society, which most of them frequented, and which on occasion they used as an alternative venue.[32] Campbell was the Society's secretary, and FitzGerald secretary of the closely related Irish Texts Society. Florence Farr, although not herself Irish, had many links with the Irish Literary Society, and acted for the Irish National Dramatic Society, appearing in Yeats's plays both in Dublin and in London. Pound later suggested that Padraic Colum, a central figure in the Irish literary scene, and a poet whom Pound much admired, had been a member of the group and one of 'Hulme's gang'.[334] No one else mentions his visiting the Tour Eiffel, although he, Pound and Hulme certainly met at the Irish Literary Society, and he was an old friend of Campbell, indeed the person who introduced him to Whitman's poetry. Yet the very fact that Pound thought Colum might have been there suggests how important the Irish presence in the group had been to him. Pound may have originally attended the Irish Literary Society in search of Yeats, but the Yeats he admired at this time was the Yeats of the Celtic Revival. Pound himself, while still a student in America, had, he said, 'been drunk with Celticism and Dowson's "Cynara"'.[34] In his first book of poems, *A Lume Spento*, published the previous December in Venice, Pound had identified his own pagan-cum-mystical beliefs with those recorded in *The Celtic Twilight*, as well as imitating Yeats's manner in several of the poems. Dorothy Shakespear had already noticed with surprise that Pound affected an Irish accent when declaiming Yeats's poetry to them, and indeed most of the time. Later in the year, after he had met Yeats, Pound gave his father an account of his usual week: 'Victor Plarr of the old Rhymers' Club ... is in on Sunday supper-and-evenings, Yeats Monday evenings; a set from the Irish Lit. Soc. eats together on Wednesdays and a sort of new Rhymers gang on Thursdays'.[35] If one remembers that the original Rhymers' Club, whose former members Pound pursued so ardently, was strongly associated with Celticism (Victor Plarr himself being described by Lionel Johnson as 'half-Celt, half-French'), it is quite a Celt-dominated week.

The Irish literary revival, as the close association with the Rhymers indicates, was in many ways a continuation of the nineteenth-century poetic return to a more appealing past, as it was of the earlier Romantic idealisation of the folk, but it was also an important bridge between those nineteenth-century traditions and Anglo-American modernism in general. It gave to the modernists a model for change that looked not simply to the past but to an alternative cultural tradition from which and by which to critique the values of the present power structures and Western modernity. The Irish had been one of the most despised groups in Britain in the nineteenth century, 'white negros' or even 'more like tribes of squalid apes than human beings': the 'Irish Yahoo' was to some the obvious candidate for the Missing Link.[36] The Celtic Revival was as much an effort to fight back against that racist valuation and to challenge British aesthetic and cultural norms, as it was to support political independence. (It was, incidentally, repeatedly invoked as a model by the New Negro and Harlem Renaissance writers in the United States.) By 1909, the year of Synge's death, divisions had appeared within the movement, between a narrow chauvinistic nationalism, which took such exception to *The Playboy of the Western World*, and was to be so mocked by James Joyce, reproducing the cultural values of their colonisers in their search for respectability; and the proto-modernist attempt, in writers like Yeats and Synge, to see Irish traditions in an alternative international context stretching from Homer to Ibsen. Pound himself was later to suggest that perhaps the real beginnings of modernism came with Synge and his impact on Yeats. In 1909, however, he admired the Celtic Revival as a continuation of the nineties.

## Campbell and Ireland

The Irish Literary Society, founded with Yeats's help in 1891, was highly politicised, much involved in debates about Home Rule and Irish independence. Politically, both Joseph Campbell and Desmond FitzGerald were Irish Nationalists, though their presence in the group shows they were artistically neither narrow nor chauvinist. FitzGerald later became something of a hero, taking part in the Easter Rising, being imprisoned, elected as a Sinn Féin MP while still in jail, Minister for External Affairs in the Irish Free State government, and eventually a Senator, though, unlike his son Garret, never Taoiseach. In his memoirs of 1913–16, FitzGerald recalls his early friendship with Pound and Hulme; Pound later insisted on several occasions that FitzGerald, for whom he clearly had considerable affection, had played a significant role in the group.[37] But the poet to whose work Pound first appears to have responded was Joseph Campbell, who published under the Gaelic name of Seosamh Mac Cathmhaiol. Campbell had been born in Belfast in 1879 into a large artisan Catholic Nationalist family, so like Flint was of lower-class origins, and, like him too, had, according to a sister, 'socialist tendencies'.[38] Before coming to England he had joined the Gaelic League, and been involved with the Ulster Literary Theatre and the periodical *Uladh*. (*Uladh* is Gaelic for Ulster: it also, chillingly, means a charnel-house.) He had translated into English the songs and traditional airs collected by his brother in Donegal, learning through this, according to the poet Austin Clarke, what he describes, in very imagistic terms, as the 'directness' and 'concentrated simplicity' characteristic of his poetry.[39] Campbell's own poems drew both on folklore and on his own observation – on walking tours – of peasant life, and his work, although deeply romantic, exhibits a powerful sense of their humanity. Austin Clarke says Campbell was the first Irish poet to experiment with free verse, though he also continued to use ballads and traditional folk forms, poems which, like Pound's, were a mixture of translation and pastiche.

In 1909 Campbell brought out his fifth book of poems, *The Mountainy Singer*, containing both free and traditional verse, named from a poem he had written a couple of years before:

> I am the mountainy singer –
> The voice of the peasant's dream,

> The cry of the wind on the wooded hill,
> The leap of the fish in the stream. [40]

As this imagery suggests, Campbell's transmuted folk songs and ballads came out of a sense of the Irish tradition which had much in common with Flint's view of the Japanese: the art of an innately poetic people, immediate and direct, capturing the ever-mobile fluidity of the natural world. Max Beerbohm had noted in a review in 1904 that the plays put on by the Irish National Literary Theatre made their appeal by combining simplicity and exoticism, a combination which was also very much the appeal of Japanese art and poetry.[41] Some of Campbell's free verse, though still on Irish subjects, is clearly influenced by the experiments with Japanese forms, like this poem from *The Mountainy Singer*:

> Night, and I travelling
> An open door by the wayside,
> Throwing out a shaft of warm yellow light.
> A whiff of peat-smoke;
> A gleam of delf on the dresser within;
> A woman's voice crooning, as if to a child.
> I pass on into the darkness.[42]

Like a haiku or tanka (although of course somewhat longer), this poem, in Hulme's Bergsonian phrase, 'pil[es] up ... distinct images in different lines'. Yet Campbell's ballads also had much in common with Pound's poetry of the period, although in a different idiom. Like Campbell's, Pound's poems were characteristically first person, spoken through a persona, colloquial, taken from an earlier, fresher tradition, drawing on myth and the past, often, as even in Campbell's free verse poem here, about someone on the move. The first poem Pound wrote after joining the group, the 'Ballad of the Goodly Fere', was based on one of Campbell's best-known poems, 'The Gilly of Christ' (1907), like it being in the voice of one of Christ's companions, but a voice far removed from conventional piety.[43] When Pound was next invited to the Poets' Club, Campbell, a tall, strikingly handsome man, read the poem for him, dressed dramatically in bardic robes. Pound told his father that 'Campbell, "the dark man from the narth" read the "Goodly Fere" splendidly. I wish I had his voice'.[44] When the poem was published later that year in Ford Madox Ford's *English Review*, it attracted a good deal of attention and earned Pound a welcome £5, which he promptly spent on an outfit which out-Yeatsed Yeats. By now, the end of 1909, Pound had learnt to discriminate between the different sections of London literary life. He recalled with pleasure the horrified reactions to his appearance: 'peak of attainment annoyed elderly brit/literatus'.[45] Also to his satisfaction, 150 readers cancelled their subscriptions in outrage at the poem's apparent blasphemy.

Pound was intrigued by the likenesses between the Irish strolling minstrels and his own medieval 'wandering singers', and was to draw on Campbell's work again. He continued to praise Campbell's work, in later years more for his experimental moments than his Celtic qualities, and in 1912 and 1913 sent some of Campbell's poems to *Poetry*, the magazine which was to be so important in promoting the imagist movement. Campbell did not appear in the 1914 anthology *Des Imagistes*. He had returned to Ireland in 1913 to join the Irish Volunteer Army, and though Pound mentions his visits back in 1914, Campbell's life was to be taken over and embittered by the struggles. Although Campbell saw a good deal of FitzGerald until 1921 (barring the prison years), even hiding him from the British after the Easter Rising, he was eventually to be imprisoned himself during the Civil War by the government to which FitzGerald belonged.

### Pound's pre-war politics

In those pre-war years, Pound's politics were shaped by the Irish question, though in the end most significantly by Yeats's views on it. The circles in which Pound moved in London outside the Tour Eiffel group were all sympathetic to Ireland's demands for Home Rule, and Pound himself arrived in England with a 'predisposition to respect the Irish nation'.[46] Although that predisposition was later to vanish, along with his interest in Celtic twilights, he absorbed an abiding scorn for British institutions, including the British Empire. Yeats had presented the American public in 1903 with, in Roy Foster's words, 'high claims for Irish culture over English materialism', and it was this binary of culture versus materialism, art versus greed, that was to remain the basis of Pound's politics.[47] The British Empire, according to Pound in 1913, was the product of English materialism, of their 'hateful and barbaric' love of property.[48] Pound's political leanings when he left the United States were akin to the Progressives, who opposed both business monopoly and union power; they, like him, were individualists, and, like him, had great faith in the power of strenuous exhortation. Although Pound was not interested in nationalism as such (it was too collectivist), he was drawn to rebels, and he was also soon to realise that monopolies and corporate money-making ran Europe as much as America. One of the most overt statements of Pound's political orientation in the pre-war period appeared in a brief letter to *The New Age* in 1912, attacking an earlier article on the Turkey-Bulgaria war:

> If Turkey has been maintained in the 'unspeakable' status quo, I should like to know by what force if not by the force of the allied monopolies of Europe? If it has not been to the interest of European capital to maintain the Turk, why has he persisted?
>
> If an oriental despotism is not lock, stock and barrel of our matter with the industrial tyrannies of Europe, to what is it allied? ... we wish we could throw off the subtle strands of the hidden tyranny of the monopolists as swiftly and cleanly as you are throwing off the yoke of a tyranny of arms.
>
> Uncivilised Montenegrins, Servians, decadent Greeks, pestilent Bulgarians, I wish you well, and I pray that you conserve your ideal of freedom better than men have done in my own 'free' country or in constitutional England.[49]

The impatience of those like Campbell with the monolithic weight of British rule, and the Celtic scorn for wealth produced by 'industrial tyrannies', undoubtedly appeared entirely understandable to him.

Pound's politics, however, differed from Campbell's in more ways than in their attitude to nationalism. Campbell said of himself in contrast to Yeats, 'I am a poet of the Prakrit (the vernacular speech) rather than of the Sanskrit (the speech of the sheltered elect).'[50] Pound was increasingly to prefer the elect, a Yeatsian aristocracy rather than the democracy favoured by Campbell and Flint. As he wrote in 1914, 'The aristocracy of entail and of title has decayed, the aristocracy of commerce is decaying, the aristocracy of the arts is ready again for its service.'[51] By 1914, Pound had abandoned his sympathy for the Irish nation as such, railing at its failure to recognise the genius of Synge and Joyce, and describing it as 'a half-educated, Zorastrian rabble of "respectable" people more stupid and sodden than is tobe found even in America'.[52] His politics were to be increasingly aesthetic rather than liberatory. He did not give up his attacks on the British

Empire, but it became for him a symbol of obtuse philistinism, which he condemned for its neglect of the artist rather than its oppression of the many. In his essay on 'Psychology and the Troubadours', he suggests there are two kinds of religion: on the one hand the intense visionary experience of the poet, and on the other 'the Mosaic or Roman or British Empire type, where someone, having to keep a troublesome rabble in order, invents and scares them with a disagreeable bogie, which he calls God'. [53] Pound's criticism of the Empire was not its treatment of the rabble, but its failure to recognise the superiority of the poet.

For all its limitations, Pound's scorn for British imperialist attitudes was part of the shift that brought about Anglo-American literary modernism. In the hierarchy of empire, the British administrative class, at home and abroad, is of a higher kind than those they administer whether or not they be poets or artists: just as for Forster in *A Passage to India*, it became important to Pound to reverse that valuation. In 1910, although Pound rejected any idea of evolutionary progress, insisting that all ages were contemporaneous and wanting 'Theocritus and Mr Yeats weighed in one balance', the cultural objects he valued were almost all in that Western trajectory from Greece to Ireland.[54] In 1912 he began to look beyond the West: he did not abandon his troubadours, but he no longer found models in the Western past sufficient; by 1914 he was to argue that 'we should develop a criticism of poetry based on world-poetry, on the work of maximum excellence'.[55] In 1912 Pound reinvented himself as the leader of an *avant-gardiste* coterie on the French model: following the Flint/Hulme trajectory of the earlier group, *les imagistes* looked to experimental modernist artists and writers on the Continent, largely in France, but like the Continental modernists sought models as well in archaic or non-European forms. This avant-garde imagism followed the example of the simple/exotic offered by the haiku, the sudden juxtaposition of images, minimal syntax, fleeting but vivid evocations, much as Flint had originally advocated. Hulme was no longer interested in poetry, nor indeed in Bergson, but he was making a similar shift away from Western traditions of representation, and was shortly to recommend the return to pre-Renaissance or 'primitive' forms for the visual arts. By 1915 he looked back at 'the change in sensibility which has enabled us to appreciate Egyptian, Indian, Byzantine, Polynesian, and Negro work as art and not as archaeology or ethnology'.[56]

## Pound and Tagore

Pound was later to find his most important model in China, but at precisely the time he was launching imagism he was for a while attracted to another alternative to the West, that represented by the Bengali poet Rabindranath Tagore. When he returned to London in late July 1912 from his Provençal walking tour, Tagore was in London, with Yeats enthusiastically promoting his work, poems which Tagore himself had translated from the original Bengali.[57] Pound, too, was immediately enthralled, writing up Tagore for the *Fortnightly Review* and for the new Chicago monthly *Poetry*, whose foreign correspondent he had agreed to become that August, and whose pages were to be so important in publicising imagism. He persuaded its editor Harriet Monroe that 'the very great Bengali poet, Rabindranath Tagore' should also have some of his poems published in *Poetry*, and they appeared there in the wake of the first proclamations of imagism.[58]

Tagore's poems, although intricately rhymed in Bengali (as Pound, to do him justice, had troubled to find out), were translated as prose poems, and again appeared to offer the combination of directness, simplicity and exoticism at which the new movement aimed. According to Pound in his piece for *Poetry*, Tagore's poems had affinities with both the troubadours and the imagists: 'If you refine the art of the troubadours, combine it with that of the Pléiade, and add to that the sound-unit principle of the most advanced artists in *vers libre*, you would get something like the system of Bengali verse.'[59] Tagore's songs, he said 'are sung throughout Bengal, more or less as the troubadours' songs were sung through Europe in the twelfth century'.[60] The Bengali poet, Pound told Dorothy, made him feel like 'a painted pict with a stone club'.[61] (As Tagore charmed everyone by his courtesy, and even Yeats described Pound as 'a headlong ragged nature … always hurting people's feelings … his voice …too loud, his stride too resounding', there were probably plenty in London to applaud the comparison.[62]) Pound particularly liked Tagore's disciple, Kali Mohon Ghose, and started to learn Bengali and to work on translations with him. It was presumably from Ghose he learnt the quite detailed information about Bengali verse that he included in the *Fortnightly Review* article. Harold Hurwitz suggests that Pound must have admired Tagore's independence, his opposition both to British imperialism and to Indian nationalist chauvinism. (Roy Foster says much the same about Yeats.)[63] Pound, however, was furious when Edmund Gosse frustrated Yeats's efforts to have Tagore elected an honorary member of the Academic Committee of the Royal Literary Society, and delighted at the Committee's discomfiture when Tagore was given the Nobel prize later in 1913. Tagore was for Pound – at any rate for a while – a perfect example of the artist whose profound importance the hacks of empire were unable to comprehend.

Pound's enthusiasm for Tagore lasted less than a year, partly no doubt because he became so popular as a religious poet, not least, to Pound's irritation, with Pound's own mother. (It may have been of her he was thinking when he wrote in 1917 that Tagore had 'relapsed into religion and optimism, and was boomed by the pious non-conformists'.[64]) Yet his admiration was undoubtedly genuine while it lasted. James Longenbach has argued that Pound was indulging in absurd posturing to impress Yeats when he asserted in *Poetry* that 'world fellowship' would be brought nearer by Tagore's visit to London.[65] But Pound had already the year before written to the Japanese poet Yoni Noguchi that 'if east and west are ever to understand each other that understanding must come slowly and come first through art'.[66] Pound's belief in the power of art should not be underestimated. Longenbach also finds preposterous Pound's claim that the West's discovery of Tagore would be for the modern world what the rediscovery of Greek had been to the Renaissance. But Pound was eighteen months later to assign this role to the Chinese. In the immediate pre-war years, he scented a new Renaissance round the corner, and believed, as he put it, that 'the first step of a renaissance is the importation of models for painting, sculpture or writing'.[67] This renaissance he hoped would come in America; for Britain he saw the situation in different terms. In England, he said, he knew he was 'perched on the rotten shell of a crumbling empire'; his little circle of literary friends in 'Kensington and its environs' were 'carried on the back of a very large and sickly elephant ... London ... is like Rome of the decadence, so far, at least as letters are concerned. She is the main and vortex drawing strength from the peripheries. Thus the finest authors ... are all foreigners.'[68]

### Pound and imperial masculinity

Pound came to think Tagore too 'mushy', just as he decided the 'Celtic imagination ... flopp[ed] about' and the Japanese were 'too damned soft'.[69] From 1912 he had been recommending poetry in increasingly masculinist terms, poetry which was 'harder', 'austere', 'like granite', 'nearer to the bone'.[70] This was a continuation of a trend, rather than a new departure. One way in which Pound's early poems often had differed from the Pre-Raphaelites and the Nineties poets had been the brash machismo tone many assumed. (The same contrast was there between 'The Gilly of Christ' and 'The Goodly Fere'.) If the earlier poets cultivated values of private sensibility and sensitivity against a public and patriotic, even jingoistic vigour, they adopted – certainly according to their critics – the place of femininity rather than masculinity, though this performance of the role of sexually ambiguous aesthete or decadent was thrown into crisis with the Wilde trial. Pound's strategy had always been different; from the beginning he wanted to create active, virile personae, like for example his favourite troubadour, Bertrans de Born, soldier, lover, poet, and general troublemaker. Pound wrote five poems about de Born before 1916 (he also appears in the *Cantos*) and read one, 'Sestina: Altaforte' at his very first visit to the Tour Eiffel, shouting at the top of his voice, 'Damn it all! all our South stinks peace./ You whoreson dog, Papiols, come! Let's to music!/ I have no life save when the swords clash.'[71] This masculinist vein was something he had in common with Hulme, who in 1908 had written that

> The latter stages in the decay of an art form are ... worth study because they are peculiarly applicable to the state of poetry at the present day. They resemble the latter stages in the decay of religion when the spirit has gone and there is a meaningless reverence for formalities and ritual. The carcass is dead and all the flies are upon it. Imitative poetry springs up like weeds, and women whimper and whine of you and I, alas, and roses, roses all the way. It becomes the expression of sentimentality rather than of virile thought.[72]

In recent years the misogyny of this aspect of modernism, with its assumption that the place of the feminine is abject and despicable, has received much comment. (Earlier, and by many Pound disciples still, it was regarded simply as the language of full-blooded men.) But, misogynistic though it was, the aim of that rhetoric was not to do women down but to promote the poet. It was aimed at other men, not at women. Modernist male writers, *pace* Gilbert and Gubar, if often far from enlightened in their sexual attitudes, did much more to assist women writers than their predecessors.[73] Escaping the image of the effeminate poet was their goal. If in the United States the place of masculinity had become that of the entrepreneur, in Britain it was that of the imperial Englishman, the Englishman as distinguished from his effeminised, inconstant, weak colonial subjects. For Pound in particular, if he was to insist on the importance of poetry, on the value of the poet against that of the businessman, the trader, the committee man, the administrator, the only language in which he could conceive of doing so was that of masculinity. Pound's opposition to empire was not to its hierarchical nature nor its asymmetrical differences: Pound, like Hulme, was already an anti-democrat. But he wished to impose a different hierarchy. The world leaders for Pound are, or rather should be, the gifted poets and artists, of whatever race or indeed gender; if he approved of a woman poet, like H.D., he described her poetry as hard as well. Pound's poetics are both an attack on the justification for empire – government by an elite whose superiority, vigour and omniscience are guaranteed by their race and nationality – and a mirror image of it, a virile artistic elite whose worth is guaranteed by their work. Before the First World War, however, Pound saw his artistic elite solely as a guerrilla force; after the war his ambitions for the arts took on their own brand of imperialism.

## Wilfrid Scawen Blunt

It is perhaps this desire to assert that the poet rather than the empire-builder should rightly be considered for the role of manly leadership which lay behind one of the most curious and comic episodes of Pound's pre-war poetry promotions, the lunch he organised in January 1914 to honour the anti-imperialist, womaniser (his biographer describes him more euphemistically as an 'amorist'), horse-breeder and poet, Wilfrid Scawen Blunt.[74] Blunt, aristocratic and handsome, had had many affairs, with, among others, Janey Morris and Lady Gregory, and was an ardent and committed opponent of the British Empire. He had been in jail for two months in Ireland as a political prisoner in 1888, and was regarded by Queen Victoria as a 'red hot revolutionary'.[75] He attacked both territorial and economic imperialism. As Pound's fascination with China was then beginning, Blunt's indignation at the treatment the Chinese received must have particularly pleased him. Among his many written denunciations of imperial policy (most of them printed at his own expense) was a pamphlet he wrote in 1900, *The Shame of the Nineteenth Century*, in which he recounted the misery and suffering brought by Britain to India, China ('in the commercial raids on China for the last sixty years it has been always Englishmen who have led the way, and who count now on securing the greater share of the commercial spoils'), Africa, the 'Pacific Isles', the Maoris and the Australians (that is, Aborigines).[76] On the Chinese 'Boxer Rebellion' of 1900, which started a Yellow Peril fever in Britain, he wrote in language which must have delighted Pound, 'The Chinese, after a long course of bullying by the Powers, worrying by missionaries, and robbing by merchants and speculators, have risen, and are, very properly, knocking the foreign vermin on the head.'[77] (Incidentally, silk painting masterpieces which were 'lost' from the Imperial Palace in Beijing during the rebellion mysteriously turned up in the possession of the British Museum in 1903: Englishmen, as Blunt points out, seizing the spoils.)

The lunch was to honour Blunt as a poet, on the grounds that he was the first to use poetry to deal with contemporary issues, and the last to be 'able to use the ... "grand style" effectively', but it was also, according to Pound, because he 'had never ceased to protest against the tyrannies and swindles of the Empire'.[78] Six poets attended: three imagists – Pound, Aldington and Flint; three Rhymers – Yeats, Plarr and Sturge Moore. (Flint was in agonies before the event, convinced his suit would not pass muster.) Blunt refused to meet them in London, but invited them to his Sussex estate, Newbuildings, met them dressed in Arabian garb, and served them peacock dressed in all its feathers, which Pound reported to his mother went well with the medieval cum Burne-Jones setting. Though flattered, Blunt was perplexed: they presented him with a sculpture by Gaudier-Brzeska, and a sample of a poem by each, all of which he cordially disliked. Pound recited a verse in his honour, but credited him with helping Mazzini, the Italian patriot, rather than Arabi, the Egyptian nationalist. Blunt had published no poetry for eight years, and although later that year he was to bring out his collected poems, it seems very unlikely this was just about Blunt's poetry, as most accounts of the incident, ignoring Pound's mention of the Empire, suggest. It is possible it was another of Pound's sudden crazes, but when he told Harriet Monroe she should publish some of Blunt's poetry it was 'for the glory of the name' rather than anything to do with the poetry itself.[79] For Pound, and in varying degrees for the others, it was more the heady mix that Blunt represented: virile, poetic, anti-establishment, anti-Empire and aristocratic. The full pleasure of the gesture came when they were told that a Foreign Office official had said he would never speak to any of them again.

Blunt himself was a flawed figure, as his wife knew only too well; he was possibly something of anti-Semite (Pound implies, but somewhat ambiguously, that Blunt described the Empire as 'a Semitic invention of Disraeli's' – it could have been someone else's phrase, even Pound's own); but Blunt's recognition of the crimes against humanity perpetrated by the Empire was admirable.[80] Similarly, for all the unsavoury elements already present in Pound's views, one should acknowledge, as for example Derrida does, that Pound in some ways at any rate pushed the growing doubts about the sufficiency of a Eurocentric view one stage further. For Derrida it is specifically the break with the notion of the superiority of alphabetic writing that he finds admirable, but that was not Pound's only move.[81] One of the aims of the modernism Pound proposed, like other modernists of the time, was to learn from the cultures hitherto so often despised by the West. As Hulme put it, there was a change in sensibility. Modernism is conventionally described as cosmopolitan, but the implications of that term generally refer only to American and European metropoles. Modernism was cosmopolitan in a far more profound sense. It was part of a changing comprehension of the world; the modernists were conscious in a new way that the West was only part of the world's culture. Raymond Williams defined the most important characteristic of the modern metropolis as its 'miscellaneity'. He writes:

> within the new kind of open, complex and mobile society, small groups in any form of divergence or dissent could find some kind of foothold, in ways that would not have been possible if the artists and thinkers composing them had been scattered in more traditional, closed societies ... the metropolis ... in the course of capitalist and imperialist development has characteristically attracted a very mixed population, from a variety of social and cultural origins ... Thus the key cultural factor of the modernist shift is the character of the metropolis.[82]

What in a homogeneous society might appear natural, this cultural mix revealed as conventional, one way of doing or saying it, but not necessarily the only or even an adequate way. It brought the realisation, as Hulme commented, 'that what were taken for the necessary principles of aesthetics' were merely localised European traditions.[83] Pound met the working-class Flint, met the Irish nationalists, met Tagore, met Ghose, met Yoni Noguchi, was soon to meet Michio Ito. His fateful meeting with Mary Fenollosa, the widow of Ernest Fenollosa, whose work on the Chinese was to change the course of his poetic life, was at the house of the Bengali poet, Sarogini Naidu. Writing to Harriet Monroe, Pound described the metropolis as 'that which accepts all gifts and all heights of excellence, usually the excellence which is *tabu* in its own village. The metropolis is always accused by the peasant of "being mad after foreign notions".'[84] Simon Gikandi has argued that 'One of modernism's most enduring achievements ... was to connect race and aesthetics at the most fundamental level'.[85] Aesthetic value had in European philosophy been by definition the property of European art; now it lay in the cultural fusions of modernism.

It was this registering of a new perception of the world which lay behind the imagist aesthetic; a world which was fragmented, heterogeneous; with moments of intensity, yes, a traditional framework, no. Much of the imagist programme – avoidance of rhetoric, presentation not description, directness of approach, importance of cadence – was in fact a continuation of the precepts of the Rhymers, particularly, as James Longenbach points out, those of Yeats. The imagist emphasis on the epiphanic moment follows Pater and Rossetti, re-conceptualised through Bergson. But the device that I would argue is the most characteristic of modernism, the collage, whose qualities of fragmentation and juxtaposition permeate so much of modernist art and literature, the qualities that it shares with the modern metropolis, enters Anglo-American poetry though the haiku. Pound was eventually to find his supreme version of this in the superimpositions of the Chinese ideogram, from which he drew, as he put it, 'a whole basis of aesthetic', his version of Hulme's earlier analogy of the chord.[86] The collages of modernism came out of a hybrid, multiracial world. In Pound's case, openness to certain other cultures was combined even at this stage with scorn for most outside the elect (elected by him, of course), and the beginnings of his anti-Semitic paranoia.

Jewish acquisitiveness, as he sees it, merges with the desire for property that he identified as the foundation of the British Empire. It was at the height of his anti-Semitism that Pound was to denounce most vehemently 'the ineffable and illimitable imbecility of the British Empire'.[87]

Pound's politics cannot and should not be justified, but their complexity has to be acknowledged. Overall, he was part of a movement that was bigger than himself, though he played a not inconsiderable role. Modernism as an artistic practice was not, I would argue, responsible for views like Pound's fascism; modernism was an artistic movement that could encompass liberatory as well authoritarian beliefs. Other modernists had different agendas. All of them had quarrels with the hierarchies they inherited: some, like Pound, went on to put equally dangerous ones in their place.

## Notes

1 This chapter comes out of the research I have done for a group biography of the imagist movement, to be published by Jonathan Cape. I have to thank the British Academy for a Research Award that helped to make the research possible. I have only had space here to give a very limited set of examples; I am particularly sorry not to have been able to discuss the relation of these ideas to H. D. and her Hellenism, but to have begun to do so adequately would have doubled the length of my chapter. It will be in the book!

2 Helen Carr, *Inventing the American Primitive: Politics, Gender and the Representation of Native American Literary Traditions, 1789–1936* (Cork, University of Cork Press/New York, University of New York Press, 1996), pp. 210–29.

3 Susan Hiller, summarising Kenneth Coutts-Smith's argument, in Susan Hiller (ed.), *The Myth of Primitivism: Perspectives on Art* (London, Routledge, 1991).

4 Lisa Lowe, *Critical Terrains: French and British Orientalisms* (Ithaca, Cornell University Press, 1991).

5 Henry Louis Gates, 'Harlem on our minds', in *Rhapsodies in Black: Art of the Harlem Renaissance* (London, Hayward Gallery with the Institute of Visual Arts and the University of California Press, 1997), pp. 164, 163; see also Michael North, *The Dialect of Modernism: Race, Language and Twentieth-Century Literature* (New York, Oxford University Press, 1994).

6 Zhaoming Qian, *Orientalism and Modernism: The Legacy of China in Pound and Williams* (Durham, N.C., Duke University Press, 1995).

7 J. B. Harmer, *Victory in Limbo: Imagism, 1908–1917* (London, Secker &

Warburg, 1975), pp. 19–21.

8 *Ibid.*, p. 21.

9 F. S. Flint, 'A history of imagism', *The Egoist*, 2:5 (1 May 1915).

10 Humphrey Carpenter, *A Serious Character: The Life of Ezra Pound* (London, Faber & Faber, 1988), p. 124.

11 Samuel Hynes, *The Edwardian Turn of Mind* (Princeton, Princeton University Press, 1968), p. 8.

12 F. S. Flint, 'A history of imagism'.

13 F. S. Flint, *The New Age*, 6 (9 December 1909) 137, quoted in Wallace Martin, '"The Forgotten School of 1909" and the origins of imagism', in J. Howard Woolmer, *A Catalogue of Imagist Poets with Essays by Wallace Martin and Ian Fletcher* (New York, J. Howard Woolmer, 1966), p. 12.

14 F. S. Flint, 'Recent Verse', *The New Age*, 3 (11 July 1908) 212–13 quoted in Cyrena Pondrom, *The Road from Paris: French Influence on English Poetry, 1900–1920* (Cambridge, Cambridge University Press, 1974), pp. 50–51.

15 Paul-Louis Couchoud, *Sages et poètes d'Asie* (Paris, Calmann-Lévy, 1916), p. 7.

16 Pondrom, *The Road from Paris*, p. 50.

17 Couchoud, *Sages et poètes*, pp. 34–5.

18 Pondrom, *The Road from Paris*, p. 50.

19 Couchoud, *Sages et poètes*, p. 8.

20 *The Collected Writings of T. E. Hulme*, ed. Karen Csengri (Oxford, Clarendon Press, 1994), p. 87.

21 Henri Bergson, *Introduction to Metaphysics*, trans. T. E. Hulme (London, Macmillan, 1913), p. 14. (Hulme did not acknowledge Flint's help.)

22 Csengri, *T. E. Hulme*, p. 54.

23 Ezra Pound to William Carlos Williams, 21 October 1908, in *Selected Letters of Ezra Pound*, ed. D. D. Paige (London, Faber & Faber, 1951), p. 36.

24 Ezra Pound to William Carlos Williams, 3 February 1909 in *Selected Letters*, p. 41.

25 Brita Lindberg-Seyersten (ed.), *Pound/Ford: The Story of a Literary Friendship* (London, Faber & Faber, 1982), p. 172.

26 David Frail, *The Early Politics and Poetics of William Carlos Williams* (Ann Arbor, U.M.I. Research Press, 1987), p. 29.

27 F. S. Flint, 'A history of imagism'.

28 See letter to William Carlos Williams, 21 May 1909, in *Selected Letters*, pp. 41–2.

29 James Longenbaum, *Stone Cottage: Pound, Yeats, and Modernism* (New York and Oxford, Oxford University Press, 1988), pp. 13–14.

30 Josephine Guy, *The British Avant Garde: The Theory and Politics of Tradition* (Hemel Hempstead, Harvester Wheatsheaf, 1991).

31 Ezra Pound, *Make It New* (London, Faber & Faber, 1934).

32 The one scholar who points this out is Ronald Schuchard, though he

sees its importance only in terms of the question of whether modern verse should be spoken or not. See Ronald Schuchard, '"As regarding rhythm": Yeats and the imagists', *Yeats: An Annual of Critical and Textual Studies*, 2 (1984).

33 Patrica Hutchins, *Ezra Pound's Kensington: An Exploration, 1885–1915* (London, Faber & Faber, 1963), p. 63.

34 Ezra Pound, 'Lionel Johnson', in *Literary Essays* (London, Faber & Faber, 1954), p. 367.

35 Longenbaum, *Stone Cottage*, pp. 12–13. Humphrey Carpenter quotes from this letter, but omits the mention of the Irish Literary Society (Carpenter, *A Serious Character*, p. 127).

36 Vincent J. Cheng, *Joyce, Race and Empire* (Cambridge, Cambridge University Press, 1995), pp. 19, 33 and 37.

37 Norah Saunders and A. A. Kelly, *Joseph Campbell, Poet and Nationalist, 1879–1944: A Critical Biography* (Dublin, Wolfhound Press, 1988), p. 64.

38 Desmond FitzGerald, *Memoirs, 1913–16* (London, Routledge & Kegan Paul, 1968), p. 21. My grateful thanks to W. J. McCormack for telling me the poet and the politician were the same person.

39 Austin Clarke (ed.), *The Poems of Joseph Campbell* (Dublin, Allen Figis, 1963), p. 1.

40 Joseph Campbell, *The Mountainy Singer* (Dublin, Maunsel, 1909).

41 Roy Foster, *W. B. Yeats: A Life*, Volume 1, *The Apprentice Mage, 1865–1914* (Oxford, Oxford University Press, 1997), p. 318.

42 Campbell, *Mountainy Singer*, p. 50.

43 Ezra Pound, *Collected Early Poems* (London, Faber & Faber, 1977), pp. 112–13; Joseph Campbell, *The Gilly of Christ* (Dublin, Maunsel, 1907). 'Gilly' means servant – the poem refers to 'The mate of Mary's son'. Pound footnotes his poem, explaining 'Fere = Mate, Companion'.

44 Harmer, *Victory in Limbo*, p. 49.

45 Hutchins, *Ezra Pound's Kensington*, p. 130.

46 Ezra Pound, 'The non-existence of Ireland', *The New Age*, 16:17 (25 February 1915), reprinted in Lea Baechler, A. Walton Litz and James Longenbach (eds), *Ezra Pound's Poetry and Prose: Contributions to Periodicals, Vol. 2, 1915–17* (New York, Garland, 1991), p. 21.

47 Foster, *W. B. Yeats*, p. 306.

48 'Through alien eyes. 1', *The New Age*, 12:11 (16 January 1913), reprinted in *Ezra Pound's Poetry and Prose: Contributions to Periodicals, Vol. 1, 1902–14*, ed. Lea Baechler, A. Walton Litz and James Longenbach (New York, Garland, 1991), p. 114.

49 Ezra Pound, 'The Black Crusade', *The New Age*, 12:3 (21 November 1912) in Baechler *et al.*, *Ezra Pound's Poetry and Prose, Vol. 1*, p. 108.

50 Saunders and Kelly, *Joseph Campbell*, p. 37.

51 'The new sculpture', *The Egoist*, 1:4 (16 February 1914).

52 'The audience. 1', *Poetry*, 5:1 (October 1914) 29.

53 Ezra Pound, *The Spirit of Romance* (1910; London, Peter Owen, revised edn 1952), p. 95.

54 *Ibid.*, p. 8.

55 Ezra Pound, 'The Renaissance' (1914), in *Literary Essays*, p. 225.

56 Csengri, *T. E. Hulme*, p. 250.

57 Roy Foster says Pound was introduced to Tagore on 7 July, but Pound was not in the country then. Foster also follows James Longenbach in misdating Pound's letter to Dorothy about Tagore to 8 May 1912, instead of 1913, thus implying Pound's enthusiasm had disappeared before it had begun, which would have been rapid even for Pound. See *Ezra Pound and Dorothy Shakespear: Their Letters, 1909–14*, ed. Omar Pound and A. Walton Litz (London, Faber & Faber, 1984), p. 224.

58 Letter to Harriet Monroe, 24 September 1912, in Paige, *Letters*, p. 44.

59 Ezra Pound, 'Tagore's poems', *Poetry*, 1:3 (December 1912) 92.

60 *Ibid.*, p. 93.

61 Carpenter, *A Serious Character*, p. 186.

62 Foster, *W. B. Yeats*, p. 475.

63 Harold M. Hurwitz, 'Ezra Pound and Rabindranath Tagore', *American Literature* 36 (1964) 56–7; Foster, *W. B. Yeats*, pp. 470–1.

64 Hurwitz, 'Ezra Pound and Rabindranath Tagore', p.58.

65 Longenbach, *Stone Cottage*, p. 25.

66 Yoko Chiba, 'Ezra Pound's versions of Fenollosa's Noh Manuscripts and Yeats's unpublished "Suggestions and Corrections"', *Yeats Annual, No. 4*, ed. Warwick Gould (London, Macmillan, 1984), p. 122.

67 Ezra Pound, 'The Renaissance', p. 214.

68 'Through alien eyes. 2', *The New Age*, 12:12 (23 January 1913), and 'Through alien eyes. 3', *The New Age*, 12:13 (30 January 1913), reprinted in Baechler *et al.*, *Ezra Pound's Poetry and Prose, Vol. 1*, pp. 115 and 116.

69 Carpenter, *A Serious Character*, p. 186; Ezra Pound, '"Dubliners" and Mr. James Joyce', *The Egoist*, 1:14 (15 July 1914), p. 400; Yoko Chiba, 'Ezra Pound's versions', p. 138.

70 Ezra Pound, 'Prologomena' *(sic)*, *Poetry Review* 1/2 (February 1912) 76.

71 Ezra Pound, *Collected Early Poems*, p. 108.

72 Csengri, *T. E. Hulme*, p. 51.

73 Sandra Gilbert and Susan Gubar, *No-Man's Land: The Place of the Woman Writer in the Twentieth Century*, 3 vols (New Haven, Yale University Press, 1987, 1989, 1994), *passim*.

74 Elizabeth Longford, *A Pilgrimage of Passion: The Life of Wilfrid Scawen Blunt* (London, Weidenfeld & Nicolson, 1979), p. 3.

75 *Ibid.*, p. 339.

76 Wilfrid Scawen Blunt, *The Shame of the Nineteenth Century. A Letter Addressed to the 'Times', December 24, 1900* (London; n.p., 1901), p. 3.

77 Longford, *A Pilgrimage of Passion*, p. 343.

78 Ezra Pound, 'Homage to Wilfrid Blunt', *Poetry*, 3:6 (March 1914) 222.

79 Ezra Pound to Harriet Monroe, 28 March 1914, in *Selected Letters*, p. 73.
80 Pound, 'Homage to Wilfrid Blunt', p. 222.
81 Jacques Derrida, *Of Grammatology*, trans. Gayatri Chakravorty Spivak (Baltimore, Johns Hopkins University Press, 1976), p. 92.
82 Raymond Williams, *The Politics of Modernism: Against the New Conformists*, ed. Tony Pinkney (London, Verso, 1989), p. 45.
83 Csengri, *T. E. Hulme*, p. 250.
84 Ezra Pound to Harriet Monroe, 7 November 1913, in *Selected Letters*, p. 62.
85 Simon Gikandi, 'Race and the modernist aesthetic', in Tim Youngs (ed.), *Writing and Race* (New York and London, Longman, 1997), p. 152.
86 Ezra Pound to Felix E. Schelling, June 1915, in *Selected Letters*, p. 102.
87 Ezra Pound to the editor of the *English Journal*, 24 January 1931, in *Selected Letters*, p. 310.

# 4

## 'Immeasurable strangeness' in imperial times: Leonard Woolf and W. B. Yeats

### Elleke Boehmer

What is it that happens when different conceptual systems interact within an imperial context? How do different 'languages' – in the Bakhtinian sense of a conceptual system or point of view – intersect across the power differentials imposed within colonial hierarchies? These questions impact directly on early-twentieth-century modernism in its effort to respond to the new and the strange introduced to Europe by colonial expansion, investigations in ethnography and myth, and new interests in mysticism and spirituality. In their attempt to work through their own internal pessimism concerning the adequacy of inherited structures of belief to interpret the cataclysmically expanding and collapsing modern world, modernist writers tested the limits of their own values and beliefs against symbolic systems imported from other, so-called primitive, intuitive, and often politically subordinate contexts. My focus in this chapter concerns some of the implications that this encounter had for their work. Did that verbal and ideological accommodation take place which, according to Bakhtin, occurs when a self-enclosed unitary language is exposed to others and decentred as a result?[1] What was the self-questioning, or the new awareness of relative value, which resulted from European writers' perception of otherness?

I want to consider these questions in relation to two writers who in different ways exposed their words and world-views to 'alien', 'dialogically agitated'[2] environments at that crucial informing moment for modernism, the years just before the outbreak of the First World

War. The writers are Leonard Woolf and W. B. Yeats, the first of whom played an influential role in modernism, not least through his work at the Hogarth Press; and the second of whom is widely recognised as one of modernism's defining voices, a poet who, especially from the time of *Responsibilities* (1914), came to stand at the very centre of experimentation with personae and reinvented tradition.

However, while this chapter will seek to place these two self-questioning writers alongside each other, from the outset the clear differences between them should be underlined. While deeply identified with the free-thinking, intellectual world of Bloomsbury, Leonard Woolf as a Jew would have been confronted with the anti-Semitism endemic to the liberal bourgeois individualism of that chosen social milieu (among others). His sense of his own difference, operating in conjunction with his colonial experiences, can persuasively account for Woolf's espousal of a radical socialist and internationalist politics (more radical than the politics of any other member of Bloomsbury) from the time of Versailles at the end of the First World War. This radicalism is expressed in powerful critiques of empire such as *Economic Imperialism* (1920) and *Imperialism and Civilisation* (1928), as well as the later two-volume *After the Deluge* (1931, 1939).[3]

For his part the Anglo-Irish patriot W. B. Yeats had worked since the early 1890s in support of Ireland's 'war' to '[affirm] her own individuality' and to oppose English materialism.[4] Though conventionally regarded as an elitist modernist, contemptuous of political involvement, Yeats's efforts across his lifetime to revivify Irish cultural traditions and build a new national literature have more recently, and correctly I feel, been placed in a broadly post-colonial context. For Yeats the way in which the Irish might overcome the debilitating effects of their colonisation was to 'awaken ... the national idea' through culture – it is an overcoming for which any number of post-colonial novelists and poets since have struggled.[5]

Yet even as both writers, though so differently, set themselves in opposition to the dominant imperial culture, they also, as we will see, remained to an extent complicit with its values and perceptions, especially with regard to race. While the challenge of cultural otherness and the possibility of alternative cultural knowledge held their attention, other peoples (for Woolf, natives in Ceylon; for Yeats, Indians as well as Irish peasants) were by and large described *en masse* or as representatives of generic groups. European-constructed differ-ence in this respect continued to obstruct a clear-eyed view of the particular social and material worlds which colonised peoples inhabited.

Leonard Woolf's letters home from Ceylon, where he worked as a colonial officer between 1905 and 1911, give us an apt point of entry to the contact zone between modernist writing at the start of this century and its imperial context.[6] Significantly, these letters – and the later story 'Pearls and Swine' (1921; composed *c.* 1912/13), which is based on material in the letters – form the first textual interrogation of colonisation in the new century to take Joseph Conrad's own ambiguous *Heart of Darkness* (1899)[7] as an informing (indeed already paradigmatic) text through which to understand empire's paradoxes.[8] The formal echoes of Conrad in Woolf are strong enough to suggest that the latter was increasingly relying on Conrad's epistemological questions, and moving away from Rudyard Kipling's colonial caricatures, in order to represent his own personal and political anxieties as an imperialist.

What is immediately striking about Woolf's letters is how markedly they contrast with the highly efficient and scrupulously factual administrative records that he was also keeping at the time.[9] In particular in the expostulations addressed to his friend Lytton Strachey, Woolf responds to his experience of governing Tamils in the manner of a Marlow who, moving into the unknown of another culture, even though cushioned by white colonial structures, is deeply shaken. In the jungle regions of Hambantota, however, Woolf finds – unlike Marlow – no secret sharer, no Kurtz through whom to seek to recuperate his illusions about the civilising mission or the value of his labours. Read chronologically, we see in the letters a growing awareness of British colonial culture as caught in a contradictory, unreal and even absurd position: confused about the purpose of their rule, people at the club act out a Kiplingesque fantasy which lacks any connection with local people.[10] This awareness, what Woolf later called an increasing 'political schizophrenia' – a resentment at 'being a ruler of the ruled',[11] no doubt exacerbated by his own outsider status – was for a hard-working colonial officer profoundly disorienting and dispiriting. It was also an awareness that back in England, with the benefit of retrospection, would transform Woolf into an anti-imperialist, a process that is dramatised in the conflict at the centre of his story 'Pearls and Swine', which I will discuss in the latter part of this chapter.

An emblematic case in point of Woolf's disorientation or ideological decentring occurs in a letter of 21 May 1905, written within the first year of his arriving in Ceylon (in October 1904).[12] From the start the Conradian notes are unmistakable: the devotion to work as giving a hold on reality despite its tedium; the pervasive sense of disgust at the white man's self-involved and therefore seemingly pointless rule in the tropics; the inevitable stereotyping of natives, here of their fatalism; and, probably the predominant mood, a profound sense of the fragility of reality as it was previously understood.[13] 'This curious mixture of intense reality and unreality', even of 'theatrical unreality', as he described it, is a perception that Woolf returns to again and again, as he does in his autobiography about the years in Ceylon, *Growing*.[14] There is 'the strange sense of a complete break with the past', and of 'no connection with yesterday'. '[O]ne feels as if one were acting in a play or living in a dream', in relation to which, significantly, not only Ceylonese life but existence back in London and Cambridge seems unreal.[15] '[A]ll Anglo-Indians and imperialists who were colonial government servants' resemble 'displaced persons': 'in a foreign country, [we] had therefore become unreal, artificial, temporary, and alien'.[16]

In the May 1905 letter, Woolf's sense of the general uncertainty of things in the foreign context is given dramatic point by his description of a great hole (presumably due to subsidence) that appears to be opening up in the Jaffna Peninsula, threatening to tumble the whole province over which he has charge into the sea. Beginning with the observation, 'A cataclysm is hourly expected here', he goes on:

> a hole had suddenly appeared in the midst of a field about 5 miles from Jaffna, that … had gradually in a few hours increased from about 3 to 90 square feet & … was still increasing … It is like a big pond with the water about a foot from the top, there is a curious heaving in the water, every five or ten minutes a crack appears in the earth round the edge, the crack widens and the earth topples over into the water which heaves & swirls & eddies. Hundreds of natives stand round, looking on with their usual appearance of complete indifference, & every time another foot of the ground disappears, a long 'aiyo, aiyo' goes up. The water is obviously from the sea … and I expect that it means that Jaffna Peninsula is going to return to the seabed from which it came.[17]

While the language is touched by a self-conscious melodrama, Woolf can be read as using the incident and the feeling of incipient disaster it evokes as a correlate for his state of mind, the profound unsettling of his world. The description ends abruptly with one of the refrains concerning his mental inertia which are recurrent in the letters to Strachey: 'I neither read nor think nor – in the old way – feel'. The curiosities of local life are 'the only realities';[18] there is nothing else of importance, other than, intriguingly, further suggestions of imminent danger and flooding, and of holes and cracks in the stability of things, in the account of an inspection of a leaky ship which follows. It is also significant in this respect that the same letter opens with another reference to uncertainty and anxiety, indeed to literal displacement, where he speaks of having been forced to move house and the fear of catching a colleague's consumption.

The implicit and perhaps even partly unconscious connections that Woolf makes in this letter between his feelings of alienation and displacement, and scenes involving a leaky earth and leaky vessels, remind us again of Conrad's Marlow in *Heart of Darkness*. At this point the parallel with Conrad allows us to gain a clearer sense of the emptying out of Woolf's preconceptions that occurs in response to the foreign unreality that is also the 'only reality'. From the beginning of his journey along the African coast, Marlow in *Heart of Darkness* registers a similar experience of perceptual shock at the seeming inscrutability of the African forest but also at the same time at the grotesque, 'objectless' farce of empire.[19] At the Outer Station, while attempting to avoid following the 'deathlike' spectacle of the chain-gang, Marlow tells us, he sidesteps a vast hole dug for no apparent purpose, and then nearly falls into a ravine dumped full of imported and broken drainage pipes before finally stumbling into the hellish grove of trees in which slaves disabled by their work lie dying. Later, at the Central Station, where he is occupied in mending the steamer which has had the bottom torn out of it, there is a fire which one of the white men attempts to put out with a leaky bucket.[20] Withheld from working by an absence of rivets, Marlow is overwhelmed by a deep sense of unreality: the brickmaker, a hollow 'papier-mâché Mephistopheles', has nothing to make his bricks with; there is a pervasive 'air of plotting about [the] station, but nothing came of it, of course'.[21] Like Woolf, he compares his experience to dreaming: 'It seems to me I am trying to tell you a dream … that commingling of absurdity, surprise, and bewilderment in a tremor of struggling revolt, that notion of being captured by the incredible which is of the very essence of dreams'.[22]

The comparison with Conrad, which Woolf's language encourages, underlines the extent to which an orientation towards, or a closeness to, the alien can produce a vertiginous disorientation, even a profound psychic agitation, on the part of the white imperialist. If we now turn to Bakhtin's analysis of dialogic decentring, in his long essay 'Discourse in the Novel', we may begin to account in more general theoretical terms for this disorientation. Bakhtin's concept of intentional, directed hybrid formations (as opposed to the 'organic' or unconscious mixtures of world-views we find in any language) offers, I believe, a helpful model for thinking about how the voice of colonial authority may open out to other voices, and begin to question itself.[23]

At the height of empire around the turn of the twentieth century, the colonial world-view, its conviction of European superiority and leadership over other races, in many ways corresponds to Bakhtin's description of the monologic utterance, sufficient to itself, aware of other utterances, if at all, only as 'objects' exterior to its internal commitments and concerns.[24] However, where this closed and self-sufficient 'voice' is confronted by another world of meaning, in such a way that the other world cannot be ignored, as for example in the colonial context, with the colonial officer or agent's involvement in trials and hangings, or proximity to native crowds and chain-gangs, what results can be described as that Bakhtinian disturbance which comes about when an utterance *addresses itself to* others. A 'qualified relationship to one's own language' emerges; the authoritative language begins to regard itself, often with disruptive effect, as if from elsewhere or 'through the eyes of another language'.[25]

A similar condition of colonial self-awareness and consequent ambivalence is described in psychoanalytic terms by Homi Bhabha in his much-cited essays collected in *The Location of Culture*, though for him the emphasis is on how colonial perception is split from the outset, constantly oscillating through aversion and attraction.[26] Differently, my focus here is on the *emergence* of colonial decentring in writing, on the dynamics of a growing disaffection on the part of those directly exposed to the alien as a result of colonial experience or an encounter with colonised self-expression. The turn of the century was, of course, the time when the British Empire was at its height and its confidence apparently unshakeable. Yet it was that very expansion of colonial rule across so many different contexts that, it seems to me, began to undercut the possibility and plausibility of its languages of power. Specifically, therefore, I am interested in those moments in texts where the decentring or unsettling of inherited cultural discourses can be seen to begin to occur – moments that register the breakdown of accepted terms, but also the first stresses of what might be termed a new dialogic perception. I am interested in where and how single-voiced imperial authority begins to admit of its own ill-adjustedness, and its own delegitimation, in confrontation with an alien or indigenous culture.

Following the Bakhtinian model, the self-aware colonial voice, such as that of Woolf or Conrad, when confronted by cultural difference, and its own seeming uselessness or superfluity in the colonial context, may be said to move from the unconscious ambivalence so well described by Bhabha towards an *intentional* hybridity or double-voicedness: a conflict of values that arises in spite of and in opposition to the reassuring separations imposed by the colonial situation within which that voice is enclosed. As a result of this growing, even if still intermittent, perception of alternative sources of meaning – in short, of perceptual noise or, taking Woolf's image, leakiness – in the foreign environment, a sense of relativity emerges whereby the colonial voice hears itself as if being spoken from another place; in other words, begins to objectify, displace and even ironise itself. We might think here of Woolf's growing sense of his own displacement as outlined in his letters, of being 'done for' with regard to England. In the reiterated phrases accentuating not only his absurdity in Ceylon, but also his sense of alienation with regard to his native land, Woolf is in effect objectifying himself, perceiving his cultural standpoint as 'only *one* among other cultures and languages', to quote Bakhtin again.[27]

A comparable, though in many cases differently generated, sense of relativity occurred also as the motor force behind much European modernist self-questioning, and behind the searches through the symbolic systems of other cultures to find alternative aesthetic potential (such as we find in Ezra Pound or T. S. Eliot's poetry of this time, or in the 'savage pilgrimage' recorded in Lawrence's novels *Kangaroo* (1923) and *The Plumed Serpent* (1926), or in primitivism in painting). The difference here was that ideas of cultural relativity within Europe were stimulated not so much by direct colonial experience as by the broader imperial context, by the cultural repercussions of a world opened up by imperialism. A further difference was that whereas for metropolitan modernist writers – the T. S. Eliot of *The Waste Land* (1922) is a clear example – the citation of alien symbolic systems was largely an appropriation to the end of shoring up a European cultural landscape already perceived to be disintegrating (though still of central importance), in Woolf's case the encounter with the other world of meaning acted directly as the disintegrating force. The proximate presence of the indigenous culture cast doubt on his own significance, and as a result cast doubt too on the system of authority (and on the justifications of that system) which he as a colonial officer represented: 'We are all doomed, I imagine', he wrote, 'we treat them as inferiors & tell them that they are their own equals'; 'They don't understand and they don't believe in our methods'.[28]

Like Woolf, and like Conrad's Marlow, the poet W. B. Yeats also used the language of dreams when speaking in 1912 of the effect on him of the Bengali poet Rabindranath Tagore: his lyrics displayed a world that Yeats '[had] dreamed of all [his] life long'.[29] As I have already suggested, as an Anglo-Irishman and an Irish cultural nationalist, Yeats's position relative to British colonialism was obviously different from that of Leonard Woolf, though both writers were positioned outside the British establishment. Yet it is interesting that in his Introduction to Tagore's self-translated *Gitanjali* (1912, which appeared just after Woolf's return from Ceylon to London, and before he began work on his 'stories of the east'), we see Yeats, too, speaking self-consciously as a Westerner, yet searching for terms that will at once evoke *and* effect the 'stirring'[30] encounter with a distant Eastern culture that Tagore's poetry seems to invite. For Yeats in the Introduction the attempt to translate the Bengali poet's mystical appeal in a way that his English-speaking metropolitan audience would understand (many of the emendations of Tagore's English translations were indeed Yeats's[31]) leads from a sense of its foreignness and remoteness,[32] through an attempt to identify on some level with its 'immeasurable strangeness',[33] and then to reflections on the lack of integration, the self-deprecating 'continual warfare' that marks public life in Europe, and more specifically in Ireland, relative to the 'completeness' of Tagore's poetic world in Bengal. Perhaps springing out of his long-standing preoccupation with Eastern thought and mysticism, there seems to be for Yeats something deeply transforming and revelatory in this connection with a distant culture.[34] As in Woolf, we again observe how directedness towards the foreign generates an objectification of the familiar and the proximate, and an expansion and reticulation of accepted modes of thought. (This expansion and multiplication of the utterances emerging out of an East–West encounter finds a parallel in the fact that Tagore's *Gitanjali* of 1912 was a version of his Bengali *Gitanjali* of 1910, with additions from two other collections, *Naivedya* and *Kheya*.)

At this point I would like to look more closely at the terms of Yeats's admiration for Tagore in the Introduction, which probably represented his most concentrated and concrete attempt to promote Tagore's writing in the West. What does he make of an art whose mystery so 'stirs his blood'? First, there is his expression of wonder, even of bafflement: he feels remote from the ceremonious wholeness of the Bengali poet's life.[35] But within a number of paragraphs he attempts to establish some sort of connection or commonality alongside that bafflement, to call the literary nationalist movement of which Tagore is a part a 'new Renaissance'.[36] He compares Tagore's culture to the more integrated traditional world combining meditation and politics, love and philosophy, that, he believes, can also be found in Europe's past. The poetry therefore sets off in him a very modernist nostalgia for a fuller, vibrant and more unselfconscious life, marked by reciprocity between the elite and the 'unlearned', and a unification of the spiritual and sensual aspects of being.[37] In this contrast between the Calcutta Renaissance and the warfare that is aesthetic and political life in Ireland, we see Yeats beginning (within a context of shared colonisation) to project his own image upon Tagore and upon Bengal. Indeed we cannot deny that this romanticising objectification of India as caught in an earlier phase of human history bears distinctly Orientalist overtones; at moments in the essay Yeats the Westerner can justly be regarded as patronising and stereotyping 'my Indians'.[38]

And yet the yearning towards a closer connection with India that moves through the writing seems also to pull against such crude stereotyping. Whilst underlining the differences that separate him from Tagore, Yeats prepares for the turning point two-thirds of the way through the essay, when he says that despite its effects of estrangement, the Indian poet's work makes its strongest impression because we find within that strangeness 'our own image ... our voice as in a dream'[39] – in effect, we encounter our dream selves. Here, once more, is Marlow claiming to recognise something in the Africans of the Congo that harks back to depths within himself.

True, this kind of European projection upon other cultural worlds is again difficult to distinguish from the self-representations and self-distancing of more overtly colonial writing. Yet what is significant about Yeats's (and perhaps also Marlow's) language is that the perceived cultural difference is not only recognised as reflecting a division within the self; the difference also seems paradoxically closer to the self, more real, more identifiable-with, than are aspects of European culture. As did Leonard Woolf, Yeats uses his suggestions of un-reality, and of a splitting of the self, to evoke the impact of a strange-ness that yet accommodates, an unhomeliness that can be welcomed home. As he goes on to say, there is more in Tagore that we might respond to than we find in Western mysticism, a greater wonder, a greater wholeness and intensity of experience. Tagore's poetry seem-ingly lies closer to the frustrations and depressions of contemporary life in Europe, especially in Ireland, than does European contempla-tive and ascetic literature. As if to embrace and enact this closeness in his own writing, Yeats devotes the final part of the Introduction to long quotations from *Gitanjali* itself which, to him, illustrate the Bengali lyricist's spontaneous intensity and unity of being.[40]

Paradoxically, it was around the time that he was thus praising Tagore that Yeats himself was trying to cultivate 'a less dream-burdened will'.[41] Tagore's devotional poetry in the Vaishnava tradi-tion of intensely personal spiritual longing[42] exemplified the type of work Yeats identified with but was seeking to divest himself of. Yet it is possible to speculate that the encounter with the Indian poet that Yeats describes – the encounter with an opposite that was also in part himself – acted as one of the catalysts of the changed, honed poetry Yeats was beginning to write. He was perhaps animated on the one hand by the coincidence between the mystical remoteness of Tagore and his own early poetry, and on the other by the contrast between this and the conflict and individuality of his own society. Moreover, the achievement that Tagore represented as the national voice of Bengal (even though this was a position Tagore himself was to disavow) may also have suggested to Yeats a model for a disciplined aesthetic that yet retained powerful cultural and political resonances.

So far I have spoken of Yeats mainly as a Western poet encountering work of suggestive cultural remoteness. In the context of colonial modernism, however, it remains important to remember the reality of Ireland's own colonised position in relation to Britain, and Yeats's particular nationalist interests as expressed in the Celtic Revival and in his labours for the Irish National Theatre. Like artists of the decolonising world since his time, Yeats confronted the question of how to give form to a national culture emerging out of a history of dispossession. In the absence of rallying symbols of identity, he realised, a writer had to attempt to forge these out of the detritus of the colonial past and the surviving myths and stories of the downtrodden. Yeats was therefore no doubt drawn to the cultural idealism of a Bengali nationalist like Tagore because of the latter's attempt to reclaim local languages and traditions: ·Yeats understood the compulsion to retrieve or reinvent images of the homeland untouched by the colonial presence.

Impelled by his ambitions for Ireland, Yeats's approach to Tagore demonstrates how Bakhtin's 'foreign' or 'alien' might also *at the same time* be the familiar, the 'already uttered', this intersection taking place not only in the unconscious world of dreams, but in the wider political sphere. In this case modernism as it emerges out of a colonial background subtly reverses the connotations of the Eastern and the exotic; strangeness in effect becomes 'measurable', captured in the forms of Yeats's own immediate experience. Or, to put it another way again, where modernist and colonial realities conjoin, as in Yeats's world, where the teaching of tradition has been a form of imposing authority, the modernist drive to 'make it new', to warp and unsettle a received tradition, might be that much more powerfully felt and expressed.[43]

Declan Kiberd has suggested that Tagore may have found models for his own work in Yeats's attempts through stylistic innovation to project new forms into the cultural void of the nation.[44] However, taking into account not only the relative ages of the two writers but also that Tagore was in part formed by the powerful nationalist movement in Bengal from the 1880s onwards, it is clear on the contrary that the influence would have operated in the other direction, from Tagore to Yeats. As part of that effort which we find in his poetry and short stories to project visions of an unspoilt pastoral Bengal, Tagore might have helped reveal to Yeats what it was in the nation that might be different from and resistant to the materialist imperial centre (and what it was in the poet that might remain separate from the fanaticism and 'baseness' of nationalism). Yet again, the foreign came to the Irish poet in the form of another colonial's mystical lyricism and revealed to him his own image.

In Yeats's Introduction to *Gitanjali* the unsettling of the Western writer's superiority over another culture is sharpened and complicated by the writer's own culturally subordinate position relative to the metropolis. In Leonard Woolf's case, however, that kind of broad cultural identification could not be immediately available. Yeats explored those pathways of mysticism and cultural nationalism through which certain forms of modernism attempted to approach other sources of cultural meaning, despite the continued existence of empire's social and political hierarchies. For Woolf the colonial officer, the Jewish Cambridge Apostle bent on trying to conform, these pathways were not similarly accessible. For him a decentring of accepted views emerged rather out of the juxtaposition, even of the clash, between different and opposing perspectives on his own colonial work, such as is movingly dramatised in the conclusion of the short story about his time in Ceylon, 'Pearls and Swine'.[45]

'Pearls and Swine' takes the form of a Conradian narrative-within-a-narrative told in the smoking room of a Torquay hotel where two returned and disillusioned Indian civil servants, the narrators, encounter a retired colonel of solid establishment views, a self-opinionated Liberal clergyman, and a pro-imperialist 'stock-jobber'. Talk about the Durbar of 1911 and attendant 'unrest' (in connection not only with the scanty Morley–Minto reforms of 1909, but probably also with the opposition to Partition in Bengal, 1905–08) goads the 'fierce' 'Anglo-Indian', whom the first narrator has not directly addressed, into telling his story. This story, a thinly fictionalised account of Woolf's own experience of nerve-deadening toil superintending a pearl fishery on the West coast of Ceylon,[46] is offered by way of setting the (once again distinctively Conradian) 'facts' straight concerning what rule really involves in India.[47]

The climax of this tale, which also forms the end of the frame-narrative, occurs on the night that an unscrupulous European dealer in pearls called White, who has gate-crashed the fishery, dies of delirium tremens in the company of the narrator (the second narrator of the story) and his young European assistant, Robson. As with the opening scene to the first narrative, it is significant that the build-up to the climax involves drawing out different European opinions with respect to empire: Robson's progressive 'scientific' humanitarianism, White's grossly exploitative and hypocritical despotism, and the narrator's own jaded indifference despite his commitment to keep working at his job, all of which are shown to be of little or no consequence against the background of the fishery, both its long history and its day-to-day drudgery and chaos.

Juxtaposing these different viewpoints, therefore, Woolf's method is to create a bricolage of voices from between the gaps and cracks of which the untenability and indeed the impossibility of 'the strong hand' and the white man's presence is allowed to shade through.[48] His interest in objectifying voices in this way is underlined by his decision to use the *Heart of Darkness*-style frame in which the unnamed first colonial officer transmits to us the story of the (again unnamed) second, while in fact there is little to distinguish the two. (Both notice, and speak in similar terms of, the solid, too-comfortable smell of horsehair and varnish, which to them characterises 'civilised' life in England.[49]) From this, it seems as though the permanent dislocation of European ideas and values cannot yet be spoken in so many words, can still only be suggested through the juxtaposition and interanimation of now contrasting, now overlapping, utterances.

The moment of starkest juxtaposition in the story follows White's night of terminal agony during which not only the dying man, but Robson too, detailed to watch over him, are seen to break down under the enormity and terror of their experience in India. In contrast to this degradation, the 'Arabs, Negroes, Tamils' involved in the fishery calmly go on with their work throughout the night, pausing only to survey, 'unastonished', the white man's writhing.[50] Like Yeats, Woolf might admittedly be criticised for surrendering to the embedded stereotypes of an ageless, 'impertuable' East in his attempt to suggest that alternative and far more viable sources of value exist in that other world. However, even in this reproduction of the already known, he is trying to say something more significant. Within moments of White's obviously symbolic ceasing, the narrator is called out to witness another death: an Arab who has expired while diving for pearls is quietly and unostentatiously brought in to the shore by his brother and work companions. The impromptu oration that is spoken over his body on the beach outlines an ordinary but dignified life of work, fatherhood and brotherliness. In comparison with this, White's death and dissolute existence, and the civilisation of which he is a representative, are seen to exhibit no redeeming virtues, are fit only to be shamefacedly set to one side. It is a strong, but not an explicit statement. Appropriately, in the light of Woolf's growing attention to qualified and layered cultural awareness, the story ends with a quoted Tamil proverb, which is applied to the white man's view of (and no doubt fate in) governing India: "'When the cat puts his head into a pot, he thinks all is darkness.'"[51]

Though they operate, as I have said, from very different social, national and vocational positions, we see how both Woolf and Yeats, writers influential in European modernism, attempt in these two texts to direct their own points of view across the cultural divides established and reinforced by colonialism. Yet, significantly, they do not, in so orienting themselves, always show awareness of the brute authority involved in maintaining those divides. It is generally assumed that the dignity, quiet inner strength and endurance of the Bengali poet or Arab fishers will carry them through and beyond colonial rule. Their status as colonised people is in this sense almost incidental. This partial blindness (if also, from another perspective, constructive indifference) to colonial structures of authority was indeed symptomatic of primitivist and exotic interests in modernism more generally: high culture sought out and identified with alternative conceptual systems believed to be regenerative, but without confronting in any substantial way the hierarchies which upheld the power and privilege of that culture. (Indeed, this charge of blindness could even be laid at Bakhtin's own door, in so far as his theory of double-voiced discourse in the novel on occasion assumes a freely responsive other understanding, a self-determination and volition on the part of the listener to whom that discourse is directed. Elsewhere, of course, Bakhtin does recognise that monologic discourse is associated with centralising power, constituted in the face of opposition.)

Against the romanticisation of the serene endurance of the other culture, however, there are in both Woolf and Yeats moments when colonial realities are confronted, or at least in part acknowledged. We might think here of the violence of White's imprecations and memories in Woolf's story, and of Yeats's apparent identification with Tagore as a cultural nationalist working against the effects of colonial occupation (in consequence, perhaps, of his idealisation of features of the oppressed culture). As I have suggested, both writers moved towards a testing of the boundedness and boundaries of their own understanding by laying side-by-side and splicing together contrasting cultural and political points of view. This admission of an internal incompleteness (and, relatedly, of the dysfunction of the imperial idea), while increasingly symptomatic of the writing of their own time, also anticipated the interactive strategies that would become typical of the hybrid post-colonial writings of the latter half of the twentieth century. Fragmented, 'double-voiced' perspectives would also be particularly evocative for other modernist writers from colonial spaces, such as Katherine Mansfield, who found that narrative strategies of incompletion provided ways of representing her own geographic displacement. Moreover, in the case of Mansfield, the memories of a magical lost world out in the Pacific, such as are evoked in *Prelude* (1917), may well have exacerbated the formal disjunctions and concern with collapsed and uncertain identity now seen as characteristic of her modernist writing.

To round off what must at this stage remain an open-ended and tentative study, we might end by looking briefly at this overlapping of modernist and colonial concerns in preoccupations with displacement. In this context it becomes telling that Leonard's wife, Virginia Woolf, represented life out in the Empire, or away from the imperial metropolis, under a dreamlike, unreal or disorientating aspect. At Clarissa's party in *Mrs Dalloway* (1925), for example, the guest Miss Helena Parry, with her one glass and one memory-clouded eye, becomes strangely abstracted, alienatingly lost at once in the past and within a dream, 'at the mention of India, or even Ceylon'.[52] More importantly, Peter Walsh, recently returned from India, wielding his knife, acts throughout as a disruptive and predatory presence in Clarissa's orderly Central London world. In an earlier work, her first novel, *The Voyage Out* (1915), in which the pro-imperial Richard and Clarissa Dalloway are first introduced as characters, Virginia Woolf is fascinated with distanced and estranging perspectives on England, a 'shrinking island', here directed from the exotic and imaginary place in the novel that is South America.[53] Crucially, in this foreign context, without the 'supporting background' of their routine-based life back home, the English travellers appear at once 'cumbrous' and insubstantial.[54]

In Virginia as in Leonard Woolf, therefore, we find moments of intense uncertainty and a questioning of received meanings from points of view external to England. It is tempting to speculate that such moments of dissolution and crisis in value, which are so central to Woolf's experiments in the anti-novel or 'novel-essay', took on the shade of Leonard's, and perhaps also Mansfield's, accounts of their own colonial disorientation. But even if this was not the case, Virginia Woolf's increasing fascination with a shrinking England (culminating in the explicit anti-imperialism of *Three Guineas* [1938]) again poses the question of whether modernism cannot be seen as an intrinsic expression of an anxiously imperial world, surveying the breaking apart of trusted cultural certainties and the emergence of new, mixed and muddled identities. Modernism, it would appear, emerged out of later colonialism. In this light it merits more extensive and concentrated study.

## Notes

1   Bakhtin discusses ideological decentring as part of his theory of heteroglot multiplicity in the novel. For the purposes of this essay, heteroglot instability will be taken as a metaphor for the meeting between the 'native' and the 'foreign' in modernism. Mikhail Bakhtin, 'Discourse in the Novel', *The Dialogic Imagination*, trans. Caryl Emerson and Michael Holquist (Austin, University of Texas Press, 1981), pp. 257–422.

2   Bakhtin, *The Dialogic Imagination*, p. 276.

3   Patrick Brantlinger, '"The Bloomsbury Fraction" versus war and empire', in Carola M. Kaplan and Anne B. Simpson (eds), *Seeing Double: Revisioning Edwardian and Modernist Literature* (London, Macmillan, 1996), pp. 149–67, gives a broad, illuminating account of Leonard and Virginia Woolf's post-war radicalism and anti-imperialism.

4   Letter to T. P. Gill of 13 November 1898, in *Collected Letters of W. B. Yeats*, vol. 2, ed. Warwick Gould, John S. Kelly and Deirdre Toomey (Oxford, Oxford University Press, 1997), p. 302.

5   See *Collected Letters of W. B. Yeats*, vol. 1, ed. John Kelly and Eric Domville (Oxford, Oxford University Press, 1986), p. 399. Declan Kiberd, *Inventing Ireland* (London, Cape, 1995) offers a spirited and encyclopedic study of modern Irish literature as post-colonial.

6   *The Letters of Leonard Woolf*, ed. Frederic Spotts (London, Weidenfeld & Nicolson, 1989), pp. 55–151.

7 Joseph Conrad, *Heart of Darkness* (Harmondsworth, Penguin, 1973).

8 Any number of anti-imperial (or uncertainly imperial) reworkings of Conrad would follow Woolf's, including those of André Gide, Graham Greene, Wilson Harris, V. S. Naipaul, and Chinua Achebe.

9 See Leonard Woolf, *Diaries in Ceylon 1908–1911: Records of a Colonial Administrator and Stories of the East* (London, Hogarth Press, 1961); also published in the *Ceylon Historical Journal* (July 1959–April 1960). Douglas Kerr, 'Colonial habitats: Orwell and Woolf in the jungle', *English Studies*, 78:2 (1997), looks *inter alia* at Woolf's various writings about Ceylon.

10 'White society in India and Ceylon, as you can see in Kipling's stories, was always suburban ... the social structure and relations between Europeans, rested on the same kind of snobbery, pretentiousness and false pretensions as they did in Putney or Peckham'. Leonard Woolf, *Growing: An Autobiography of the Years 1904–1911* (London, Hogarth Press, 1961), p. 17. The point about colonial superfluity is differently made in the native-centred *The Village in the Jungle* (1913; Oxford, Oxford University Press, 1981).

11 See Leonard Woolf, *Growing*, p. 158, and *Beginning Again: An Autobiography of the Years 1911–1919* (London, Hogarth Press, 1964), p. 100.

12 This is one of the five or so letters that Woolf later quoted in his autobiography *Growing* as evoking 'very vividly the atmosphere and savour of those early days in Jaffna' (p. 58).

13 In its stress on the redeeming reality of work, and the absurd farce of the white man's presence among watchful and inscrutable natives, Woolf's story 'Pearls and Swine' also exhibits clear resonances of the Conrad, as I will show.

14 Woolf, *Growing*, pp. 21, 23.

15 *Ibid.*, pp. 26; *The Letters of Leonard Woolf*, p. 137; Woolf, *Growing*, pp. 21, 23.

16 Woolf, *Growing*, pp. 23, 46, 47. See also the letters of, for example, 20 December 1904, in *The Letters of Leonard Woolf*, pp. 68–9; 5 January 1905, pp. 70–1; and 4 June 1905, p. 92. Throughout the time in Ceylon, Woolf speaks of a deepening depression at the general 'futility' of existence as experienced in Ceylon, and in particular at British authoritarianism disguised as liberal humanitarianism. See the letter to Strachey of 25 September 1905, in *The Letters of Leonard Woolf*, pp. 101–2.

17 Letter to Lytton Strachey, 21 May 1905, in *The Letters of Leonard Woolf*, p. 90.

18 *Ibid.*

19 Conrad, *Heart of Darkness*, p. 22.

20 *Ibid.*, pp. 30, 33.

21 *Ibid.*, pp. 40–1, 35.

22 *Ibid.*, p. 39.

23 On intentional hybridity or 'double-languagedness' in novelistic discourse

    – that is, utterance which is intentionally hybrid because it both takes into account and is *directed towards* a listener – see Bakhtin, *The Dialogic Imagination*, pp. 355–362.

24 *Ibid.*, pp. 285–6.

25 *Ibid.*.

26 Homi Bhabha, *The Location of Culture* (London, Routledge, 1995). See also Robert Young's discussion of hybridity in both Bakhtin and Bhabha in *Colonial Desire* (London, Routledge, 1995), pp. 20–6, in which the emphasis on how hybridity emerges in the colonial situation is again slightly different. For Young, Bhabha's crucial intervention is to show how in any colonial context discursive hybridity is dramatised and laid bare in the presence of indigenous cultures.

27 Bakhtin, *The Dialogic Imagination*, pp. 276, 296–301.

28 Letters to Lytton Strachey of 3 March 1907 and 28 April 1907, in *The Letters of Leonard Woolf*, pp. 125 and 128.

29 W. B. Yeats, 'Introduction', in Rabindranath Tagore, *Gitanjali (Song Offerings)* (London, Macmillan, 1913), p. xiii. The book was first issued in a limited edition by the London Indian Society in 1912.

30 *Ibid.*, p. vii.

31 See Roy Foster, *W. B. Yeats: A Life: I. The Apprentice Mage 1865–1914* (Oxford, Oxford University Press, 1997), p. 471.

32 W. B. Yeats, 'Introduction', pp. vii–xiii.

33 *Ibid.*, p. xvii.

34 Already in the late 1880s Yeats had begun to seek in the 'maze of eastern thought', as he said in his opening address for the Dublin Hermetic Society, answers to the question of the immortality of the soul. His contact with the Indian Theosophist Mohini Chatterji led to a three-year involvement with Madame Blavatsky's Theosophical Society that encouraged his interest in dreams, symbols and the unseen. Theosophy was for Yeats a philosophy that 'confirmed my vague speculations and seemed at once logical and boundless'. In his first collections, the significantly entitled *Crossways* (1889) and *The Rose* (1893), we find meditations on the nature of God that reach beyond Christianity and towards the East ('The Indian Upon God'), and a pervasive interest in dream-like states in which, as he said, 'only body's laid asleep' ('To Ireland in the Coming Times'). See Richard Ellmann, *Yeats: The Man and the Masks* (Harmondsworth, Penguin, 1979), pp. 44, 68.

35 W. B. Yeats, 'Introduction', pp. ix–xii.

36 *Ibid.*, p. ii.

37 *Ibid.*, pp. xiv, xv.

38 *Ibid.*, p. xiii.

39 *Ibid.*, p. xvii.

40 *Ibid.*, pp. xx–xxii.

41 He was turning to a greater precision of form and impersonality in his

own work. There was, it is important to remember, much hype in the promotion of Tagore by Yeats and Pound. It was, as Pound put it, 'a piece of wise imperialism' – 'in honouring him we honour India'. See James Longenbach, *Stone Cottage* (Oxford, Oxford University Press, 1988), p. 17.

42  See Mary Lago, *Rabindranath Tagore* (Boston, Mass., Twayne Publishers, 1976).

43  As the modernist Marxist Walter Benjamin so powerfully put it, in effect reworking Pound's well-known formulation: 'In every era the attempt must be made anew to wrest tradition away from a conformism that is about to overpower it.' See Walter Benjamin, 'Theses on the Philosophy of History', in Dennis Walder (ed.), *Literature in the Modern World* (Oxford, Oxford University Press, 1992), pp. 362–4.

44  Kiberd, *Inventing Ireland*, pp. 4–7, 117–18.

45  First published in *Stories of the East* (London, Hogarth Press, 1921). The story appears in Saros Cowasjee (ed.), *Stories from the Raj: From Kipling to Independence* (London, Bodley Head, 1982). The original story can be found in Elleke Boehmer (ed.), *Empire Writing: An Anthology of Colonial Literature 1870–1918* (Oxford, Oxford University Press, 1998).

46  As described to Lytton Strachey in two letters of March 1906, in *The Letters of Leonard Woolf*, pp. 113–16.

47  Cowasjee (ed.), *Stories from the Raj*, p. 186.

48  *Ibid.*, pp. 183 and 192.

49  *Ibid.*, pp. 181–2, 193.

50  *Ibid.*, pp. 197–8.

51  *Ibid.*, p. 200.

52  Virginia Woolf, *Mrs Dalloway* (Harmondsworth, Penguin, 1982), pp. 195–6. This purblindness can clearly be seen as a signifier of imperial self-delusion associated with the Raj. For further discussion under this heading, see Jenny Sharpe, *Allegories of Empire: The Figure of the Woman in the Colonial Text* (Minneapolis, University of Minnesota Press, 1993).

53  Virginia Woolf, *The Voyage Out* (Oxford, Oxford University Press, 1992), p. 29.

54  *Ibid.*, pp. 246, 350.

# 5

# Latin, arithmetic and mastery:
# a reading of two Kipling fictions

**Janet Montefiore**

## Kipling and modernism

Kipling is known as an imperialist not a modernist. His familiar attributes – Tory politics, plain-man anti-intellectualism, preference for odd genres like the children's story, the tall story, the adventure story, the popular song – hardly resemble the fragmentary avant-gardism normally associated with modernist writing. Fredric Jameson rules out 'the writings of Kipling, Rider Haggard, Verne, Wells' from his discussion of imperialism and modernism because the 'literature of imperialism … is by and large not modernist in any formal sense, and, emerging from subcanonical genres like the adventure tale remained "minor" or "marginal" during the hegemony of the modern and its ideology and values'.[1] Yet Kipling's relation to modernism is much more complex and substantial than is generally recognised. Jameson's description is so ill-informed (indicating that his acquaintance with Kipling's work may not go much beyond *Kim*) that it could well prompt a defence of Kipling as an unrecognised modernist, given the alertness to the new technologies of the twentieth century displayed in, for instance, *Actions and Reactions* (1908), whose stories thematise radio ('Wireless'), the motor car ('They') air transport ('With the Night Mail') and above all the moving photographic image (defined by Jameson as *the* modernist topos) in 'Mrs Bathurst'. Obliquely related to a narratorial 'I' by a half-comprehending witness, the Conradianly multiple narrative method(s) of this riddling story of destructive sexual passion are as modernist as its cinematic motif.[2] More generally, Kipling's many-voiced stylistic virtuosity, mastery of the pared-down short story (itself a characteristically modernist form), and avoidance of narratorial authority through the creation of first-person narrators, all have strong affinities with the modernist aesthetic.[3] Proto-modernist mimicry is closely bound up with Kipling's imperial theme through the way his writing 'layers' its standard English against lively oral vernaculars: the Irish brogue and stage cockney spoken by his soldiers (turned later to very different modernist ends by T. S. Eliot and Bertolt Brecht)[4] and the rich, archaised English which is Kipling's approximation to the Indian vernacular mixture of Urdu and Hindi spoken over North India in the nineteenth and twentieth centuries (also, in various contexts, Punjabi, Sanskrit, Pushtu, and even animal speech).[5] I have shown elsewhere how Kipling's fictions, by contrasting the clipped British idiom of the officers against the Indians' eloquence, and thus creating a symbolic English-speaking 'daylight' world as opposed to the shadowy 'night-time' realm of India, make the colonial rulers look sadly insensitive and inarticulate compared with their subjects.[6]

It might be tempting to claim further that Kipling's highly wrought verbal contrasts anticipate the fragmentary plural voices of such texts as *The Waste Land*, or at least that, as Stephen Bann argues in an early essay, Kipling undercuts the authority of conventional realism. Bann describes Kipling as 'extraordinarily, and for his time perhaps uniquely, sensitive to the non-natural, conventional nature of language'.[7] But any claim that his writing tends to subvert linguistic law and order, as opposed to being aware of their potential fragility, would surely be disingenuous. The 'native vernacular' in Kipling's Indian fictions is certainly alluring, powerful, and subversive – which is why it needs to be kept in check by the formal hegemony of a Standard English framework. *Kim*, his most seductive imperialist fiction, shows the colourful diversities of Indian street-life flourishing in the safety of a *Pax Britannica* secured both by the subtle-minded players of the Great Game *and* by crass, uneducated British soldiers like the drummer-boy who tells Kim 'You talk the same as a nigger, don't you?' Similarly, that same conventional language of English law evaded by the hero from the start – 'He sat, *in defiance of municipal orders*...'[8] (my emphasis) – guarantees the civil society where Kim moves among those Indian languages, customs and cultures whose subtleties the municipal lawgivers will never understand.

To explore the full aesthetic and ideological meanings of Kipling's potentially subversive ironies would need a whole book. This chapter deals with a smaller subject, namely the ideological issues implied by the scenes of instruction in two of his fictions, *Kim* (1900) and the short story 'Regulus' (1917), where English schoolboys are shown acquiring specifically imperialist authority by learning certain languages: in 'Regulus', Latin verse; and in *Kim*, the humbler rules of arithmetic.

Education was closely linked to imperialism in late-nineteenth-century English 'public' schools whose curriculum consisted of classical languages and literature, representing both an intellectual discipline and a European ideal, and team games, supposedly inculcating courage, *esprit de corps*, obedience to orders and general 'manliness'.[9] Cricket and what would now be called 'rugby' football were given a moral, almost religious significance by imperial ideologists. Lord Baden-Powell told the boys of his old preparatory school in 1900 that the lesson of 'do[ing] your duty ... to obey the orders of your Captain' in the rugby team would teach them, when they were grown up, 'never [to] dream of trying to save your own life if your duty requires you to risk it'.[10] The same message appears in Sir Henry Newbolt's famous 'Vitaï Lampada' (1908), describing a military disaster miraculously redeemed by sportsmanship:

> The river of Death has brimmed his banks
> And England's far and Honour's a name
> But the voice of a schoolboy rallies the ranks,
> 'Play up! play up! and play the game!'[11]

The academic part of the public-school curriculum carried an equally strong ideological charge. The teaching of Roman history and Latin literature (Greek was only for the abler boys) was 'geared', as Gauri Viswanathan has written, 'to instruct learners in the principles of law, government and society ... These languages were a pre-requisite for social leadership and, more subtly, the means by which social privilege was protected.'[12] Classical literature was preferred because its inspiring examples of patriotism and public spirit ('role models', as we say now), would inspire the young gentlemen to emulate the aristocratic Roman virtues of *gravitas* and authority. As Louis MacNeice wrote sardonically:

The classical student is bred to the purple, his training in syntax
    Is also a training in thought
And even in morals; if called to the bar or the barracks
    He always will do what he ought.[13]

Edward Said has written that by the late nineteenth century 'it was almost a commonplace of British imperial theory that the British empire was different from (and better than) the Roman Empire in that it was a rigorous system in which order and law prevailed, whereas the latter was mere robbery and profit.'[14] For the school-masters' purposes, however, the analogy went the other way: the grandeur that was Rome at once prefigured and ennobled the 'Pax Britannica' with the glamour and prestige of the past. Thus J. C. Welldon, headmaster of Harrow, addressing the Royal Colonial In-stitute on 'The Imperial Aspects of Education' in 1894, cited Virgil in the *Aeneid* prophesying the responsibilities of imperial destiny:

Tu regere imperio populos Romane memento
Hae tibi erunt artes pacisque imponere morem
Parcere subjectis et debellare superbos.

'Remember, O Roman, it shall be your destiny to have dominion over the nations, to impose the arts of peace, to spare the humble and to cast down the arrogant.'[15]

## Latin verse in 'Regulus'

Virgil's epic of imperial destiny lies at the heart of Kipling's story 'Regulus' (1917),[16] whose prosaic concision belies its sophisticated articulation of the ideals (and limits) of imperial identity. Because this story of classical education and public service is not as well known as *Stalky & Co.* (1899), whose setting and characters it shares, a summary is in order. It begins with an italicised epigraph:

*Regulus, a Roman general, defeated the Carthaginians in 256 B.C., but was next year defeated and taken prisoner by the Carthaginians, who sent him to Rome with an embassy to ask for peace or an exchange of prisoners. Regulus strongly advised the Roman Senate to make no terms with the enemy. He then returned to Carthage and was put to death.*

The Fifth Form had been dragged several times in its collective life, from one end of the school Horace to the other. Those were the years when

Army examiners gave thousands of marks for Latin, and it was Mr. King's hated business to defeat them.

Behold him now, on a wet November morning...[17]

The long opening scene shows the boys struggling to translate a notoriously difficult Horace ode (Book III, number 5) calling Romans to emulate Regulus's heroic patriotism. In the second half of the story, they live out these 'Roman' values in practice. A hitherto virtuous boy called Winton lets loose a mouse in the next lesson, is reported to the Head and sentenced to write out five hundred lines of Virgil by tea-time. He will therefore have to miss compulsory football practice, which entails another punishment: 'It was law in the school ... that any boy outside the First Fifteen who missed his football for any reason whatever, and had not a written excuse ... would receive not less than three strokes with a ground-ash from the Captain of Games, generally a youth of between seventeen and eighteen years, rarely under eleven stone ... and always in hard condition' (Kipling as usual writes of punishment with rather detestable relish). Winton has played for the First Fifteen but is not yet an official team member. Worse, Mullins the present Captain of Games is his 'study-mate', they being 'cousins and rather close friends'.

This is all so unfair that King, his housemaster, asks the Head to relent; he is refused on the grounds that the too-spotless Winton badly needs to un-learn his own virtuous complacency. Still sympathetic to his ewe lamb, King turns up while the boy is writing out his lines, and dictates the 'rich Virgilian measures' to him, beginning with those three lines about imperialist destiny which were quoted in real life by Welldon to the Royal Colonial Institute (and, no doubt, by many an unrecorded headmaster and guest speaker to innumerable public schoolboys at prize-day assemblies and the like). He adds 'There you have it all, Winton. Write that out twice and yet once again.'[18] Kipling gives no translation, possibly because he considered the lines too well known to need one, but more likely because he preferred to leave the naked expression of imperialist pieties in the decent privacy of Latin. The unspeakable vulgarity of broaching these ideals is emphasised in an earlier school story about the boys' embarrassment when a crass public speaker invokes 'matters like the hope of Honour and the dream of Glory, that boys do not discuss even with their most intimate equals'. This 'Jelly-Bellied Flag-flapper' is dismissed by his outraged audience as 'beyond question born in a gutter and bred in a Board-School, where they played marbles' – as opposed to the manly game of football.[19]

Having finished writing his lines, Winton is about to take his humiliating punishment when the other footballers return to the classroom. The mistimed sympathy of the sub-prefect Paddy Vernon moves Winton to murderous rage; he first attempts to 'batter him into pulp', then threatens to 'lick' him with the ceremonial ground-ash, and finally tries to throw him out of the upstairs window. Four other boys combine to prevent this, and Winton batters them heavily too. Then they all mop up, he apologises, and goes off to be flogged by his study-mate Mullins with 'Roman' nonchalance – '"stand clear of our photo-bracket, will you?"'[20] The story ends happily with Winton's promotion to sub-prefectship and official membership of the First Fifteen.

The analogy between Winton and Regulus, made several times in the story by different characters, is that both honourably submit themselves to physical violence: Regulus patriotically refusing the chance of ignoble safety, Winton refusing to be let off the beating he has earned by his 'cad's trick'. Just as gentlemanly is Mullins the Captain of Games carrying out to the letter his imperial duty to 'spare the downtrodden' (he deals kindly with a frightened junior boy) and to 'cast down the proud', including his best friend. And both Paddy Vernon, muttering offendedly that 'he would see Winton and all the school somewhere else' when urged to report his injuries to the school authorities, and his bruised comrades who agree to explain their bloody noses by saying that 'we got all these pretty marks at footer – owin' to the zeal with which we played the game', are equally men of honour.[21] Less overtly than in Newbolt's 'Vitaï Lampada', the message is the same: just as the mock battles of the school playing fields prepare the boys for the real thing, so these boys (who are nearly all destined to be Army officers) will die for England, should she need their deaths as Rome needed that of Regulus.

This powerfully implied message could hardly have been missed in 1917 when 'Regulus' was first published in *A Diversity of Creatures*, whose stories allude constantly to the spectres of dead or dying youth in the Great War of 1914–18, especially Kipling's own son John whose death in 1915 is commemorated in the grieving poem 'The Children'.[22] 'Regulus' appears after the story 'In the Presence', about Sikh soldiers' loyalty and bloodthirsty honour, and before 'The

Edge of the Evening', in which a German spy is accidentally killed by civilians – a theme powerfully taken up in the final story 'Mary Postgate', whose bereaved spinster heroine experiences a release of unmistakably sexual pleasure while listening to the death rattle of a wrecked German airman. Kipling appears to condone her ecstasy of hatred with the book's tight-lipped *envoi* 'The Beginnings', whose refrain is 'When the English began to hate'.[23]

The serious patriotic subtext of 'Regulus' first surfaces in the comic opening scene of (mis)translation. In demanding accurate, elegant language from his reluctant pupils, even if he doesn't get it, the schoolmaster King is not just coaching them for exams; he is teaching them moral – and cultural – values. These burst into explicit clarity when a pupil renders *scilicet* as 'forsooth': an infelicity which provokes a textbook outburst of reactionary rhetoric:

> 'Regulus,' he said, 'was not a leader-writer for the penny press, nor, for that matter was Horace. Regulus says: "The soldier ransomed by gold will come keener for the fight – will he by – by gum!" *That's* the meaning of *scilicet*. It indicates contempt – bitter contempt ... Regulus *was* in earnest. He was also engaged in cutting his own throat with every word he uttered. He knew Carthage which (your examiners won't ask you this so you needn't take notes) was a sort of God-forsaken nigger Manchester. Regulus was not thinking about his own life. He was telling Rome the truth. He was playing for his side. Those lines from the eighteenth to the fortieth ought to be written in blood ... Horace knew a very great deal. *He* knew!'[24]

King's racist jibe turns Horace's ode into a political allegory, equating the ancient North African metropolis with the industrial and intellectual centre of nineteenth-century liberal capitalism, itself the epitome of the cheap vulgarities of 'the penny press' and (what King sees as) 'futile' democracy.[25] For the 'pre-eminently commercial state' of Carthage was the Mediterranean rival of republican Rome, contesting its power in three 'Punic Wars' between 264 BC and 146 BC. These ended with the demolition of Carthage by the victorious Roman armies who killed most of the inhabitants and enslaved the rest, about a century before Horace wrote his *Odes*.[26] Since King is bent on schooling his pupils in the high-minded imperial values of honour, patriotism and courage, and anyway regards 'evil-minded commercial Carthage'[27] as the enemy of civilisation, he naturally ignores this episode of Roman barbarism.

So far, 'Regulus' may appear to be little more than a piece of unusually well-written right-wing propaganda. There are, however, several interesting discrepancies. First, the Roman pieties which King seeks to inculcate in his pupils through close reading of Horace are destabilised by the farce of the boys' mistranslations:

'Er – a disgraceful husband – *conjuge barbara* – with a barbarous spouse.'
    'Why do you select *that* disgustful equivalent out of all the dictionary?' King snapped. 'Isn't "wife" good enough for you?'
    'Yes, sir ... *Et*, and, *consenuit*, has he grown old – *in armis*, in the – er – arms – *hostium socerorum*, of his father-in-law's enemies.'
    'Who? How? Which?'
    'Arms of his enemies' fathers-in-law, sir.'
    'Tha-anks. By the way, what meaning might you attach to *in armis*?'
    'Oh, weapons – weapons of war, sir.' There was a virginal note in Beetle's voice as though he had been falsely accused of uttering indecencies.

The charming verbal play arises from Kipling's layering of different verbal registers: the elegant Latin clumsily parsed into near-senseless phrases, the just-averted mistranslation of '*in armis*', and the graceful, slightly *risqué* adjective 'virginal' following Beetle's ham-fisted translations. Worse is to follow from the even more incompetent Paddy Vernon: 'He [Regulus] is related to have removed from himself the kiss of the shameful wife and of his small children as less by the head, and, being stern, to have placed his virile visage on the ground', which provokes King into a Ciceronian defence of 'the passion, the power, the – the essential guts of the lines which you have so foully outraged in our presence'.[28] Such irreverent play with classical tradition resembles the parodies of English prose in the 'Oxen of the Sun' chapter in *Ulysses*, or still more the puns and mistranslations in Pound's *Homage to Sextus Propertius* and *Hugh Selwyn Mauberley*. (So, even more, does the proleptic moment of 'postmodernist' intertextuality in another 'Stalky' story where the boys 'scramble' another Horace ode to create nonsense Latin phrases like '*Mutatosque deos in antro* ... Mute gods weepin' in a cave'.[29]) True, Kipling's mockery of the classics differs from that of Pound or Joyce in that his parodies and mistranslations, however pleasurably transgressive, don't represent a conscious, ironic break with the past; 'Regulus' thematises continuity, not fragmentation. Yet since the ideal of cultural continuity is constantly thwarted by the boys' failure to live up to it, Kipling's comedy also bears witness to a genuine rupture of meaning between Augustan Rome and the modern classroom.[30]

Furthermore, the identification which 'Regulus' proposes between the modern schoolboy and the Roman general becomes shaky when looked at closely. Winton, unlike Regulus, is not only in the wrong but distinctly unheroic. Far from bearing his punishment with Roman stoicism, he worries constantly that it may '"count against me"', explodes with envious rage against the innocent Vernon, then collapses into apologies and finally a sleep of emotional exhaustion. After this, he still can't stop apologising and takes his incipient hysteria to the chaplain, who briskly prescribes 'Epsom salts'. (The sequence of events and responses – anxiety, rage, beating, unconsciousness – also strongly suggests a homoerotic subtext of the kind analysed by Peter Middleton, in which love between males is displaced into violence.[31]) He thus, as the wise Head intended, learns a salutary lesson in self-knowledge. A future officer whose 'only fault is a certain costive and unaccommodating virtue'[32] needs to learn the hard way that he too can fall into disgrace and be punished; only then can he safely be given the authority to rule and to punish others. Hence the story's thrice-repeated Horatian motto *Dis te minorem quod geris imperas*, 'Thou rulest because thou bearest thyself lower than the Gods',[33] which could apply to all members of ruling elites (including Komsomol recruits in the old USSR, or members of the US Peace Corps) as well as to Winton. But the story's subtlety is only for rulers; its implied attitude towards rebellious subjects is given in King's notorious description of Carthage as 'a sort of God-forsaken nigger Manchester',[34] the coarse racism of whose phrasing betrays a hidden violence. The ultimate destiny of the Carthaginians was to be killed or enslaved for challenging the Roman republic, Cato's historical demand 'Delenda est Carthago' ('Carthage must be destroyed') prefiguring Conrad's Kurtz, who wished to 'Exterminate all the brutes!'[35] The analogy between ancient and modern empires may thus be more apt and less flattering than King supposes.

### Chlorine gas and the threshold of modernism

'Regulus' has another characteristically modernist theme, also paralleled in Conrad's *Heart of Darkness*: the release of dangerous, barbaric energies when self-control collapses, signalling that 'internalized conflict between the civilized and the regressively primitive' which for Christopher Butler defines the modernist conception of human psychology.[36] Contained by the story's framework of prosaic comedy, violence erupts for a sinister moment where death hovers over the desks:

> 'Will you,' said Winton very slowly, 'kindly mind your own business, you cursed, clumsy, fat-headed fool?'
> The form-room was as silent as the empty field in the darkness outside.

That outer darkness into which Winton tries a few seconds later to throw the battered Paddy, condenses several meanings. Most obviously, the 'empty field' connects with the previous afternoon's games practice which Winton has missed while writing his lines and overhearing his victim 'calling the roll and marking defaulters' – including, of course, Winton himself. Also, since rugby football is supposed to be both a mock battle and a training for the real thing, the 'empty field' suggests a battleground abandoned to its dead at night. The window thus represents a threshold between the lighted, orderly space of school and the unfriendly dark of the world outside; also between the boy's conventionally good character and the unadmitted savagery of his divided psyche, for he does intend murder. Appropriately enough, the threshold between metonymic naturalism (the football pitch, the battlefield) and metaphoric otherness (the unacknowledged violence of a mind which 'can't think what's the matter with me')[37] is occupied by the motif of the form-room window, a naturalistic detail which is also a figure of liminality.

That window introduces several unobtrusive but very telling allusions to chlorine gas, the text's metonymic shorthand for science and technology (then known in public schools as the 'Modern Side'). King's Latin lesson is twice interrupted by chlorine gas seeping in from the chemistry lesson next door, making everyone cough badly even after the windows are opened to let the smell out. Of course, the association of science with 'stinks' is a schoolroom cliché, but canisters of chlorine are fairly unusual equipment for beginners' experiments. (Sulphuretted hydrogen would be a more typical source of bad smells from a school laboratory.) The pollution of his classroom by 'unheavenly gases' provokes King into several rhetorical flights addressed first to the boys and later to the science master Hartopp, in which chlorine symbolises both modernity and the crass pretensions of science.[38]

Chlorine gas was, of course, very 'modern' indeed when 'Regulus' was published in 1917. The first of the poison gases used in the trench warfare on the Western Front, it was then the latest way of killing men in large numbers.[39] Moreover, this 'filthy weapon' (as Kipling accurately called it) was first deployed by the British Army at the Battle of Loos, 1915, when Kipling's son John was 'reported missing, believed killed'.[40] Even more menacingly than that silent darkness outside, the gas invades the protected world of the school story as a subtextual cloud no bigger than a man's hand, making 'the Form cough as more chlorine came in'.[41] According to the military historians Harris and Paxman, 'at thirty parts per million of air, chlorine gas induces a rasping cough'. In fiction, this can be remedied by letting in fresh air; in real life, soldiers were dying horribly by the same gas in the air itself: 'At one part per thousand, it is fatal.'[42]

This wartime context gives a chilling edge to the friendly sparring between Hartopp and King about 'classical *versus* modern', with each man accusing the other's discipline of 'unrelated' knowledge. King attacks 'your modern system of inculcating unrelated facts about chlorine', to which the science master Hartopp replies that classical studies are irrelevant to life; all King's efforts merely equip his unfortunate victims with 'a dozen – no, I'll grant you twenty – one score of totally unrelated Latin tags'. King answers with the Arnoldian argument that classical literature humanises its students by giving them 'balance, proportion, perspective – life. Your scientific man is the beast without background. Haven't you realized *that* in your atmosphere of stinks?'[43]

This dispute was hardly new in 1917. English educationists had debated humanism versus utilitarian practicality from the 1790s onwards, and there was vigorous public debate on the value of 'the grand, old, fortifying, classical curriculum'[44] in the 1860s and 1870s, Matthew Arnold famously making the case for poetry as 'a criticism of life'.[45] Half a century after 'Regulus' appeared, the debate between C. P. Snow and F. R. Leavis revived the argument, Snow blaming literary intellectuals for ignoring science and Leavis attacking Snow for his 'complete ignorance of human creativity'.[46] 'Regulus' appears to endorse King since his argument is borne out by its linking of Latin poetry with schoolboys' lives, the boys even quoting bits of Horace and prompting the schoolmaster's modestly triumphant 'You see. It sticks. A little of it sticks among the barbarians.'[47]

Yet King doesn't quite have the last word, for his cherished classical values are playfully undermined in the poem which follows the story. Entitled 'A Translation: Horace Bk. V *Ode* 3' (another insider's joke, for Horace's *Odes* stop at Book IV), it dismisses biology (the cultivation of 'broths impure'), chemistry ('whose study is of smells') and physics ('the heated wheel'). The 'incurious' poet notices as little whether he travels 'by the power/ Of wheels or wings' (i.e. by literal or mythological machinery) as he does the slave bringing 'logs for my fire'.[48] Such Olympian smugness comes oddly from the man who had written 'The Sons of Martha' (1908) in praise of the engineers who enabled intellectuals to travel 'pleasantly sleeping and unaware', and whose later story 'The Eye of Allah' (1928) would sympathetically portray the intellectual excitement of medieval scientists viewing bacteria under a forbidden microscope.[49] A second look at that studied Horatian elegance may read it as a parody of the kind of gentlemanly leisure which prides itself on ignoring petty practicalities but would notice soon enough if the slave let the fire go out.

The motif of chlorine also implicitly subjects the story's pedagogic values to a less literary, far more devastating critique. For the self-sacrificing patriotism recommended by King's beloved 'Roman Odes'[50] was memorably questioned in the same year that 'Regulus' appeared, by Lieutenant Wilfred Owen of the 2nd Manchester Regiment in the now famous poem 'Dulce Et Decorum Est' about a soldier dying hideously from poison gas. That the gas was chlorine is clear both from the poem's nightmare vision of the man seen drowning 'through thick green light … as under a green sea' (chlorine is greenish-white), and its clinically accurate description of how 'the blood/ Come[s] gargling from the froth-corrupted lungs,/ Obscene as cancer, bitter as the cud/ Of vile, incurable sores on innocent tongues'.[51] As Harris and Paxman explain, 'Chlorine does not suffocate; it poisons, stripping the lining of the bronchial tubes and lungs. The inflammation produces a massive amount of liquid that blocks the windpipe, froths from the mouth and fills the lungs … [the victim] being "drowned in his own exudation".' [52] Owen's rendering of these ghastly details culminates in a bitter repudiation of 'the old Lie, *Dulce et decorum est/ Pro patria mori*' – 'to die for the fatherland is sweet and fitting', a phrase from the second ode of Horace's third book. (Mr King's pupils, who were being 'dragged through the school Horace' in preparation for their Army examinations,[53] would presumably have 'done' this a week or so before tackling the fifth ode.)

Owen's reversal of King's pieties is so neat that it looks intentional, but it is not; his poem was in fact directed at Jessie Pope, author of the recruiting poem 'The Call' ('Who longs to charge and shoot,/ Do you, my laddie?').[54] Yet in the light of his withering irony, King's blend of classical humanism and imperialist story does look intellectually and morally bankrupt – as, equally, does Hartopp's positivist belief that he unlike King is educating boys adequately for the modern world. For all their kindly concern, these two schoolmasters appear to be educating their little victims into a deadly obedience – King's classical moralism inculcating the obedience, while Hartopp teaches the means of death.

True, the horrors of chlorine gas and the nonsense it will make of King's Horatian pieties belong only to the margin of 'Regulus', not its centre. They are subtextual threats suggesting an implied 'latent content' – which is not the same as a 'true message' – contradicting though not finally subverting its overt militarist values. Still, the story remains much less assured of certain certainties than it looks at first, more aware that, as Kipling wrote bitterly in 'The Children', the young men 'believed us, and perished for it'. Or, as he made the dead soldiers say in 'Common Form', 'If any question why we died,/ Tell them, because our fathers lied.'[55]

## Arithmetic and the colonial subject

A different kind of mastery, having more to do with power than duty, is evoked by another scene of instruction in *Kim* where imperialist values are mediated by a specifically English form of knowledge: the language of elementary arithmetic, which enables the hero to assert his autonomy against the forces of 'native' irrationality. Kim famously belongs to two worlds; by birth lower-class Irish–English,[56] by breeding Indian (a dual allegiance which for Kipling is not contradictory, Irishmen and Indians being subjects of the English Crown), he can fit in anywhere in India, act any role he pleases, his double, triple or quadruple identities making him the perfect recruit for the 'Great Game' of spying. When his 'Sahib' parentage is discovered, both the Tibetan Lama whose *chela* [disciple] he has become and the chaplains of his father's regiment agree that he must be educated accordingly. Thanks to the generous lama's access to the wealth of a Tibetan monastery ('I ask for that I need'), Kim escapes the dismal prospect of the Military Orphanage, instead receiving a public-school education at 'St Xavier's in Partibus in Lucknow', recommended by the Catholic chaplain Father Victor as 'the best schooling a boy can get in India'. This sounds very grand, but, despite its imposing appearance, 'the great old school of St Xavier's in Partibus, block on block of low white buildings standing in vast grounds' actually caters for the lower echelons of the colonial elite, 'the sons of subordinate officials, warrant officers, planters, missionaries, and a few wealthy Eurasians'.[57] This suggests a good second-rank institution rather than an Indian Eton – correctly, for the school's original, La Martinière College in Lucknow, is not named in Mangan's list of top public schools in Victorian India, the cheapest of whose fees is more than double the 300 rupees charged by St Xavier's.[58]

Kim's public-school Jesuit education resembles that of Stephen Dedalus at Clongowes in Joyce's *Portrait of the Artist*, where the well-off Catholic 'fellows' are shown learning rugby football, cricket and Latin grammar with competing teams called 'York' and 'Lancaster' after rival English dynasties. The empowering potential of this curriculum appears when Stephen, unfairly punished by the prefect of studies, overhears an older boy remarking 'The senate and the Roman people declared that Dedalus had been unjustly punished' and is encouraged to protest like 'some great person … in the books of history'.[59] Kim, however, does not learn Latin since he needs to retain his fluency in Indian 'vernacular' rather than learning a dead language (besides, his lower-class hybrid parentage presumably makes his status as a gentlemanly 'Sahib' too uncertain for him to receive the classical education reserved for future governors).[60] He does, however, shine at 'mathematical studies and map-making', winning a prize 'for proficiency therein', for he will need these skills when spying out enemy territory. He is once shown making practical use of this knowledge when Mahbub Ali orders him to make a map of 'the wild walled city of Bikanir' for British Intelligence. Kim's report is duly filed in a government office and 'was on hand a few years ago',[61] but little is made of it. Far more significant is the episode when his English schooling gives him the strength to resist 'Indian' magic in the form of hypnosis.

This episode occurs in the school holidays when Kim takes a 'native' (i.e. Indian) identity and is instructed in the techniques of the 'Great Game'. The mysterious 'Lurgan Sahib' subjects Kim to several tests of willpower, culminating in an order to smash a water jar followed by an almost successful attempt to hypnotise the boy into seeing it as whole:

> There was one large piece of the jar where there had been three, and above them the shadowy outline of the entire vessel. He could see the veranda through it, but it was thickening and darkening with each pulse. Yet the jar – how slowly the thoughts came – the jar had been smashed before his eyes. Another wave of prickling fire raced down his neck, as Lurgan Sahib moved his hand.
> 'Look! It is coming into shape!' said Lurgan Sahib.
> So far Kim had been thinking in Hindi, but a tremor came on him, and with an effort … his mind leaped up from a darkness that was swallowing it and took refuge in – the multiplication-table in English!
> 'Look! It is coming into shape,' whispered Lurgan Sahib.
> The jar had been smashed – yess, smashed – not the native word, he would not think of that – but smashed – into fifty pieces, and twice three was six, and thrice three was nine, and four times three was twelve. He clung desperately to the repetition. The shadow-outline of the jar cleared like a mist after rubbing eyes. There were the broken shards, there was the spilt water drying in the sun, and through the cracks of the veranda showed, all ribbed, the white house-wall below – and thrice twelve was thirty-six![62]

Kim's triumph is the simple but all-important faculty of seeing *what is there*. The syntax of that final sentence emphasises detail, separation and clarity – 'there were the shards, there the spilt water' – as opposed to the 'thickening, *darkening* outline' of the jar (my emphasis), while the figurative 'darkness that was swallowing' Kim's mind is dispelled by the literal daylight showing through the planks, which he can see only by thinking in English – 'not the native word, he would not think of that.' The chant of 'twice three is six, thrice three is nine' which enables him to see the jar steadily and see it shattered is 'magical' art in the sense defined by R. G. Collingwood: 'a representation where the emotion evoked is valued on account of its function in practical life, evoked in order that it may discharge that function, and fed by the generative or focusing magical activity into the practical life that needs it.'[63] Kipling of course presents the spell as simple fact: Western Enlightenment concentrated in the multiplication table works its magic simply (so we are invited to believe) because it is true. This mastery of reality endows the 'Sahib' boy, 'strong enough to make anyone do anything he wants',[64] with power against the Indian world of magic, intuition, the supernatural. The pupil whose shoulder tingled at the movement of his teacher's controlling hand is now at least his equal.

Kipling's glorification of Western forms of knowledge does not mean that he shows Indians as ignorant. An earlier scene shows a Brahmin priest casting a horoscope with mathematical calculations far more complex than anything Kim attempts; but his magic, more beneficent than hypnotism, is still associated with darkness and mystery:

> 'Fetch me a twig, little one.' He knitted his brows, scratched, smoothed out, and scratched again in the dust mysterious signs – to the wonder of all save the lama, who, with fine instinct, forbore to interfere.
>
> At the end of half an hour he tossed the twig from him with a grunt. 'Hm! Thus say the stars. Within three days come the two men to make all ready. After them follows the Bull, but the sign over against him is the sign of War and many armed men.'

The priest's prophecy of 'war and armed men – many hundreds' turns out even truer than Kim thinks: he already knows that the letter he carried for Mahbub Ali has sent eight thousand men to war, but cannot guess that the 'Maverick' regiment is shortly to claim him as Kimball O'Hara's son.[65] Yet this scene, however lovingly and sensitively delineated (the fine tact of the fellow-expert is an especially nice touch), implies no equality of knowledge between Indians and their rulers. It adheres to the classic 'Orientalist' double standard whereby *our* simple arithmetic connotes the daylight mastery of reality, while *their* mysterious calculations are part of night-time magic.

That Western myth of intellectual mastery which is at stake in the contest of wills between Kim and Lurgan Sahib can be further clarified by looking at George Orwell's brutally ironic rewriting of this scene in the famous incident in *Nineteen Eighty-Four* where the hero is tortured into accepting that two plus two equals five if the 'Party' says so.[66] Orwell, one of a generation brought up on Kipling,[67] knew his work well, as appears in his 1942 essay comparing Kipling's imperialist conservatism with the brutal *realpolitik* that succeeded it. Emphasising Kipling's old-fashioned belief in law and order, Orwell finds him a 'pre-Fascist' innocent compared with the cynical moral nihilism prevailing now that 'no one believes in any sanction greater than military power ... There is no "law", there is only power. I am not saying that that is a true belief, merely that it is the belief which all modern men do actually hold.'[68] *Nineteen Eighty-Four* reformulates that bitter perception into O'Brien's explanation of his Party's true sadistic intentions: 'We are not interested in the good of others; we are interested solely in power ... The object of torture is torture. The object of power is power'; also, more concisely, in the Party's three nonsense-slogans: WAR IS PEACE, FREEDOM IS SLAVERY and IGNORANCE IS STRENGTH, the last of which deliberately contradicts the old Enlightenment tag 'Knowledge is Power'.[69]

The meaning of this last paradox is spelt out when Orwell re-writes Lurgan's attempted subjugation of Kim as an unequal contest between orthodox Party officer and tortured heretic – only this time, the attempt succeeds. The delicately homoerotic relation that Kipling suggests between pupil and master[70] becomes a sadomasochistic bond between torturer and victim whose intimacy of mutual understanding goes 'deeper than friendship'. Whereas Lurgan's light hand on Kim's neck 'held the boy as in a vice', O'Brien has Winston strapped to a real machine – 'Even the back of his head was gripped in some manner'. The 'wave of prickling fire' roused by a movement of the master's hand becomes a terrible 'wave of pain' invading Winston's body at 'a slight movement of O'Brien's hand' on the lever of a dial.[71] And the English formula which enabled the hero literally to see through the irrational power of 'native' magic is now defeated by a sadistic embodiment of European totalitarian dictatorship, its power no longer opposed to but growing out of the Western technology represented by the dial and lever by which pain is inflicted. The free Western mind is thus reduced to abject obedience, unable to per-ceive any reality which contradicts the Party's word.

The political implications of the repeated arithmetical mnemonic are clarified and emphasised in Orwell's text almost to the point of fable. Whereas the symbolic significance of 'twice three is six' is left unobtrusively implicit in *Kim* (as it needs to be if its magic is to work on the reader), Orwell's 'twice two is four' stands, famously, both for objective reality *and* for the autonomy of the free mind that perceives it. Subjected to ever more violent waves of pain, Winston protests 'How can I help seeing what is in front of my eyes? Two and two are four.' But not, it turns out, if the pain of seeing is great enough. Turning the 'pain-dial' to its highest point, O'Brien holds up four fingers and tells his victim to see them as five; through the fog of pain Winston finds himself unable to count. After a massive electric shock he is completely amenable: 'He did see them, for a fleeting instant ... a moment of luminous certainty, when each new sugges-tion of O'Brien's had filled up a patch of emptiness and become absolute truth, and when two and two could have been three as easily as five, if that were what was needed.'[72] So the once-rational subject yields himself to a 'luminous certainty' like a hellish parody of a modernist epiphany: no light, but rather darkness visible.[73]

### A modern unconscious?

The fact that the relation between *Nineteen Eighty-Four* and *Kim* is at least as much oppositional as parallel might suggest that Kipling's relation to modernity is only a matter of oblique intertextuality. On a thematic level, the distinction drawn by Orwell's essay between Kipling's 'pre-Fascist outlook' and the lawless belief in power 'which all modern men do actually hold' would seem to support a reading of Kipling as a pre-modern conservative. If 'modernism' means a break with the past, then how can Kipling, so urgently insistent on tradition (in *Kim*, the power of English certainties; in 'Regulus', the continuities between the 'present' of English schoolboys and the 'past' of Roman history), possibly qualify as a modernist?

The question looks unanswerable because it is too simple. It ignores the other side of Kipling: the perception of the potential fragility of laws and traditions, of the darkness of the psyche, which can make his readers feel that, as Lionel Trilling put it, 'the ramparts of empire are being erected against the mind's threat to itself'.[74] The defeat of rationalism portrayed in Orwell's dystopian rewriting of *Kim* was already potentially present in the earlier book (an imperialist identity defining itself through mastery of an irrational other always risks being itself mastered, should the other prove unruly enough), while even 'Regulus' acknowledges the savagery underlying the safe world of school. Kipling's intuition of the potential instability of the certainties dear to 'mine own people'[75] and his perception of the internal divisions of rationalist subjectivity do link him with canonical modernists like Conrad, Joyce, Pound and Eliot. What separates him is the fact that he never explores these powerfully felt intuitions to the limit. His conservative commitment to law, order and the *Pax Britannica* does not permit him to focus directly on the unstable, divided imperialist subject or the fragility of the laws by which his men create order. And neither Kipling's talent for parody nor his sensitivity (noted by Stephen Bann) to the 'conventional nature of language'[76] has the effect of making his voice disappear into that Mallarméan 'language-construct within which the reader is invited to play the game of interpretation' that Butler has defined as central to modernist poetics.[77] Modernity, it would seem, is Kipling's unconscious, the other side of his apparently unswerving conservative imperialism.

## Notes

1   Fredric Jameson, 'Modernism and imperialism', in Seamus Deane, Terry Eagleton, Fredric Jameson and Edward W. Said, *Nationalism, Colonialism and Literature* (Minneapolis, University of Minnesota Press, 1990), p. 43.

2   See Jameson, 'Modernism and imperialism', pp. 56–66; Rudyard Kipling, *Actions and Reactions* (London, Macmillan, 1908). Louis Menand gives a subtle reading of 'Mrs Bathurst' as a work of post-Paterian modernist relativism, 'Kipling and the history of forms', in Maria DiBattista and Lucy MacDiarmid (eds), *High and Low Moderns: Literature and Culture 1889–1939* (New York, Oxford University Press, 1996), pp. 148–66.

3   For a percipient Barthesian reading of the *mise en abîme* in 'A Matter of Fact' and '"The Finest Story in the World"' (Rudyard Kipling, *Many Inventions* [London, Macmillan, 1893]), see Stephen Bann, 'Il compenso di Kipling' ['The rewards of Kipling'], trans. Franco La Polla, *Paragone/ Letteratura*, 284 (October 1971) 62–83.

4   For Kipling's influence on Eliot, see the pub conversation in *The Waste Land* (Part II) as well as the light verse of *Old Possum's Book of Practical Cats* (London, Faber & Faber, 1936) and the thoughtful introduction to Eliot's *A Choice of Kipling's Verse* (London, Faber & Faber, 1941). Brecht, for whom 'Kipling remained till the last among those few twentieth-century authors for whose work [he] had any deep regard', drew on *Barrack Room Ballads* for the 'Soldiers' Song' in the *Threepenny Opera* and rewrote Kipling's 'The Incarnation of Krishna Mulvaney' (*Life's Handicap* [London, Macmillan, 1891]) into the play *Mann Ist Mann* (John Willett, *The Theatre of Bertolt Brecht* [London, Eyre Methuen, 1997], pp. 90–1.)

5   I am indebted to Professor Suvir Kaul for this definition of the mixed-origin North Indian vernacular. For references to Punjabi, Urdu, Hindustani and Pushtu, see *Kim* (1900; London, Macmillan, 1960), pp.

6, 7, 276 and 407 respectively. Sanskrit is (presumably) the language spoken by the Hindu Gods in 'The Bridge Builders' (*The Day's Work* [London, MacMillan, 1898]). The idiom of the animals in *The Jungle Book* is modelled on the North Indian 'vernacular' which gives the Hindi/ Urdu word *dewanee*, meaning 'madness', as the animals' word for rabies: 'We call it hydrophobia, but they call it *dewanee* – the madness – and run' (Kipling, 'Mowgli's Brothers', *The Jungle Book* [1893; Harmondsworth, Penguin, 1990], pp. 36–7).

6  See Janet Montefiore, 'Day and Night in Kipling', *Essays in Criticism*, 27:4 (October 1977) 299–314.

7  Stephen Bann, p. 67. My quotation is taken from p. 6 of the unpublished English MS. I thank Professor Bann for kindly giving me copies of both English and Italian versions.

8  Kipling, *Kim*, pp. 145, 1.

9  Corelli Barnett and other social historians have emphasised the connections between the standard public-school curriculum of classical literature, cricket or rugby football and the imperialist ethic. See T. C. Worsley, *Barbarians and Philistines* (London, Faber, 1940); David Newsome, *Godliness and Good Learning: Four Studies in a Victorian Ideal* (London, Oxford University Press, 1973); Corelli Barnett, *The Collapse of British Power* (London, Eyre Methuen, 1972); J. A. Mangan, *The Games Ethic and Imperialism* (New York, Viking Press, 1985); and Joseph Bristow, *Empire Boys: Adventures in a Man's World* (London, HarperCollins, 1991).

10  Lord Baden-Powell, open letter to the boys of Cottesmore Preparatory School, 22 July 1900, quoted by Mangan, *The Games Ethic and Imperialism*, p. 48.

11  Henry Newbolt, 'Vitai Lampada', *Collected Poems, 1997–1907* (London, John Murray, 1908), p. 132.

12  Gauri Viswanathan, *Masks of Conquest: Literary Study and British Rule in India* (London, Faber & Faber, 1989), pp. 55, 69.

13  Louis MacNeice, Canto XIII of *Autumn Journal* (London, Faber & Faber, 1939). Reprinted in E. R. Dodds (ed.), *The Collected Poems of Louis MacNeice* (London, Faber & Faber, 1966), p. 127.

14  Edward Said, *Culture and Imperialism* (New York, Viking, 1993), p. 186, citing E. Cromer [Lord Baring], *Ancient and Modern Imperialism* (London, John Murray, 1910) and Joseph Conrad, *Heart of Darkness, Youth and Other Stories* (1899; London, Blackwood, 1927).

15  Mangan, *The Games Ethic and Imperialism*, p. 34, quoting Virgil's *Aeneid*, Book VI, lines 851–3 (my translation).

16  The date of composition for 'Regulus' is given as 1908. Rudyard Kipling, *A Diversity of Creatures* (London, Macmillan, 1917), p. 239.

17  Kipling, *A Diversity of Creatures*, p. 239.

18  *Ibid.*, pp. 253, 254, 256, 256.

19  Rudyard Kipling, 'The Flag of their Country', *Stalky & Co.* (London,

Macmillan, 1899), pp. 212, 214, 213.

20 Kipling, *A Diversity of Creatures*, pp. 259, 266.

21 Kipling, 'Regulus', pp. 256, 263, 260.

22 Kipling agreed in January 1917 to undertake the regimental history of the Irish Guards, published as *The Irish Guards in the Great War* (2 vols, London, Macmillan, 1923). He was therefore researching this work, which he wrote partly as a memorial to his son John Kipling who had been a 2nd Lieutenant in the Irish Guards, during 1917, while he was seeing *A Diversity of Creatures* through the press. See S. Brown, Preface to *The Irish Guards in the Great War* (London, Spellmount, 1996) vol. 1, p. iii.

23 See Kipling, *A Diversity of Creatures*, 'The Children', pp. 129–30; 'The Honours of War', pp. 105–28, featuring a grown-up 'Stalky', 'now Lieutenant-Colonel A. L. Corkran, I.A.' (p. 105); 'In the Presence', pp. 217–36; 'The Edge of the Evening', pp. 273–98; 'Mary Postgate', pp. 419–40; 'The Beginnings', pp. 441–2.

24 Kipling, *A Diversity of Creatures*, pp. 244–5.

25 *Ibid.*, p. 250. See also: 'The democracy stood about futilely pitying him and getting in the way', p. 248.

26 Sir Paul Harvey, *Oxford Companion to Classical Literature* (1937; London, Oxford University Press, 1975), p. 91, entry on Carthage. The first three books of *Odes* 'reflecting the political events of 33–23 BC' by Horace (Quintus Horatius Flaccus, 65 BC–8 BC) appeared in 23 BC (see p. 214), 123 years after Carthage was sacked in 146 BC (see p. 354).

27 Kipling, *A Diversity of Creatures*, p. 250.

28 *Ibid.*, pp. 241, 246. The Latin text mangled by Vernon goes:

> fertur pudica coniugus osculum
> parvosque natos ut capitis minor
> ab se removisse et virilem
> torvus humi posuisse vultum...

> [They say he drew back from the kiss his true wife
> And little children begged, and like a prisoner
> Deprived of civil rights
> Bent an austere gaze grimly on the ground...]

*The Odes of Horace*, translated by James Michie with the complete Latin text (Orion Press, New York, 1963), pp. 146–7.

29 Kipling, 'The Last Term', *Stalky & Co.*, p. 230. Beetle and Stalky are rearranging the text of Horace's 'Ad Pyrrham' ode (Book I, no. 5, *Quis multa gracilis* ['What slender youth...']), which King has set for a school examination. Their ungrammatical surrealist phrase suggests the defeated Titans in Keats's *Hyperion*, and also the fallen angels in *Paradise Lost*, Book 1.

30 I am grateful to Laura Marcus for pointing this out to me.

31  Peter Middleton, *The Inward Gaze. Masculinity and Subjectivity in Modern Culture* (London, Routledge, 1992). See, especially, chapter 2, 'Boys will be men', pp. 17–42.

32  Kipling, *A Diversity of Creatures*, pp. 266, 268, 269–70, 252.

33  The line (Horace, *Odes*, Book III, Number 6, stanza 2, line 1) is first quoted by King with 'full voiced' emphasis (Kipling, *A Diversity of Creatures*, p. 250), repeated by Stalky (p. 251), by King again, reproving Winton (p. 256), and again by a teasing Stalky (p. 270). Michie translates the line a little differently: 'Only as the servant of gods in heaven/ Can you rule earth' (Michie, *Odes of Horace*, p. 149).

34  This racism is noted in Randall Jarrell's poem 'The Night before the Night before Christmas' where a leftish girl reluctantly reads to her brother 'about Regulus leaving, full of courage/ For that nigger Manchester, Carthage./ She reads it, *that Negro Manchester*', Randall Jarrell, *The Complete Poems* (London, Faber & Faber, 1971), p. 42.

35  Joseph Conrad, *Heart of Darkness*, p. 134. For Cato, see Plutarch, *Life of Marcius Cato*, translated by Dryden, ed. A. H. Clough (5 vols, Liverpool, John Young, 1910): 'CARTHAGE, METHINKS, MUST BE UTTERLY DESTROYED' (vol. II, p. 351).

36  Christopher Butler, 'The modernist self', in *Early Modernism: Literature, Modernism, Painting in Europe 1900–1916* (Oxford, Oxford University Press, 1994), p. 95.

37  Kipling, *A Diversity of Creatures*, pp. 258, 256, 260.

38  *Ibid.*, pp. 247, 249–51, 257, 261–2.

39  See Robert Harris and Jeremy Paxman, *A Higher Form of Killing: The Secret Story of Chemical and Biological Warfare* (New York, Hill & Wang, 1982), pp. 1–29.

40  Kipling, *The Irish Guards in the Great War* (1923), reprinted as vols 27 and 28 of the *Sussex Edition of the Complete Writings of Rudyard Kipling in Prose and Verse* (London, Macmillan 1938). The information here comes from vol. 2, p. 55. Kipling describes the 'clouds of gas and screens of covering smoke' at Loos in vol. 1, p. 140, but indicates that 2nd Lieutenant John Kipling was not gassed; machine-gun fire left him 'wounded, believed missing' (vol. 2, p. 16). For a detailed account of a gas attack at Loos, see Robert Graves, *Goodbye to All That* (1929; London, Penguin, 1988), pp. 127–31.

41  Kipling, *A Diversity of Creatures*, p. 249.

42  Harris and Paxman, *A Higher Form of Killing*, p. 1.

43  Kipling, *A Diversity of Creatures*, pp. 269, 261–2.

44  Matthew Arnold, *Friendship's Garland* (London, Smith & Elder, 1871), p. 49. For educational debates, see David Newsome, *Godliness and Good Learning*, pp. 59, 62–3 and Visnawathan, *Masks of Conquest*, pp. 18–19.

45  Matthew Arnold, 'On the study of poetry', *Essays in Criticism. Second Series* (London, Smith & Elder, 1888), p. 5.

46  C. P. Snow, *The Two Cultures and the Scientific Revolution* (Cambridge, Cambridge University Press, 1959); F. R. Leavis *Two Cultures? The Significance of Charles Snow* (London, Chatto & Windus, 1962), p. 10. On the Leavis–Snow debate, see Hubert Butler, *The Children of Drancy* (Mullingar, Lilliput Press, 1988), pp. 188–95; also Ian MacKillop, *F. R. Leavis: A Life in Criticism* (London, Allen Lane, 1995), pp. 314–25.

47  Kipling, *A Diversity of Creatures*, p. 270.

48  Kipling, 'A Translation', *A Diversity of Creatures*, pp. 272–3.

49  See Kipling, 'The Sons of Martha' (1907), in *The Complete Verse of Rudyard Kipling* (London, Kyle Cathie, 1990), p. 308; also 'The Eye of Allah' in *Debits and Credits* (London, Macmillan, 1928).

50  The first six poems in Book III of Horace's *Odes*, all on patriotic themes, are known to classicists as the 'Roman Odes'.

51  Wilfred Owen, 'Dulce Et Decorum Est', *Collected Poems of Wilfred Owen*, ed. C. Day Lewis (London, Chatto & Windus, 1963), p. 55. This edition gives August 1917 as the date of the poem's composition ('In a letter to his mother dated August 1917, Owen wrote "Here is a gas poem, done yesterday"' [Owen, *Collected Poems*, p. 56]). But Jon Stallworthy dates it to October 1917 at Craiglockhart Hospital (*Wilfred Owen: A Biography* [London, Oxford University Press, 1970], p. 226).

52  Harris and Paxman, *A Higher Form of Killing*, p. 2. Chlorine, named from the Greek *chlorus* ('pale green'), works instantly, as Owen describes; whereas the phosgene and mustard gases used later in the Great War take one or two days to show their effects (pp. 17–29).

53  Horace, *Odes*, Book III, number 2, line 13; Kipling, *A Diversity of Creatures*, p. 239.

54  Drafts of the poem show that it was addressed *To Jessie Pope* and, alternatively, *To a Certain Poetess* (Owen, *Collected Poems*, p. 55). Jessie Pope's 'The Call', first published in her *War Poems* (London, Grant Richards, 1915), is reprinted in C. Reilly (ed.), *Scars Upon My Heart: Women's Poetry and Verse of the First World War* (London, Virago, 1981), p. 88.

55  Kipling, 'The Children', *A Diversity of Creatures*, p. 130; Kipling, 'Epitaphs of the Great War 1914–1918', in *Complete Poems*, p. 314.

56  Kim is the 'poor white' son of downwardly mobile members of the well-to-do working class. His mother 'had been a nursemaid in a Colonel's family and married Kimball O'Hara, a young colour-sergeant of the Mavericks, an Irish regiment'. The shadowy ex-nursemaid who died young of cholera is presumably English; Kim's Irish father is first a respectable NCO, and then a 'gang-foreman' on an Indian railway before declining into drink, opium and early death (Kipling, *Kim*, pp. 1–3).

57  Kipling, *Kim*, pp. 304, 133, 171, 175.

58  Angus Wilson, *The Strange Ride of Rudyard Kipling* (London, Secker and Warburg, 1975), p. 92; J. A. Mangan, *The Games Ethic and Imperialism*, pp. 122–41. St Xavier's annual fee of 300 rupees (Kipling, *Kim*, pp. 133,

148–9) is small compared to the 780 rupees (for an 'ordinary boy with horse') at Mayo College, the cheapest school fee listed by Mangan, *The Games Ethic*, p. 129.

59 See James Joyce, *A Portrait of the Artist as a Young Man* (1916; Harmondsworth, Penguin, 1960), pp. 8–10, 12–13, 52, 53–4, 59–60.

60 Kipling seems to be sociologically accurate here; neither Mangan's *The Games Ethic and Imperialism* nor Viswanathan's *Masks of Conquest* describes Victorian Indian schoolboys learning Latin.

61 Kipling, *Kim*, pp. 233, 239–40.

62 *Ibid.*, pp. 218–19.

63 R. G. Collingwood, *The Principles of Art* (Oxford, Clarendon Press, 1938), p. 68.

64 Kipling, *Kim*, p. 245.

65 *Ibid.*, pp. 57, 120.

66 George Orwell, *Nineteen Eighty-Four* (1949; Harmondsworth, Penguin, 1962), pp. 256–72. For a differently angled reading of Orwell's novel as a combative response to modern novels, see Edward Mendelson, 'How Lawrence Corrected Wells; How Orwell Refuted Lawrence' in Dibattista and MacDiarmid (eds), *High and Low Moderns*, pp. 166–75. Readers can also find in Sylvia Townsend Warner's novel *Mr Fortune's Maggot* (1928; London, Virago, 1978) a much gentler scene of mathematical instruction between master and 'native' pupil. Mr Fortune tries to comfort the godless Polynesian boy Lueli with mathematics, believing that 'if anything could minister to a mind diseased, it would be the steadfast contemplation of a right angle … that no human tears could blur, no blow of fate deflect' (p. 169); but mathematics mean nothing to the boy, who is simply bored. For an analysis of this pedagogic relationship, see Nigel Rigby's chapter in this volume.

67 Kipling was standard reading at Edwardian preparatory schools, including St Cyprian's which Orwell (Blair) attended. See Cyril Connolly, *Enemies of Promise* (1938; Harmondsworth, Penguin, 1963), p. 182.

68 Orwell, 'Rudyard Kipling' (1942, revised 1945), reprinted in Andrew Rutherford (ed.), *Kipling's Mind and Art* (London, Oliver & Boyd, 1964), p. 72.

69 Orwell, *Nineteen Eighty-Four*, pp. 275–6, 6. The slogan 'Ignorance is Strength' is explained, somewhat longwindedly, in Goldstein's 'secret book', pp. 209–26.

70 As Angus Wilson has pointed out (*The Strange Ride*, p. 131), Lurgan's homosexuality is suggested by the presence in his house of a 'soft-eyed Hindu' boy with 'scarlet lips', who is mortally jealous of Kim as a potential rival (Kipling, *Kim*, pp. 212, 215).

71 Orwell, *Nineteen Eighty-Four*, pp. 256–7.

72 *Ibid.*, pp. 255–6, 263–4, 270–1.

73 I am grateful to Howard Booth for pointing out to me the parallel

between this vision and a Joycean epiphany.

74  Lionel Trilling, 'Kipling', in Rutherford (ed.), *Kipling's Mind and Art*, p. 91.

75  Subtitle of Kipling's first collection, *Plain Tales from the Hills, Being Stories of Mine Own People* (London, Macmillan, 1887).

76  Bann, 'Il compenso di Kipling', p. 67. (Bann, 'The rewards of Kipling', p. 6.)

77  Butler, *Early Modernism*, p. 5.

**6**

# Modernism, Ireland and empire: Yeats, Joyce and their implied audiences

## C. L. Innes

Given Ireland's long and continuing history of struggles for independence and self-definition as a nation, it is surprising that readings of Irish literature within a post-colonial context have arrived so belatedly on the scene. Despite a burgeoning interest over the past thirty or forty years in general or comparative discussions of colonial, nationalist and post-colonial writing from India, Africa, the Caribbean, Australia and Canada, the example of Irish nationalist and post-nationalist writing has been almost invariably absent from such discussions. This may be because the political impact in their own time of many of the extraordinary works produced by Joyce, Synge, Yeats and O'Casey had been defused, at least as far as British and American critics were concerned, by the time the literary canon and literary criticism began to feel the effects of the great wave of independence and cultural nationalist movements in the late 1950s and early 1960s. Joyce and Yeats have both been appropriated as stars of the European and English modernist pantheon, and their writing has been acclaimed in proportion to the degree it can be tied and confined to aesthetic concerns, with an emphasis on reflexivity, self-containment and self-consciousness about the form and media of art, to the exclusion of political concerns. Joyce's wry comment on the appropriation of Irish writing by the British retains its force: 'Condemned to express themselves in a language not their own [the Irish] have stamped on it the mark of their own genius and compete for glory with the civilised nations. This is then called English literature...'[1]

While some critics do acknowledge that Yeats and Joyce had an awareness of contemporary Irish and European politics, they are often anxious to reassure us that the literary value of these two writers rests largely on their ability to dismiss and rise above the politics of their time. As Declan Kiberd points out, many critics have assumed that Joyce's critique in *Ulysses* of aspects of Irish nationalism is from the 'vantage point of a European humanist', and that he did not himself espouse or condone any partisan politics, including Irish nationalism.[2] Steven Connor in his recent study of Joyce summarises three stages in the history of critical views of *Ulysses*. On its publication it was berated as a distressing and shocking surrender to what Yeats deemed 'the filthy modern tide'. Between the 1930s and 1970s, however, it was explicated and celebrated as a work which 'immerses itself in the destructive element of modernity in mass culture in order precisely to transform that destructiveness into art' and thus express 'a rich and complex refusal of that modernity'.[3] Critics such as Harry Levin, Hugh Kenner and Samuel Goldberg were leading proponents of this redemptive exercise. From the 1970s, Connor sees an increasing understanding among critics of a postmodern perspective in relation to Joyce, with an emphasis on 'the politics of voices, both in narrative and social life'.[4]

Connor himself goes on to explore the ways in which *Ulysses* exemplifies the use of the novel form as 'a sounding board or receiving apparatus for the manifold voices, styles and idioms which throng about and permeate modern subjectivity'.[5] *Ulysses* and *Finnegans Wake* are both analysed as texts which radically question concepts of authority and authorial presence. Neither Ellmann and earlier critics in their celebration of Joyce's 'European humanism', nor Connor and more recent critics in their emphasis on Joyce's 'postmodernism', give more than a passing mention of Joyce in terms of colonial or post-colonial perspectives.

In recent years, however, a number of critics have constructed post-colonial readings of Joyce and Yeats, seeking in different ways to resituate the modernist techniques and concerns of these two writers in the contexts of Irish and other anti-colonial movements. In particular, Fredric Jameson's influential essay 'Modernism and imperialism' makes a distinction between the modernism of metropolitan writers such as Forster and Woolf and the modernism of Joyce.[6] The first section of this chapter responds to several post-colonial readings of Joyce's *Ulysses*, including Jameson's, and draws comparisons with readings of Yeats as an anti-colonialist writer. It then discusses other characteristics of these two Irish writers which distinguish them from British and European modernists and relate them to other post-colonial writers. These characteristics include their insistent reference to autobiographical and personal experience, and their awareness and recurrent reminders not only of a double consciousness on the part of the author but also of a double audience: British and Irish.

## Post-colonial rereadings of Joyce and Yeats

Several important essays and monographs on Joyce published during the 1990s have been influenced by post-colonial studies. Of these one of the most recent is included in Declan Kiberd's *Inventing Ireland*, published in 1995, which argues in its chapter on Joyce that a close reading reveals that Joyce's stance is more anti-colonialist than anti-nationalist. Kiberd maintains that Joyce's modernism is distinct from European modernism and more akin to the project of Salman Rushdie in what he terms its 'radical modernism' and above all in its concern to 'write a narrative of colonisers and colonised in which the symbiotic relationship between the two becomes manifest', thus revealing what has been repressed in texts written from the imperial centre.[7] According to Kiberd, Bloom is portrayed as the epitome of the colonised subject, and the attitudes of characters in *Ulysses* towards him reveal the ways in which Irish citizens and nationalists have been complicit with English imperialism in what Fanon would describe as an interdependent psychological identity established between colonised and coloniser and an essentialist construction of each.[8] Joyce's project, in Kiberd's view, is a post-nationalist one, which will engender a community that allows for a multiplicity of voices and perspectives and which also elevates voice and speech above writing. 'Caught on the cusp between the world that spoke and the world that read,' Kiberd proclaims, 'Joyce tilted finally towards the older tradition'.[9] And so Joyce is restored to a recognisable community of cultural nationalists, including African and Caribbean and Australian, who insist on the centrality of oral tradition as a distinguishing feature from the book and newspaper culture of the colonisers. (In his chapter in this collection, John Nash analyses the importance of newspaper culture to Joyce in his creation of *Ulysses*.)

David Lloyd, in his chapter on Joyce in *Anomalous States: Irish Writing and the Postcolonial Moment*, although he also places Joyce's fictions within a post-colonial frame, differs from Kiberd in his reading of the play of written and spoken discourse in *Ulysses*.[10] In the 'citizen' section above all, according to Lloyd, Joyce presents the disintegration of voice, as one form of discourse rapidly elides into and contaminates another. Here adulteration is a stylistic principle, a distinct modernist technique, where the autonomy of the speaking subject is constantly undermined. Lloyd argues that such adulteration and the threat it presents is analogous to the threat presented by adultery to the patriarchal family and the nation-state. (And so style and technique in *Ulysses* are linked to the preoccupation with adultery which haunts the relationship between Molly and Leopold Bloom.) He links contiguity and hybridisation as devices which contest racial essentialisation and cultural assimilation, and thus contest both imperialism and monologic nationalism whose symbiotic project is to produce simple and single-voiced subjects.[11] In *Joyce, Race and Empire*, a detailed study of Joyce's fiction, Vincent Cheng is more concerned with content and allusion than narrative technique, documenting thoroughly, from the essays as well as the fiction, Joyce's full and subtle awareness of the pervading ideologies which underpinned European imperialism, and the consequences for the colonised. Like Kiberd and Nash, he takes the Cyclops episode as the one which most clearly demonstrates the mirroring of imperial attitudes and racism in the anti-Semitic comments and behaviour of the citizen and his cronies.[12]

Whereas Kiberd, Lloyd, Nash and Cheng explicitly or implicitly relate their readings of Joyce to other colonial and post-colonial writing, Fredric Jameson in his essay 'Modernism and imperialism,' is more concerned with distinguishing between the modernism of 'metropolitan' writers and the modernism of Joyce as a colonised Irish writer, and it is this analysis I wish to pay particular attention to. Jameson identifies the closedness of Dublin, the continuing existence of 'a classic urban community', rather than the content or reference to other colonised subjects, as the mark of its peculiar status as a modernist fiction mapped onto a colonised space.[13] In a different sense, therefore, Jameson shares with Kiberd the view that

*Ulysses* manages to unite the narratives of both the colonisers and the colonised. Despite this superficial agreement, however, they disagree radically in their reading of the novel. For Kiberd the colonial experience is expressed through the *lack* of community and communication revealed, the contrast between the richness of interior monologue and the sparseness of external speech, the frequent misunderstandings, and the marginalisation or exclusion of the main characters, Stephen and Bloom. Jameson finds community and communication and the continuities and interrelationships of village life in the continuing existence of pubs: 'The very fact of the pub itself, or public space in which you meet and talk, is itself a happy survival of an older urban life, which will have no equivalent in metropolitan literature, where meetings between disparate characters must be more artificially arranged, by means of receptions and summer houses.'[14] Jameson's 'metropolitan' examples are Forster's *Howards End* and (briefly) Woolf's *Mrs Dalloway* and *To the Lighthouse*. Arguably, the absence of meetings in pubs in the metropolitan London portrayed by Forster and Woolf has more to do with the gender and class of the main characters than the necessities of metropolitan literature. The fact that meetings in the novels of Woolf, and in this particular novel by Forster, take place in private salons, summer houses and drawing rooms rather than public spaces is not unrelated to the fact that women were generally excluded from the latter. Equally, Jameson seems to have overlooked the absence of women in Joyce's pubs – except as barmaids. The distinctions Jameson draws between the literatures of colonising modernists and colonised modernists are far from coherent or persuasive, based as they are on such highly selective examples. Indeed he seems to conflate two different kinds of reactions to modernisation. As Emer Nolan remarks in her exemplary study of Joyce, '[B]oth modernism and nationalism might be defined by their ambivalence towards modernization … Nationalism seeks to recreate a sense of traditional community within contemporary mass culture; modernist writing exploits the relentless energy of commercial civilization, but it may also record or lament the progressive abolition of local difference in the modern world.'[15] In the passages cited above, it appears that Jameson is himself caught up in the very nostalgia for a seemingly lost organic community which he discerns in the metropolitan writers he discusses.

Jameson comments on Forster's 'ethos of place, as "the basis of all earthly beauty'", which is linked to what he sees as a character-istically metropolitan modernist 'style' of conjoining place or spatial signifiers with a metaphysical concept, implying and intertwining both aesthetic and moral significance. He quotes Margaret Schlegel's recipe for salvation: 'either friends, or the country, ... either some very dear person or some very dear place seems necessary to relieve life's daily grey, and to show that it is grey. If possible, one should have both.'[16] Jameson goes on to say:

> [T]he place is of course the country house itself, the Howards End of the title; and the 'dear person' the late Mrs Wilcox, who begins to merge with her dwelling to the point of becoming almost literally a 'genius loci.' Yet the representational dilemma remains, as in our earlier figure; Mrs Wilcox as a character draws her possibilities from the concrete place that is Howards End, while this last draws its evocative power from the spirit of Mrs Wilcox. The transformation of chance encounters ('only connect') into a utopian social community presided over by a woman who is a providential spirit in a virtually literal sense; and the recovery of a utopian landscape ..., the combination, indeed, the identification of these two visionary constructions is Forster's political as well as his aesthetic agenda in his novel.[17]

I have quoted this extract from Jameson's essay at length because his description of the identification of the 'dear place' and its 'dear person', his analysis of the role of the country house in terms of the author's political and aesthetic agenda, seems to me exactly appropriate as a description of Yeats's series of poems on Coole Park and in praise of Lady Gregory, or 'A Prayer for My Daughter', which desires that she may be 'Rooted in one dear perpetual place'. Yeats would have his daughter fulfil a role like that of Mrs Wilcox and Lady Gregory (and also Virginia Woolf's Mrs Ramsay, with whom Jameson com-pares Mrs Wilcox), as a presiding and providential presence: '...all her thoughts may like the linnet be,/ And have no business but dispensing round/ Their magnaminities of sound.'[18] Similarly the em-phasis on the 'greyness' of the city and 'life's daily grey', and of the meaninglessness of chance encounters within the city, is reminiscent of Yeats's evocation of urban life in the first stanza of 'Easter 1916':

> I have met them at close of day
> Coming with vivid faces
> From counter or desk among grey
> Eighteenth-century houses.

> I have passed with a nod of the head
> Or polite meaningless words...[19]

Jameson also cites from Forster's novel a vision of an age of rootlessness, a 'nomadic civilization', for which 'trees and meadows and mountains will only be spectacle, and the binding force they once exercised on character must be entrusted to Love alone'.[20] Twenty years later, Yeats would lament in similar terms the obliteration by a 'nomadic civilization' of a rooted and utopian world, a great house 'where travelled men and children found/ Content or joy':

> A spot whereon the founders lived and died
> Seemed once more dear than life; ancestral trees,
> Or gardens rich in memory glorified
> Marriages, alliances and families
> And every bride's ambition satisfied.
> Where fashion or mere fantasy decrees
> We shift about – all that great glory spent -
> Like some poor Arab tribesman and his tent.[21]

These similarities between the interdependent aesthetics and politics of Forster and Yeats suggest that the particular contrasts between colonisers and colonised proposed in Jameson's essay need to be qualified and revised, although it seems to me that the point about place as the locus for a politicised aesthetic remains a valid one. But how are we to reconcile the anti-colonial project of Yeats with his difference to Joyce and his affinities with the imperialist novelist Jameson discerns in Forster? That reference to 'travelled men' who 'find content' (in both senses of the word) in Coole Park subtly reminds us of the links Sir William and Lady Gregory did have with the imperial project, as representatives of the British government in Egypt and Ceylon, among other colonial possessions. It is also a reminder perhaps that the Anglo-Irish were embroiled in the imperial enterprise, not merely as victims, but also as perpetrators, and sometimes as both at once. That hybrid role, as victim and perpetrator of the imperial project, is depicted repeatedly in Kipling's works, where Irish soldiers and regiments make themselves at home in India or South Africa, and above all in that most hybrid of characters, Kim (born Kimball O'Hara).

Jameson argues that imperialism, or rather European consciousness of imperialism in relation to colonised states, belongs mainly to the post-First World War period, and that previously (that is from 1884) the consciousness of imperialism is concerned with the relationship between European imperial powers. Jameson's argument is scarcely tenable if one pays attention to anything other than the modernist works he chooses precisely because references to empire are not explicit, ignoring writers such as Kipling, Conrad, and (largely) Forster's *A Passage to India.* Jameson also ignores the avid interest in 'the primitive' which characterised much modernist art, the constant and well-publicised visits of nationalist intellectuals and writers such as Rabindranath Tagore prior to 1914, and the fact that the European ruling and intellectual groups were for a good two hundred years before this period personally involved as governors, administrators, civil servants, educators, missionaries and traders with those areas now referred to as the Third World. Moreover, as Said points out, for the colonised themselves the difference between the technical term 'empire' and early forms of colonial subjection was far less clear than it seems to be to contemporary historians and theorists. As Said remarks, 'I don't think it much matters to an Indian or an Algerian that in the first half of the nineteenth century he or she did not belong to the age of imperialism whereas after 1850 both of them did. For both of them their land had been dominated by an alien power for whom distant hegemony over non-white peoples seemed inscribed by right in the very fabric of European and Western Christian society, whether that society was liberal, monarchical, or revolutionary.'[22]

Said might have added that Ireland's experience of colonial domination extends over an even longer period, and that at varying times one might have substituted for 'non-white' the terms 'non-Anglo-Saxon', 'non-Protestant'. Certainly, as Said goes on to argue, many 'Third World' nationalist writers saw in the Irish literary and cultural revival a model for their own cultural nationalist movements. He maintains that Yeats belongs with those other 'great nationalist artists of decolonization and revolutionary nationalism, like Tagore, Senghor, Neruda, Vallejo, Cesaire, Faiz, Darwish'.[23] In all these writers several main motifs recur: among them the determination to 'distance the native American, Indian, or Irish individual from the British, French, or (later) American master'; and the recovery, at first in the imagination, of the land occupied by the coloniser, for 'if there is anything that radically distinguishes the imagination of anti-imperialism it is the primacy of the geographical in it'.[24] Said goes on to give examples of the ways in which colonisation caused the land to be not only possessed, but renamed and altered so as to mirror the coloniser's homeland.

## Renaming and reclaiming the territory

Brian Friel's play *Translations* is a remarkable representation of the colonial process of renaming and remapping in its earlier stages. The process of reclaiming places as Celtic rather than English is illustrated in many of Yeats's poems, especially earlier ones. For example, 'The Man Who Dreamed of Fairyland' invoking Dromahair, Lissadell, the 'well of Scanavin', 'the hill of Lugnagall' in *The Rose*, and 'The Hosting of the Sidhe' in *The Wind Among the Reeds* where Celtic place names such as Knocknarea and Clooth-na-Bare are used and specified as belonging within a whole system of rooted Irish culture and identity. In these early poems Yeats is remapping Ireland as a possession of a distinctively Celtic people. Joyce's insistent, indeed almost excessive, mapping of Dublin in *Dubliners* and *Ulysses* has a similar function, I would claim, but here the fact of dispossession is simultaneously acknowledged with the act of reclamation. In *Dubliners* the names of streets such as Great Britain Street and Little Britain Street, in *Ulysses* the Martello tower, the Viceregal procession, Nelson's column, the presence of the sailors (from HMS *Belle Isle*), and the soldiers in the 'Night Town' episode, are among the constant reminders of England's occupation. However, Stephen Dedalus and Bloom repossess and claim the city step by step, they re-vision it, and they and their companions also at times rename it. Nelson is retitled and deflated as the 'one-handled adulterer'; his column becomes a mere device for an embryonic *Dubliners* story, a site from which very ordinary Dubliners might gaze upon and reclaim their city ('A Pisgah Sight of Palestine') – and enjoy eating plums.

Seamus Deane has argued, and Said agrees with him, that 'Yeats's early and invented Ireland was amenable to his imagination ... [whereas] he ended by finding an Ireland recalcitrant to it.'[25] While not disputing this claim, I would want to complicate the line of argument by adding that whereas Yeats was able to reimagine and reclaim Ireland geographically in his early poems, the tension and changes arise when he seeks to confront history, or, rather, to weld together the historical and the geographical. The pressure to do this comes with the First World War (and Robert Gregory's involvement in it), the Easter Rising, and then the establishment of the Irish Free State, all events which force him to see Ireland as not merely space to be reclaimed, but a state involved in and making contemporary history. Those poems and writings in which the tension becomes most powerfully expressed, even when they may also become almost inexpressible, and the problem of expressing them most foregrounded, are also those writings which one might see to be his most modernist. There is of course, *The Vision*, which flees from place and space to a metaphysics of history, but I am thinking more of poems where the stasis of place provokes a desire to escape out of time and out of history: 'The Tower', 'Sailing to Byzantium', 'Easter 1916', 'A Prayer for My Daughter', 'Coole Park and Ballylee', and 'Meditations in a Time of Civil War'. Each of these poems begins with an invocation of a particular place and a particular historical or biographical moment. Each (except 'Sailing to Byzantium') then invokes earlier history or biography, and each turns to visions of empty space and time or to visions out of space and time in response to the torment of history. Despite the differences in politics and class, Yeats and Stephen Dedalus share the desire to escape the consequences of history as it has impacted upon Ireland. Stephen's response is expressed in the claustrophobic atmosphere of Deasy's office and its icons of colonial rule, 'History is a nightmare from which I am trying to awake'.[26]

Yeats and Joyce may seem to compare with some English modernist writers such as Woolf, Eliot and (perhaps) Forster in their *foregrounding* of place in relation to time over plot or narrative, and in their insistent linking of the relationship between place and personal identity. As I have tried to show, however, this linking of place and time has a distinctly different function in their works from that of metropolitan writers. They also differ in their emphasis on relationships between specific places and autobiographical experience or personal history. In his early poems, Yeats draws on certain place names (Innisfree, Lissadell, Clooth-na-Bare, Ben Bulben) not merely because they are Celtic, but because they are in or near Sligo and associated with his childhood. Similarly the persons explicitly or implicitly named in later poems are not merely figures from the Irish social and political scene, but the people *he* knew – Lady Gregory,

Synge, Hyde, Constance Markiewicz, Pearse, MacDonagh and, of course, Maude Gonne (although she is never explicitly named). Throughout his poetry, the making of Irish history, the possession of Ireland and its historical narrative, is linked by Yeats inextricably with his own personal history and place.

Such a refusal to distinguish between his own story and Ireland's might be seen – indeed has been seen – as extraordinarily arrogant, but my argument is that this is both a typical and perhaps a necessary move in an anti-colonial context. A similar assertion of personal and national identity is made by Stephen Dedalus in *A Portrait of the Artist as a Young Man*: 'This race and this country and this life produced me ... I shall express myself as I am.'[27] The leading twentieth-century Australian poets Judith Wright and Les Murray likewise return again and again to the naming and renaming of the land, and the linking of their parents and grandparents with very specific geographical areas in northern New South Wales. One could also compare Yeats and Joyce with other nationalist writers who insistently make these links: Wole Soyinka in his poetry and three volumes of autobiography links his family's history with the history of colonisation and resistance in Nigeria; Derek Walcott's long poem *Another Life* retraces his life story with reference to the developing of a nationalist consciousness in St Lucia and the Caribbean; Leopold Senghor, celebrating in his poems and essays the dual consciousness which was a consequence of European colonisation of Africa, presented himself as representative and spokesman for Senegal, the country of which he became president. For these and many other anti-colonial writers the telling of personal autobiography is a means of retelling communal and national history – a new starting point from which to sidestep the overwhelming colonial narrative.[28] In the case of Ireland and other settler colonies, such as Australia and Kenya, these autobiographical links between place and a new foundational history may well be contested by subsequent autobiographical works. The title and narrative of *My Place*, a family autobiography by the Australian Aboriginal author Sally Morgan, challenges not only the autobiographies of 'pioneering settlers' such as the Drake-Brockmans in Western Australia but also the implicit claims made by other settler descendants such as the novelist Katherine Susannah Prichard, and the poets Judith Wright and Les Murray. *Dubliners*, *A Portrait of the Artist as a Young Man* and *Ulysses* all implicitly, and at times explicitly, challenged the claim staked by Yeats and his generation and class to a founding narrative set in rural Ireland and the milieu of landed gentry, their friends and families.

## Community and audience

In all these cases the establishment of an inextricable relationship between place and personal and communal identity is not merely a means of repossessing the land, of asserting who has claims to it; it is also a means of defining an inside community against an outsider community, those who belong against those who do not. Like other anti-colonial nationalist writers, Irish writers differ from English and European modernist and postmodernist writers in their sense of a double audience, one existing as an immediate community within or identified with the Irish nation, the other an outside or metropolitan readership. For the immediate community, reading is largely an act of *recognition* and bonding – naming becomes an assertion and (re)creation of this intimate inside community. The small group of people who originally received copies of Yeats's 'Easter 1916', from its privately printed run of twenty-five copies, did not *need* to be told the names; they knew who was being referred to by 'That woman … who rode to harriers,' 'This man' who kept a school, 'This other his helper…', 'This other who seemed…'. Among the ways in which those participants in the Easter Rising have 'changed, changed utterly' is that they have become not only members of an inside community, but *also* members of an outside community, for which they become *merely* the names invoked at the end of the poem. (One might note that women remain barred from that outside community; 'that woman', although she is the first to be described, is not named in the final stanza along with 'MacDonagh and MacBride/ And Connolly and Pearse'.)

While 'Easter 1916' in part commemorates the changing status of Ireland from colonised and marginalised community to the status of nation that speaks its own history and names its own heroes, other poems by Yeats retain their address to a private community, about which only insiders can speak with authority. Many critics have noted Yeats's change of style, and with it a change from late Romantic to modernist techniques and aesthetics, marked by the poem, 'A Coat', which records the casting aside of song as a 'coat/ Covered with embroideries/ Out of old mythologies', in order to 'walk naked'.[29] 'A Coat' is the penultimate poem in the volume *Responsibilities*, for which 'Pardon Old Fathers' is the Preface announcing the new unclothed Yeats. Here indeed 'old mythologies' are cast off to allow the display of personal history and experience: a series of ancestors who were merchants and scholars, or soldiers 'that withstood/ Beside the brackish waters of the Boyne/ James and his Irish when the Dutchman crossed'; a poet now aged forty-nine who seeks 'Pardon that for a barren passion's sake' he has no child.[30] The poem underlines not just a move from myth to history, but also a move to a particular ancestral history which will provide the new foundation for 'a book' to 'prove' the continuity between their blood and his. For Irish readers the invocation of the Boyne would have had particular resonances, as would Yeats's declaration that his ancestors withstood 'James and *his Irish*' (my emphasis). Here Yeats asserts his identity within and against an Irish context. Such assertions are made again in 'The Tower', in the proclaimed links with Mrs French on the one hand, and Burke and Grattan on the other, in 'Meditations in a Time of Civil War', and in 'Nineteen Hundred and Nineteen'. Similarly poems such as 'Among School Children', 'In Memory of Eva Gore-Booth and Con Markiewicz', 'Blood and the Moon', 'Coole Park, 1929', and 'The Municipal Gallery Revisited' forge links between specific places, personal acquaintances and Irish history so as to assert a community of insiders, whose names and lives are to be recognised and affirmed by a wider, but always Irish, community. In all these poems, the emphasis on biographical and local detail serves not only as a means of asserting the authority of local readings of the texts and reversing the previous relationship between definer and defined, but such details also allow Yeats and selected Irish writers, artists and political icons to create a different foundation from which to rebuild and reinvent a community outside of the categories imposed by the English colonisers.

The issue of a double audience and insider knowledge is also relevant to the writing of James Joyce, and particularly to *Ulysses*. For Joyce's Irish contemporaries, the act of reading *Ulysses* was in many ways an act of recognition, the retracing and hence the sharing and repossession of familiar places, names and persons. The novel is peopled with actual Dubliners, with familiar figures, and passing references to familiar places, events, anecdotes. Some are explicitly named (like Eglinton, George Russell, Nanetti [who was to become Mayor of Dublin] and Best); others (like Buck Mulligan and the citizen) are given names and characteristics which disguise only to reveal. *Ulysses* is a novel for which inside knowledge and authority as a reader comes from being part of a community, which Joyce seeks to extend but also to define. In this novel, Haines is not only a caricature of the English imperialist, with his nightmares about guns and panthers, his collecting of folklore and his amateur anthropological and philological interests; he is also a figure of the *excluded* or outside reader, who fails to 'get' Stephen's jokes or to understand the nuanced references in the speech and chatter of the Dublin community.

The distinction being made here between Haines as 'excluded' or outside reader and the insiders who share jokes and understanding to which he has no access has to do with 'constructed' or fictional readers, rather than 'real' ones. The issue of Joyce's actual readership is a complicated one, but nevertheless it could be argued that Joyce sets up a tension between a number of implicit readers and his actual readers – if only in terms of disengagement. In seeing how Haines 'misreads' Mulligan, Stephen and the old woman who brings the milk, we can perhaps become more nuanced readers ourselves. Most of the contemporary critics I mentioned earlier in this essay have shown the significance of the multiplicity of voices in *Ulysses*, and have commented in varying ways on the problem of locating an authoritative voice in this novel. A corollary of the multiplicity of voices and the question of the authoritative speaker is the multiplicity of listeners and the question of the authoritative reader.

*Ulysses* is a book noteworthy for the number of listeners who inhabit it, and for the number of scenes which draw attention to the listener hovering on the margins of conversations. In the first two episodes of the novel, Stephen suffers the chatter of Mulligan, the earnest commentary of Haines, the preaching of Deasey, the halting mistranslations and misreadings of his pupils; he himself says remarkably little, although his silent responses to Mulligan, Haines and Deasey suggest how we should read what they say. In the ninth episode, Stephen is heard, but he also frequently overhears himself, and at certain points nudges his readers towards sceptical detachment from his autobiographical readings of Shakespeare. Indeed this central episode in the Dublin National Library is as much about reading and misreading as it is about authorship, whether of Shelley, Shakespeare or Irish writers. The 'Aeolus' episode, set in the newspaper offices, also shows Stephen and Bloom as listeners and readers, both at times seeking to insert themselves into the community of speakers. In his contribution to this volume, John Nash demonstrates the interplay and clash between modes of writing displayed in this episode, and Joyce's use of the London *Times* as a source for news which reveals here and in the 'Cyclops' episode Joyce's awareness of London as a centre of empire. But this chapter also invokes a series of readings dependent on 'insider knowledge' which is unavailable to Londoners. Beginning with that resounding phrase 'In the heart of the Hibernian metropolis',[31] with its playful insistence on Dublin as a centre, not only of paralysis and a mimic culture, but also of a history and 'Hibernian' counter-culture of its own making, Irish metropolitan readers finds themselves in an almost entirely known world, amidst a familiar series of place names and a group of speakers who assume both a mastery of Greek, Latin and Judaic-Christian oral and written cultures and an insider knowledge of Irish history and affairs. The references to lines from 'The Boys of Wexford,' a ballad well known to Irishmen and women, to the Wild Geese, Isaac Butt, [James] Whiteside, John Philpott Curran, the mass meetings held by Daniel O'Connell at Tara and Mullaghmast, newssheets such as *Paddy Kelly's Budget* and *The Skibbereen Eagle,* invoke a specific national history and culture which has little or no meaning for readers outside Ireland. The anecdote narrated by Myles Crawford about the reporting of the Phoenix Park assassinations in coded form, whose decoding depended on access to the Irish *Freeman's Journal* and a ready knowledge of Dublin's streets and suburbs, can be seen as paradigm (perhaps a 'gnomon') for the reading of many sections of *Ulysses,* in which incidents, names, phrases signify differently for Irish and non-Irish readers. The effect is not to make those sections meaningless to those who do not share the knowledge of Irish place and history; it is rather to create an awareness among Irish readers of a shared knowledge and history, over which they have authority and mastery, and which non-Irish readers must be taught.

The fact that communal histories and stories are parodied and subverted in the 'Cyclops' episode does not detract from that sense of a shared culture and history; rather, it emphasises it. For the recognition of what is being parodied and mocked in this section depends on a fairly thorough immersion in a whole store of nationalist texts, stagings and rewritings. Moreover it is important to remember that the contemporary Irish audience for *Ulysses* was not an audience living in the Dublin of 1904, but an Irish audience, which like the British, European and American audiences who first read the novel in 1922, had seen the shattering effects of the First World War. William McCormack is one of the few critics to have made the point that *Ulysses* is a *historical* novel, and that the gap between the composition of this work and its setting is much greater than in either *A Portrait of the Artist* or *Dubliners*. As McCormack comments, 'It is not enough merely to place the object in its historical context; the reader, the subject (so to speak) of criticism is also historically placed'.[32] In the Cyclops episode the Irish reader of 1922 and later is particularly likely to be aware of the tension between 'then' and 'now', of the historical events which have grown out of and superseded the world of the citizen, the Gaelic League and the Gaelic Athletic Association – which was led in 1904 by 'Citizen' Michael Cusack. In particular, the Easter Rising has taken place, reiterating and also transforming the rebellions referred to and invoked time and again in the talk and consciousness of Stephen, Bloom and the other citizens of Dublin. Throughout *Ulysses* and especially in the 'Cyclops' episode, Robert Emmet is recalled. Irish readers would be quick to recognise the events and the restaging of events (there existed at the time some forty plays and numerous ballads and popular novels with Emmet as the central character).[33] He was a role model for Padraic Pearse, who spoke thus of him:

> Here at St Enda's we have tried to keep before us the image of Fionn during his battles – careless and laughing, with that gesture of the head, that gallant, smiling gesture, which has been an eternal gesture in Irish history; it was most memorably made by Emmet when he mounted that scaffold in Thomas Street, smiling, he who had left so much, and most recently by those three who died at Manchester. I know that Ireland will not be happy again until she recollects that old proud gesture of hers, and that laughing gesture of a young man that is going into battle or climbing a gibbet.[34]

This particular speech about Emmet was made by Pearse in 1913, and is reiterated in other speeches around the same time. Lennox Robinson's play about Emmet, *The Dreamers*, which represents the hero in a similar light, was staged in Dublin in 1915. Emmet's marriage to Sarah Curran on the eve of his execution may well have inspired Joseph Plunkett to wed his fiancée Grace Gifford the day before he was executed for his part in the Easter Rebellion. Joyce and his Irish readers must surely have had both the Easter Rebellion and the post-1904 iconography of Emmet in mind when writing or reading the parodic account of Emmet's death in the 'Cyclops' episode: 'She would never forget her hero boy who went to his death with a song on his lips as if he were but going to a hurling match in Clonturk park ... Oblivious of the dreadful present, they both laughed heartily, all the audience, including the venerable pastor, joining in the general merriment.'[35]

Joyce's burlesque of this sentimentalised and romantic heroism speaks to a European and American audience which has seen the deaths of thousands of young men in the First World War; but it speaks more directly and intimately to an Irish audience which has witnessed the replaying of Emmet's story on the streets of Dublin, and would have recognised the Easter Rebellion in that context, and indeed in the wider context of a series of heroic martyrdoms and rebellions, remarked by Leopold Bloom in his dispute with the citizen about 'the point, the brothers Sheares, and Wolfe Tone beyond on Arbour Hill and Robert Emmet and die for your country, the Tommy Moore touch about Sarah Curran and she's far from the land'.[36] Bloom's detailed consciousness of Irish history, culture and places, his consciousness of himself as an Irishman rather than an 'other', unites him with the Irish readers of *Ulysses* and the community depicted by Joyce. Writing *Ulysses* in the years between 1914 and 1921, Joyce may have wished to construct an Irish readership that would be ready to identify Bloom as one among themselves, and to reject as they recognised it an outdated and xenophobic nationalism that was unable to acknowledge Bloom as an insider. It might also be a readership growing towards the affirmation of Ireland as an independent nation, writing and reading itself into its own version of history.

Seamus Deane has commented on the doubleness of language, culture and audience in Ireland as providing a productive dilemma for both Yeats and Joyce:

> Caught between two cultures, two languages, and two audiences, English and Irish, [earlier Irish novelists] had been mired by history. Joyce,

inheriting these divisions, overcame them by bringing history into the ambit of fiction and revealing thereby the essentially linguistic and therefore ductile nature of both activities. In this respect he emulated Yeats.[37]

Both writers, but Joyce more insistently so, assert ownership of a 'double' language or idiom, one which asserts mastery over standard literary English, and another which asserts the distinctiveness of Irish English, and so implicitly excludes a constructed British reader such as Haines from its community. In writing to a double audience, these two authors in different ways reverse the relationships between centre and periphery. The Irish audience possesses the 'inside' knowledge which allows it to recognise key references to a Dublin/Irish inner circle, Irish history, geography, culture, and personal biography; British readers become, and are made to feel themselves, outsiders, lacking the knowledge and authority which will allow them to 'possess' these Irish texts. Paradoxically, it may have been the unacknowledged desire to suppress recognition of their marginalised status as readers which propelled many 'outsider' critics to categorise them as English or European modernists, and to insist that the politics of Ireland's colonial and post-colonial status were irrelevant to the appreciation of the works of Joyce and Yeats.

## Notes

1 Richard Ellmann, *James Joyce* (Oxford, Oxford University Press, 1965), p. 26.
2 Declan Kiberd, *Inventing Ireland: The Literature of the Modern Nation* (London, Chatto & Windus, 1995), p. 345.
3 Steven Connor, *James Joyce* (Plymouth, Northcote House in Association with the British Council, 1996), p. 71.
4 *Ibid.*, p. 72.
5 *Ibid.*
6 Fredric Jameson, 'Modernism and imperialism', in Seamus Deane, Terry Eagleton, Fredric Jameson and Edward W. Said, *Nationalism, Colonialism and Literature* (Minneapolis, University of Minnesota Press, 1990), pp. 43–68.
7 Kiberd, *Inventing Ireland*, p. 344.
8 For further discussion of Irish cultural nationalism in the context of Fanon's analysis of colonial psychology see C. L. Innes, *The Devil's Own Mirror: The Irish and Africans in Modern Literature* (Washington, D.C., Three Continents Press, 1990).
9 Kiberd, *Inventing Ireland*, p. 355.

10 David Lloyd, *Anomalous States: Irish Writing and the Post-Colonial Moment* (Durham, N.C., Duke University Press, 1993).

11 *Ibid.*

12 Vincent Cheng, *Joyce, Race and Empire* (Cambridge, Cambridge University Press, 1995).

13 Jameson, 'Modernism and imperialism', p. 62.

14 *Ibid.*, p. 63.

15 Emer Nolan, *James Joyce and Nationalism* (London, Routledge, 1995), p. xii.

16 E. M. Forster, *Howards End* (Harmondsworth, Penguin, 1973), pp. 150–1.

17 Jameson, 'Modernism and imperialism', pp. 55–6.

18 W. B. Yeats, *Collected Poems* (London, Macmillan, 1982), pp. 212–13.

19 *Ibid.*, p. 202.

20 Quoted in Jameson, 'Modernism and imperialism', p. 57.

21 Yeats, 'Coole Park and Ballylee, 1931', *Collected Poems*, p. 276.

22 Edward Said, 'Yeats and decolonization', in *Nationalism, Colonialism and Literature*, p. 71.

23 *Ibid.*, p. 73.

24 *Ibid.*, p. 77.

25 Quoted by Said in 'Yeats and decolonization', p. 80.

26 James Joyce, *Ulysses* (Harmondsworth, Penguin, 1986), p. 28.

27 James Joyce, *A Portrait of the Artist as a Young Man* (Harmondsworth, Penguin, 1986), p. 203.

28 For a fuller discussion of the links between autobiographical and national narrative in African literature, see James Olney, *Tell Me Africa: An Approach to African Literature* (Princeton, Princeton University Press, 1973).

29 Yeats, *Collected Poems*, p. 142.

30 *Ibid.*, p. 113.

31 Joyce, *Ulysses*, p. 96.

32 W. J. McCormack, 'Nightmares of history', in W. J. McCormack and Alastair Stead (eds), *James Joyce and Modern Literature* (London: Routledge & Kegan Paul, 1982), p. 78.

33 For a description of some of these works, see Maureen S. G. Hawkins, 'The dramatic treatment of Robert Emmet and Sarah Curran', in S. F. Gallagher (ed.), *Women in Irish Legend, Life and Literature* (Gerrards Cross, Colin Smythe, 1983), pp. 125–37.

34 Quoted by Ruth Dudley Edwards, *Patrick Pearse: The Triumph of Failure* (London, Faber & Faber, 1979), p. 177.

35 Joyce, *Ulysses*, p. 254.

36 *Ibid.*, p. 251.

37 Seamus Deane, *A Short History of Irish Literature* (London, Hutchinson, 1986), pp. 186–7.

# 7

# The anti-colonial modernism
# of Patrick Pearse

## Máire ní Fhlathúin

During a literary, political and pedagogical career spanning the years
1898–1916, Patrick Pearse worked with the consistent aim of restoring
Irish political autonomy and reclaiming an Irish cultural heritage. In
this chapter I want to consider Pearse in his most obvious role as
an anti-colonial writer and revolutionary, and also in a context less
immediately apparent: literary modernism. His revolutionary career
culminated in his execution in 1916 for his part in the Easter Rising,
leading to his silhouetted portrait becoming instantly recognisable in
Irish school history lessons and his name acquiring its own explanatory footnote to Yeats's 'Easter 1916'. As writer and literary critic,
he consistently wrote against the hierarchies inherent in the colonial
relationship, by attempting to recover – or reinvent – a native Irish
history and culture, and by advocating the ideals of self-sacrifice and
redemption through suffering common to an Irish Catholic heritage
and to a contemporary, anti-colonial mode of thought.[1] A similarly
anti-colonial effort is also apparent in the themes and concerns of
his fiction, in which the basic colonial hierarchy is reversed, as the
west coast of Ireland becomes the centre, replacing the colonial
metropolis of London or its outposts of Dublin or Galway. The
apparatus of a patriarchal colonial state is opposed to a family- and
mother-centred sentimental nationalism; and the texts are often
written in Irish, not English, which is an obvious de-colonising
practice. But while Pearse saw himself – in the early years of his
career at least – as a voice of authentic Irish culture, opposed to any

form of modernity, his tactics and his literary works can be seen as characteristically modernist in form.

European modernism is notable for the attempts of writers and artists to revitalise Western culture by the incorporation of elements of other cultures and traditions, its representative texts being Eliot's *The Waste Land* (1922) and Picasso's *Les Demoiselles d'Avignon* (1907). The techniques of these artists and writers produced an effect of instantly recognisable textual ambiguity, where the European framework vies for attention and emphasis with the non-European elements of the work. In its Irish context, modernism has always involved the attempt to look to an Irish cultural tradition, and also to look outside Ireland: both are present in the central modernist texts of Yeats's poems and Joyce's *Ulysses* (1922). Patrick Pearse, writing in the first sixteen years of the century, had his own literary and political agenda, incorporating a rejection of the modern together with an attempt to reappropriate the authentic voice of Irish culture by writing in the Irish language and using the style and subject matter of 'naive' folk literature. In so doing, however, he introduced contemporary themes and characters to his fiction and adapted the structures he found to a more consciously 'European' narrative form. In effect, he pre-empted many of the themes and techniques now described as modernist, and produced a set of writings in which ambiguities of language, presentation and context draw attention to the rootless nature of his work. Despite its superficially nationalist and linguistic specificity, his work belongs to a mode of engagement with the world which draws on a multiplicity of cultural forms and sources.

A reading of his early literary essays makes the idea of Pearse-as-modernist look distinctly odd, however. In 'The Intellectual Future of the Gael' (1897), he is to be found making the case that an unhealthy interest in the modern is precisely the failing of the literature of the time:

> The truth of the matter is that the intellectual and literary tastes of the world have been carried away by a craving for the un-real, for the extravagant, for the monstrous, for the immoral. Men's tastes have become vitiated. There is no healthy out-of-door atmosphere in modern literature. Literature has arrived, in short, at a state of unnatural senility, and the time seems not far off when either of two things must happen – either intellect and literature must disappear from modern life, and with them everything that makes modern life worth living, or some new and unpolluted source

must be opened up, some new blood must be infused into the intellectual system of the world, which has become prematurely worn out.

The 'new blood' he had in mind was, naturally, to come from 'the Gaelic race – a race whose literature is as different from the unnatural literature of to-day as the pure radiance of the sun is different from the hideous glare of the electric light'.[2] His later work, while it maintained the effort to continue writing in this tradition, was characterised also by an attempt to merge it with elements of the contemporary culture he had earlier found so distasteful. It is in this merging of cultural modes, together with Pearse's own status as a figure multi-contextual both by birth and by practice, that his links to modernism can be discerned.

Terence Brown's work on 'Ireland, Modernism and the 1930s' makes a convincing case for a coincidence of technique and theme between the Irish Literary Revival – of which Pearse's work forms a part – and the modern movement, arguing that:

> the Irish Literary Revival in its nationalist context was contiguous with modernism rather than merely concurrent. Text and context formed a culture in which the kinds of technical devices and the sense of reality modernism would internationalise were contemporaneously aspects of the Revival project and probably influenced, consciously and unconsciously, the Irish contribution to the general movement.

Brown's work refers to a period postdating Pearse, when the work produced by Yeats, Joyce *et al.* had already defined the boundaries of Irish Revival literature and Irish Modernism. At the same time, his argument is important, and relevant, to the earlier years of the century, in particular for the view that

> the Revival and modernism can be seen as exhibiting parallels of outlook and method. At moments in the work of the Irish modernists the literary historian is conscious of overlappings, points of contact as well as parallels and similarities. And the Revival context can be seen as one likely to produce writers who, formally at the very least, can be reckoned as contributors to the international phenomenon of modernism.[3]

Patrick Pearse was just such a writer. This chapter will examine the intersection of his literary writings and his political career, with the aim of showing how both aspects of his life and work manifest the strategies of anti-colonialism and the attributes of literary modernism.

The drive towards anti-colonialism underlies all Pearse's work, whether political, literary or critical. It is most openly stated in his political writings and pamphlets,[4] but it also informs the themes and structures of his plays and short stories, where he, like most of the Irish Revival writers, engages in a thematic revaluation of the colonial relationship. A key metaphor of colonialism is the mapping of the patriarchal family onto the colonial world, where the coloniser is gendered male, given the status and duties of the father, and opposed to the feminised, child-like figure of the colonised. The corresponding anti-colonial strategy may be described as a partial revision of this structure, where the identification of the colonised with the female or the child is retained, but the hierarchy which places these figures below the patriarch is reversed. Declan Kiberd identifies 'the revolt of an artistic son against an unsatisfactory father' as 'a leitmotif that spanned the literature of Europe in the early years of the twentieth century'; but also notes that this revolt is particularly in evidence in Ireland, together with a comparable pattern where 'women assert their independence of fathers and husbands, often appearing more manly than their partners: this masculinization may be found in many classic works of the Irish revival'.[5] The result is a consistent fictional theme: the idealisation of the woman and the child, together with a lack of emphasis on the father or mature adult male figure, who can often be read as representing the oppressive figure of the coloniser. In Pearse's work, as often in the Irish tradition, the female figure foregrounded is usually the mother, and the child is the idealised figure of a young boy. Developing his use of these themes, the following analysis concentrates mainly on the short story 'An Bhean Chaointe' (1907) and the play *The Singer* (1915).[6]

In the words of Elizabeth Butler Cullingford, 'Mariolatry in Ireland must be understood as the deliberate identification of a conquered people with a cult which was anathema to their Protestant oppressors.'[7] Pearse's work displays abundant evidence of the adoration and worship of the mother, using her in plays and stories such as the two mentioned above, and in the poem 'The Mother', to establish the principle of sacrifice, a sacrifice perceived by him as both good in itself and, in some cases, offering hope for political or cultural freedom from British rule. In *The Singer*, the narrative is centred on Maire, the mother: it is she who plays the main part in the opening scenes, and the driving force of the play is her relationship with her

son MacDara. He was compelled to depart from his mother's house
when he attracted the notice of the colonial state for his songs 'full
of terrible love for the people and of great anger against the Gall
[the English]': 'word came down from Galway or from Dublin that
he would be put in prison, and maybe excommunicated if he did not
go away.' The events of the play take place on the night of his return.
In the dialogue between his mother, his sister and the other characters,
MacDara's heroic status is revealed to the audience, together with
news of a revolutionary figure called the Singer. Eventually the two
are identified as the same person, and MacDara sets off, with his
mother's blessing, to mount his own fight for freedom; his younger
brother Colm (his rival in love but his follower in politics) has already fought, and been defeated. The final scene links the religious
with the political through the idea of sacrifice, as so often in Pearse's
work. Maire willingly gives up her son, and MacDara his life, as he
leaves with a speech of renunciation: 'One man can free a people as
one Man redeemed the world. I will take no pike, I will go into the
battle with bare hands. I will stand up before the Gall as Christ hung
naked before men on the tree!' The stage directions underline the
cost and the effect of his actions: 'He moves through them, pulling
off his clothes as he goes. As he reaches the threshold a great shout
goes up from the people. He passes out and the shout dies slowly
away. The other men follow him slowly. Maire ni Fhiannachta sits
down by the fire, where Sighle still crouches.' The relationship
between mother and son – both sacrificial victims, both willingly
sacrificing – represents the hope of liberation from masculine/patri-
archal forces: the priest who 'counselled [MacDara] to go' into exile,
and the British soldiers who meet and defeat his brother in unequal
combat. The play serves as illustration of its own statement, Mac-
Dara's assertion that 'to serve and suffer as women do is to be the
highest thing'.[8] The self-sacrifice identified by Daniel O'Neil as one
of the 'fundamental themes' of anti-colonialism[9] is thus associated
with the most evocative figure of suffering womanhood, the mother
who gives up her son.

The foregrounding of the child has a similar, anti-colonial function in Pearse's work. In the majority of his plays and stories, the
central, iconic figure is a young boy – prepubescent, innocent,
childishly wise – who, like the mother-figure, represents both actual
goodness and potential freedom: Giolla na Naomh in the play *An*

*Rí* (1912), Iollann in *The Master* (1915), the protagonists of 'Íosagán' (1906) and 'An Gadaí' (1916).[10] The preoccupation with the child-figure has generally been explained in terms of Pearse's sexual naivety and latent attraction to young boys: Seán Farrell Moran is a representative voice when he refers to Pearse's 'lack of a clearly defined sexual identity';[11] and Ruth Dudley Edwards argues that 'Pearse was an innocent, but there can be little doubt about his unconscious inclinations. His prose and poetry sing when he speaks of young male beauty.'[12] It is impossible to disagree with such assessments, and in this respect Pearse fits easily into the category of 'Uranian' poets described by Timothy d'Arch Smith, notable among them only for the idealised, unselfconscious quality of his writing.[13] Unlike these writers, however, his work was directed to a political end.

In his focus on youth, his figuring of Ireland, her saviours, his protagonists and himself as youthful (a race 'as yet young and vigorous and healthy'[14]), Pearse is taking the quality of childishness, familiar in the discourse of colonialism as one of the defining attributes of the colonised, and revaluing it. If the coloniser, as father and governor, is to be rejected, the colonised, the child, in Pearse's work is not a lesser being who needs teaching, or civilising – he is an example to be emulated. Like the narrative structure of his stories, offering the peasant mother's household as a moral centre of opposition to the invisible forces of the coloniser, the emphasis on youth reverses the moral value-structure of colonialism. The word 'young' recurs, like a mantra, in Sighle's reveries in *The Singer*: 'I am proud other times to think of so many young men, young men with straight, strong limbs, and smooth, white flesh, going out into great peril because a voice has called to them to right the wrong of the people. Oh, I would like to see the man that has set their hearts on fire with the breath of his voice! They say that he is very young.'[15] The imagery echoes Yeats's famous *Cathleen Ni Houlihan* (1902), with its young protagonist going out to fight for an Ireland personified as a woman; it also foreshadows Pearse's own image of himself, in 'The Fool', as a revolutionary whose impulse to 'scatter, not save' is part of his 'hot youth'. In this poem, again, youth is opposed to 'wise men', prudence, 'lawyers … in council' and 'men with … keen, long faces' – the patriarchal, judicial aspect of the coloniser.[16]

The opposition of youth to a colonial parent-state found its final, practical expression in the boys from Scoil Éanna who listened to

Pearse's speeches and took part in the Easter Rising, an event anticipated by Pearse with a mixture of horror and delight in his recounting of a dream:

> I dreamt that I saw a pupil of mine, one of our boys at St Enda's [Scoil Éanna], standing alone upon a platform above a mighty sea of people; and I understood that he was about to die there for some august cause, Ireland's or another. He looked extraordinarily proud and joyous, lifting his head with a smile almost of amusement; I remember noticing his bare white throat and the hair on his forehead stirred by the wind, just as I had often noticed them on the football field. I felt an inexplicable exhilaration as I looked upon him, and this exhilaration was heightened rather than diminished by my consciousness that the great silent crowd regarded the boy with pity and wonder rather than with approval – as a fool who was throwing his life away rather than as a martyr that was doing his duty. It would have been so easy to die before an applauding crowd or before a hostile crowd: but to die before that silent, unsympathetic crowd![17]

In this vision, the complex variety of Pearse's depiction of youth is most apparent: again, the youth – the fool – is opposed to the practical masses, the individual opposed to the 'mighty sea' of people. It is a vision that recalls one of the themes described by d'Arch Smith as typical of 'Uranian' love – that is, the 'angelic vision' where a dream-figure, usually a young boy, appears to the sleeping poet.[18] In Pearse's mind, the figure carries a political as well as an erotic charge: the young boy on the stage becomes the focus of the school-master's idealised love for his pupil, but also an image of individual sacrifice for a political 'august cause'.

This same revaluation is clear in the treatment in Pearse's work of two other fields where the colonial centre is normally opposed to a dependent, colonised periphery. These are the areas of geographical space and of language. The centring of marginal elements – the bog, the mountainside, the peasant home – is evident in Pearse's literary work as far back as 1898, when he wrote on 'The Folk Songs of Ireland'.[19] The authors of these folk songs, he said, were 'peasant men and women ... born and bred in the middle of a bog, per-chance, or in a mud-cabin on a mountain-side'. Such locations, however, are the spiritual centre of Ireland, and the people who live there are 'poets taught by nature herself', their ignorance of the English language not a handicap but a positive quality. The rest of this passage makes uneasy reading, as Pearse embarks on a characteristically fanciful set of comparisons – the folk songs are 'spotless as the driven snow, like the souls and lives of those who sing them', musical 'as the ripple of the streamlet'[20] – but alongside the guileless-ness is apparent again the reversal of the priorities of a colonial enterprise: the marginal and the unsophisticated are recast as the original and unadulterated. This pattern of sentimental centrality is also apparent, though less naively expressed, in his later consideration of the nation as opposed to the Empire, in 'The Sovereign People' (1916). As might be expected, he uses the analogy of kinship, the household, to describe the nation: 'The nation is a natural division, as natural as the family, and as inevitable ... A nation is knit together by natural ties, ties mystic and spiritual, and ties human and kindly; an empire is at best held together by ties of mutual interest, and at worst by brute force. *The nation is the family in large*; an empire is a commercial corporation in large.'[21]

As the centre moves from the macrocosm – the colonial state, the Empire – to the microcosm, the family, so it moves also from the geographical heart of the Empire to the periphery. All Pearse's stories are set in or around the Connemara Gaeltacht (Irish-speaking area), on the west coast of Ireland, the margin of the Empire. They were written in Irish, and never translated by Pearse himself, though he translated much of his own work. *The Singer* (a play published after his death) is written in English, but an English designed to give the impression of literal translation from Irish, sometimes with the 'colour' and archaism of literal translation exaggerated for literary effect. The result, as in Synge's better-known plays, is to foreground the language as a distinctly 'unEnglish' English, something apparent from the very first lines, when the response to Maire's 'Are you cold?' is 'The feet of me are cold'.[22] This effect is further intensified by the literal use of Irish nickname forms ('Diarmaid of the Bridge'), and the occasional interpolation of Irish words: 'My name was in many a song that he made. Often when I was at the *fosaidheacht* [herding] he would come up into the green *mám* [hillside] to me, with a little song that he had made. It was happy for us in the green *mám* at that time.'[23] Where the text is in the Irish language, as in the short stories, the process of defamiliarisation is complete: the world is named and defined through the medium of a language which has no officially-recognised part in the colonised state of Ireland.

A story like 'An Bhean Chaointe', written in Irish, is a good example of the anti-colonial refusal to accept that the English language is *the* natural instrument for representing the world, or that London, the 'home' point of the British Empire, is the location by which others are defined. This story has a 'Chinese box' narrative structure, where a young boy is told by his father of how the Keening Woman lost her son to prison when he was sentenced to life imprisonment for the murder of a landlord. The mother, desperate to free him, goes to London to ask the Queen for help, is sent back home and told to await a letter. The letter never arrives, and after many days waiting she is told that her son has died in prison.

The son, Cóilín, was framed, it is implied, by a government agent: 'an fear dubh'. 'An fear dubh' translates as 'the dark man', but 'an Fear Dubh' is the devil, and references to evil and the diabolic proliferate around him, as do references to betrayal: the representative of empire is also representative of evil. Against this, the boy-narrator's mother's continual invocation of the rosary, and refusal to allow a curse, places her and her family on the side of good, thus inverting the more common colonising narrative where the centre is a force for good and civilisation while the colonised state is a locus of evil, savagery and darkness.

The central passage of the story – framed both by the boy's narrative and, within that, by his father's – is the Keening Woman's account of her journey to London in quest of her son's freedom. This is quoted here in full:

> I went to Galway. I saw the prison Governor. He told me he could do nothing, that it was the Dublin people who could let him out of prison, if such could be done. I went on to Dublin. Lord! hadn't I walked many stony hard roads, and hadn't I seen many fine big towns before I got to Dublin. 'Isn't Ireland a big country' I'd say to myself every evening when I'd be told that I'd so-many miles to walk before I'd see Dublin. But, thanks be to God and the Glorious Virgin, I walked in the Dublin road at last, on a cold, rainy evening. I found lodgings. The following morning I inquired for the Castle. I was told of it. I went there. I wouldn't be let in at first, but I kept at them until I was allowed to talk to a man. He sent me to another man, one higher-up than himself. He sent me to another man. I said to all of them that I wished to see the Queen's Lord Lieutenant. At last I saw him. I told him my story. He said to me that there was nothing he could do. I bestowed my curse on Dublin Castle and went out the door. I had one pound in my pocket. I boarded a ship and next morning I was in Liverpool, England. I walked England's long roads

from Liverpool to London. When I got to London I asked directions for the Queen's Castle. I was given them. I went there. I was not allowed in. I went there every single day in the hope that I'd see the Queen coming out. After a week I saw her coming out. There were soldiers and great people around her. I went over to the Queen before she got into the coach. I had a paper a Dublin man wrote for me in my hand. An official got hold of me. The Queen spoke to him and he let me go. I spoke to the Queen. She did not understand me. I held out my paper to her. She gave the paper to the official and he read it. He wrote some words on the paper and he gave it back to me. The Queen spoke to another woman who was with her. The woman took out a crown and gave it to me. I gave her back the crown and said it wasn't money I wanted, but my son. They laughed. In my opinion, they didn't understand me. I showed them the paper again. The official put his finger on the words he had written. I curtseyed to the Queen and went away. A man read the words the official had written for me. It was that I'd be written to about Cóilín without delay. I took the road home hoping that maybe there would be a letter waiting for me.[24]

There is apparent in this passage a structural opposition of the Irish against the English worlds which distinguishes Pearse's work from that of other Irish Revival writers, such as Synge and Lady Gregory. 'An Bhean Chaointe' echoes in many respects the plot of Lady Gregory's play *The Gaol Gate* (first produced in 1906); this play also features a young man imprisoned, his mother travelling (in this case to the prison gate) to inquire for him, only to be told in the end that he is dead. In *The Gaol Gate*, however, the son is imprisoned in Galway, and the gatekeeper who talks to the mother is as Irish as she is. Injustice is thus located within Ireland; there is no straightforward opposition of a victimised people to an oppressive colonial state. Similarly, the supposed victim of the son's 'crime' is never specified as English or as an agent of the state, so his death is not linked to any anti-colonial impulse, unlike that of Pearse's hated landlord.[25] In Pearse's story, the Keening Woman, the colonised mother, is immediately contrasted to the Queen, the mother of the Empire. Family love and commitment is located in Ireland, but allied to weakness; absolute power and maternal incapacity in England – the Queen cannot or will not look after her subjects. At the same time, the narration of events makes the Keening Woman, not the Queen, the centre of attention: the royal waiting-woman, the officials, the nameless civil servants are all displayed by the naive gaze of the Irishwoman. It is left to the reader, who knows the function of the woman by the Queen and the official with the paper, to supply even their roles.

On the level of language, the centrality of the Irish experience is again apparent. In a reversal of the technique familiar through the work of writers like Kipling, the story is told in Irish, the language of the colonised, with certain untranslatable concepts – untranslatable because they are supposed not to exist in the Irish world-view – presented in transliteration, as if spelled out by an Irish-speaker. In this story, centred on the margin, it is the English words that need explanation: 'Liverpool' becomes 'Libherpúl Shasana', the adjective 'Sasana' added to make it clear that the place is in England. The prison Governor becomes 'Gobharnóir an phriosúin', and the Lord Lieutenant is 'Lord Leifteanant na Banríona'. Elsewhere in the story, we find the word 'traein' for 'train', and the policeman from Dublin Castle rendered as the 'pílear [peeler, as in English slang] ó Chaisleán Bhaile Átha Cliath'.[26] The story was published under an Irish pen name, 'Colm Ó Conaire'.[27] In all these respects, the story appears to be a successful attempt at reversing the effect of colonialism, presenting the experience of the colonised as the standard and reconfiguring the symbols and the language of the coloniser to fit this new/old world-view. It is an easy, and attractive, transition to move from this point to the Easter Rising, when Dublin becomes a centre set up in opposition to the Imperial centre of London, initial failure becomes ultimate success when the sacrifice of the rebels is recognised, and Patrick Pearse becomes an icon of a new Ireland.

There is an alternative view. It is possible to see in the story a pathetic, misjudged and already-too-late effort to reclaim and re-create a dead language and culture. The Irish transliterations may not be the equivalent of Kipling's appropriation of Indian words and phrases, but evidence of the poverty of a language no longer spoken.[28] Pearse's linguistic and literary abilities, acquired by a diligent study of Irish starting when he was twelve years old, were viewed with suspicion by many of his contemporaries, keen to point out the fact that the Irish language was not his mother tongue. His first story, 'Poll an Phíobaire' (1906), published under the pseudonym Colm Ó Conaire in *An Claideamh Soluis*, was acutely skewered by the etymologist Fr Dineen as 'a certain Irish storyette' reminiscent of 'the margarine of the slums' rather than the 'genuine mountain butter' of Connemara – an image which indicates the issues of authenticity, urban versus rural, and 'real' versus 'fake' Irishism current at the time. Pearse certainly aimed to produce 'Connemara butter', but was never accepted as the real thing.[29] Even more to the point, the reading I have constructed of this story, above, is possible only if it is read through the medium of Irish in the first place: the story in English loses the defamiliarising force of the original, as English terms are applied to Irish concepts with no hint of strangeness. In Ireland itself, Pearse's work is more likely to be read in English than in Irish, except perhaps by schoolchildren reading set texts. Elsewhere, there is no question of its status: whilst researching this article in the British Library in London, I noted the pristine state of the volume of Pearse's Irish-language writings, in contrast to the well-used aspect of the Campbell translations of the same material.

Whatever the status of the language, in the story the English terms, transliterated, are also evidence of a contemporary need to come to terms with a mixed tradition, one incorporating the Queen's Lord Lieutenant as well as the boy-narrator staying away from school to ferry home reeds for the thatched roof. In this, the story parallels the attempts made by all the writers of the Irish Revival, but Pearse in particular, to reclaim an old Irish literary tradition – one which inevitably turns out to be as inauthentic, in places, as 'an pílear' from Dublin Castle. This is partly to do with the impossibility of recovering a past uninfluenced by the present, but it is also a product of the unashamedly political aims of Pearse's literary archaeology. The figure of the Singer has a resonance outside the eponymous play, as an analogue for Pearse and a demonstration of the nature of the work he had undertaken.

The parallels between *The Singer* and Pearse's life are obvious, and the play (written in autumn 1915) appears prophetic in the same way as the poem 'Renunciation', both looking forward to the speaker's sacrificial death.[30] It would seem an extreme reading to ascribe even to the self-centred and visionary Pearse an identification of himself with both Christ and Singer. Raymond Porter, however, remarks that '*The Singer* does give expression to the ideas and ideals that informed Pearse's life', and describes the play as 'a literary analogue for the events of Easter Week, 1916'.[31] Another analogue is to be found in the title of the play. Pearse's attempts to evoke revolutionary fervour from his unresponsive compatriots were not confined to his political speeches: in the collection of 'Songs from the Irish Rebels', he offered a selection of Irish poems together with English translations (some of them his own); these were written between 1573 and 1652, and their titles include 'On the Fall of the Gael', 'Róisín Dubh' and 'On the Cromwellian Clearances'.[32] One of these, titled 'Ceathramhna Gríosuighthe' or 'Some Rebel Quatrains', was annotated by him as follows: 'Just as in early Irish manuscripts, Irish love of nature or of nature's God so frequently bursts out in fugitive quatrains of great beauty, so in the seventeenth and eighteenth century manuscripts we find Irish hate of the English (a scarcely less holy passion) expressing itself suddenly and splendidly in many a stray stanza jotted down on a margin or embedded in a long and worthless poem.'[33] Here, of course, Pearse is busily creating the tradition he seeks to explicate, presumably with the intention of eliciting rebellious sentiments from his readers as the Singer did from his audience. Of the three Quatrains, the first marks the passing of earlier empires – 'Alexander, Caesar, and all that shared their sway' now 'scattered like dust' – and looks forward to a similar fate for the British Empire: 'And even the English, perchance their hour will come!' The second combines most aptly the two sentiments – love of nature and hatred of the English – that Pearse ascribed to the Irish. The poem reads:

> Good is thy fruit, O tree!
> The luck of thy fruit on every bough;
> Would that the trees of Innisfail
> Were full of thy fruit every day!

This hymn to nature takes on a different slant when read alongside the explanatory note: the 'fruit' is in fact 'an Englishman hanging upon a tree', the speaker 'a dispossessed Gael'. It is doubtful whether Pearse would have acknowledged, or cared about, a distinction between literary archaeology and propaganda. Certainly, when he came to write the pamphlet 'Ghosts' in 1915, he included these 'Rebel Quatrains' and used them to argue that 'The "secret songs" of the dispossessed Irish are the most fiercely Separatist utterances in any literature.' Rather disingenuously, he continued: 'I do not defend this blood-thirstiness any more than I apologise for it. I simply point it out as the note of a literature' – a 'note' offered by his own careful selection which is used to prove his later assertion that the 'student of Irish affairs who does not know Irish literature is ignorant of the awful intensity of the Irish desire for Separation as he is ignorant of one of the chief forces which make Separation inevitable'.[34] Reading his attempts to create the character of a nation, and prove that it had always existed, we see the focus move from the literary critic to the creative writer – from tradition to the individual talent – from Pearse's work to Pearse himself.

In this, we see the congruity between Pearse's work and literary modernism. Taking apart the previous order, and replacing it in new patterns, modernism refixed its new order on the person of the poet. In Pearse's case, the elements of interculturality and the evidence of two traditions are to be found in his life as well as in his work. His English father and Irish mother represented both sides of the cultural context in which he found himself, a duality which may be traced throughout his career, from the two languages in which he wrote to the different forms of his name, where Patrick Pearse is sometimes Pádraic Mac Piarais, and occasionally Colm Ó Conaire as well.[35] Campaigning for educational reform, he looked to Belgium for his model; trying to revolutionise literature in the Irish language, he recommended a study of both the old Irish narratives and the modern European short story.[36] While his early critical writings yearned for the 'new blood' of a pure, Gaelic alternative to the English tradition, this eclecticism epitomises, for Declan Kiberd, the refusal to see tradition as necessarily opposed to innovation.[37] The manifesto 'The Forces of the Irish Republic', issued from the GPO in Dublin during the Easter Rising, was written 'on post office notepaper bearing the Royal Arms of England on the top left corner'[38] – a hybrid document appropriate to the dual character of the man who produced it. Pearse himself, however, liked simplicity,[39] and in the Easter Rising and its aftermath he found the unproblematic role of self-sacrificing revolutionary, something that had been anticipated in his later writings.

Daniel O'Neil's account of anti-colonialism makes the point that the ideals of sacrifice and revolutionary activity appeal in particular to those who might be accused, or might accuse themselves, of being less than authentic as opponents of the colonial state: 'The anticolonial effort demands and gets sacrifice from individuals who have enjoyed a privileged position under the Imperial order. Sons of the traditional native elite who have enjoyed economic and educational opportunities often work out their identity problems through revolutionary flirtations.' This idea is particularly applicable to the leaders of the Easter Rising, many of them distinct from other Irish people in personal background as well as in social class. O'Neil points out that, of the seven signatories to the Proclamation of the Irish Republic,

> Five of the seven – Pearse, Connolly, Clarke, Plunkett, and MacDonagh – had been associated with journals and had written books, while three – Pearse, Plunkett, and MacDonagh – were poets. Pearse's father was an English convert to Catholicism; Connolly was born in Edinburgh and had served in the British army; Tom Clarke was born in England, having a Protestant soldier father; MacDonagh's mother was a Unitarian convert to Catholicism; and Ceannt's father was a Royal Irish Constabulary RIC sergeant [*sic*].

For them, in O'Neil's view, their commitment to military action was, among other things, a means of solving their 'individual identity problems'.[40] Subsequent versions of history showed the validity of this view: with their execution, the dual nature of the revolutionaries was collapsed into singularity; their status as uneasy members of two cultures changed as they cast off and were cast out from any English identity and became central to the myth of Irish history. There they have remained, fixed in the moment of the Easter Rising in a story essentially unchanged since Yeats first celebrated their transformation in 'Easter 1916'.

Some of the names have become, with time, less resonant. But in the case of Patrick Pearse, the most visible of the revolutionaries, the narrative is still being retold. In a talk entitled 'Pádraig Mac Piarais Fealsamh' ('The Philosopher Patrick Pearse') given to the 1992 May Symposium held in Áras Bhord na Gaeilge in Dublin, Pearse was described in the most uncritical terms as one who had a true appreciation of Irish culture, and was its successful advocate and defender.[41] The complexity and complicity of his work is lost in assessments such as this, when it is asserted that Pearse's creative writing 'was wrung from [his] understanding of the dramatic qualities of the Irish people'. In his writings, 'there is apparent under the veneer of sentimentality and romanticism an account of matters relevant to the way of life in Pearse's time, and to the basic human conflict with the self, the environment and one another.' Such a description, in its insistence on Pearse's realism, denies what appears to me the saving grace of his work: its fantastic expression of the emotional and imaginative concerns of anti-colonialism and anti-realism. Most tellingly, the symposium paper ends with an indictment of the modern Irish state, listing its inadequacies with reference to such features as unemployment, poverty, emigration, the threat of closer involvement with Europe and its accompanying spectres of legalised abortion and loss of neutrality. It concludes: 'If it is worth trying to bring about a new era one could do no better than engage in a careful re-reading of the works of the philosopher Pádraig Mac Piarais.'[42]

The appeal of such an assessment lies in its simplicity: Pearse as synonymous with and emblematic of a 'real' Irishness is an attractive figure in the same way as Pearse the anti-colonial revolutionary. In his own time, occupying as he did a position in the multiplicity of cultures and traditions which characterised both the modernist mode of thought and early-twentieth-century Ireland, this clarity of definition escaped him. Within and outside Ireland, the modernist impulse was to focus on the artist as a figure centred and decentred – collecting images from a variety of traditions to shore up the ruins of Western culture, but also incorporating them into a new version of that Western thought, where individuality and insistent personality have defined Modernism in literature. Pearse, also, was a central and a marginal figure: English and Irish, a subject of the Empire and first 'President' of the Irish Republic, for a few days, until his execution. At this point, he ceased to occupy this multiplicity of roles, mainly because he had ceased to be in any sense an actor, and become a symbol – to be invoked by others as he had in his political speeches evoked the names of Emmet, Lalor and O'Donovan Rossa. His character, like the familiar portrait, presented one aspect of him to the audience: the Irish revolutionary.

Events and history have dealt perversely with Patrick Pearse. The obsessive speaker for Irish cultural tradition, who saw his role and that of Irish literature as opposing a venal modernity, appears, from a vantage point eighty years on, to have worked consistently in the mode that became known as modernism. The Irish literature he so passionately advocated came to be, after his death, but was written for the most part in English, not in Irish. He claimed, at his court martial, to have 'kept faith with the past, and handed on a tradition to the future'. In the post-colonial context of twentieth-century

Ireland, past and future appear to be not unitary elements, but aspects of the moment; and Pearse's concept of an autonomous nation and literature lasted only the brief time of his own life.

## Notes

1 Daniel J. O'Neil, *Three Perennial Themes of Anti-Colonialism: The Irish Case* (Denver, University of Denver, Monograph series in World Affairs, vol. 14, 1976). O'Neil describes the three 'fundamental themes' of anti-colonialism as 'self-reliance, self-sacrifice, and exploitation' (p. 3). He regards 'the act of revolt against overwhelming odds where there is virtual certitude of failure and martyrdom' as the 'ultimate form' of the self-sacrifice theme (p. 17); and chooses Pearse (pp. 63–80) to exemplify this theme in the Irish case.

2 *Collected Works of Pádraic H. Pearse: Songs of the Irish Rebels and Specimens from an Irish Anthology, Some Aspects of Irish Literature: Three Lectures on Gaelic Topics* (Dublin, Cork and Belfast, Phoenix, n.d.), pp. 233–4, 234.

3 Terence Brown, 'Ireland, modernism and the 1930s', in Patricia Coughlan and Alex Davis (eds), *Modernism and Ireland: The Poetry of the 1930s* (Cork, Cork University Press, 1995), pp. 36, 37.

4 See Padraic H. Pearse, *Collected Works: Political Writings and Speeches* (Dublin and London, Maunsel & Roberts, 1922).

5 Declan Kiberd, *Inventing Ireland* (London, Jonathan Cape, 1995), pp. 383, 384.

6 'An Bhean Chaointe' – 'The Keening Woman' – was first published as 'Bríd na Gaoithe' in *An Claidheamh Soluis*, reprinted in Séamus Ó Buachalla, *Na Scríbhinní Liteartha le Pádraig Mac Piarais* (Dublin and Cork, Mercier, 1979), pp. 77–93. (This volume is cited in future as *Scríbhinní.*) It is available in Joseph Campbell's translation in Padraic H. Pearse, *Collected Works: Plays, Stories, Poems* (Dublin and London, Maunsel, 1917). 'The Singer' is written in English, dedicated to Pearse's mother and first published after his death in *Collected Works: Plays, Stories, Poems*. Ó Buachalla's 'Scríbhinní Liteartha an Phiarsaigh – Treoir do na Foinsí' (*Scríbhinní*, pp. 9–19) may be consulted for further bibliographical information; the English version of this essay is 'The Literary Works of Pearse – A Bibliographical Guide', in *The Literary Writings of Patrick Pearse* (Dublin and Cork, Mercier, 1979), pp. 7–21.

7 Elizabeth Butler Cullingford, '"Thinking of Her … As … Ireland": Yeats, Pearse and Heaney', *Textual Practice*, 4:1 (Spring 1990) 2.

8 *Collected Works: Plays, Stories, Poems*, pp. 21, 44, 31.

9 O'Neil, *Three Perennial Themes*, p. 3.

10 *An Rí* became *The King* in the English version; the short stories 'Íosagán' and 'An Gadaí' ('The Thief') are available in translations by Joseph

Campbell (*Collected Works: Plays, Stories, Poems*), while the translation of the play *Íosagán* in the same volume is by Pearse.

11 Sean Farrell Moran, 'Patrick Pearse and the European revolt against reason', *Journal of the History of Ideas*, 50:4 (1989) 629.

12 Ruth Dudley Edwards, *Patrick Pearse: The Triumph of Failure* (1977. London, Faber & Faber, 1979), p. 127.

13 Timothy d'Arch Smith, *Love in Earnest: Some Notes on the Lives and Writings of English 'Uranian' Poets from 1889 to 1930* (London, Routledge & Kegan Paul, 1970).

14 *Collected Works of Padraic H. Pearse: Songs of the Irish Rebels and Specimens from an Irish Anthology* (Dublin and London, Maunsel, 1918), p. 224.

15 *Collected Works: Plays, Stories, Poems*, p. 10.

16 *Ibid.*, pp. 334–6.

17 *An Macaomh* (May 1913), quoted in Edwards, *Patrick Pearse: The Triumph of Failure*, p. 143.

18 D'Arch Smith, *Love in Earnest*, pp. 174–5.

19 *Collected Works: Songs, Three Lectures*, pp. 197–216.

20 *Ibid.*, pp. 214, 215.

21 'The Sovereign People', in *Collected Works: Political Writings and Speeches*, p. 343.

22 *Collected Works: Plays, Stories, Poems*, p. 3.

23 *Ibid.*, p. 8; italics in the original.

24 *Scríbhinní*, pp. 90–1. This passage is my translation; for the story in Campbell's translation see *Collected Works: Plays, Stories, Poems*.

25 Lady Gregory, *The Gaol Gate*, in Ann Saddlemeyer (ed.), *The Tragedies and Tragi-comedies of Lady Gregory* (Gerrards Cross, Colin Smythe, 1970), pp. 5–10.

26 *Collected Works: Plays, Stories, Poems*, pp. 90, 79, 93.

27 See Ó Buachalla, *Scríbhinní*, p. 10.

28 This is not to suggest that Kipling simply appropriated Indian words. As Janet Montefiore points out elsewhere in this collection, Kipling's use of language is a complex issue.

29 Dineen, review of 'Poll an Phíobaire' in the *Irish People*, quoted in Edwards, *Patrick Pearse: The Triumph of Failure*, p. 95.

30 See *Scríbhinní*, p. 29 for the Irish original, 'Fornocht a Chonaic Tú'.

31 Raymond J. Porter, *P. H. Pearse* (New York, Twayne, 1973), p. 111. See also Edwards, *Patrick Pearse: The Triumph of Failure*, pp. 262–3.

32 Pearse worked intermittently on these collections for a long time; they were published after his death in *Collected Works: Songs* and *Collected Works: Songs, Three Lectures*. See Edwards, *Patrick Pearse: The Triumph of Failure*, pp. 203–4.

33 *Collected Works: Songs*, pp. 34–5.

34 *Collected Works: Political Writings and Speeches*, pp. 235, 236, 237.

35 This, together with the various spellings of his name in Irish, represents

a problem of consistency. I have followed Pearse's directions to a correspondent: 'I would prefer if you referred to me as "P. H. Pearse" if you are writing in English than as "Pádraig Mac Piarais"; I deem it very strange to have an Irish form of a foreign name in an article ... written in English.' Séamus Ó Buachalla (ed.), *The Letters of P. H. Pearse* (Gerrards Cross, Colin Smythe, 1980), p. 242. In quoting or referring to other texts and critical material, I have retained their spelling; I have followed the same principle with regard to the presence or absence of diacritical marks in Irish words and names.

36  Pearse's writings on literature span many years, were frequently written in Irish, and are most often to be found in *An Claidheamh Soluis* and *An Barr Buadh*. See Raymond J. Porter, 'Language and literature in Revival Ireland: the views of P. H. Pearse', in Raymond J. Porter and James D. Brophy (eds), *Modern Irish Literature: Essays in Honor of William York Tindall* (New York, Iona College Press and Twayne, 1972), pp. 195–214.

37  Kiberd, *Inventing Ireland*, p. 134.

38  Xavier Carty, *In Bloody Protest: The Tragedy of Patrick Pearse* (Dublin, Able Press, 1978), p. 25.

39  'He always liked fundamentally simple answers...', Edwards, *Patrick Pearse: The Triumph of Failure*, p. 38.

40  O'Neil, *Three Perennial Themes*, pp. 14, 76.

41  Ciarán Ó Coigligh, 'Pádraig Mac Piarais Fealsamh', in Ciarán Ó Coigligh and Diarmuid Ó Gráinne (eds), *An Fhealsúnacht agus an tSíceolaíocht* (Dublin, Coiscéim, 1992), pp. 53–63.

42  Ó Coigligh, 'Pádraig Mac Piarais', pp. 57, 59, 62. The quoted passages, in Irish, read as follows: 'Ba chumadóireacht iad a fáisceadh as tuiscint an Phiarsaigh ar cháilíocht dhrámata an phobail Ghaelaigh' (p. 57). 'Faightear faoi screamh thanaí an mhaoithneachais agus an rómánsachais cur síos ar nithe a bhaineas le coinníollacha na beatha le linn an Phiarsaigh agus le buanchoimhlintí an duine leis féin, lena thimpeallacht agus lena chomhdhuine' (p. 59). 'Más fiú féachaint le ré nua a thabhairt chun cinn níorbh fhearr rud a dhéanfadh duine ná athléamh cúramach ar chuid scríbhinní Phádraig Mhic Phiarais fealsamh' (p. 62). The English versions in the text are my translations.

# 8

## 'Hanging over the bloody paper': newspapers and imperialism in *Ulysses*

### John Nash

Joyce's thorough documentation of Edwardian Dublin, then known to some as the Second City of the Empire, is well known, and his moulding of factual sources into the multi-layered narrative of *Ulysses* provides a particular illustration of the techniques adopted within literary modernism to explore the vicissitudes of imperial relations. Joyce's peculiar vantage point – writing from a Europe devastated by war and beset by competing nationalisms – allows him to construct an image of British imperialism in Ireland from the different perspectives of a displaced Irish-Hungarian Jew and the inhabitants of middle-class Catholic Dublin. The range of narrative voices in *Ulysses* makes it the most daring as well as the most thorough work of modernist fiction, and this cacophony of voices is paramount to any reading of the novel. The exciting variety of styles in *Ulysses* comprises not only literary parodies but also includes the emergence and convergence of other narrative media, such as newspapers and advertising, as well as different spoken uses of English, from the scrupulousness of Stephen Dedalus to the slang and invective of the Irish citizen. This vast repertoire of narrative voices is not necessarily harmonious, indeed one of the principal problems facing the reader of *Ulysses* lies in identifying the relative authority of the different narrative positions. When, as in 'Cyclops' – a chapter riddled with parody – the subject matter is explicitly political and imperial, then the necessity, but also the difficulty, of identifying the authority of the speaking voice is all the more keenly felt.

This chapter examines Joyce's use of the London *Times* as source material for the composition of 'Cyclops'. It deals in turn with the issue of authority, with the history of *The Times*, and with Joyce's use of that newspaper in 'Cyclops'. The production and consumption of news plays a significant role in *Ulysses*, as Bloom traverses the shared offices of the *Freeman's Journal* and *Evening Telegraph* in 'Aeolus' (a chapter narrated in headlined fragments) and, most notably, as the papers provoke discussion in 'Cyclops'. The imperial history of *The Times* makes it a fitting medium for Joyce's moulding of historical documentation into the intimate nuances of everyday Edwardian Dublin, as news stories from London circulate through Joyce's writing and are recontextualised in Dublin. In fact, newspapers (imperialist or not) can be read as a peculiar form of modernist text, juxtaposing different stories and styles, weaving reportage with opinion, conscious of the economics of their own composition and dissemination. The anti-imperial ends of Joyce's parodic method show how closely modernism and imperialism are entwined.

## Parody and politics

'Cyclops' consists of some thirty-three parodies interspersed with the anonymous narrator's account of events. Those thirty-three episodes parody general literary or newspaper styles (rather than a specific target), mainly Irish nineteenth-century mythology and sentimental nationalism. These parodies, usually of a grotesque and comic exaggeration, provide an indirect commentary on the narrator's story, often rephrasing the very events he has narrated. The chapter takes place in Barney Kiernan's pub on Little Britain Street, where a diverse group, led by the Irish citizen, swap gossip and discuss hanging, imperial brutality, and the nature of violence.[1] The narrative form of 'Cyclops' directly questions the reliability of narration and the suitability of style to content, issues which are also raised by the organisation of the book as a whole.

The explicit problem raised by this practice – more so than elsewhere in the book – is one of interpretive determination, a problem exacerbated by the overtly political character of 'Cyclops'. It can clearly be seen in this pronouncement by Philip Herring:

> It is clear that Joyce abhorred the 'Citizen's' political stance and recognized the nobility of the liberal humanitarian sentiments of Bloom. But

all sociopolitical positions are indiscriminately undercut by Joyce's use of exaggeration ('gigantism' is the technique here) and irony … it is impossible in this episode to take anything seriously.[2]

The political problem posed by Joyce's parody would appear to be reconciling (i) an apparent 'clear … political stance' with (ii) the effect that 'all sociopolitical positions are indiscriminately undercut'. What is far from clear is how Herring maintains both these positions. Two recent studies of Joyce's politics illustrate the difficulty of this problem.

Vincent J. Cheng's *Joyce, Race and Empire* argues that all the characters of 'Cyclops' are enmeshed within the hegemony of British imperial rule: all are (to some extent) racist, imperialist and ethnocentric. The citizen, for instance, is seen by Cheng as a ranting xenophobe whose nationalism only mirrors the violence of the British imperial rulers. It is only Bloom, Cheng argues, who can see beyond the constraining dualism of us/them in his 'unceasing' sceptical questioning of stereotypes, which is 'in stark contrast to … his xenophobic fellow Irishmen'. Bloom, it appears, is both constructed by the imperial hegemony and able to overcome it. Cheng's conclusion is oddly conservative: Bloom emerges as the humanist ('multiple vision') hero and the citizen as the nationalist ('monologic vision') villain, perhaps as bad as the British he mimics. By stating that the persuasive hegemony of imperialism is universally applicable in *Ulysses* and in the world ('a pervasive and unavoidable discursive mind-set absorbed (and recycled) by the members of the culture'), Cheng's argument is analogous to the political problem posed by parody.[3] For if such hegemony exists, how can one identify a voice that escapes it? The answer is that such a saturating hegemony cannot exist: applied to turn-of-the-century Ireland it is a disabling straitjacket that prohibits identification of the range of positions that have contributed to British imperialisms and Irish nationalisms. But if imperial rule does not saturate a culture, its effects are of course still felt, and, likewise, it is not only Bloom who questions it; so too do others.

The most recent original and provocative attempt to disentangle the problem of authority in 'Cyclops' has come from Emer Nolan's *James Joyce and Nationalism*, which provides an account of the chapter's politics that goes some way towards redressing the myth once popular in Joyce studies that Joyce and Bloom are like-minded internationalists and that Joyce had no truck whatsoever with Irish nationalism.

She argues that although *Ulysses* as a whole veers towards 'the realm of postmodern pastiche', the 'Cyclops' chapter exposes and mocks 'the endlessly levelling discourse of the modern'. It does so by placing greater authority and credibility in the voices of the citizen and 'the citizens generally' than in the parodies.[4] Nolan argues that there is a sort of common language shared by the citizen, his cronies and Joyce, citing an early essay by Joyce, part of which the citizen repeats. Nolan argues that it is here, in what Raymond Williams calls a 'community of speech', that the politics of the 'Cyclops' chapter can most accurately be read.[5] However, such a grouping implies a forced homogeneity, for Joyce's coincidence of language with the citizen is brief; Joyce could not be held to the xenophobic, anti-Semitic or violent exhortations of the citizen. In addition, the supposed community (that Nolan disingenuously calls 'the citizens generally') in Barney Kiernan's is not so united: the nameless narrator and others betray a variety of differences from the citizen, and from each other, ranging from distrust to religious and class difference.

Nolan's argument proceeds from a distinction between, on the one hand, 'levelling discourse' (the idea that all voices merge equally) and, on the other hand, the 'community of speech'. It is the mundane speech of the characters 'which is continuously used to mock and combat the endlessly levelling discourse of the modern which appears unable to render the reality of conflict'. That 'reality of conflict', Nolan argues, is 'occluded by the levelling modern discourse of the newspapers', yet it is these newspapers which provoke the group's anti-imperial discussion, including much of the citizen's speech. Although they are superficially similar, Nolan distinguishes the voice of the citizen from the modern discourse of the newspapers: 'His [the citizen's] discourse ... resembles the modernism of sheer textual production exemplified by the interpolations; but it also resists the consequent assimilation of all styles into empty and abstract equivalence which is suggested by such a practice of parody.' In Nolan's reading, then, it is the citizen who emerges as the voice of authority through which the chapter's otherwise bewildering parody can be read. Thus 'the text cannot parody the citizen ... for his language of violence is its language as well'.[6]

Although both Nolan and Cheng share the same ostensible target of imperialism in their quite different readings of 'Cyclops', each attempts to rescue from the cacophony a voice that will prove reliable and authoritative. Each operates a false dichotomy: between either 'levelling discourse' and 'community of speech' (associated by Nolan with the citizen); or between 'pervasive and unavoidable' hegemony and 'sympathetic imagination' (associated by Cheng with Bloom). These are false dichotomies because in each of them the first term is merely a convenient myth from which to distinguish a supposedly authoritative language (be it the citizen's invective or Bloom's caution). As can be seen from tracing Joyce's use of source material, parody does not imply either a loss of target or a 'levelling' of language, rather, the entire chapter of 'Cyclops' is parodic. The citizen draws on an anti-imperial newspaper parody (discussed in the final section of this chapter) while also being himself a mocking parody of xenophobia; and, as Cheng unwittingly remarks, Bloom is 'almost a walking parody of ecumenical tolerance and cultural pluralism', and the parodic narrator mimics Bloom's uncritical sentimentality in the brilliant aside, 'Love loves to love love'.[7] In this episode, no single character or language-use holds a voice of authority that fully escapes the parody. It is therefore not possible to identify a constant voice of authority; instead, reading 'Cyclops' demands reading with both eyes the ebb and flow of the text.

By following Joyce's deployment of *The Times* in composing 'Cyclops', it is possible to trace a conjunction between this modernist form of parody and the imperial relations that crisscross the text. Joyce had no access to an Irish newspaper for June 1904 prior to 1919, when he began writing the 'Cyclops' chapter in Zurich. Joyce instead read *The Times* with meticulous care. Although Joyce had limited use of the *Irish Independent* from 1919 onwards, it was *The Times*, bastion of the British Empire and printed in London, that most influenced the composition of 'Cyclops'. Despite the 'genetic' identification of sources for the chapter, the significance of the use to which Joyce puts them has not been explored. In particular, the imperial context of the London *Times* is an important thread in the construction of Joyce's modernist narrative. It is remarkably underacknowledged that, for Joyce, no newspaper could ever be only historical reportage, and one such as *The Times*, with its anti-Parnellite and pro-imperial stance, provided not just material to be written *from*, but also to be written *against*. Joyce's use of *The Times*, then, is likely to be of some importance, both for that paper's history in Irish and imperial affairs, and for its contemporary news coverage. Indeed, where Joyce explicitly borrows from this source, his concern is fundamentally with imperialism.

## The Times and imperialism

It is a curiosity of *Ulysses* that for a story of a Dublin newspaper ad-canvasser, there is remarkably little reference to Irish newspapers. In 'Cyclops', the citizen and others in Barney Kiernan's bar directly refer to a variety of newspapers and journals: the *Freeman's Journal*; the *Irish Independent*; *Stubb's Weekly Gazette*, *National Police Gazette*, *The Times*; and the *United Irishman*. The 'Cyclops' chapter – by no coincidence the most explicitly political chapter – 'is the most newspaper-like episode in *Ulysses*'.[8] Whenever newspapers are referred to in this chapter it is always in a national, racial or imperial context. Reading from the announcements of 'the births and deaths in the *Irish for all Ireland Independent* and I'll thank you and the marriages' (on 16 June 1904) the citizen finds several English names and addresses. 'How's that for a national press, eh?' (pp. 384–5) he asks. The extent to which *The Irish Daily Independent* – 'founded by Parnell to be the workingman's friend' (p. 384) as the citizen says – did not hold an inclusive national audience is suggested not only by the amount of English addresses but also by Cockburn's simultaneous appearance in the death column of *The Times* (alongside one 'Lazarus').[9] The citizen's complaint implies that Ireland lacks a truly national newspaper, protesting at British influence. His reading of names from the announcements (although he omits all the Irish and a few more English names) implies that the *Independent* caters for an English readership. Indeed, an Irish national press was lacking: the *Independent*, founded by Parnell in 1891, was floundering; the *Irish Times* was heavily biased towards Dublin and the middle classes; the *Freeman's Journal* was distrusted by nationalists; and Griffith's *United Irishman* was unable to cover current events to the same extent as daily newspapers and was dominated by a sentimental nationalism. It would not be until the following year, 1905, that William Martin Murphy's revamped *Irish Independent* became the 'first halfpenny popular paper in Ireland'.[10]

A measure of Joyce's reliance on *The Times* can be shown from the very few news stories discussed in 'Aeolus'. In his notebook, Joyce records notes on two stories he read in *The Times*: first, the assassination in Finland of the (tyrannically imperial) Russian Governor-General Bobrikoff (17 June); and second, the prosecution of hawkers for trying to sell mementoes of the Phoenix Park murders to tourists (9 June).[11] In 'Aeolus' a parallel is drawn between the two events. J. J. O' Molloy asks, 'Or was it you shot the lord lieutenant of Finland between you? … General Bobrikoff'. (U. 171). Almost immediately, discussion turns to the infamous Phoenix Park murders. But J. J.'s use of the title 'lord lieutenant' – when Bobrikoff was actually 'Governor General' – draws a parallel with British imperial rule in Ireland and recalls to the minds of those present the Invincibles' assassination of Chief Secretary Cavendish and Under-Secretary Burke in 1882. The parallel suggested by the juxtaposition of these news stories has further interest because of their shared source: the anti-Home Rule and pro-imperial London *Times*. However, something of the complexity and duplicity of imperial relations may be gauged from the leader column from which Joyce took his information, for *The Times* was indignant at the atrocious treatment by Russian imperialism in general, and Bobrikoff in particular, of the Finnish people, 'against whose traditions, whose language, and whose laws he has conspired'.[12]

There is a peculiar history to *The Times* with which Joyce was no doubt familiar, for the involvement of *The Times* in Irish and other Imperial policy, and specifically its unfounded charges against Parnell, led directly to its great slump in sales at the end of the nineteenth century – a slump which prompted a series of modernising measures in the early twentieth century, including the huge promotion of a subscription savings offer in the summer of 1904 in the copies that Joyce used in writing *Ulysses*.

The 'Irish question' was of paramount importance to the owners and editors of *The Times* in the nineteenth century, in whose minds it was indissolubly linked with the future of the Empire: if the Union could not hold at home, how could the Empire function across the world? The stance of the paper was always imperialist: to maintain stability, which would, when appropriate, allow further expansion. In the late nineteenth century the paper carried a hegemonic function as 'one of the principal agencies by which the nation was taught to "think imperially"'.[13] However, it was in the notorious case of Richard Pigott's forged letters – purporting to be by Parnell – that *The Times* most clearly expressed its imperial attitude to Ireland (and in so doing was castigated by the Royal Commission).[14]

*The Times* had been a leading and vociferous campaigner against Home Rule, singling out Parnell and condemning him as complicit in violent agitation. It ran a series, 'Parnellism and Crime', leading up to its intended exposé of the leader with the publication of Pigott's letters. It printed a facsimile of Pigott's 'letter no. 2' in April 1887. Parnell refused to instigate legal action until he eventually sought libel damages in an Edinburgh court the following year, launching the inquiry that proved them to be forgeries by Pigott. Had *The Times* any local knowledge of Dublin, it would have been immediately suspicious of the letters it bought for £1,780: Pigott was a notoriously shady not to say disreputable character, as any journalist working in Dublin in the late 1880s could have said. Towards the end of the trial, Pigott shot himself with a revolver known and engraved as 'The British Bull Dog'. All along, and against all evidence, the owner of the British 'Thunderer', John Walter, steadfastly refused to believe letter no. 2 a forgery. Although Parnell was vindicated by the inquiry, its findings nonetheless enabled *The Times* to continue to imply the political complicity of Parnell in others' violence, calling the Irish Home Rule Party 'in no true sense a political party ... but a parasitic growth'.[15]

At the close of the trial, the newspaper's defence was, in the words of their lawyer, that it had acted not for a class, 'but on behalf of the whole Irish nation, on behalf of those who have most need of protection', arguing that the paper had long supported Irish causes, singling out their coverage of the Famine of the 1840s as 'taking a leading part in the relief of distress'.[16] This was at best a disingenuous argument and at worst a shameful lie, for *The Times* was ruthless in its pursual of English economic interest and it only softened somewhat after the worst of the Famine was over.[17] In 'Cyclops' the only explicit mention of *The Times* concerns this point: the citizen condemns *The Times* for having 'rubbed its hands' (p. 428) at the depopulation caused by death and emigration during the Famine, and there should be no doubt on which side Joyce's sympathy lay.

The treatment of Parnell by Britain's most powerful and conservative newspaper, a proclaimed supporter of imperialism, brought into question the stance taken by *The Times* towards Ireland throughout the nineteenth century. Moreover, the case brought by Parnell was to have a lasting impact on the history of that newspaper. Its editor at the time, Buckle, considered it his duty to report the daily proceedings of the trial and when this was placed in addition to the parliamentary debates, which *The Times* reported extensively, little room was left for other news or features. Understandably, the paper's competitors were improving their circulation at the expense of *The Times*. It is important that the failed case against Parnell was a very public and costly method of admitting fallibility. As the official history of *The Times* concedes, because of the Parnell case, 'The mid-Victorian legend of the inerrancy of *The Times* was exploded'.[18] In addition to this loss of prestige came near-crippling legal costs of over £200,000, forcing *The Times* to contemplate measures of popularisation. Thus in terms of both public esteem and its own character, the imperial attitude of the newspaper towards Ireland and especially towards Parnell led to irrevocable changes to *The Times*.

Joyce's lifelong admiration for the 'uncrowned king' is well-known. That Parnell's reputation was so strongly challenged and ultimately, and ironically, strengthened, by one of the prime agents of British imperial hegemony was known to Joyce, who referred to the Pigott letters – and their medium, *The Times* – in his essay 'The Shade of Parnell', written in Italian in Trieste in 1912.[19] As part of the fallout from the Parnell case, *The Times* set about a process of modernisation, which included a major promotional campaign run by the newspaper in the summer of 1904. Announced at the end of May, there were frequent, obtrusive reminders of this campaign through June, and Joyce could not fail to have been aware (reading in 1919) of the changes that had been in process at *The Times*. A new system of newspaper distribution was to be inaugurated in July 1904, whereby subscribers could save money and delivery was made direct to the doorstep ('the theory of direct dealing between a newspaper and its readers'). Meanwhile, *The Times* continued to attempt to maintain its traditional standards, and was happy to cite the testimony of the *Daily Mail* that its pages were 'a matter of national and even of Imperial importance', indeed 'part of British civilization' and belonging 'to the historic greatness of the race'.[20] This scheme addresses a significant juncture in the relationship between modernity and empire. *The Times* was of course subject to the pressures of modernisation, as it lost financial muscle along with readers: the subscription scheme is in effect a belated effort to shore up its readers against the ruins of modernity.[21] Yet it is apparent that, although the prestige of *The Times* was dented by its ill-advised participation in the conspiracy against Parnell and Home Rule, it remained very much the organ of the British establishment, and its standing as a pro-imperial newspaper steadfastly remained.

In terms of policy, there was some slight change, as following the settlement of the Boer War a new 'New Imperialism' was announced: an empire in which all people were to be, as a leading article put it, 'citizens in no unreal sense'.[22] American independence was denounced as a sham, and the debacle of the Boer War suddenly made imperial 'co-operation' seem attractive. In truth, the British economy was feeling the squeeze from its rivals and sought trade alliances among the nations of the Empire. Having supported German imperialism in the 1880s, the early years of the new century saw *The Times* wince at German naval strength. *The Times* took to supporting the new Empire Day, which was first launched in 1904, on the basis that for imperial unity to stand any chance of success the public 'at home' would first have to be educated. It even, guardedly, talked about recognising 'the just and powerful claims of national feeling among each people in the Empire'.[23] The importance of the Empire remained its priority, of course, although there is some strategic reconsideration of imperial relations. Reading this shortly after the First World War, Joyce must have been able to view the recent history of British imperialism in a manner quite removed from its reportage.

The 1900s proved a significant decade for *The Times* as it sought to continue its 'great Imperial mission' while enduring the inevitable fallout (in terms of imperial policy and modernisation) from its disastrous handling of the Pigott/Parnell letters and of Irish politics in general.[24] It is against this history that Joyce's use of *The Times* as source material should be approached. To read *Ulysses* in the context of its use of newspapers is to engage the critical conjunction between imperialism, modernity and modernism. Joyce's reliance upon the imperialist London *Times* to forge fiction from history is in itself an apt comment on the situation. Yet the documents that Joyce relied upon could never be just documents; in the case of *The Times*, the pro-imperialist history of that institution and its stance against Parnell make Joyce's use of that source itself an act of political significance within an ongoing imperial relationship.

## Reading the news in 'Cyclops'

It is possible to follow Joyce's concern with the relationship between imperialism and newspaper reporting in a relatively early text, written twelve years prior to 'Cyclops', but which nonetheless can be read as a telling introduction to the chapter. Joyce's Triestine newspaper article from 1907, 'Ireland at the Bar', describes the Maamtrasna murders of 1882 and the subsequent trial of Myles Joyce, who was executed for a murder he did not commit. Myles Joyce spoke little or no English.

> The court had to resort to the services of an interpreter. The questioning, conducted through the interpreter was at times comic, and at times tragic. On one side was the excessively ceremonious interpreter, on the other the patriarch of a miserable tribe unused to civilised customs, who seemed stupefied by all the judicial ceremony. The magistrate said:
> 'Ask the accused if he saw the lady that night.' The question was referred to him in Irish, and the old man broke out into an involved explanation, gesticulating, appealing to the others accused and to heaven. Then he quieted down, worn out by his effort, and the interpreter turned to the magistrate and said:
> 'He says no, "your worship".'

Joyce's point is that Myles Joyce is 'a symbol of the Irish nation … unable to appeal to the modern conscience of England and other countries'.[25] Crucial to this partition are the newspapers that act as the medium of understanding between cultures. 'The English journalists act as interpreters between Ireland and the English electorate', who are, Joyce says, distrustful of the Nationalist MPs in the House of Commons. In a striking image, Joyce says that 'Skimming over the dispatches from London (which, though they lack pungency, have something of the laconic quality of the interpreter mentioned above), the public conceives of the Irish as *highwaymen* with distorted faces.'[26] English newspapers, in other words, are largely responsible for producing an image of Ireland as a country of outlaws.[27]

In 'Cyclops', this concern with representations of Ireland is addressed through a parodic conflation of fact and fiction. The early part of the chapter is dominated by two images of barbarous execution: the lengthy parody of Emmet's beheading; and the letters apparently from a British hangman, Rumbold, whose entreaty, '*i have a special nack of putting the noose once in he can't get out*' (p. 392) may recall the struggle of Myles Joyce, whose executioner 'was obliged to press the body with his foot' (as *The Times* reported), or 'kicked at the miserable man's head' (as Joyce put it).[28] This introduction to the chapter establishes a recurrent concern with barbarity, especially in an imperial context, and its reportage.

Later in the chapter, Joyce presents the citizen, at a different kind of bar, engaging issues of imperialism in the newspapers, and Joyce's striking image from 'Ireland at the Bar' is alluded to in the conversation between the citizen and others as the citizen performs an ironic mimicry of a highwayman. The first time he appears he is seen by the narrator 'up in the corner having a great confab with himself' surrounded by 'his load of papers' (pp. 380–81). It is significant that from the first the citizen is associated with newspapers and their role in public image-formation. Moreover, the citizen enacts a highwayman's question-and-answer formula when greeting the newcomers:

> – Stand and deliver, says he.
>   – That's all right, citizen, says Joe. Friends here.
>   – Pass, friends, says he. (p. 381)

This allusion to highwaymen is given in the language of the outlaw: 'Stand and deliver' was the supposed demand of the highway robber, the most notorious of whom was Dick Turpin (an Englishman), who is listed in the following parodic interlude as an Irish hero of antiquity (p. 383). The citizen's mini-charade, portraying himself in the position of the highwayman, recalls Joyce's newspaper article. The image of the citizen, then, is depicted to coincide with what Joyce had described as the popular English perception of the Irish, created by English newspapers. The citizen's absorption in newspapers and their effects comes across in his very next line: 'says he: – What's your opinion of the times?' (p. 381). These men are almost desperate for news. The narrator asks Joe, 'anything strange or new?' (p. 378), and on their entrance to the pub, having passed the highwayman's code, they are immediately confronted with a further request for news. The citizen may just as well be asking, 'what's your opinion of *The Times*?', for this chapter is not only built from newspapers but is also centred around newspapers for its characters' discussion.

*The Times* of June 1904 sets the agenda for a debate centred on imperialism in that Joyce takes several significant stories and grafts them into the fabric of 1904 Dublin. Two of these – disciplinary flogging in the British Navy, and Roger Casement's report on the Congo Free State – concern barbaric brutality; while the other, the parody on the Alake of Abeokuta, concerns the propagation of imperial relations by non-violent means. Joyce's post-war and post-1916 perspective would of course provide a knowledge of Casement's death, and of the subsequent history of Abeokuta: trajectories into the future that colour the discourse of 1904. A reading of Joyce's adaptation of these news stories, and the form of their inclusion in *Ulysses*, provides an illustration of the complex interaction between modernism and imperialism.

The citizen and Joe have already objected to that 'barbarous bloody barbarian', the hangman Rumbold, and Bloom has apparently offered a *defence* of capital punishment 'with the why and the wherefore' mentioning 'deterrent effect and so forth and so on' (p. 393), when the discussion turns to corporal punishment.[29] Ned suggests that the British Navy 'keeps our foes at bay' (p. 426), indicating that the colonisation of Ireland should be seen within the context of the Union. The citizen informs him of 'the revelations that's going on in the papers about flogging on the training ships … A fellow writes that calls himself *Disgusted One*' (p. 426). A Nationalist MP, John MacNeil, had brought up this issue in the House of Commons, and letters to *The Times*, including one from George Bernard Shaw (which was noted by Joyce), debated the question. Once more, attention here is directed at the victims of brutality, only this time they are seamen (often boys) in the Royal Navy. The citizen recognises the barbarity of flogging 'the bloody backside off the poor lad' but it is Bloom who answers 'isn't discipline the same everywhere? I mean wouldn't it be the same here if you put force against force?' (p. 427). Against the citizen's objections, Bloom seemingly endorses both capital and corporal punishment; but the citizen cannot help rising to the bait of Bloom's question and launches into an invective against imperial oppression (which includes his attack on *The Times*).

The citizen relates naval flogging to the 'great empire they boast about of drudges and whipped serfs'. However, sympathy for the victims of violence is tempered, for 'the tragedy of it is … they believe it. The unfortunate yahoos believe it' (p. 427). This analysis leaves no room for those other, British, citizens who have little reason to believe in the greatness of empire, and the irony is that this debate is lifted from the letters pages of *The Times*, a primary organ of imperial hegemony in the production of news, and that such letters – even to *The Times* – can form a voice of dissent. As the narrator remarks in a different context, 'Someone that has nothing better to do ought to write a letter *pro bono publico* to the papers' (p. 403).

The second example of Joyce reworking *The Times* into the group's discussion concerns direct imperialist violent oppression by 'those Belgians in the Congo Free State' (pp. 434–5), referring to the reports filed by Roger Casement.[30] On this occasion it is J. J. O'Molloy who implicitly condemns 'raping the women and girls and flogging the natives on the belly to squeeze all the red rubber they can out of them' (p. 435). Casement's reports (filed the previous February) were then under discussion in Parliament, and Joyce noted that 'Sir Char Dilke' repeated Casement's charges of 'grave maladministration and ill-treatment'.[31] This is a rather euphemistic way of describing the slavery and even cannibalism inflicted by Congolese forces (under Belgian administration) which Dilke highlighted from Casement's report. Again, their information comes from *The Times*, which on the same day devoted its Leader to condemning the atrocities. In this case, both the Irishmen and the British imperial newspaper are united in their disgust, and united also in their hypocrisy: once more, the citizen's revulsion at barbarity is tempered by his racist dismissal of Bloom as 'that whiteyed kaffir' (p. 435); and *The Times* could hardly claim innocence of racism and imperial bloodshed.

These two examples display the group in 'Cyclops', including both Bloom and the citizen, extending humane sympathy to the victims of imperial violence, although Bloom has already appeared to condone legitimated violence; seemingly, however, it is only Bloom who does not succumb to racism. In fact, a condemnation of imperialism is perhaps the only thing that everyone in Barney Kiernan's can agree upon. Significantly, these two examples show facets of imperial violence that are sometimes overlooked: violence within the imperial force, and that committed by the colonised in service of the coloniser. It is also possible to see some overlap between the pro-imperial *Times* and Joyce's characters in their condemnation of imperial violence. Importantly, though, the moral authority of the text is not located solely within any one character.

Joyce's most elaborate reshaping of a news story from *The Times* shows the workings of imperialism in a non-violent context, and it is here that one can see most fully his dissection of imperial

**Plate 2**    Thomas Jones Barker, *Queen Victoria Presenting
a Bible in the Audience Chamber at Windsor, c.* 1861

journalism. The citizen reads aloud 'that skit in the *United Irishman*
today about that Zulu chief that's visiting England' (p. 433). However, there was no such piece in the *United Irishman,* of that day or
any other; rather, the parody was composed with the aid of reports
in *The Times.* Its peculiar mixture of fact and fiction displays Joyce's
careful moulding of the imperialist *Times* into its direct opposite, a
humorous and anti-imperial newspaper. The citizen takes out 'one of
his paraphernalia papers' (p. 433) and reads:

> A delegation of the chief cotton magnates of Manchester was presented
> yesterday to His Majesty the Alaki of Abeakuta by Gold Stick in Waiting,
> Lord Walkup on Eggs, to tender to His Majesty the heartfelt thanks of
> British traders for the facilities afforded them in his dominions. The
> delegation partook of luncheon at the conclusion of which the dusky
> potentate, in the course of a happy speech, freely translated by the British
> chaplain, the reverend Ananias Praisegod Barebones, tendered his best
> thanks to Massa Walkup and emphasised the cordial relations existing
> between Abeakuta and the British Empire, stating that he treasured as

one of his dearest possessions an illuminated bible, the volume of the word of God and the secret of England's greatness, graciously presented to him by the white chief woman, the great squaw Victoria ... after which he visited the chief factory of Cottonopolis and signed his mark in the visitor's book, subsequently executing an old Abeakutic wardance ... amid hilarious applause from the girl hands. (pp. 433–4)

There are four significant areas in which this parody shows the influence of reports in *The Times*: trade, translation, the Bible, ceremony and etiquette. Each of these details symbolizes a key factor in imperial rule: economic exploitation, linguistic dominance, religious persecution, the extension of imperial values.

*The Times* carried several reports of the Alake's visit to England in May–June 1904. The first report that Joyce read observes that, 'The Alake spoke at some length, and at the close his secretary informed the committee of the tenor of his remarks.' The Alake's father had written to Queen Victoria, who sent him 'two bound volumes of the Word of God, saying that that book was the secret of England's greatness'.[32] There was indeed a painting of Victoria presenting a bible to a suitably grateful African recipient painted in the 1860s (Plate 2). The British monarchy puffed itself up in this manner, and the representation of such acts was designed to dignify the Victorian and Edwardian notions of imperial relations, making such gestures as the presentation of a bible into an 'allegory of Empire'.[33] The Alake shares the title 'His Majesty' with Edward VII to whom he was presented at the beginning of his visit. *The Times*'s report of that occasion observes that the Alake 'has had his most ardent desire fulfilled' by the meeting. On entering the Throne Room, the Alake 'advancing to the Royal presence between two rows of Gentlemen-at-Arms, made three separate pauses, kneeling at each'. The 'Gold Stick in Waiting' was the official emblem of the Captain and Gold Stick of His Majesty's Body Guard of the Honourable Corps of Gentlemen-at-Arms, but this detail Joyce took not from a report on the Alake but from the small print of the court circular. Joyce's parodic name, 'Gold Stick in Waiting, Lord Walkup on Eggs' mocks the venerable attitude of *The Times* towards the pomposity of royal etiquette. By conflating elements from different reports Joyce is able to show a conjunction between imperial and monarchic values, and the role in creation and support of those values played by *The Times*.[34] Such pomp marks the heyday of the Empire in a manner that may well betray a certain amount of anxiety, and that would have appeared quite ridiculous to Joyce in 1919.

According to *The Times*'s report, King Edward told the Alake that he was 'greatly pleased at the prosperity' of Abeokuta. After the appointment, the Alake added that 'it was only after his gracious reception by the King that he realized the greatness of the British Empire'. Speaking of his visit to Britain, he added, 'its results will be most valuable to my country'.[35] One such result was the stimulation of cotton trade links: the Alake hoped to establish 5,000 acres of cotton farms in Abeokuta. As the citizen notes, 'that's how it's worked ... Trade follows the flag' (p. 434). The skit also seems to carry some criticism of the Alake himself as a lackey of British imperialism. However, not everyone in Abeokuta was as pleased as the Alake with this result of his visit. It was his concurrent attempt to 'modernize' Egbaland that led him, as Gailey has argued, 'further than any other West African ruler in attempting to learn about and emulate British forms ... upon his return to Abeokuta the Alake was more pro-British than ever'.[36]

Joyce goes to some lengths to establish a provenance for his parody, citing it in the *United Irishman* and attributing it to an anonymous scribe: 'Is that by Griffith? ... No, says the citizen. It's not signed Shanganagh. It's only initialed: P' (p. 434). However, Arthur Griffith, who founded *Sinn Fein* in 1904, did write parodies of a not dissimilar kind in the *United Irishman*, and used both 'Shanganagh' and 'P' as pseudonyms, although Joyce seems to be trying to establish that the parody is not Griffith's, perhaps because of Griffith's support for black slavery. Joyce is careful to distance both the citizen and Griffith from authorship of the parody, presumably not wanting their racism to detract from its target, which is clearly the economy and pomposity of British imperialism. It is interesting that, as Gifford suggests, 'P' may indicate 'the spirit of Parnell'.[37] The actual source of the skit, and Joyce's reference to its fictional origin, points to the critical difficulty in reading this chapter: who speaks, and what authority can be attributed to the different voices of the text? Joyce purposely sets his politically argumentative chapter in the context of newspaper parodies in order to address these questions.

Central to the problem of attributing authority to a voice is Joyce's habitual method of composition, for his writing is so often composed from elements of other texts, whether factual or fictional.

Joyce did not need to go far to find news material to furnish a chapter on imperialism, as a reading of *The Times* from June 1904 shows, but crucially the attacks on imperialism made in 'Cyclops' are also attacks on the source of Joyce's news. For Joyce is fundamentally concerned not just with news stories but with their manner of narration. It is by reading the form that the problem of voice may be answered, for parody necessarily implies a targeted text. The ultra-dry London *Times* with its reluctant struggle to confront contemporary journalism as a facet of modernity, while clinging desperately to British imperialism and Unionism, provides a fitting target for the aim of Joyce's parodic pen. Its reverence and moderation is exploded by the exaggerated invective of the citizen and others, and especially by the Alake skit, which is not the citizen's but is instead attributed to the shade of 'P' in the *United Irishman*. This skit is a fictional parody of a real text within a larger fiction; it is composed neither by the narrator nor by the citizen who reads it. It is a parody apart, quite distinct from the thirty-three parodies that intersperse the chapter's action, and as such it is the only parody that is shared by the characters. Whereas those thirty-three parodies are mostly aimed at a general style, the 'skit' is derived from a particular text: coverage of the Alake's visit by *The Times*. It is therefore possible to establish, through reading the form of Joyce's work, at least one specific and determinate target for his parody – that is, the organ which attempted to suppress Parnell, which was one of the principal media of British imperialism, and which acted as interpreter of Ireland at the bar of British public opinion: *The Times*.

## Conclusion

*Ulysses* exemplifies the interaction of literary modernism with the discursive formations of modernity – the competing plurality of voices in the city, in newsprint, in communities – which vie for textual space. Meanwhile, the attempt to establish a form of imperial hegemony is reliant upon those same discursive formations. A newspaper such as *The Times* illustrates the uneasy adaptation of a conservative institution to the demands of its modern form: the pro-imperial attempt to 'educate' an audience in a form which inherently carries the possibility of dissent. In Joyce's hands, literary modernism adopts and exposes this condition through its focus on the social construction of narrative. It is the very political character of the form of modern discourse that provides the impetus to modernism's engagement with imperialism, for it is here that the contestation of history is dramatised. Neither imperial hegemony nor the modernist variety of styles can ever be 'levelled', then, because plurality does not imply equality. Instead, both modernist parody and imperial hegemony highlight the dilemma of textual authority and thus present their readers with the problem of disentangling textual threads and locating authority. Joyce's adaptation of pro-imperial reports from *The Times* – one of the primary tools of imperialist 'education' for a British public – into the mouth of the Irish citizen provides a fitting example of the cross-cultural mutation undergone by 'the news' as Joyce's parody challenges the veracity of legitimated modes of representation. The use to which Joyce puts *The Times* is not just a criticism of that particular institution but also an indication of the extent to which modernism and imperialism collide; a collision which renders necessary, as much as it renders difficult, a reading of their historical matrix.

## Notes

1 The citizen (not Citizen, as some critics have it) is modelled on the nationalist Citizen Cusack, as he called himself, who co-founded the GAA in 1884.
2 Philip Herring, *Joyce's Ulysses Notesheets in the British Museum* (Charlottesville, University Press of Virginia, 1972), p. 14.
3 Vincent J. Cheng, *Joyce, Race and Empire* (Cambridge, Cambridge University Press, 1995), pp. 177, 184, 170.
4 Emer Nolan, *James Joyce and Nationalism* (London, Routledge, 1995), pp. 118, 107, 118.
5 Raymond Williams, *The Country and the City* (1973; London, Hogarth Press, 1993), p. 245.
6 Nolan, *James Joyce and Nationalism*, pp. 106–7.
7 Cheng, *Joyce, Race and Empire*, p. 182. James Joyce, *Ulysses* (1922; London, Penguin, 1992), p. 433. Subsequent references to *Ulysses* are to this edition, and are included in the text.
8 Danis Rose and John O' Hanlon, *James Joyce: The Lost Notebook* (Edinburgh, Split Pea Press, 1989), p. xxiv.
9 *The Times*, 16 June 1904, p. 1. The name Cockburn appeared elsewhere (p. 10) in that day's *Times*. Listings under 'TODAY'S ARRANGEMENTS' included the 'League of Empire: Annual general meeting' and

'Compatriot's Club: Sir J. Cockburn on "The Evolution of Empire"'. The *Irish Daily Independent* was planned by Parnell, but he died (5 October 1891) before it began publication (18 December 1891).

10 Hugh Oram, *The Newspaper Book: A History of Newspapers in Ireland, 1649–1983* (Dublin, MO Books, 1983), p. 100. The *Independent* became known for its innovations, and so successful was it that for many years rumours persisted in Dublin that it was owned by Harmsworth (who owned the *Daily Mail*) and was staffed by English journalists! The modernisation processes undertaken by the *Irish Independent* helped to create a nation-wide audience which, despite the rumours, in turn became more able to sustain a discourse of nationhood. It was the first national paper to have a significant effect on the locals, mainly because it arrived in the morning. By 1908 sales were eight times that of the old *Irish Daily Independent* (see Oram, *The Newspaper Book*, pp. 100–9). The new owner, Murphy, became notorious for his merciless treatment of workers in the great lock-out of 1913.

11 Joyce's notes from *The Times* for June 1904 are in notebook MS VI.D.7, edited as *The Lost Notebook*.

12 *The Times*, 17 June 1904, p. 9.

13 *History of the Times, Volume 3: The Twentieth Century Test 1884–1912* (London, The Times, 1947), p. 15.

14 That Joyce knew this case well is beyond question, for he was a loyal Parnellite and frequently averted to the case of Pigott's give-away misspelling ('hesitency') in *Finnegans Wake* (e.g. 35.20).

15 *The Times*, 14 February 1890, p. 9. For a 'full summary' of the Commission's report, see pp. 5–8.

16 *History of the Times*, vol. 3, p. 72.

17 As Gifford notes, *The Times* changed tack, as it put it, 'with great reluctance', on 8 February 1849. Don Gifford, *Ulysses Annotated* (Berkeley, University of California Press, 1988), p. 358.

18 *History of the Times*, vol. 3, p. 75.

19 It was not so much *The Times* as the Irish press that met with Joyce's censure, for their 'envy' which contributed to Parnell's betrayal. See 'The Shade of Parnell', in *The Critical Writings of James Joyce*, ed. Ellsworth Mason and Richard Ellmann (Ithaca, Cornell University Press, 1989), p. 227.

20 *The Times*, 28 May 1904, p. 6.

21 New technologies also effected this modernisation, such as the wireless telegraphy which was pioneered (and advertised) during the paper's coverage of the Russo-Japanese war, alongside its promotional campaign.

22 *The Times*, 2 June 1902, p. 11; cited in *History of the Times, Volume 4, part 1: The 150th Anniversary and Beyond* (London, The Times, 1952), p. 3.

23 *The Times*, 25 March 1909, p. 11; cited in *History of the Times*, vol. 4, p. 17.

24 *The Times*, 2 June 1902, p. 11.

25 He may also have had in mind Parnell, who had a 'speech defect', 'lacked eloquence' and was betrayed by the Irish press. See 'The Shade of Parnell', p. 225.

26 James Joyce, 'Ireland at the Bar', *Critical Writings*, pp. 197–8 (my emphasis). First published as 'L'Irlanda alla Sbarra', in *Il Piccolo della Sera*, Trieste, 16 September 1907.

27 On English newspaper representations of the Irish in the nineteenth century, see L. P. Curtis, Jr., *Anglo-Saxons and Celts: A Study of Anti-Irish Prejudice in Victorian England* (Bridgeport, Conn., University of Bridgeport, 1968), and *Apes and Angels: The Irishman in Victorian Caricature* (Washington, D.C. Smithsonian Institution Press, 1971).

28 *The Times*, 16 December 1882, p. 6; James Joyce, 'Ireland at the Bar', p. 198. Robert Emmet was beheaded, but only after having been hanged first. Sir Horace Rumbold was the British Minister to Bern in 1918–19; Rumbold ignored Joyce's request for assistance in a litigation with Henry Carr, a British consular official in Zurich, an event which aroused his hostility to British bureaucracy (see Herring, *Joyce's Ulysses Notesheets*, p. 15).

29 The unnamed narrator gives a jaundiced description of what Bloom says, including a reference to the 'deterrent effect', which would suggest that Bloom defends capital punishment. The popular view, repeated by Cheng, that Bloom opposes the death penalty, seems to require a more forced reading of the passage. It is important to note, though, that the narrator – as on many occasions – uses reported rather than direct speech.

30 Casement (who was born a stone's throw from the Martello tower at which the opening of *Ulysses* is set) was then serving as British Consul in Boma. The British Government published his report in February, 1904, by which time Casement was already working for Irish nationalist groups. In April 1916 he was arrested smuggling arms from Germany into Ireland to assist the Easter Rising. He was tried and executed (by hanging) in London, August 1916.

31 Rose and O'Hanlon (eds), *The Lost Notebook*, p. 17. Joyce copied this from *The Times*, 10 June 1904, p. 6.

32 *The Times*, 15 June 1904, p. 10.

33 *Victorian Portraits* (London, National Portrait Gallery, 1996), p. 17.

34 During the reigns of Victoria and Edward VII monarchic traditions were revived or invented to shore up the monarchy against its waning political power. See David Cannadine, 'The context, performance and meaning of ritual: the British monarchy and the "Invention of Tradition", c. 1820–1977', in Eric Hobsbawm and Terence Ranger (eds), *The Invention of Tradition* (Cambridge, Cambridge University Press, 1983), especially pp. 120–38.

35 *The Times*, 31 May 1904, p. 6.

36 H. A. Gailey, *Lugard and Abeokuta* (London, Frank Cass, 1982), pp. 40–1. There was considerable opposition to the 'modernisation' that Britain and the Alake attempted to introduce. Abeokuta was in Egbaland, just north of Lagos. It had been independent since 1893. In January 1904 some judicial powers were passed to British control and in 1914 Egbaland was brought under British sovereignty. For a fictional reworking of this colonial encounter, see the three novels in Chinua Achebe, *The African Trilogy* (London, Picador, 1988).

37 Gifford, *Ulysses Annotated*, p. 366.

# 9

# Lawrence in doubt:
# a theory of the 'other' and its collapse

## Howard J. Booth

Racist and pro-colonial statements can be found in D. H. Lawrence's writing, but he can also be seen questioning negative Western attitudes to the racial 'other'. Between 1917 and 1925 Lawrence developed the view that engaging with other cultures and peoples could renew the self and Europe. He pursued this theory in extended travels and in writing, oscillating between insisting on his position and, increasingly, doubting it. At the end of the period Lawrence withdrew back to Europe and concentrated on thinking about the future in terms of the past of the continent. He worked through a series of positions while other major modernist writers – for example, Pound and Eliot – drifted, after a radical start to their careers as poets, into the racist and reactionary positions which they then held for many years. Lawrence continually pushed lines of thought as far as they would go and, when they began to fail to satisfy, moved on. He did not, of course, explore all the positions in relation to imperialism and race available, and he never found a stance that transcended the prevailing colonialist discourses. Assumptions remained in place about the right of the Western subject to develop fantasy constructions of the 'other'. Yet Lawrence took on, stretched and probed many of the possibilities of thought around colonialism available. As with other issues, such as sexuality and gender, few writers take us further into the shaping of thought and language in the modernist period than Lawrence, however uncomfortable it might sometimes be to follow his thinking.

## Corruption and the Edwardians

In his early career Lawrence responded to what he believed was wrong with the preceding generation of novelists. He agreed with them in seeing the problem with Britain and Europe in terms of decay and decline, but they were, he believed, too pessimistic, offering no way forward. The comments Lawrence made on older writers also sought to establish a space for himself as an author, and they were to provide the ground on which his attitudes to race and empire were built. In a 1912 letter from Italy, Lawrence condemned Arnold Bennett's *Anna of the Five Towns* (1902), a study of how capitalism, with non-conformist religion colluding, distorts and ruins relationships and lives: 'I hate England and its hopelessness. I hate Bennett's resignation. Tragedy ought really to be a great kick at misery. But *Anna of the Five Towns* seems like an acceptance – so does all the modern stuff since Flaubert. I hate it. I want to wash again quick, wash off England, the oldness and grubbiness and despair.'[1] Condemning the novel for its failure to tackle the problems of modern life, Lawrence is concerned, characteristically, with what the novel says rather than with issues of form. The diagnosis of the West, and most of all England, notes its decay, which writers with their self-consciousness have added to rather than opposed. As Lawrence said in another letter from the same year, about Conrad (he was probably referring to *Under Western Eyes* and *'Twixt Land and Sea*), 'But why this giving in before you start, that pervades all Conrad and such folks – the Writers among the Ruins.'[2] The final phrase of this quotation echoes the title of Browning's 'Love among the Ruins' (1855).[3] In the Browning poem, new love begins on the grassed-over ruins of a capital city of the past. Lawrence clearly felt that later authors had taken to picking over the remains rather than welcoming, as Browning had advocated, love and the future.

Lawrence's interest in dissolution and decay can be linked to degeneration theory, which is explored in relation to both modernist writing and colonial discourse by Rod Edmond in his chapter in this volume. There are differences between Lawrence's interest in dissolution and theories of degeneration, though, as Lawrence did not work within the scientific discourse of the degenerating race or individual. Instead he applied to lives, and indeed whole cultures, metaphors drawn from plant life – the decline, decay and eventual reuse by new life of rotted vegetable matter. This theme of dissolution in Lawrence was for long obscured by F. R. Leavis's contention that Lawrence's writing shows everywhere a 'life reverence'. G. Wilson Knight and especially Colin Clarke, in his excellent *River of Dissolution* (1969), recognised the importance of decay to Lawrence, particularly in *Women in Love* (1920).[4] Dissolution and good and bad forms of new growth had in fact been an issue for Lawrence from the start of his career. His first novel *The White Peacock* (1911) is full of references to what David Bradshaw has called 'freakish tumescence', an abnormal and excessive growth on the edge of corruption.[5]

The issues raised by dissolution can be seen in the deeply ambivalent close of *Sons and Lovers* (1913). It may appear to be simply positive as Paul, despite his mother's death, walks towards 'the faintly humming, glowing town, quickly'. But the light is artificial, and is described in terms of 'gold phosphorescence'.[6] Lawrence often used the word 'phosphorescent' when writing about decay, and as a keen biologist he used it in the contemporary scientific sense of the emission of light by matter in the process of decay – he did not take it right back to the element phosphor and the emission of light in the dark.[7] For Lawrence, decay exercises an attraction and is ambivalent: as he put it at the end of his life, in *Apocalypse*, there are two forms: 'the consciousness of man always tends to revert to the original levels; though there are two modes of reversion: by degeneration and decadence; and by deliberate return in order to get back to the roots again, for a new start.'[8] The problem here is of knowing the path one is taking: is it a decay towards death, or a process of breaking down that will lead to rebirth and renewal?

The text by an author of the preceding generation that Lawrence responded to most strongly was H. G. Wells's *Tono-Bungay*.[9] The novel draws heavily on discourses of degeneration, and it sees the corrosion of values and attitudes at work in business, mass media and love. Lawrence read the novel as it was being serialised in Ford Madox Hueffer's *English Review*, and he told his friend Blanche Jennings, in a letter shortly after the last of the four parts had appeared, that it was 'the best novel Wells has written – it is the best I have read for – oh how long. But it makes me so sad ... He is a terrible pessimist'. Wells, like the other 'Writers among the Ruins', is too resigned. In a move that characterises Lawrence's reading throughout his career, he believes that he perceives something in Wells's material that the novelist himself has not seen, namely what is remarkable – indeed showing a level of 'mysticism'[10] – in Edward Pondevero's collapse and despair, which is the great power unleashed by decay.

*Tono-Bungay* has been described by David Lodge as being in a line of 'Condition-of-England' novels.[11] Given the links it makes between degeneration and colonialism it is better described as a 'Condition-of-Empire' novel. (It is worth remembering that the *English Review* often contained articles on political, social *and* imperial issues, as well as new creative writing.[12]) The 'African' section of the text comes near its close, when the businesses of Edward Pondevero, built around the quack tonic 'Tono-Bungay', are approaching collapse. To stave off disaster his nephew George, the novel's narrator, undertakes to go to an island off West Africa to steal deposits of a potentially valuable radioactive element, 'quap', which will help Edward Pondevero to 'show value' at his 'London and African' company shareholder meeting.[13] In describing the trip Wells links the evils of a new capitalist order (with its emphasis on advertising and consumerism), the unstable elements that science was identifying, and colonialism. These are connected to modern ways of loving and conducting relationships, shown in the visit that George makes before he leaves Britain to see Beatrice, his first and main love. Here and elsewhere in the novel, the way that people are affected by modern capitalism, the changing values and social structures, are reflected in the geography of the modern world. Wells constructs a moral map of Edwardian Britain and its empire, by examining the imprint society leaves on the land. This approach was to be taken up by Lawrence in *The Rainbow* (1915), especially in the text's opening pages.

There are a number of links between the 'How I Stole the Quap from Mordet Island' chapter of *Tono-Bungay* and *Heart of Darkness*, though Conradian values are presented only to be undermined. Beatrice is George's 'Intended', but her affections are anything but total and constant. The things in life that, for Conrad, make it bearable are shown to be insufficient for George Pondevero on the trip. The Eastern European captain and the mate, with his character 'of impenetrable reserve',[14] are so irritating that George wishes to be violent. For him 'There's no romance about the sea in a small sailing ship as I saw it'.[15] The account of the trip down the coast of Africa again parallels Conrad's text: the emphasis is on the 'decay' George senses in the jungle, 'a world of steamy fogs and a hot smell of vegetable decay ... All my former ways ceased, all my old vistas became memories'.[16] Another foundational text is echoed and recast, this time *Robinson Crusoe*, when George comes across an African man and shoots him in the back. This modern reworking of the encounter between Crusoe and Man Friday is described by George as 'the most unmeaning and purposeless murder imaginable'.[17]

George's closing thoughts at the end of the novel on his new found work on destroyers (Wells clearly relishing the name) depicts the evening lights on the Thames estuary going out in a degenerating imperial land: 'Out to the open we go, to windy freedom and track-less ways. Light after light goes down. England and the Kingdom, Britain and the Empire, the old prides and the old devotions, glide abeam, astern, sink down upon the horizon, pass – pass. The river passes – London passes, England passes ...'[18] Lawrence was right to see the novel as a gloomy and pessimistic text – for all that Wells is often depicted as the spokesman for a facile belief in the positive effects of scientific progress.[19] As he sought for an answer, Lawrence would not see sexual relationships and the interracial encounter as being at the end of a chain of cause and effect, inevitably damaged by capitalism. Rather, he believed it was possible to focus on them in their own right as offering the possibility for renewal *beyond* the terms of debate defined by economic change.

## Lawrence's answers to decay

The first response that Lawrence produced to the 'Writers among the Ruins', and one that many erroneously associate with Lawrence's life and work as a whole, was that new life comes from engaging with another person in a heterosexual relationship. This position was only dominant between 1913 (the 'Foreword' to *Sons and Lovers*) and 1917, and again in the late 1920s, when it returned in a somewhat different and simplified form with *Lady Chatterley's Lover* (1928) and a number of polemical texts. In the first of these periods, the 'lesser' theme of racial otherness and national difference underwent a shift in the way it was treated. From being associated with negative events and atti-tudes, difference gained in attractiveness. Lawrence responded strongly to Germany and Italy after he eloped to the Continent with Frieda Weekly in 1912; nevertheless, it was some time before these countries were viewed favourably in his work. Continental Europe was associated with the sadism and violence of military life in the short story 'The Prussian Officer'. In *Women in Love*, Germany is used to explore modern art and perverse sexuality through the figure of Loerke, and the Alps are associated with the death of that energetic but degenerate industrial male, Gerald. The positive effects of Lawrence's early travels can be seen in the project that resulted in *Twilight in Italy* (1916), which contributed some of the thought, particularly around the use of binary oppositions, that was to influence *The Rainbow*. In fiction, though, it was not until after 1917 – and here one thinks of *The Lost Girl* (1920) and *Aaron's Rod* (1922) – that the rest of Europe, and specifically Italy, began to function more positively. In Lawrence's own life the final escape from Britain in November 1919 to such locations as Florence, Capri, Taormina and Sardinia involved increasing levels of difference from the North of Europe, away from industrialisation and the modern. Yet Lawrence started to see the whole continent as exhausted, and a move beyond Europe's boundaries became increasingly likely.

In *The Rainbow* Lawrence is interested in how a past England, imagined mythically as unchanging and socially constant, was affected – down to its personal and sexual relationships – by industrialisation and the political changes in Europe that allowed, in the 1860s, Tom Brangwen to meet and marry the Polish Lydia Lensky. Poland is reintroduced, two generations on, through Anton Skrebensky and his relationship with Ursula. Skrebensky hides his own weakness and lack of identity in his commitment to 'the nation' and to fighting as a soldier in colonial wars. Ursula, who gains more authorial support, takes an individualist line and says of the Sudan conflict, 'we don't care about Khartoum'. Ursula's rejection of Skrebensky's offer of marriage is also a refusal to go to India with him. She has a horror of the 'European population of India'[20] – unlike Adela Quested, in *A Passage to India*, Ursula does not visit India to see what married life there would be like. While Ursula's position is anti-colonial, it is also based on ignoring 'otherness' – she thinks about India in terms of its 'European population' alone. Accounts of Skrebensky's African experiences in the Boer War draw on the link established in colonial discourse between Africa, decay and sensuality. He tells her 'about Africa, the strange darkness, the strange blood fear', and 'the negro, with his loose soft passion that could envelop one like a bath'. The darkness is seen as having 'possessed his own blood', and his talk about Africa has the effect of 'conveying something strange and sensual to her'.[21] Lawrence is clearly using 'Africa' to represent an extreme of decayed physicality, something at once attractive and deathly. Ursula will reject this darkness in Skrebensky.

The colonial tropes that managed to link Africa to what is wrong with the West were taken up again in extended form in *Women in Love*. In the 'Fetish' chapter the pregnant Possum is compared to a (probably wholly invented) statue of an African woman in childbirth, linking her to a sensual degeneration.[22] The most important references to Africa in the novel, though, come in the 'Moony' chapter when Birkin remembers another sculpture. He opposes the sensual degeneration seen in African art with Nordic, abstract, idealised degeneration, which he connects with Gerald.[23] These two ongoing forms of decay are seen as pressing in upon modern man. While a text like *The Rainbow* seems to reflect a generally anti-colonial stance, Lawrence is also drawing in his writing on images of Africa to represent modern Western decay.

In 1917, the year when the last substantial alterations to *Women in Love* were made, Lawrence's thinking shifted away from arguing for a positive change through heterosexual relationships towards the view that engaging with racial difference and cultural otherness could offer a transformative encounter. In a recent article the Lawrence biographer Mark Kinkead-Weekes has pointed to a number of major changes in 1917 that saw Lawrence move from the concerns of *The Rainbow* and *Women in Love* towards an interest in masculine singularity and other cultures.[24] Marriage came to seem less attractive to Lawrence. There were strains in his relationship with Frieda, and in Cornwall Lawrence was spending time with other men, due in part to a sexual attraction. He hoped that in working on the land he would discover the male comradeship he found described in American literature. The encounter with the Mecklenburgh Square set, after his expulsion from Cornwall, including Richard Aldington, H. D., Dorothy Yorke and Cecil Gray, led to a revulsion from the modern world of sex and relationships. (Lawrence drew on these experiences in *Aaron's Rod*.) There was to be both a misogynistic turn in Lawrence's writing and a turning inwards as he began to think about what constituted a complete person.

The main new writing project undertaken in 1917, the first

versions of his essays on American literature, reflected the change of direction (four of these pieces have only recently resurfaced).[25] It was here that Lawrence began to develop the ideas that resulted in both *Studies in Classic American Literature* (1923) and his books *Psycho-analysis of the Unconscious* (1921) and *Fantasia of the Unconscious* (1922). Lawrence used ideas in Hindu thought about the 'chakras' – centres of psychic energy in different parts of the body – to think about how consciousness resides in various bodily centres, and how so-called 'psychological' problems result from an imbalance between them. He began to think not only about the self, but about the relations between people from different cultures, particularly in the American context, and as described in American writing. Lawrence felt that as the United States had moved furthest down the path of industrial development, it was the most degenerate, and therefore the place from which renewal might spring. He had written in a November 1916 letter to Catherine Carswell, 'America has dry-rotted to a point where the final *seed* of the new is almost left ready to sprout.'[26] Rather than the America of capitalist development, what most caught Lawrence's attention was the treatment in the country's writing of the interracial encounter, be it the settler engagement with Native American culture found in Fenimore Cooper, or the American encounter with the Pacific described in Melville. Lawrence was beginning to feel that, with his faith in the regenerative potential of the heterosexual relationship waning, hope for the rebirth of individuals and societies lay in the Western encounter with other races and cultures. Leaving Europe was not only a means of escape from a war-ravaged continent; he believed that hope resided elsewhere in the world.

## Lawrence's theory of renewal for the West

The view that something new and different could emerge from the interracial encounter was explored by Lawrence in his first published essay on Fenimore Cooper's Leatherstocking novels, probably from 1917, which appeared in the *English Review* of March 1919. Lawrence describes Natty and Chingachgook in *The Last of the Mohicans*:

> They are isolated, final instances of their race: two strangers, from opposite ends of the earth, meeting now, beholding each other, and balanced

in unspeakable conjunction – a love so profound, or so abstract, that it is unexpressed; it has no word or gesture of intercommunion. It is communicated by pure presence alone, without contact of word or touch. This perfect relationship, this last abstract love, exists between the two isolated instances of opposite race.

And this is the inception of a new race. Beyond all expression, save the pure communion of *presence*, the abstract love of these two beings consummates itself in an unimaginable coalescence, the inception of a new psyche, a new race-soul that rises out of the last and first unknowable intercommunion of two untranslatable souls. That which Chingachgook was, Natty was not; nor could he ever know. In the same way, Natty himself was the untranslatable unknown to Chingachgook. Yet across this insuperable gulf in being there passed some strange communion between the two instances, invisible, intangible, unknowable – a quality of pure unknowable embrace. And out of this embrace arises the strange wing-covered seraph of new race-being. From this communion is procreated a new race-soul, which henceforth gestates with the living humanity of the West.[27]

The unknowability of the 'other' is stressed, but there is a 'yet': something can result from the contact that is new and joint. The meeting is between males and, unusually for Lawrence, is praised for staying on an intense, 'abstract' and spiritual level. I have written elsewhere on Lawrence's view of the interracial engagement, which draws on the belief in balanced human relationships set out in his psychoanalysis books, and compared it with the model of the colonial encounter described by Frantz Fanon in *Black Skin, White Masks*.[28] The model suggested by Lawrence's work is that equal and positive engagements are possible, as opposed to the internalisation of fierce hierarchies of power described by Fanon. Many of the problems with Lawrence's position are present in the passage quoted above, however. If the races are separate and their difference is respected, how can something joint result? Who confers the authority on the Western subject to use the 'other' to help revivify an exhausted culture? What of the wishes of the racial 'other' and the colonial subject? Lawrence was to find the presumption of authority harder to sustain after his departure from Europe. New and different landscapes could also, Lawrence believed, suggest a new way of living for Western people. He wrote of locations that he only knew from novels or in fantasy, and imagined a utopia: 'And the lovely American landscape is the pure landscape of futurity: not of our present factory-smoked futurity, but of the true future of the as yet unborn, or scarcely born, race of Americans'.[29]

In addition to accounts of the individual encounter and the engagement with place, Lawrence also addressed the rise and fall of whole societies and cultures, beginning with the essay 'The Spirit of Place', which appeared in 1918.[30] The fullest sense of how Lawrence conceived of cultural change and transformation before he left Europe, though, can be found in the myth of human history he develops in the 'Preface' to *Fantasia of the Unconscious*, from October 1921. Opposing conventional science, which he felt to be the study of what is dead, he called for a return to the 'subjective science' of 'sure intuition' that he believed once held sway: 'Just as mathematics and mechanics and physics are defined and expounded in the same way in the universities of China or Bolivia or London or Moscow today, so it seems to me, in the great world previous to ours a great science and cosmology were taught esoterically in all countries of the globe, Asia, Polynesia, America, Atlantis and Europe.'[31] Lawrence claimed that he found 'hints' for his argument about a deep well-spring of true life in the subject obscured and distorted in modern life in 'the Yoga and Plato and St John the Evangel and the early Greek philosophers like Herakleitos down to Frazer and his "Golden Bough", and even Freud and Frobenius'.

Lawrence believed that such travel and contact was possible before the ice melted and the sea rose. Constructing his own account of the past, he maintains that after an 'interchange' between parts of the world that was 'complete, and science was universal over the earth, cosmopolitan as it is today' came a decline, a degeneration towards what is conventionally called civilisation:

> Then came the melting of the glaciers, and the world flood. The refugees from the drowned continents fled to the high places of America, Europe, Asia, and the Pacific Isles. And some degenerated naturally into cave men, neolithic and palaeolithic creatures, and some retained their marvellous innate beauty and life-perfection, as the South Sea Islanders, and some wandered savage in Africa, and some, like Druids or Etruscans or Chaldeans or Amerindians or Chinese, refused to forget, but taught the old wisdom, only in its half-forgotten, symbolic forms. More or less forgotten, as knowledge: remembered as ritual, gesture and myth-story.[32]

This borrows without thought a number of things from racist, imperial and evolutionary discourse about the places and peoples mentioned, seeing some people as more degenerate than others. But it also reverses some of the expected tropes. Degeneration is not seen as having set in comparatively recently at the centre, as located at the margins, or in terms of a complex interchange between centre and margins. Nor are there two different poles of ongoing degeneration, as in *Women in Love* with its stress on Nordic abstraction and African sensuality. Rather, decay has occurred in the old, once-universal civilisation. What is now, *everywhere*, is degenerate; but degeneration had proceeded at a greater pace in some peoples than in others. Narratives of Western civilisation and improvement are being questioned here. In some cultures old and better forms of knowledge remain, hidden but present as symbols.[33]

In the place of narratives of continual improvement is a theory of history as marked out by convulsions and interruptions, a series of civilisations that rise and then collapse, and where people then use the surviving earlier precedents to start building up again.[34] This argument is intended as a counter-blast to theories of evolution:

> Floods and fire and convulsions and ice-arrest intervene between the great glamorous civilizations of mankind. But nothing will ever quench humanity and the human potentiality to evolve something magnificent out of a renewed chaos.
>
> I do not believe in evolution, but in the strangeness and rainbow-change of ever-renewed creative civilizations.

Lawrence maintains that it is the role of the individual subject to help 'spark'[35] new civilisations and possibilities out of collapse. The word 'strangeness' here also suggests the necessity of engaging with what is different, and the 'rainbow-change' reminds us that such shifts from floods and shocks into new life and possibility *at a personal level* had been the subject of Lawrence's fiction since *The Rainbow* and *Women in Love*. In the 'Preface' to *Fantasia of the Unconscious* change for whole societies has been added to individual change.

When Lawrence left Europe, and his engagement with difference was no longer through his reading, the theory he had developed came under strain and eventually collapsed. The assumptions and fantasies developed working from books were placed in question, and Lawrence at times compensated for the instability of self that resulted by drawing on stock colonial and racist responses to the 'other'.

### Engagements with difference

Lawrence's experiences of travelling need to be seen in terms of *a journey*, and not, as often happens in work on the author as a series of separate residences in different locations. He was interested in approaching the United States from the West, and avoiding the industrial East Coast. It will help if this journey is briefly summarised. Lawrence left Sicily in February 1922, going first, via the Suez Canal, to Ceylon, as it then was, where he stayed for six weeks, before spending time in Australia. He stayed two weeks in Western Australia before living in New South Wales for two and a half months. After stopovers in Wellington, the Cook Islands and Tahiti he arrived in San Francisco in September. He settled in New Mexico, though he visited other parts of the USA, and spent two long periods in Mexico. Lawrence made one trip back to Europe during this time, and he settled there again in late 1925. In Taos in New Mexico, with its American, Spanish and Native American cultures, he was again in a situation that was, in many ways, 'colonial' in nature. During his time in Mexico he was fascinated by the clash between the Indian and Spanish settler cultures.

One of Lawrence's characteristics as a writer, in terms of his career as a whole, is his responsiveness to the new and the different. But what has never been given due emphasis is that on encountering cultural and racial difference in these years of travel Lawrence in large measure closed down. He recoiled away from the very thing that had so fascinated him before he left Italy, and that had contributed to his making the journey. Certainly before he arrived in New Mexico, and even there it took him some time, there is but limited engagement with other peoples and places. He found the encounter with difference unsettling and it was difficult for him to adjust. In what engagements with 'otherness' there were, Lawrence deploys constructions of other peoples that show a marked degree of fantasy. However, the racially and culturally different were no longer as controllable and malleable as they had been before he left Europe, when they were only 'known' through texts.

Lawrence's attitude to imperialism was now different from the withering scepticism of Ursula in *The Rainbow*. He was impressed by it, and upset by evidence of the British Empire's decline. Critical of liberal attitudes towards the 'unruly native', the solitary colonial administrator fascinated him.[36] The Englishman abroad could be seen as the resolute single male, while so much English masculinity was, he felt, weak and vacillating. As Lawrence came from a very different social background to the colonial administrators, there was also perhaps an element of cross-class identification. Lawrence's account of his first encounter with a colonial possession, Malta in 1920, shows him moved by the perceived glory of the Empire, but upset by its decay. He wrote in the *Memoir of Maurice Magnus*, completed in January 1922, 'One felt the splendour of the British Empire, let the world say what it likes. But alas, as one stays on even in Malta, one felt the old lion had gone foolish and aimiable [*sic*]. Foolish and aimiable, with the weak aimiability of old age.'[37] The repetition here captures the sense of mental decay affecting Britain, and the result for the Empire is a lack of 'aim'.

The view that the British Empire is weakening as its masculinity declines is also expressed in the only creative writing that Lawrence dated from his time in Ceylon, the poem 'Elephant'. The Prince of Wales, then on his Far East visit, is described as a weak modern European male, a 'dispirited Prince ... his nerves tired out'. At the Pera-hera he is unable to fulfil his responsibility, lacking the strength to respond to the feelings sent up to him: 'As if the homage of the kindled blood of the east,/ Went up in wavelets to him, from the breasts and eyes of jungle torch-men,/ And he couldn't take it.'[38] The Ceylonese are rapidly and stereotypically written in here, as Lawrence focuses on Europe and its problems, embodied in the figure of the Prince.

There was more involved than a diagnosis of the state of masculinity and the weakness of British colonialism: Lawrence was personally unsettled by Ceylon. The engagement with the country produced a sudden and complete (if temporary) reversal of the position set out before he had left Europe. Lawrence's letters show a wish to return home, a belief that Europe is the most advanced place, and the deployment of racist discourses to describe the racial 'other' who, it had been hoped, would help renew an exhausted and decayed West. The anger at a liberal colonial policy that is present is fuelled by this unsettlement of the self. To cite some key sections from this correspondence:

> But I do think, still more now I am out here, that we make a mistake forsaking England and moving out into the periphery of life. After all, Taormina, Ceylon, Africa, America – as far as *we* go, they are only the

negation of what we ourselves stand for and are: and we're rather like Jonahs running away from the place we belong ... The east, the bit I've seen, seems silly. I don't like it one bit. I don't like the silly dark people or their swarming billions or their hideous little Buddha temples, like decked up pigsties – nor anything. I just don't like it. It's better to see it on the cinema: you get there the whole effect, without the effort and the sense of nausea ... Europe is, I fancy, the most satisfactory place in the end ... I think Frieda feels like me, a bit dazed and indifferent – reckless. – I break my heart over England when I am out here. Those natives are *back* of us – in the living sense *lower* than we are. But they're going to swarm over us and suffocate us. We are, have been for five centuries, the growing tip. Now we're going to fall. But you don't catch me going back on my whiteness and Englishness and myself. English in the teeth of all the world, even in the teeth of England. – How England deliberately undermines England. You should see India. Between Lloyd George and Rufus Isaacs etc we are done.[39]

Lawrence here sees the colonies as the 'periphery' and the 'negation' of the West: this is a long way from the Lawrence of the 'Preface' to *Fantasia of the Unconscious*. From offering the potential of renewal, other races are now described as 'silly dark people'. He feels 'dazed and indifferent' and he co-opts Frieda's responses in support of his own. Europe is the most 'satisfactory place', but it is under threat from colonial hordes flooding into the centre. The coloniser, holding on despite an ever increasing level of pressure, is further damaged by a perceived 'enemy within'. Lawrence makes disparaging references to Lloyd George and Rufus Isaacs, then Viceroy of India (anti-Semitism perhaps showing here). They are seen as failing to cope with the challenges of colonial policy in the region – specifically, this involved how to deal with Gandhi and the uprisings in Madras and the Punjab. But Lawrence also seems to be opposing the general tendency of early-twentieth-century British 'reform' in India, such as the 1921 Government of India Act, which was attempting to buy off Indian political aspirations with no intention of handing over significant power. It should also be remembered that Lawrence's statements come three years after the Amritsar massacre, and in the context of violently repressed demonstrations in East Africa and the establishment of the Irish Free State.[40] When Lawrence fears that because of Lloyd George and Isaacs – both Liberal politicians – '*we* are done' (my emphasis) he is identifying as a beleaguered British imperialist.

There is further evidence here of Lawrence being disturbed by Ceylon. The engagement with Ceylon is described as having direct physical effects, of rendering him both nauseous and suffocated. Lawrence is left arguing for 'contact' with the colonial subject through cinema, a medium he usually loathed,[41] believing it to show the worst in the modern. Lawrence's unsettlement leads, by way of compensation, to the extreme form of his views about the threat to the Empire. But while these statements may in large measure be born of a destabilising of the self, the effect is that the discourses of colonialism are once again recycled. At this stage Lawrence did not return to England, as his letters from Ceylon had threatened; rather, he went on to Australia. However, the questioning of the theory with which he left Europe had begun, and it was to intensify.

The extent to which Lawrence knew, while writing his novel *Kangaroo* (1923), of the right-wing political movements that had sprung up in post-war Australia has been much debated. The argument that Lawrence had high-level contacts with these groups while in Australia remains unproven, despite Robert Darroch's considerable energies.[42] Lawrence's engagement with Australian politics may often have been in fantasy, given the short time he spent there, his isolation and his work rate on the novel. Rather than being seen in utopian terms, as the American landscape had been, place and native peoples were now perceived as evil and dangerous, and the Spirit of Place as malign. The Lawrence figure in the novel, R. L. Somers (the name sees Lawrence linking himself with that other writer-traveller R. L. Stevenson) goes for a walk into the bush in Western Australia:

In Europe, he had made up his mind that everything was done for, played out, finished, and he must go to a new country. The newest country: young Australia! Now he had tried Western Australia, and had looked at Adelaide and Melbourne. And the vast, uninhabited land frightened him. It seemed so hoary and lost, so unapproachable...

And then one night at the time of the full moon he walked alone into the bush. A huge electric moon, huge, and the tree-trunks like naked pale aborigines among the dark-soaked foliage, in the moonlight. And not a sign of life – not a vestige.

Yet something. Something big and aware and hidden! He walked on, had walked a mile or so into the bush, and had just come to a clump of tall, nude dead trees, shining almost phosphorescent with the moon, when the terror of the bush overcame him. He had looked so long at the vivid moon, without thinking. And now, there was something among the trees, and his hair began to stir with terror, on his head. There was a presence.

The trees are said to be 'like … pale aborigines' and are then made the locus of the presence: Lawrence reads the landscape in terms of the threatening native. The 'electric' moon, which suggests the mechanical in Lawrence's writing, is to be described a little later as 'unnatural'. It makes the trees 'phosphorescent': the glow of dissolution is used to represent a malign Spirit of Place. What is 'other', be it in the form of people or landscape, is seen in terms of evil. As Somers walked back home, 'He felt it was watching, and waiting. Following with certainty, just behind his back. It might have reached a long black arm and gripped him'.[43] The 'alien' white people become its potential 'victim': 'It was biding its time with a terrible ageless watchfulness, waiting for a far-off end, watching the myriad intruding white men'.[44] On arrival in Australia Lawrence represents the 'other' as withdrawn, angry and on the edge of violence.

## A loss of faith: exploring uncertainty in *St Mawr*

The period in the American continent saw Lawrence oscillating between two extremes. One pole was the assertion of possibilities of renewal and transformation through Western contact with a young, growing culture; the other was an increasingly well articulated sense of doubt and uncertainty about this project. After the shock to the self of the first contact with non-European cultures came other questions, around the imposition of the will in the encounter with the 'other', and whether modernisation had not now affected all life, everywhere. Lawrence at times blamed the West for the pressure his theory was coming under. He also deployed racist and colonial discourses in an effort to hold the racial 'other' responsible.

A new answer to the question of how the difference of the 'other' could be maintained in any transformative interracial contact was produced. Rather than the Western subject imposing his or her 'will', the possibility was explored of them lapsing into submission to the culturally different. This Lawrence depicted in the short story 'The Woman Who Rode Away' (written in the early summer of 1924), and in the two versions of his Mexican novel. Both texts of the novel use indigenous belief to imagine a way of living beyond Christianity and Mexico's troubled political history. There are a number of differences between the first draft of the novel (written in the spring and summer of 1923 and first published in America in 1995 under Lawrence's preferred title for the project of *Quetzalcoatl*) and the second version, written in 1924–5 and published as *The Plumed Serpent* in 1926.[45] The final text sees the religious element in any effort to regenerate a decayed society emphasised more strongly, as the central protagonist, Kate, enters further into the new religion and way of living that are depicted as taking off in Mexico. In *The Plumed Serpent*, Kate enters into a marriage with one of the leaders of the movement, Cipriano, and agrees to become a living goddess of the new religion. At the end of the novel she is less likely to return to Europe than in the first version. David Ellis has pointed out that in the effort to envisage a society that moves past the effect of Spanish culture on Mexico both versions of the novel can be termed 'post-colonial'.[46] However, the depiction is of a post-coloniality written by a Western subject, and focalised through the eyes of the European character, Kate. (Lawrence shows some sensitivity to this by relating Kate, through her 'European' marriage, with Irish Republicanism.) This post-coloniality is not for the colonised – their *post*-colonial experience is now being colonised by a Western author – but for the needs of a threatened European.

*The Plumed Serpent* was the extreme point in Lawrence's effort to imagine the 'other' transforming and changing a decayed society. I will prioritise here the Lawrence that questioned and doubted his earlier theory, as this is an aspect of Lawrence's writing in this period that has received little attention. The focus will be the short novel *St Mawr*, which Lawrence wrote in the summer of 1924 when in New Mexico, between writing the two versions of the Mexican novel. It not only registers doubt and despair about Lawrence's project in these years; it is among his most 'modernist' texts. The fragmentary, shifting nature of its narrative challenges and often frustrates the reader, brilliantly juxtaposing different voices and capturing the ennui of modern cosmopolitan life. The possibility of an anthropological or symbolic reading is at once offered and continually frustrated and ironised. Such contentions might be held to support the recent critics who have begun to talk about Lawrence's writing of the 1920s not only in terms of modernism but also of *post*modernism.[47] However, it is easy to get Lawrence wrong by trying too readily to make him our contemporary. He represented the lack of a whole society and the difficulties of attaining such a state by using these devices; yet while Lawrence registered uncertainty around the sign in a number of his texts he was a writer who would always 'fain see a sign'. With Yeats perhaps the last major literary system-builder and 'prophet' before the collapse of grand narratives noted by postmodern theory, Lawrence used the strategies available to a modernist writer to register the strain and problems of finding a belief system in the first half of the twentieth century, but he did not give up the search.

*St Mawr* depicts a failed journey to find a better way of living, sought in cosmopolitan society, in different places and in people, and indeed animals, that might offer the hope of access to a more meaningful and grounded way of life. The central characters, Mrs Witt and her daughter Lou, fail to find what they are searching for in London, in Shropshire (for Lawrence, as for Forster and Housman, the very wilds of England), and in Texas and the Southwest of the United States. The horse St Mawr has for much of the text provided a possible symbol for a new masculinity and way of living, but in the end he too is found wanting.

Rather than a world where distances between the centre and margins are clear and fixed, Lawrence sees modern communications, travel and interracial contacts as having already collapsed particularity and difference. While he might have wanted unique and pristine interracial contacts himself, he is annoyed at the effects of too much interchange undertaken by others. He feels that miscegenation has mixed up the world's races. The margins have collapsed into a Europe that is degenerate, old and being destroyed by the modern; but that is not to say that the 'outsider' offers the solution. The uncertainty of the reader over the direction of the text when reading *St Mawr* – particularly when the main characters are shipped to America – reflects the crisis in reading the world of late colonialism experienced by the writer.

Many of the text's main points are economically made in the opening pages. Lou is an American with a 'queer familiarity with foreign cities and foreign languages', a 'lurking sense of being an outsider everywhere' and 'like a sort of gipsy, who is at home anywhere and nowhere'.[48] She comes from a Louisiana family who had moved to Texas, though her childhood was European, moving between France, Italy, Switzerland, Austria, Germany and England. Her husband Rico represents what is wrong with modern European masculinity. He is an artist brought up across a colonial-European axis. His real first name is Henry, and he is Australian by birth: he gained the name Rico in Rome, where Lou first met him. But this colonial with an Italian name is also a figure of the Establishment. Rico's father was a baronet, and he succeeds to the title. Rico and Lou Carrington have a house in Westminster, and they are thus able to 'settle into a certain layer of English society'.[49]

Mrs Witt, Lou's mother, remembers growing up in the old South and her memories of the Black servants of that time in her life recur through the text. Her servant and groom, whom she calls Phoenix, is a further example of the dizzying range of backgrounds and experiences introduced at the start of the novel:

> Out of the débâcle of the war she had emerged with an odd piece of débris, in the shape of Geronimo Trujillo. He was an American, son of a Mexican father and a Navajo Indian mother, from Arizona. When you knew him well, you recognised the real half-breed, though at a glance he might pass as a sunburnt citizen of any nation, particularly of France.[50]

Phoenix, further, is pictured as being somewhat disorientated by living in Europe, suggesting that difference and travel confuse rather than offer a possible site where something new and positive can emerge.

Lawrence's view at this time that it is impossible to produce a positive 'hybridity', a bringing together of different cultures, is shown in his reaction, in the summer of 1924, to Forster's *A Passage to India*. He was positive about Forster and his achievement in the novel. He wrote to him on 23 July, with characteristic tree imagery to the fore, 'there's not a soul in England says a word to me – save your whisper through the willow boughs'. Yet Lawrence later critiqued Forster's views on interracial encounters. In a letter to John Middleton Murry of 3 October he argued for the final separateness of the races, of the impossibility of knowledge of the 'other': 'All races have one root, once one gets there. Many stems from one root: the stems never commingle or "understand" one another. I agree Forster doesn't "understand his Hindu".'[51]

*St Mawr* displays a nostalgia for a world imagined as having had fixed racial groups and hierarchies of power. The vision of the world to which the novel tends is misanthropic and hopeless. Lawrence is left with a view of the world not dissimilar to that of the Edwardian writers he had set out to respond to at the start of his career. He is also ready to blame everyone, of whatever race and culture, for what he sees as a rising tide of degenerate modern evil. After Mrs Witt and Lou leave London and travel to Shropshire there is the possibility, Lou feels, of finding life 'straight from the source' and locating the 'pure animal man'.[52] This section's set-piece scene occurs when the party visit the Devil's Chair on the English/Welsh border. It is a place 'where the spirit of aboriginal England still lingers, the old savage England, whose last blood flows still in a few Englishmen, Welshmen, Cornishmen'. In a passage with complex symbolism the horse St Mawr, linked to Pan and to the 'red horse' of the Book of Revelation,[53] rears on encountering a dead snake, which perhaps represents the evil in the world. Rico, who is riding the horse, makes the situation worse by pulling the horse back on himself. He is depicted as responsible for the injuries he suffers; modern man brings his crises upon himself. Yet the most remarkable and strange passage occurs after the accident, in Lou's reaction. She watches, does not act, and a long sermon on the nature of evil in the modern world is ascribed to her. The narrative grinds to a halt: a temporal dislocation occurs to add to the collapse of space and cultural difference dramatised elsewhere in the text. The account sees the modern as a flood of evil which is still rising. It is a bleaker view of decay than that offered in the 'Preface' to *Fantasia of the Unconscious*. Decay is happening now and everywhere, and none is exempt:

> There was no relief. The whole world was enveloped in one great flood. All the nations, the white, the brown, the black, the yellow, all were immersed in the strange tide of evil that was subtly, irresistibly rising. No-one, perhaps, deliberately wished it. Nearly every individual wanted peace and a good time all round: everybody to have a good time.

Lawrence goes on to locate the centre of evil in the 'core of Asia' – perhaps associating it with his Ceylon experiences and fantasies.[54]

This leaves the means of bringing about an alternative to modern forms of life more difficult to find than ever. The description of the ranch – based on the Lawrences' own property – with which the short novel ends is an account of how a malign Spirit of Place can defeat encroaching representatives of the modern. It is depicted as the last place of retreat for someone who wishes to avoid the reach of modernity, and what produced fear in *Kangaroo* now becomes the weapon against the modern world. The only protection against decay is an isolation spent resolutely hoping, despite the evidence, for rebirth:

Every new stroke of civilisation has cost the lives of countless brave men, who have fallen defeated by the 'dragon,' in their efforts to win the apples of the Hesperides, or the fleece of gold. Fallen in their efforts to over-come the old, half-sordid savagery of the lower stages of creation, and win to the next stage.

For all savagery is half-sordid. And man is only himself when he is fighting on and on, to overcome the sordidness.

And every civilisation, when it loses its inward vision and its cleaner energy, falls into a new sort of sordidness, more vast and more stupen-dous than the old savage sort. An Augean stables of metallic filth.

And all the time, man has to rouse himself afresh, to cleanse the new accumulations of refuse. To win from the crude wild nature the victory and the power to make another start, and to cleanse behind him the century-deep deposits of layer upon layer of refuse: even of tin cans.[55]

What saves man from 'savagery' – be it of the margins or the new form from the centre – is a kind of Conradian resolution despite the odds and the sense of despair. Lawrence seems to have come close to coming to rest as a 'Writer among the Ruins'. Yet, as David Ellis has pointed out, it would be wrong to map Lou's feelings at the end of *St Mawr* on to Lawrence as his firm resolution.[56] He was trying out a position rather than finally adopting one, and was shortly to go south to Mexico to make one last attempt to assert more strongly than ever the possibility of a new start gained from a different, older culture in the final version of the Mexican novel. Nevertheless, in *St Mawr* doubt about leaving home and finding the new in the 'other' had been strongly stated and explored, and, after the final counter-assertion in *The Plumed Serpent*, a return to Lawrence's own 'roots' was to win out.[57] This is prefigured in the cultural references used in the above quotation: they are from Europe's past and classical civilisation. In the return home of Mrs Witt and Lou to America Lawrence had taken a step towards imagining his own journey back to Europe.

## Conclusion: Lawrence's 'Greater Day'

Lawrence's view of the necessity of withdrawing from what is 'other' and different back to the 'home' culture and place can be seen in 'The Flying Fish' from March 1925. Lawrence began by dictating this unfinished text, from just after the completion of the final version of *The Plumed Serpent*, to Frieda while critically ill in Mexico City. It appears to be the opening of a short novel. The main character, Gethin Day, is lying ill in the south of Mexico when he receives a telegram saying 'Come home else no Day in Daybrook'. He realises that it means that his elder sister is either dead or dying back at the family seat. Lawrence was using two events close to him at this time: his illness and the death of his own father, Arthur Lawrence, in September 1924. Daybrook is the old Elizabethan manor house that Day owns, and where his sister lived while he went 'wandering' around the world.[58] The (invented) intertext for the story is his Elizabethan ancestor's *Book of Days*. This is used to establish a true, vital England, to contrast with the modern country. Day is fiercely critical of Mexico, he feels ill and that he has no place there, and sees the 'Greater Day' of the Mexican Indians as being turned towards the deathly by the 'lesser day' of the Spanish settlers.[59] He sets off back to his place of birth, we can assume to try and find the Greater Day of England depicted in the *Book of Days*, and to 'come into his own', both in terms of development and inheritance.[60] If returning to Europe could perhaps be seen as a defeat for a strong 'masculine' subject, in this text a purposeful male's return to Europe is seen instead in terms of facing up to responsibility, of no longer avoiding the true challenge. The text breaks off – Lawrence said that it was written on the edge of death (and a renewal of active life) and that it was impossible for him to take up the writing again.

Lawrence was exploring a return to Europe to take the place of the father and a certain male role, the act of coming into one's own in one's own area. In *Sketches of Etruscan Places* (1932), *The Escaped Cock* (*The Man Who Died*) (1929) and *Apocalypse* (1931), all composed between 1927 and his death in March 1930, Lawrence kept his belief in a return to the past and the different to enable renewal, but now this was sought within a Western frame. Further, heterosexual relations regained much of their earlier significance. The historical axis of difference gained precedence over the geographical axis. The racial 'other', different places and cultures, had been seen as offering so much, and yet on contact a strong sense of doubt and insecurity was registered, an uncertainty that contributed to the force of the racist and imperialist statements. The theory of a necessary engagement with what is 'other' and non-European as the means by which dissolution and decay might be reversed, with which Lawrence left Italy in 1922, collapsed as a result of his journeying.

Lawrence could be constructed as having seen the error of his ways – returning to his own continent, he no longer imposed himself on someone else's. However, such a return can also be presented as an assertion of the primacy of the Western cultural past over other cultures. The narrative of Lawrence's journey given here, for all the range of positions adopted, suggests that there was always a reliance, to some degree, on colonialist assumptions. But could it have been otherwise: was it possible to think and write in the modernist period wholly outside colonial and racist discourses? I think not – though it must be stated that some positions at the time were certainly better than others, and that a number of writers were pushing in strongly anti-colonial directions. The challenge for historically aware work on modernism is to explore the shaping of possibility in the period.

## Notes

I would like to thank David Ellis, Lee Grieveson and, especially, Janet Montefiore for their comments on this chapter.

1 Letter to Arthur MacLeod, 4 October 1912 in *The Letters of D. H. Lawrence*, vol. 1, ed. James T. Boulton (Cambridge: Cambridge University Press, 1979), p. 459.

2 *Ibid.*, p. 465 and n. 3.

3 Lawrence has Birkin half remember the opening lines of Browning's poem in *Women in Love*. D. H. Lawrence, *Women in Love*, ed., David Farmer, Lindeth Vasey and John Worthen (Cambridge, Cambridge University Press, 1987), p. 61.

4 F. R. Leavis, 'Lawrence after thirty years', *Valuation in Criticism and Other Essays*, ed. G. Singh (Cambridge, Cambridge University Press, 1986), p. 110; G. Wilson Knight, 'Lawrence, Joyce and Powys', *Essays in Criticism*, 11:4 (October 1961) 403–17; Colin Clarke, *River of Dissolution: D. H. Lawrence and English Romanticism* (London, Routledge & Kegan Paul, 1969).

5 David Bradshaw, Introduction to D. H. Lawrence, *The White Peacock* (Oxford, Oxford University Press, 1997), pp. vii–xxxii. The phrase quoted comes from p. xi.

6 D. H. Lawrence, *Sons and Lovers*, ed. Helen Baron and Carl Baron (Cambridge, Cambridge University Press, 1992), p. 464.

7 See *Sons and Lovers*, note to p. 464, line 35 on p. 575; and the *Oxford English Dictionary*, 2nd edn.

8 D. H. Lawrence, *Apocalypse and the Writings on Revelation*, ed. Mara Kalnins (Cambridge, Cambridge University Press, 1980), p. 137.

9    H. G. Wells's *Tono-Bungay* was first serialised in the *English Review*, 1:1 (December 1908) to 1:4 (March 1909). It was published in book form in London by Macmillan in 1909. The modern edition referenced here is H. G. Wells, *Tono-Bungay*, ed. John Hammond (London, Dent, 1994).

10   *The Letters of D. H. Lawrence*, vol. 1, p. 119.

11   David Lodge, '*Tono-Bungay* and the Condition of England', *Language of Fiction: Essays in Criticism and Verbal Analysis of the English Novel* (2nd edn; London, Routledge & Kegan Paul, 1984), pp. 214–42; see especially pp. 234–8.

12   As well as carrying new work by Conrad, James, Bennett, Galsworthy, Wells, Hardy and Lawrence (whose first major publication the journal published in November 1909), the *English Review* also took pieces on contemporary politics. Imperial issues were often discussed: there was a section entitled 'The Empire' in *English Review*, 1:3 (February 1909) 569–93 (the same issue that contained the third of the four serialised sections of *Tono-Bungay*), and J. A. Hobson (the author of the critique of the economics of imperialism, *Imperialism: A Study* (1902)) had a piece on 'South Africa as an imperial asset' in *English Review* 3:2 (September 1909) 324–34.

13   H. G. Wells, 'Tono-Bungay', *English Review* 1:4 (March 1909) 724, 725; *Tono-Bungay*, ed. Hammond, p. 279.

14   *English Review* (March 1909) 727; *Tono-Bungay*, p. 282.

15   *English Review* (March 1909) 737; *Tono-Bungay*, p. 292.

16   *English Review* (March 1909) 737; *Tono-Bungay*, p. 293.

17   *English Review* (March 1909) 745; *Tono-Bungay*, p. 300.

18   *English Review* (March 1909) 790; *Tono-Bungay*, p. 352.

19   Edward Mendelson is particularly strong on the difference between the public 'official views of Wells' and the 'uncomfortable, subversive views in his novels and stories, which, at their best, as in *The Time Machine* and *Tono-Bungay*, saw human aspiration decline into hopeless chaos'; see his article 'How Lawrence corrected Wells; how Orwell refuted Lawrence', in Maria DiBattista and Lucy McDiarmid (eds), *High and Low Moderns: Literature and Culture, 1889–1939* (New York, Oxford University Press, 1996), pp. 166–75: 171.

20   D. H. Lawrence, *The Rainbow*, ed. Mark Kinkead-Weekes (Cambridge, Cambridge University Press, 1989), pp. 288, 439.

21   *Ibid.*, p. 413.

22   D. H. Lawrence, *Women in Love*, pp. 74, 78–9. For the issue of whether there are precedents for such subject matter in African statuary, see the note to p. 74 line 13 on p. 538.

23   D. H. Lawrence, *Women in Love*, pp. 252–4; see further the note to p. 253 line 11 on pp. 559–60.

24   See Mark Kinkead-Weekes, 'The genesis of Lawrence's psychology books: an overview', in Howard J. Booth, Elizabeth M. Fox and Fiona Becket

(eds), Special Issue on 'D. H. Lawrence and the Psychoanalytic', *D. H. Lawrence Review*, 27:2–3 (1997–98) 153–70; and his *D. H. Lawrence: Triumph to Exile 1912–1922*, Volume 2 of *The Cambridge Biography of D. H. Lawrence* (Cambridge, Cambridge University Press, 1996). Given space constraints what follows here is inevitably somewhat reductive.

25 For a description of the unpublished essays, see Kinkead-Weekes, *Triumph to Exile*, pp. 438–57.

26 *The Letters of D. H. Lawrence*, vol. 3, ed. James T. Boulton and Andrew Robertson (Cambridge: Cambridge University Press, 1984), p. 25.

27 D. H. Lawrence, *The Symbolic Meaning: The Uncollected Versions of 'Studies in Classic American Literature'*, ed. Armin Arnold (Arundel, Centaur Press, 1962), p. 103.

28 Howard J. Booth, '"Give me *differences*": Lawrence, psychoanalysis and race', *D. H. Lawrence Review*, 27:2–3 (1997–98) 171–96.

29 D. H. Lawrence, *The Symbolic Meaning*, p. 111.

30 This is an early version of what became the introductory essay to *Studies in Classic American Literature*. It appeared in the *English Review* for November 1918, and is reprinted in Lawrence, *The Symbolic Meaning*, pp. 16–31.

31 D. H. Lawrence, *Fantasia of the Unconscious, Fantasia of the Unconscious. Psychoanalysis and the Unconscious* (Harmondsworth, Penguin, 1971), p. 12.

32 *Ibid.*, p. 13.

33 Lawrence noted the link between symbols and psychoanalysis in the first published 'The Spirit of Place' essay (Lawrence, *The Symbolic Meaning*, p. 18). The possible role of Jungian thought here requires further work. While it may have been one of his borrowings, Jung is not, as we have seen, listed in the 'Preface' to *Fantasia of the Unconscious* among the authors that influenced Lawrence.

34 There are clearly possible similarities here between Lawrence and the Yeats of *The Vision*, though there are, on examination, also many differences. The best effort to compare the thinking of the two writers is Phillip L. Marcus, 'Lawrence, Yeats, and "the Resurrection of the Body"' in Peter Balbert and Phillip L. Marcus (eds), *D. H. Lawrence. A Centenary Consideration* (Ithaca, N.Y., Cornell University Press, 1985), pp. 210–36.

35 Lawrence, *Fantasia of the Unconscious*, p.14.

36 See, in particular, the essay 'On coming home' which stems from Lawrence's trip to Europe in late 1923/early 1924. D. H. Lawrence, *Reflections on the Death of a Porcupine and Other Essays*, ed. Michael Herbert (Cambridge, Cambridge University Press, 1988), pp. 177–83; especially pp. 182–3.

37 D. H. Lawrence, *Memoir of Maurice Magnus*, ed. Keith Cushman (Santa Rosa, California, Black Sparrow Press, 1987), p. 84.

38 *The Complete Poems of D. H. Lawrence*, ed. Vivian de Sola Pinto and F. Warren Roberts (1964. Harmondsworth, Penguin, 1977), pp. 388, 389.

39  *The Letters of D. H. Lawrence*, vol. 4, ed. Warren Roberts, James T. Boulton and Elizabeth Mansfield (Cambridge, Cambridge University Press, 1987), pp. 219, 221, 222, 234.

40  See *ibid.*, p. 234 n.1 and Dennis Judd, *Empire: The British Imperial Experience, from 1765 to the Present* (London, Fontana, 1997), pp. 258–72.

41  See Linda Ruth Williams, *Sex in the Head: Visions of Femininity and Film in D. H. Lawrence* (Hemel Hempstead, Harvester Wheatsheaf, 1993), pp. 1–5.

42  To list just two texts here: Robert Darroch, *D. H. Lawrence in Australia* (Melbourne, Macmillan, 1981); David Ellis, 'D. H. Lawrence in Australia: the Darroch controversy', *D. H. Lawrence Review*, 21 (Summer 1989) 167–74.

43  D. H. Lawrence, *Kangaroo*, ed. Bruce Steele (Cambridge, Cambridge University Press, 1994), pp. 13–14.

44  *Ibid.*, pp. 14–15.

45  See further, D. H. Lawrence, *Quetzalcoatl*, ed. Louis L. Martz (1995; New York, New Directions, 1998); D. H. Lawrence, *The Plumed Serpent*, ed. L. D. Clark (Cambridge, Cambridge University Press, 1987).

46  David Ellis, *D. H. Lawrence: Dying Game 1922–1930*, volume 3 of *The Cambridge Biography of D. H. Lawrence* (Cambridge, Cambridge University Press, 1998), p. 219.

47  See further, Joyce Wexler, 'D. H. Lawrence through a postmodernist lens', *D. H. Lawrence Review*, 27:1 (1997 and 1998) 47–64; and Macdonald Daly, Introduction to D. H. Lawrence, *Kangaroo* (Harmondsworth, Penguin, 1997), pp. xiii–xxxi.

48  D. H. Lawrence, *St Mawr and Other Stories*, ed. Brian Finney (Cambridge, Cambridge University Press, 1983), p. 21.

49  *Ibid.*, p. 23.

50  *Ibid.*, pp. 24–5.

51  *The Letters of D. H. Lawrence*, vol. 5, ed. James T. Boulton and Lindeth Vasey (Cambridge, Cambridge University Press, 1989), pp. 77, 142.

52  Lawrence, *St Mawr and Other Stories*, pp. 61, 62.

53  See *ibid.*, p. 31 and Revelations vi, 4. Lawrence wrote in *Apocalypse* that 'The red horse is choler: not mere anger, but natural fieryness, what we call passion.' Lawrence, *Apocalypse*, p. 102.

54  Lawrence, *St Mawr and Other Stories*, p. 78.

55  *Ibid.*, p. 151.

56  Ellis, *Dying Game*, pp. 193–4.

57  Before he left New Mexico after finishing *St Mawr* to head south and work on *The Plumed Serpent*, Lawrence wrote an Epilogue in September 1924 for the second edition of his history book for schools, *Movements in European History*. In the end the content made the Epilogue unpublishable, and it did not appear in print for forty-five years. It is his most extended response to 1920s' politics, and begins by using tree

imagery to suggest that each of the world's races are like separate branches. However, this image is clearly hierarchical and Lawrence goes on to argue that 'For a thousand years, surely, we may say that Europe has been the growing tip on the tree of mankind' (D. H. Lawrence, *Movements in European History*, ed. Philip Crumpton (Cambridge, Cambridge University Press, 1989), p. 256). But decay set in, and the war 'blew away forever our leading tip our growing tip'. Lawrence talks about a new branch coming to prominence, and also about how the old must be 'grafted with a new idea' (p. 257) – in other words, how another culture could be used to revivify Europe. However, he soon drops this line of thought, and for the rest of the Epilogue it is Europe and its politics that assume the centre ground.

58 Lawrence, *St Mawr and Other Stories*, pp. 207, 208.
59 *Ibid.*, p. 214.
60 *Ibid.*, p. 210.

# 10

## 'Not a good place for deacons': the South Seas, sexuality and modernism in Sylvia Townsend Warner's *Mr Fortune's Maggot*

**Nigel Rigby**

> The South Seas, as they used to say of Paris ... is not a good place for deacons.
>
> Anon[1]

Sylvia Townsend Warner's second novel, *Mr Fortune's Maggot* (1927),[2] is about a friendship between a middle-aged English missionary and a Polynesian boy on a fictional South Pacific island, just before the First World War. Warner's biographer, Claire Harman, has described the novel as fitting 'into the voguish Twenties genre of the "fantasy novel"', but she argues, however, that *Mr Fortune's Maggot* has a great deal more depth than the mixture of 'cleverness, oddity and pathos' which is typical of the genre, and Harman sees Warner's concerns in the novel being specifically English and literary.[3] Warner's Polynesia is entirely textual, anecdotal and imaginary: she never travelled to the Pacific; indeed, apart from one visit to America, she never travelled outside Europe. Her island landscapes are impressionistic; her Polynesian characters are undeveloped, with the exception of the boy, Lueli; and her depiction of Polynesian culture is sketchy. She herself wrote in her diary thirty years later that she had to resist giving *Mr Fortune's Maggot* 'life instead of art'.[4] The aspiration to privilege aesthetics over realist narrative form – part of modernism's search for a greater 'truth' to life through art – might suggest that Warner is merely appropriating the South Seas. I will argue, however, that her modernist aesthetics, even in such an imagined, text-based fiction as *Mr Fortune's Maggot*, engage closely with issues of imperialism, and are subtly subversive of its ideologies.

Other contributors to *Modernism and Empire* have noted the critical tendency to detach the works of the 'great' modernist writers from any suspicion of contamination by imperial writing,[5] although even before publication of this volume, which addresses the intersections in depth over a range of writing and in a number of different contexts, the conceit of a modernism untouched by empire had begun to look increasingly unconvincing. Jane Marcus has pointed out recently in her study of *The Waves* that even Virginia Woolf, one of the highest of the 'high modernists', admitted to being moved to tears after watching the Hollywood imperial epic *Lives of a Bengal Lancer*, in 1935.[6] Whether they were tears of laughter, of course, is more difficult to determine, but her point is that empire was simply a part of life in between-the-wars Britain, whatever one's social class, habits or politics, and that all writers were inevitably exposed to the wide range of imperial narrative being produced at the time. *The Waves* pushes modernist form to its limits – it is in many ways the ultimate expression of an anti-realist text – but Marcus argues that the challenging structure of *The Waves* is, in fact, a sustained and unambiguous attack on empire. The lack of ambiguity about imperialism that Marcus sees in Woolf has in turn been challenged by Patrick McGee, who argues persuasively that her attitudes to empire were far more complex than Marcus allows.[7] The broader implication of Marcus's argument, however, that Woolf is representative of a more general modernist concern with imperialism is, I would agree, far more convincing than the image of the modernist artist living in Olympian detachment from such 'mundane' issues.

I will argue in this chapter that Warner develops her critique of imperialism through the subversion of its forms of writing. Imperial narrative gains much of its ideological force through the deployment of familiar tropes. Hayden White has argued in *Tropics of Discourse* that understanding of the new and unfamiliar – which is one of the fundamental attractions of imperial writing – is a tropological process, following the traditional progression of knowledge from metaphor (the naive statement that one thing is like another) through metonymy, synecdoche, and finally to a rational cognisance, at which point the initial naive and irrational understanding of the new is recognised as false, and can be ironised.[8] White argues, however, that despite this apparent progression, rational knowledge is never entirely free from that first irrational metaphor. In terms of imperial writing, the developing knowledge of other cultures and situations that comes through continued contact and colonisation is constantly moderated, mediated and informed by irrational and emotional tropes, and throughout imperial narrative the same tropes surface time and again – the empty land, the treacherous savage, the dying native, the European who 'goes native', the white 'god' ... (the list is a long one). Following White's argument, a double understanding of empire emerges which knows rationally that 'natives' do not really think of white explorers as gods, and yet where narratives of first contact between Europeans and indigens are still informed by that ideologically charged image.[9] The appeal to the trope of the empty land, as Abdulrazak Gurnah shows elsewhere in this volume, provides settler writing with a way of maintaining a moral claim on the land, even when the text reveals the falsity of the claim. Warner engages particularly with the set of tropes that built up around the Pacific – the interracial love affair, the dying native, Nature's savage, and others – in which the issue of land was less central and which were important parts of an integrated imperial discursive structure.

Warner's works, as Janet Montefiore has noted in her recent study of writing in the 1930s, have been shamefully neglected,[10] and *Mr Fortune's Maggot* especially has received scant critical attention. As it is a relatively little known text, I shall begin with a brief resumé of the plot. Timothy Fortune is a bank clerk who is left a legacy which allows him to quit his job and become a missionary in the Raratongan islands. There is no suggestion of evangelising zeal in Timothy's decision to go to the Pacific, and Warner unobtrusively reverses the structure of an imperial novel in which the hero sets off on his travels in order to make his fortune. After ten unfulfilled years in Raratonga Timothy, always an able mathematician, goes full circle, and ends up keeping the mission's accounts. There is a strong echo in Timothy's disenchantment at colonial Raratonga of Paul Gauguin's disappointment with a Europeanised colonial Tahiti on his first arrival in the Pacific. Gauguin's Tahitian journal, *Noa Noa*, had been published in 1919, with his *Intimate Journals* following four years later, and it will become clear that Warner was familiar with the text. Gauguin's Polynesian paintings had first appeared in England at the Post-

Impressionist exhibition of 1910 (famously described by Virginia Woolf as the date on which human nature began to change, and a 'modernist' sensibility to emerge),[11] and they had had a profound effect on Warner's artist friend, Duncan Grant. Warner herself mentioned that *Mr Fortune's Maggot* owed a debt to 'Duncan's painting, which at that time was particularly brilliant and free', which would indicate Gauguin's influence also coming indirectly through Grant. Another related source is also likely to have been Somerset Maugham's novel *The Moon and Sixpence* (1919), which was based on Gauguin's life.

Timothy is quickly disenchanted with colonised Raratonga, and like Gauguin, who leaves the 'degenerate' town of Papeete for the interior of Tahiti, he wants to move on to find the 'true primitives' of Polynesia – Gauguin, of course, does not travel to the South Seas to 'civilise' the 'savage' either, but to escape civilisation and himself become a savage. Timothy's Archdeacon in Raratonga is 'sorry to hear that Mr Fortune (who was now a priest) had felt a call to go to the island of Fanua' (p. 3) where there is no mission station, and no other European. Warner's style is deceptive, and she can make an apparently simple sentence work hard. Here she confirms economically that the Archdeacon values Timothy for his skills as an accountant more than for his contribution to the spiritual life of the mission; second, Warner, by noting that Timothy '(... was now a priest)' rather as Mrs Ramsay dies in parenthesis in *To the Lighthouse*,[12] undercuts both the usual markers of time passing, and the importance of religion to Timothy; third, we only hear the Archdeacon's reported response to what Timothy has said to him – two removes from what Timothy may have actually thought. This multiple 'layering' of the narrative, which renders reality uncertain and dependent on perspective, is central to the development of Warner's subversion of a single, and imperial, voice in the novel.

For example, when Mr Fortune arrives on Fanua, 'he turned briskly inland' to explore the island, an authoritative narrative voice tells us that 'The island of Fanua is of volcanic origin ... It rises steeply out of the ocean, and seen from thence it appears disproportionately tall for its base.' This could have come straight out of a guidebook, travelogue or missionary account of the Pacific. Warner's narrator shares the knowledgeable tone of the missionary, Thomas Williams, in his introductory remarks on the Fiji group: 'A good idea of the general appearance of these islands is obtained by regarding them as the elevated portions of submerged continents. The interior is, in many instances, as single hill or mountain…' – similar examples could be found in nearly all missionary writing.[13] But Warner's sternly objective description competes with different voices: the birds 'seem to float like fragments of coloured paper'; 'there seemed to be no end to the marvels and delights of his island'; 'this gay landscape [could well] have been coloured out of a child's paint-box' – which reflect a more child-like pleasure in the beauty of the island (pp. 10, 12 and 16). Warner studiously avoids giving the island a single reality, and, more significantly, her narrative voices eschew the possession of the islanders' thoughts which is typical of imperial writing. Whilst the narrative drifts in and out of Timothy's consciousness, any moves into the islanders' heads are both clearly marked and tentative: 'Lueli's thoughts went something like this…'; or, whilst eating some biscuits that Timothy has given them, the islanders' 'expressions were those of people struck into awe by some surprising novelty: Mr Fortune wondered whether he were that novelty, or Huntley and Palmers' (pp. 197 and 14).

From the first, Timothy's attempts to convert the islanders on Fanua are unenthusiastic, and in three years he only makes one convert, Lueli. However, he is happy on the island, and his happiness is almost exclusively centred on Lueli: the other islanders play little more than walk-on parts in the novel. Then Timothy discovers with a shock that Lueli is no convert at all, but has 'been playing a double game, betraying him, feigning to be a Christian, and in secret, in the reality of secretness, worshipping an idol' (p. 111). The language strongly implies that Timothy sees Lueli's behaviour as a personal, indeed sexual, betrayal. Although there is no suggestion of physical sex between Timothy and Lueli, the relationship between them is overtly sexualised, as I will discuss below, and Timothy behaves here more like a spurned lover than a wrathful saver of souls. At this point there is an earthquake, as the volcanic island becomes active once again. Timothy revels in the destruction of the island, sitting 'on the reeling mountain side with but one sensation: a cold-hearted excitement, a ruthless attentive craving that at the height of horror would welcome another turn of the screw, another jab of the spur, another record broken' (p. 124).

Timothy has been losing his faith since he first arrived on the island. He is not long there before he remembers 'uneasily how in visiting the village that morning he had not breathed a word of conversion' (p. 34); when an old print depicting the Good Shepherd helping a lost sheep out of a pit falls out of his Bible, Timothy is suitably chastened, having 'a shrewd suspicion that this incident was intended as a slightly sarcastic comment on his inadequacies as a shepherd' (p. 36). In fact, from the moment that Timothy arrived on the island and 'found himself taken charge of and shepherded in the right direction' by the islanders, it is he rather than the Fanuans who has been straying (p. 8). Although his faith is gradually eroded, like Gauguin's 'civilisation' which falls from him 'little by little' on Tahiti,[14] Timothy's realisation that he no longer believes in God comes upon him suddenly, when he discovers that Lueli has been worshipping his wooden god during the entire period of his apparent conversion to Christianity; Timothy's loss of faith is mirrored by the physical destruction of Lueli's wooden god in the fire that follows the earthquake. Whilst Timothy's loss of faith is something of a relief and a release (when he finally realises what the reader has known about him for some time), Lueli is devastated by the loss of his god, and attempts to kill himself. Finally, Timothy leaves the island, having first symbolically relinquished his claim on Lueli by carving him a new god.

Daniel Defoe's *Robinson Crusoe* (1719) is an important text here – although the same could be said of virtually any fictional or factual Pacific island narrative, for whom *Crusoe* is often a self-consciously foundational text. In a letter to David Garnett, Warner admitted as much, describing *Mr Fortune's Maggot* being written in 'alternate layers of [Theodore] Powys and Garnett, [writers who were close friends of Warner] both imitated to the life. I roar with laughter at it and write on feverishly. The Rev. Crusoe is Theo, of course, and Man Friday is you. Oh, I forgot, there is scenery out of a child's paintbox. *That* is Bernardin de St. Pierre.'[15] *Crusoe* is referred to directly and indirectly throughout the novel: when Timothy nervously asks his archdeacon whether the Fanuans are cannibals, Crusoe's fear of being eaten on his island is recalled; the list of goods that Timothy takes to Fanua evokes Crusoe's obsessive desire to inventory everything and order his world; Timothy chides himself for not being more like Crusoe, bringing order and civilisation to the island, but he thinks of Lueli as Friday, his sole convert to the blessings of the West. The quotation from Warner's letter describes the intertextuality of *Mr Fortune's Maggot* simply in terms of a comic pastiche of literary and artistic influences, however, and does not suggest her more profound ironisation of *Crusoe*.

Despite its light tone, the ultimate message of *Mr Fortune's Maggot* is profoundly bleak, and is the complete antithesis of Crusoe's confident vision of the future of Western civilisation. Where Crusoe forges a strong religious, personal and imperial identity on the island, Timothy Fortune finds despair, loss and fragmentation. Where Crusoe introduces a European order to the wilderness, Timothy finally understands that not only does European colonisation succeed through the destruction of colonial difference, but that Europe is also destroying itself through its intolerance. Warner's rewriting of *Robinson Crusoe* can certainly be placed within the context of post-war modernist fears of the collapse of civilisation. Although the passing of time in *Mr Fortune's Maggot* is not marked in any conventional terms, the novel is set quite precisely in the first fourteen years of the twentieth century: Timothy is ten years on Raratonga, three and a half years on Fanua, and the novel finishes just as Timothy hears of the outbreak of war in Europe. The parallels between the events on Fanua and those about to happen in France are further suggested in one of the final scenes of the novel when Timothy peers into the core of the erupting volcano, seeing 'thick smoke' hanging over the lava, heavy shell-like impacts with 'splash[es] and a leap of fire' and 'thin gaseous flames' flickering on the surface (p. 218), images which are at the very least evocative of Flanders.

Gregory Woods, who has glanced briefly at *Mr Fortune's Maggot* in the context of women's writing on male homosexuality, argues that the novel is optimistic, its subjects being 'harmony and hope': when 'the genteel missionary eventually leaves the island and his beloved boy behind', Woods suggests, 'he leaves enchanted and enriched'.[16] Woods reads *Mr Fortune's Maggot* essentially as being a 'coming-out' novel; this leads, in my view, to only a partial understanding of its themes. The bleakness of the ending is clear to see, and Timothy's utter devastation as he leaves the island is underlined by Warner's perhaps guilty 'Envoy': 'My poor Timothy, good-bye! I do not know what will become of you' (p. 250). The emptiness of Timothy's future is developed in the story that Warner wrote some years later as a sequel to the novel, 'The House of Salutation'.[17]

Woods accepts Warner's playful writing *about* the novel too readily.

Why Warner did not wish to draw attention to its more serious themes is not clear. It is possible that she began writing a lighthearted pastiche of missionary writing, which become progressively more sombre as Warner herself came to see the interconnections of culture and colonisation. Certainly, the plot becomes more sober almost exactly halfway through the novel, when the earthquake begins. But although the narrative darkens, Warner's treatment remains light and playful throughout. It was not until she wrote the Preface for the Virago edition of *Mr Fortune's Maggot*, shortly before her death in 1978, that Warner even began to suggest that imperialism had a bearing on the novel. Here she recalled that her original source book was a volume of letters written by a woman missionary to Polynesia, which she had borrowed from Paddington Public Library some seven years before beginning *Mr Fortune's Maggot*: 'it had the minimum of religion, only elementary scenery, and a mass of details of everyday life. The woman wrote out of her own heart – for instance, describing an earthquake, she said that the ground trembled like the lid of a boiling kettle.'[18] After a gap of fifty years Warner could not remember the title of the book, but it was, in fact, Isabella Bishop-Bird's *Six Months in the Sandwich Islands*, first published in 1875. Bird was not a missionary but a traveller, although her description of the land trembling like a kettle lid was actually a direct quotation from one of Bird's hosts on Hawaii, the wife of an American missionary called Mrs Sarah Lyman.[19] Warner drew on Bird quite extensively. The description of the lava flowing to the south[20] came directly from 'the public library lady', as she calls Bird in her preface; one of Warner's friends, Bea Howe, also gave Warner an account of an earthquake in Valpariso which supplemented Bird's descriptions. Bird relates the story of Kapiolani, the Christian princess of Hawaii who 'tamed' the volcano on Mauna Loa, which Timothy recalls as he walks up the mountain (although it was actually a well-known story, Tennyson also having written a poem about her).[21] Although not wishing to stretch the links between Warner and Bird too far, Timothy is the complete antithesis of another of Bird's hosts, a revivalist missionary with the delightful name of Titus Coan, whom Bird describes as baptising '1705 persons, formerly heathens' on one particular Sunday.[22]

Warner is not so much quoting Bird as a source of authentic material on the Pacific, however, as suggesting similarities between herself and Bird in terms of narrative voice and gender vis-à-vis colonialism. I would argue that Warner reads Bird virtually as a proto-feminist and proto-modernist, claiming that the subjectivity and domesticity of Bird's imagery allow her to step outside the predominantly male colonial discourse of missionary writing. Bird's elementary scenery, like Warner's, refrains from making a colonial claim on the landscape, and Bird here avoids subscribing to larger 'imperial truths' through a tone of gentle incongruity: the very absurdity of a boiling kettle lid in the context of an earthquake works in a very different way to the Reverend Titus Coan's interpretation of the same volcanic eruption. For him, the 'rending [and] the raging' of the land made it seem as if 'the ribs and pillars of the earth were being shattered', and the lava streams 'creep[t] softly and silently like a serpent' towards the islanders' houses.[23] For Coan, the volcano is contradictorily both a metaphor for the savagery kept in check by a Christian civilisation and God's punishment for sinners, but at bottom the natural world and Christianity combine to support an imperial world-view.[24] I do not suggest that Bird was attacking Coan's particular description, for his book was not published until five years after *Six Months in the Sandwich Islands*, but that Warner was seeing that Bird's domestic imagery, which she saw as specifically female, offered possible ways of avoiding the assumptions of male imperial narrative.

Warner's claim should not be accepted uncritically, for her memoir was written for the Virago edition at a time when there was considerable interest in reclaiming Victorian and early women's writing. The reprinting of Warner's own novel was, of course, a part of the same process. As Sara Mills has pointed out, contemporary feminist critics have sometimes treated Victorian women travel writers 'as if they travelled simply as individuals and were not part of colonialism as a whole', and have ascribed to the Victorians a post-colonial position nearer to their own; in order for women travellers to appear distanced from the colonial process, Mills continues, certain parts of the text have to be highlighted, and certain parts ignored.[25] This would certainly appear to be the case with Bird, who is as capable of aligning herself uncritically with imperial power structures as Titus Coan, casting a proprietorial colonial eye on the landscape. Bird, for example, sees the story of Kapiolani taming the volcano in terms of Christianity conquering pagan savagery, whereas Timothy recalls the myth as an example of a naive pre-Darwinian faith in the power of good which is exposed as redundant in the modern world. However, Bird does layer her narrative with similar effect to Warner: Bird's letters are interwoven with other people's voices, and in the one in which she describes the volcanoes of Hawaii she moves from herself to Sarah Lyman, to myth, to Titus Coan, to the English missionary William Ellis with ease. A firm narrative voice does emerge – as, for example, when Bird laments: 'Poor people! It would be unfair to judge of them as we may legitimately be judged of, who inherit the influences of ten centuries of Christianity'[26] – but it is equally clear that this voice is not unproblematically Bird's.

At issue for Warner is the question of narrative authority, and this has implications both for modernist aethestics – which subverted the tradition of the omniscient narrator and the unified world-view – and for imperial ideology. The white men who 'really understand the natives', like Titus Coan, are common figures of imperial narrative, reaching their apogee, perhaps, in Edgar Wallace's Commissioner Sanders, who is able to rule wisely and well through his intimate knowledge of the native mind. 'Understanding' the 'native' channels difference and diversity through a single imperial perspective, and this narrative authority is both metaphor and manifestation of imperial control. One of the features of Pacific writing is that it frequently undermines this form of imperial knowledge through what Mary Louise Pratt has described as the 'anti-conquest'.[27] In the exotic island romances of Pierre Loti and Charles Warren Stoddard, written during the beginnings of high imperialism in the last quarter of the nineteenth century, the European hero is an enlightened individual who leaves civilisation to immerse himself in native tradition and culture – not to rule, but to record before it is destroyed by advancing colonialism. Since the publication of Edward Said's *Orientalism* (1978) we have come to recognise that European imperial power was expressed in a complex array of interconnected discourses, and we can see that Loti's and Stoddard's sentimental exoticism establishes a different form of knowledge and power over the imperial subject through a myth of reciprocity. However, although it is important to acknowledge the shortcomings of their critiques, and to recognise the place of island romances in the dissemination of imperial ideologies, they were also part of a sentimental literary tradition critical of the excesses of empire that flowered during Abolition, and on which later anti-imperial writing was to build.

In his recent study, *Representing the South Pacific*, Rod Edmond has argued that Gauguin's stance against Western civilisation in *Noa Noa* has not been taken with the seriousness it deserves. Gauguin claims in *Noa Noa* that in order to liberate himself from the old traditions of European art, he has to immerse himself in Tahitian culture, to become a 'savage', as he puts it repeatedly. This means, in practice, living with young Tahitian women, and through sex uncovering the 'lost' traditions of Polynesia. The artist seeks to rejuvenate the 'customs, fashions, vices, and absurdities' of degenerate European civilisation with the elusive 'purity' of the Tahtitian 'primitive', and *Noa Noa* can all too easily be read within the terms of 'anti-conquest' writing. Edmond argues, however, that the narrator's attempt to re-create himself as 'a savage' should not be taken at face value, for it is a pose which is repeatedly ironised in the book. Ultimately, Gauguin is unable to gain access to the culture of Polynesia, which remains frustratingly 'other' to him.[28] Knowing that the other's culture is different, yet not being able to understand its difference – as the beachcomber, Tommo, can see everything but comprehend nothing of Marquesan culture in Herman Melville's *Typee* (1846) – encapsulates Gauguin's challenge to the authoritative and knowing traditions of European aesthetics.

'Difference' – cultural, personal and sexual – is the central theme of *Mr Fortune's Maggot*. In a lengthy musical set piece, Timothy and Lueli play together, with Timothy on a harmonium and Lueli on 'a wooden pipe, rather like a flageolet' (p. 67). The shared interest in music is, on the face of it, an image of cross-cultural harmony which evokes comfortable missionary propaganda; but playing together proves 'not feasible, for the harmonium was tuned to the mean tone temperament and Lueli's pipe obeyed some unscientific native scale; either alone sounded all right, but in conjunction they were painfully discordant' (p. 70). Pre-twentieth-century European music follows a rigid tonal structure which can ultimately be reduced to a mathematical formula, whereas much non-European music is atonal, following a completely different system. The narrative voice traces the traditions behind the harmonium, which 'has a repertory of its own, pieces that can only be properly rendered on this instrument' (p. 66), and confidently describes Timothy's 'repertory of many classical larghettos and loud marches, besides, of course, the usual hymns and chants. Haydn was his favourite composer' (p. 67). Lueli's tunes, on the other hand, 'were very long tunes, though the phrases composing them were short; the music seemed to waver to and fro, alighting unexpectedly and then taking another small flight, and listening to it was like watching a bird flitting about in a bush' (pp. 68–9), and the narrative voice cannot describe Lueli's music other than in terms of 'nature'.

Although Timothy has rather 'superior accomplishments', a 'cultivated [musical] taste', and a 'grasp of musical theory', he 'was not so truly musical as Lueli', who is able to reproduce European music with facility (p. 69). Warner connects in this scene with the familiar imperial trope of civilisation encountering nature, rationality meeting intuition, age and youth. But although Warner is working with the trope, she is also complicating it. Lueli is certainly cast as 'natural man', in touch with the rhythms of life, but this is ironised by his love of music being seen to be neither indiscriminate nor simply instinctive, but having the ability to recognise, reproduce and respond to new forms and structures.

The narrator alludes in passing to the music being produced for the harmonium by 'such recent composers as Schoenberg or Max Reger' (p. 66), which Timothy has never heard of, and would not appreciate anyway. Schoenberg was a modernist composer experimenting with atonal forms of composition, while Reger was more of a traditionalist, but what both Schoenberg and Reger shared was an interest in exploring contrapuntal structures in which two melodies could play alongside one another and harmonise, but still retain their own distinct musical identities. 'In the counterpoint of Western classical music,' as Edward Said has said in *Culture and Imperialism*, 'various themes play off one another, with only a provisional privilege being given to any particular one; yet in the resulting polyphony there is concert and order, an organized interplay that derives from the themes, not from a rigorous melodic or formal principle outside the work'.[29] Said uses counterpoint as one of the structuring images of his book, which argues that imperialism and nineteenth-century 'high' European culture should be seen as intertwined rather than separate themes. Warner is using counterpoint rather differently, setting it alongside the tonal tradition of European classical music to show the destructive 'colonial' ethos of a traditional European culture which subsumes difference. (Lueli's approach to music stands as its opposite, being a metaphor for a more admirable native culture which does not seek to 'convert', but to accommodate otherness.) That

European music is already experimenting with forms which celebrate difference suggests that an avant-garde European culture is already trying to break away from a suffocating tradition: the ideological structures of modernist aesthetics are not only shown to be anti-imperial in this scene; they are also able to change imperial ways of thinking.

Timothy's rigid adherence to a regimented European musical form is part of the symbolic structure of the novel, in which mathematics stands for European rationality. In symbolism that recalls Kim's use of maths to defeat the 'irrational' force of the Orient, which Janet Montefiore discusses in this volume, mathematics and not Christianity is the true religion of the West in *Mr Fortune's Maggot*. Where Lueli is destroyed when his god is burnt, Timothy's loss of religious faith is unimportant because ultimately it is the truths of maths rather than religion that he finds ideal, eternal and universal. Timothy tries to teach mathematics to Lueli in the hope that understanding the 'order of things' will divert the boy from his misery. In a scene which is both gloriously funny and sober at the same time, Timothy embarks on his mathematics lesson by prodding a hole in the sand with his umbrella in order to demonstrate that a point 'has position but not magnitude' (p. 173); Lueli remains politely uninterested and completely uncomprehending of the 'point' of it all. The scene demonstrates both the fundamentally different organising structures of the two cultures, and Timothy's inability to be able to cure himself of the desire to dominate and control: immediately after the lesson a despairing Lueli tries to drown himself.

Timothy's failure to teach the truths of mathematics to Lueli is also a failed attempt to re-create Plato's Academy on the beach of Fanua. From the very early days of European arrivals in the Pacific it had been a commonplace to represent Polynesia as a version of Ancient Greece: the classically educated Louis-Antoine de Bougainville and Sir Joseph Banks began the trend in the 1760s, and the American artist La Farge was still describing the Samoans in terms of Greek gods as late as the end of the nineteenth century. In the case of *Mr Fortune's Maggot*, however, Timothy's tutorial to a beautiful young man on a beach is more closely associated with the homoerotic fantasy behind the Athenian Academy, for it is through 'homosexuality' that Warner fully develops her critique of imperialism.

The homoerotic theme is handled lightly and comically at first in

*Mr Fortune's Maggot.* Lueli is keen to oil Timothy, for 'Lueli oiled himself as a matter of course, and so did everybody on the island'. Timothy, however, sternly resists it: 'Oiling, and all that sort of thing, was effeminate, unbecoming, and probably vicious. It was also messy' (p. 94). Eventually, Timothy gives in and allows himself to be oiled; although 'For some weeks he confined the area of effeminacy to his left knee' (p. 94), he tells himself that 'there was nothing but what was manly and might quiet him in Elliman's Embrocation – used extensively by many athletes and as far as he could remember by horsedoctors' (p. 95), and he finally 'stretch[es] himself out for Lueli's ministrations' on a daily basis. Rather as Tommo's injured leg improves when he is receptive to the valley in *Typee*, the oiling rejuvenates Timothy, for 'his face had come alive ... and instead of wrinkles had rather agreeable creases that yielded and deepened when he laughed' (p. 96). One of the slogans of Elliman's Embrocation was 'No stiffness here', and whilst I hesitate to read too much into this, Timothy's response to the island, and his relationship with Lueli, is clearly being eroticised through the oiling.

Timothy's changing perception of what is or is not manly runs throughout the novel: it is Timothy's voice which appears to criticise Lueli for 'coquetting like a girl' (p. 20) in front of a mirror; he is, however, approving of 'Lueli's maidenly demeanour' (p. 29) when comparing it to that of a group of young girls who trap Timothy in a small bathing pool; Timothy explains his own behaviour in going walking in the rain in terms of masculinity, for 'We should think it very effeminate [in England] to stop indoors and sleep' (p. 53). Timothy bolsters his own masculinity, but he simultaneously shows his homosexual attraction to Lueli by constructing him as a recognisably effeminate figure, much like Gauguin's feminised male Polynesian figures.

In a moment that is reminiscent of Gauguin's homosexual lust for the Tahitian woodcutter – 'why was it that there suddenly rose in the soul of a member of an old civilisation a horrible thought?'[30] – Timothy is furious at being temporarily abandoned by Lueli, and reflects that 'all the time his longing had been to thrash the boy or to smite his body down on the grass and ravish it' (p. 43). In a small glade near their house Timothy finds 'Something slim and dusky and motionless ... reared up' in front of him (p. 111). It is the wooden god which Lueli has been worshipping whilst, in Timothy's view, professing to be a Christian. The idol is clearly representative of a young boy's phallus, Lueli's youthful masculinity which Timothy has been ignoring in his fantasy. The destruction of the idol in the earthquake is, then, both a sexual and a religious loss for Lueli, and one in which the colonised subject is not simply feminised, but symbolically emasculated. The symbolism makes explicit the destruction of Lueli's sexual and cultural difference, and his reconstruction in European terms as a recognisably 'homosexual' figure.[31]

Love stories between European men and island women were the dominant form of narrative fiction set in the Pacific. The Pacific's association with an explicitly female sexuality began with the sexualised welcome scenes that were reported by the early European voyagers to Tahiti; the image was indelibly imprinted on European imaginations with the *Bounty* myth; island romances such as Herman Melville's *Typee* and Pierre Loti's *The Marriage of Loti* (1880) reinforced this reputation, and laid the foundations of a literature in which sexuality became the defining factor. As both Peter Hulme and Mary Louise Pratt have shown, similar stories were found in one form or another wherever there was imperial contact: the interracial love plots, with their promise of 'cultural harmony through romance', as Peter Hulme phrases it, appear to offer a critique of imperialism which, ultimately, is never fully developed. Whilst the texts are both sympathetic towards a native point of view and critical of European 'civilisation', the European eventually returns to prosper in his society, and the woman to die in hers, and finally the imperial power structures are reinforced rather than challenged.[32]

Warner works within this tradition, and *Mr Fortune's Maggot* ironically follows the structure of most interracial romances, but where island romances ultimately restore the imperial equilibrium Warner destabilises it. The return of the hero of an island romance to the fold of civilisation realigns him with a confident male, imperial perspective. Quite literally, in *The Marriage of Loti*, Loti returns to the masculine world of his ship which has been specifically associated with spoiling 'my Tahiti, by picturing it from their point of view'.[33] In *Mr Fortune's Maggot*, however, the sense of a unified European self existing outside the island is quite exploded:

> Now the secretary [on the launch sent to fetch Timothy from Fanua] was abusing the French; and from them he passed to the Turks, the Italians, and King Ferdinand of Bulgaria. Mr Fortune could not yet gather who

was fighting who, still less what they were fighting about. However, there seemed no doubt but that it was a very comprehensive dog-fight. (p. 248)

The Great War creates Europe in terms of violence, fragmentation and an obsessive desire to destroy difference. It is a mirror image of Timothy's look into the volcano in which he sees a stream of lava emerging from an 'imprisoned original frenzy that lies in the heart of the earth' (p. 126), in one single direction, obliterating everything in its path, and any deviation from its path. Where Kapiolani and the missionary, Titus Coan, see the volcano as the evil which a Christian civilisation has a duty to control, Warner uses the volcano as a symbol of the savagery that lies deep within civilisation. Timothy sees, and understands, the lust to control and destroy in both himself and the 'civilising mission'.

Timothy is, to an extent, also a victim of his society's desire to obliterate difference, for just as Timothy has constructed Lueli as a recognisably European homosexual, Timothy has himself been artificially constructed by society as a heterosexual man. As a boy he reads his sister's books 'secretly and rather bashfully' (p. 89); we learn that his father died when he was a young boy, and thus it is suggested that he had to assume the male role in the family; when most of Timothy's clothes are lost after the earthquake, he wears 'a kilt and a mantle of native cloth, soberly contrived without any fringes or fandangos' (p. 157). At the end of the novel Timothy's destructive urge is partly redeemed by carving Lueli a new god, 'creating' a new Lueli, symbolically restoring his masculinity, celebrating his difference, and recognising Timothy's own love for the boy.

Through Timothy's changing perception of both himself and Lueli, Warner outlines a difference between a destructive, 'colonising', male lust which seeks to control and subordinate otherness to desire, and 'homosexual' love which, through its perceived moderation of masculine sexual aggression by more tolerant feminine qualities, is receptive to difference. Lueli stands here as an exemplar of a sexuality that can accommodate both male and female characteristics equally and harmoniously. Lueli is conceived by Warner in terms of the 'third sex' combining male and female qualities, which had been a popular discursive figure since the late nineteenth century, and which, as the androgyne – Eliot's Tireseus and Woolf's Orlando, for example – would become such a potent figure of literary modernism's desire to break down the reductive and destructive binaries through which

European civilisation constructed itself. Modernists such as Woolf, Warner and Eliot were writing within an intellectual climate which, partly through the work of Freud and Havelock Ellis in the early twentieth century, had begun to understand sexuality in its modern sense as the dominant human drive. The scientific study of homosexuality has until recently been seen as an exclusively European intellectual movement, and in *The Geography of Perversion* Rudi Bleys outlines this version of the history of sexuality:

> From around 1860, a new discipline, sexology, emerged from the hotbed of intellectual innovation in bourgeois Europe. Sexuality became the exclusive focus of attention of scientists, who felt that its study ought to be detached from the moral rhetoric of religious authorities. Instead of upholding a single boundary between virtue and vice, they gradually promoted an image of 'polymorphous desire', some of which was socially acceptable, most of which was not. Male 'homosexuality' as one among the newly defined 'perversions', would soon attract the attention of many a physician and psychiatrist.[34]

The study of sex developed during the period of high imperialism, and like modernism has largely continued to be seen in terms of a purely European history of ideas, uninfluenced and uncontaminated by Europe's contact with empire. Exemplifying this view is Havelock Ellis's comment in *The Psychology of Sex* (1910) that 'the travellers and others on whose records we are dependent have been so shy of touching these subjects, and so ignorant of the main points of investigation, that it is very difficult to discover sexual inversion in the proper sense in any lower race.'[35] The conception of an insulated and isolated European sexuality underpins Michel Foucault's influential study *The History of Sexuality* (1976), which traces the interwoven histories of power and sexuality in Europe from the seventeenth century, but which hardly considers at all the contact with, knowledge of, and power over other cultures that resulted from European imperial expansionism during the same period. The history that Foucault traces is insistently and exclusively that of Western civilisation. The imperial 'margins' remain, in Foucault's account, little more than a place where one could find sexual opportunities unobtainable in Europe. The power relations within empire certainly meant that such opportunities existed, and distance protected those who took advantage of them: the distant imperial setting of *Mr Fortune's Maggot* undoubtedly permitted its sexual themes to be treated more explicitly than they could have been in a domestic setting, just as historical novels enjoyed a similar sexual licence. Yet Bleys argues that the study of homosexuality during the nineteenth century, which moved from the belief that it was a bestial or violent 'act', to believing it to be a *condition* which could be understood within influential Darwinian and degenerationist theories, inevitably 'called for clarification of how this manifested itself *outside* the "civilized world"'.[36] Although this 'clarification' was based on mainly untheorised descriptions and incidental reports of travellers, missionaries and soldiers who came into contact with non-European male to male sexuality, there was clearly a considerable body of imperial knowledge about homosexuality available on which the developing European study of sex drew.

Although the image of the Pacific as a heterosexual paradise drew on a tradition reaching back to the first European contact with Tahiti, there was an equally long tradition of writing on Polynesian 'homosexuality' available to Warner. As Rod Edmond has demonstrated, 'male homosexuality was … common in Polynesian cultures. It took different forms, varying from the transvestism or social effeminacy of the Tahitian *mahu* to the undifferentiated identities of the *tayo* and the Hawaiian *aikane*.'[37] Polynesian sexuality did not stigmatise sexual relations between men, and this was, for European travellers, one of the most striking differences of Polynesia, although it was often described obliquely in their writings. Robert Morris has shown in his study of Cook's visits to Hawaii on the third voyage that there are many references to *aikane* in the official journals kept by Cook and his officers.[38] In the context of first contact it is also worth considering how Polynesians would have understood the arrival of a ship filled exclusively with men, where it was usual in Polynesian societies for men and women to voyage together. The conclusion that the men *chose* to voyage without women, and thus preferred the company of men, must have occurred to at least some Polynesians, however briefly.[39] The central relationship in John Martin's early Pacific beachcomber narrative *An Account of the Natives of the Tonga Islands* (1816) is between the teenage English castaway, William Mariner, and the Tongan king, Finau, and there is a certain amount of internal evidence that the relationship is sexual, at least initially. Missionaries, who began writing about the Pacific from the 1830s, were guarded about, but obviously fascinated by, the various forms of Polynesian homosexuality, and references to it are often found in their accounts.[40]

Bearing in mind that Melville's *Typee* has become virtually an archetypal narrative of a sailor's idyll in a female Pacific paradise, it is ironic that the novel is predominantly concerned with homosexuality. Tommo's descriptions of the definitive Polynesian 'nymph' Fayaway are heavily and obviously eroticised, but these are juxtaposed with a more subtly presented attraction to Marnoo – a beautifully tattooed male Marquesan traveller who, unlike Tommo, is able to cross cultural and sexual boundaries with ease. Melville uses Tommo's fascination with Polynesian male beauty to set Tommo apart from his European colonising culture, to make him more receptive to cultural difference. In this, Melville was followed by the American writer, Charles Warren Stoddard, whose popular *South Sea Idyls* were published in 1873. Stoddard makes explicit the homoerotic attraction of the islands which Melville cloaks with symbol and metaphor, and Stoddard suggests that his own sexuality gives him a greater affinity with the Polynesians, and like Melville uses this perceived affinity to take up a stance against European colonisation. Again, like Melville, Stoddard's attack is particularly directed at the missionaries who were busy 'stamping out' Polynesia's different sexualities.

Although there was a tradition of using Polynesian sexuality to critique imperial expansion, it was also a tradition that was contained within certain limiting tropes. Whilst Tommo is attracted to the beautifully tattooed figure of Marnoo, he is also terrified of being tattooed himself. This is partly a fear of being marked permanently as a Typee and thus being unable to return to civilisation, but there is also an association in Tommo's mind between the threatened assault to his body through tattooing, the consumption of his body through the cannibalism of the brutal savage, Mow-Mow, and the threat of male rape – also an assault, a puncturing and a form of consumption which will brand him.[41] Tommo's feelings towards the Typees have always veered between attraction and fear and he is finally driven from the valley by the threatening emergence of the brutal savage – attraction to the other is ultimately controlled by fear. This is compounded by Tommo's conviction that the Typees are also a beautiful but biologically doomed 'race'[42] – a familiar trope in imperial narrative and one which is repeated endlessly and tastelessly in many of Stoddard's short stories – and Tommo leaves the valley scared that if he stays he too will decay. The trope appears to be replicated in *Mr Fortune's Maggot* when Timothy leaves Fanua, for he reflects that 'there would soon be plenty of white men to frighten the children of Fanua, to bring them galvanised iron and law-courts and commerce and industry and bicycles and patent medicines and American alarm clocks, besides the blessing of religion' (p. 233). Timothy reads the colonial future of the Pacific accurately enough and, like Tommo, sees the Polynesians as doomed children. The death of the Fanuans, however, is clearly marked as Timothy's view. As was shown in the musical scene, there is a level of knowledge in the novel which is denied to the unintellectual Timothy and he cannot understand that although the Fanuans may assimilate elements of European culture, this does not automatically mean the complete destruction of their own. Fanuan culture is able to accommodate the new and different because it is not fixed in a destructive and ideologically charged system which sees male and female, new and old, nature and civilisation, good and evil, as polar opposites.

There are, of course, problems with Warner's depiction of Polynesian culture. Where Melville's Tommo finally fears that the Typees will brand him indelibly as one of their own, Warner's Fanua is seemingly endlessly pliant and shows no interest whatsoever in converting the outsider. This partly reflects the different Pacifics that existed in the 1840s and 1920s, for when Melville was in the Marquesas European power in Polynesia was still limited, and the islands were considerably more threatening to lone beachcombers than they were to twentieth-century missionaries. But it is also a product of Warner's modernism which presents Fanua as a primitive and natural alternative to a rigid and all-consuming Western culture, and it can certainly be argued that the integrity of the island suffers from her conscious artistic decision not to explore the island society in any depth.

Warner's concern has been consistently with the many forms of European writing and thinking about empire rather than with the realities of empire itself. As I have already suggested, there was already a long tradition of writing that was critical of the excesses of imperialism – Conrad's *Heart of Darkness* and Forster's *A Passage to India* were two of the best known and relatively contemporary examples; yet, where Kurtz's excesses and the intolerance of the Anglo-Indians are to a certain extent moderated by Marlow's work ethic and Fielding's liberalism, which provide solid and recognisable platforms of belief in Europe, the broken figure of Timothy and the fragmented world to which he returns provide no such reassurance. Although Warner's style in her island romance is playful, the exploration of European social and sexual identity in the novel is sharp, challenging and fundamentally critical of both the 'idea' of empire (in Marlow's sense) and the 'idea' of Europe. Undoubtedly, Warner was writing from within a modernist intellectual tradition that was deeply suspicious of traditional forms of representation and she uses recognisably modernist techniques to pursue her themes. Central to her attack on the destructive rigidity of Western rationality is her deployment of homosexual love – an increasingly important feature of much modernist writing of the day. However, it is also clear that Warner was drawing on an existing, imperial tradition in which homosexuality was deployed for similar thematic purposes, and which raised equally troubling questions about the nature of European identity. Where these earlier narratives were ultimately tied to the tropes that permitted a relatively secure view of European society to be maintained, the emergence of modernist styles in the early years of the twentieth century allowed these tropes to be effectively ironised. At a deeper level it can also be seen that modernism's questioning of a secure European identity was not an insulated European intellectual development, but something which also drew on the uncertainties and insecurities raised by the often fraught meetings with the other found in those earlier imperial narratives.

## Notes

1  The quotation is from a review of Charles Warren Stoddard's *South Sea Idyls* (1873), in *Nation*, 17 (December 1873) 411; quoted by John W. Crowley, 'Charles Warren Stoddard: Locating Desire', paper given at the University of Hawaii at Manoa.
2  Sylvia Townsend Warner, *Mr Fortune's Maggot* (1927; London, Virago, 1990). References are to this edition, and are included in the text.
3  Claire Harman, *Sylvia Townsend Warner: A Biography* (London, Minerva, 1991), p. 71.
4  26 September 1954, *The Diaries of Sylvia Townsend Warner*, ed. Claire Harman (London, Chatto & Windus, 1994), p. 211.
5  See Rod Edmond's and Janet Montefiore's chapters in this volume.
6  Jane Marcus, 'Britannia rules *The Waves*', in Karen R. Lawrence (ed.),

*Decolonizing Tradition: New Views of Twentieth-Century "British" Literary Canons* (Urbana and Chicago, University of Illinois Press, 1992), pp. 136–62, 145.

7  Patrick McGee, 'The politics of modernist form; or, who rules *The Waves*', *Modern Fiction Studies*, 38:3 (1992) 631–41.

8  Hayden White, *Tropics of Discourse: Essays in Cultural Criticism* (Baltimore and London, Johns Hopkins University Press, 1990). See especially pp. 1–10.

9  The death of one 'white god', Captain James Cook, on Hawaii in 1779 has become the battleground for a heated debate between two distinguished anthropologists, Marshal Sahlins and Gananath Obeyesekere. Sahlins claimed in *Islands of History* (Chicago, Chicago University Press, 1985) that Cook died because he was believed by the Hawaiians to be the returning year-god, Lono, who is ritually killed each year at the end of the Makahiki festival. European myth had long accepted that Cook was taken to be an Hawaiian god, but Sahlins took this further, finding evidence to interpret Cook's death through Hawaiian mythology. Obeyesekere argued in *The Apotheosis of Captain Cook* (Princeton, Princeton University Press, 1992) that Cook was never taken to be a god, that Sahlins is merely trying to rationalise one of the more common imperial tropes, and that the rituals which Sahlins identifies as designed to install Cook as the god Lono were, in fact, giving him temporary status as a chief – although Obeyesekere agrees that there was a post-mortem deification of Cook. Sahlins has replied to Obeyesekere convincingly in *How 'Natives' Think: About Captain Cook, For Example* (Chicago and London, Chicago University Press, 1995). It is a complex argument, with mutual accusations of Eurocentrism abounding, and one which is particularly relevant to this essay in terms of the difficulties in freeing oneself from culturally shaped ways of thinking about empire.

10  Janet Montefiore, *Men and Women Writers of the 1930s: The Dangerous Flood of History* (London, Routledge, 1996), p. 143.

11  Virginia Woolf, 'Mr Bennett and Mrs Brown', in Rachel Bowlby (ed.), *A Woman's Essays* (Harmondsworth, Penguin, 1992), pp. 69–87, 70.

12  Virginia Woolf, *To the Lighthouse* (Harmondsworth, Penguin, 1992), p. 140.

13  Thomas Williams, *Fiji and the Fijians*, and James Calvert, *Missionary Labours Among the Cannibals* (London, Hodder & Stoughton, 1870), p. 6. As Christopher Herbert has pointed out in *Culture and Anomie: Ethnographic Imagination in the Nineteenth Century* (Chicago, University of Chicago Press, 1991), Thomas Williams's responses to Fiji and the Fijians are complex, and Herbert develops an interesting argument around the fracturing of Williams's authoritative narrative voice; see ch. 3, pp. 150–203.

14  Paul Gauguin, *Noa Noa: The Tahitian Journal* (New York, Dover, 1985), p. 17.

15  Sylvia Townsend Warner to David Garnett, 11 November 1925, *Sylvia*

*and David: The Townsend Warner/Garnett Letters*, selected and edited by Richard Garnett (London, Sinclair Stevenson, 1994), p. 26. Henri Bernardin de Saint-Pierre (1737–1814) was a French novelist. Warner almost certainly refers to his popular novel, *Paul et Virginie* (1788), which contains colourful and sentimentalised descriptions of Ile de France (Mauritius). He had visited the island in 1773, giving a less sentimental description in his travelogue, *Voyage à l'Isle de France*. Bernardin de Saint-Pierre's works contributed to the taste for nature and exoticism in French writing at the end of the eighteenth century.

16  Gregory Woods, 'The other or more of the same? women's representations of homosexual men', in Gabriele Griffin (ed.), *Difference in View: Women and Modernism* (London and Philadelphia, Taylor & Francis, 1994), pp. 27–38, esp. 28.

17  Sylvia Townsend Warner, 'The house of salutation', in *The Salutation* (London, Chatto & Windus, 1932). Although the missionary is never named in this story, the main character is clearly Timothy. After leaving Fanua, he quit the mission and spent several years doing a variety of menial jobs on board ships. Profoundly unhappy, he is ill and has lost the will to live as the story opens with his arrival at a ranch in the South American pampas.

18  Preface to Virago edition of *Mr Fortune's Maggot*, written in 1978.

19  See Isabella Bird, *Six Months in the Sandwich Islands* (Honolulu, University of Hawaii Press, 1964), p. 113. I am very grateful to Dr Nancy Morris at the University of Hawaii in Manoa for suggesting Bird as a source of Warner's elusive 'public library lady'. Sarah Lyman kept an earthquake diary on Hawaii from shortly after her arrival in the islands in the 1830s; it was kept after her death by her daughter-in-law. Lyman's journal was quoted by several visitors to Hawaii, including Charles Wilkes, commander of the United States Exploring Expedition to the Pacific between 1838 and 1842. It is considered today to be a unique account of volcanic activity on Hawaii, and has recently been published in its entirety.

20  The lava flowing to the south is actually a small factual error in *Mr Fortune's Maggot*, for Warner and Bird are describing the Coriolis effect, which would drive the lava to the south in the Hawaiian islands in the northern hemisphere, but to the north in the southern hemisphere. As the Raratongan islands are in the South Pacific, the lava in the novel should actually be flowing to the north. It is, of course, possible that this is a deliberate error on Warner's part.

21  Alfred Lord Tennyson, 'Kapiolani', *Tennyson: Poems and Plays*, ed. T. Herbert Warren (Oxford, Oxford University Press, 1991), p. 826.

22  Bird, *Six Months*, p. 108.

23  Titus Coan, *Life in Hawaii* (New York, Anson Randolph, 1882), pp. 317, 318.

24  Although missionaries are commonly seen as the forerunners and

supporters of colonisation, their attitudes to it were often ambivalent. Many missionaries were outspoken in their condemnation of colonisation and colonists, yet their narratives undoubtedly helped in the construction of the ethos of the 'civilising mission' which gave meaning to nineteenth-century colonialism and imperial expansion.

25  Sara Mills, *Discourses of Difference: An Analysis of Women's Travel Writing and Colonialism* (London, Routledge, 1991), p. 29.
26  Bird, *Six Months*, p. 111.
27  Mary Louise Pratt, *Imperial Eyes: Travel Writing and Transculturation* (London, Routledge, 1992); see particularly chs 3, 4 and 5.
28  Rod Edmond, *Representing the South Pacific: Colonial Discourse from Cook to Gauguin* (Cambridge, Cambridge University Press, 1997), p. 247.
29  Edward Said, *Culture and Imperialism* (London, Chatto & Windus, 1993), pp. 59–60.
30  Gauguin, *Noa Noa*, p. 20.
31  I am indebted to Rod Edmond's reading of the woodcutter scene in Gauguin's *Noa Noa*, which appears to me to be an important source for the development of Warner's theme at this point in the novel. See Edmond, *Representing the Pacific*, pp. 251–2.
32  Peter Hulme, *Colonial Encounters: Europe and the Native Caribbean, 1492–1797* (London, Routledge, 1992), p. 253.
33  Pierre Loti, *The Marriage of Loti: Tahiti* (1880; London, Kegan Paul International, 1986), p. 15.
34  Rudi C. Bleys, *The Geography of Perversion: Male-to-male Sexual Behaviour outside the West and the Ethnographic Imagination 1750–1918* (London, Cassell, 1996), p. 145.
35  Havelock Ellis, *Studies in the Psychology of Sex* (1910; New York, Random House, 1936), vol. 2, part 2, p. 8.
36  Bleys, *The Geography of Perversion*, p. 160.
37  Edmond, *Representing the Pacific*, p. 69. Polynesian sexuality and the way it was dealt with in European writing is also discussed within the context of beachcomber narratives and Melville's *Typee* in my Ph.D. thesis, 'A sea of islands: tropes of travel and adventure in the Pacific, 1846–1894', University of Kent, 1995. The theme of homosexuality in Melville is dealt with at length in Robert K. Martin's *Hero, Captain, and Stranger: Male Friendship, Social Critique, and Literary Form in the Sea Novels of Herman Melville* (Chapel Hill and London, University of North Carolina Press, 1986). Caleb Cain's article, 'Lovers of Human Flesh: homosexuality and cannibalism in Melville's novels', *American Literature*, 66:1 (1994) is an excellent examination of Melville's integrated use of the two themes.
38  See Robert J. Morris, '*Aikane*: accounts of Hawaiian same-sex relationships in the journals of Captain Cook's third voyage (1776–80)', *Journal of Homosexuality*, 19:4 (1990) 21–54.
39  The idea certainly occurred to the Maori, who repeatedly offered male

sexual partners to Cook's crew.

40 See, for example, Havelock Ellis's quotation of the missionary Turnbull, who found in Tahiti that 'there are a set of men in this country whose open profession is of such abomination that the laudable delicacy of our language will not admit it to be mentioned.' Ellis, *Studies in the Psychology of Sex*, vol. 2, p. 18. Rod Edmond has also discussed William Ellis's mention of Tahitian homosexuality in *Polynesian Researches* (1831) in Margarette Lincoln (ed.), *Science and Exploration* (London, Boydell & Brewer, 1998), p. 158.

41 See Cain, 'Lovers of human flesh'.

42 As Mark Williams also remarks in this volume, the topos of the 'dying race' was particularly strong in European representations of the Pacific.

# 11

# Mansfield in Maoriland: biculturalism, agency and misreading

## Mark Williams

Everything new belongs to us too.
> Patricia Grace, *Cousins*

James Clifford introduces *The Predicament of Culture* (1988) with a reading of William Carlos Williams's poem 'To Elsie'. Clifford sees Elsie, Williams's domestic servant with her 'dash of Indian blood', as a representative figure of 'the condition of rootlessness and mobility' produced by and identified with modernity.[1] Voiceless, victimised, observed and recorded by the detached, faintly disgusted eye of her employer, Elsie already moves among the 'urban archipelagoes' that have progressively disenfranchised the old orders of rural, native and traditional life:

> By the 1920s a truly global space of cultural connections and dissolutions has become imaginable: local authenticities meet and merge in transient urban and suburban settings – settings that will include the immigrant neighborhoods of New Jersey, multicultural sprawls like Buenos Aires, the townships of Johannesburg.[2]

Patricia Grace's 1992 novel *Cousins* opens with another Elsie, this time a middle-aged Maori woman, Mata, who has spent her life in menial occupations, drifting between worlds she cannot inhabit. In a sense Grace's response to the displacement and ethnic blurrings of modernity is akin to Williams's, as described by Clifford. Even in as distant a setting as 1980s' Wellington, Mata is a passive recipient of advertising for the impure products of global capitalism. She is culturally dislocated, cut off from the rich worlds of belonging signified by words like 'tradition', 'place', 'nature' and 'race'. She feels herself to be without family, culture, hope or future, broken away from her Maori heritage. Her rootlessness, her mobility, her lack of racial grounding are all signs of her fallenness, her brokenness – her modernity. Yet Grace's novel adopts a very different stance towards modernity from that in Williams's poem. *Cousins* judges modernity and its Elsies not from the standpoint of a distanced intellectual mourning the loss of traditional life but from that of those who have refused to become Elsies. They have done so not by ignoring modernity or retreating into an idealised version of the traditional past but by adapting modernity (albeit not without strain or loss or reversion) to their own cultural priorities and needs. *The Predicament of Culture* concludes with a lengthy account by the ethnographer, Clifford, of the legal battle fought in Boston by a native American tribe required to prove their identity in order to establish the legal right to sue for the loss of their land. Grace's novel recounts the struggle of Maori people for legal redress for land that has been alienated and for recognition of Maori language in the voice of Makareta, a character who can move fluently between the two main cultures in New Zealand. She rescues Mata as the novel closes and restores her to her family and place. Mata, the lost one, is thus viewed from a perspective utterly opposed to that of the narrator in Williams's poem.

At issue here is not the degree of dilution of 'blood' (of Elsie or Mata), or the problem of whether any culture subject to colonisation or the sudden impact of an alien modernity can retain a sense of its pure sources, but rather the matter of agency. If the traditional culture is to exercise any control over the forces of modernisation, it must choose how to assimilate modernity and adapt it to its particular purposes. As a character in *Cousins* puts it, 'It's not sticking to the old ways that's important, … it's us being us, using all the new knowledge our way'.[3] In this context 'the new knowledge' embraces not only the range of technologies that progressively transformed social and economic life in New Zealand but also the introduced cultural forms, including the novel itself, which have impinged so dramatically and extensively on Maori life.

Recent post-colonial literary criticism has focused on the ways in which contemporary indigenous writers have effectively contested the global reach of cultural forms, choosing their own deployments of modernism or postmodernism, and subverting the available metropolitan models.[4] It is certainly true that a process of revision and adaptation is at work in Grace's novel. The opening section of *Cousins* reads like a pastiche of high modernism: passages of interior monologue interrupted by the blaring intrusions of advertising messages as an alienated woman walks through an urban landscape. Elsewhere in the novel Grace seems to employ a species of magic realism when an unborn child is given a narrative voice. Yet in both these cases the capacious descriptive categories 'modernism' or 'postmodernism' miss the point of Grace's peculiar disposition of the techniques within the novel's total economy. In the magic realism exemplified by García Márquez, Rushdie and Carey such fantastic events are flagrantly metafictional but they establish a parallel with historical representation; rather than rupture the real, they serve to complicate and deepen its presence in the novel. In the novels of indigenous fabular realists like Keri Hulme or Ben Okri the departures from realistic expectation serve to represent the continued force of alternative constructions of the real, which include spirits, magical beliefs and visitations by the ancient gods. In Grace's novel the voice of a dead foetus has a place in the novel because belief in such spiritual presences has continued force in Maori life.

It is not that modernity is being denied or that some wholly nostalgic vision is being asserted. However, modernity is being judged from the standpoint of those who have accommodated it in very different terms from those of modernist intellectuals like Williams. How different may be judged by comparing the opening section of *Cousins* with another key modernist text, written just over a decade after Williams's poem and seventy years before the publication of Grace's novel, William Faulkner's *Light in August* (1932). The disgruntled condition of being 'off center among scattered traditions' that Clifford detects in Williams is more acutely present in Faulkner.[5] Like *Cousins*, Faulkner's novel opens with a woman, who has been walking alone through an unfamiliar world, pausing. Lena Grove, simple, poor, pregnant, is journeying by foot to find the father of her imminent child in Jefferson. Lena is patient, 'sheeplike', unhurried and unanxious.[6] Her consciousnesss is moved and shaped by natural process. She is part of nature, her being intimately related to the landscape. Her simplicity is uncorrupted; her fecundity connects her to the world of nature. If Mata is Elsie after the irruption of modernity into traditional rural lives, Lena is Elsie before that irruption.

However, while Faulkner's Lena Grove walks through a natural landscape observed and assisted by country people, Grace's Mata has been walking through a city, utterly alone and disconnected. Reminiscent of Faulkner, Grace applies a form of stream of consciousness – a literary technique usually associated with educated sensibilities – to a very simple consciousness:

> All day. But now in the middle of the tarry road she sat, pitchy-footed, feet and ankles speckled with spotchy tar, breathing in and out, huffs and whiffs of breath going to wherever they would go. Sitting. Middle of the tarry road. Middle of the undark night, which was orange coloured, lit by the orange street lights and the spiky stars.
>   Down, tar. Up, stars. Tar stars. Stars, stares. After everyone had gone there'd been one bus, one late bus. Running girl gone, boy on a bike gone. The lost kids and the old men had stepped into doorways, alleys, school-yards, parks, and gone.[7]

What connects Lena and Mata is the use of stream of consciousness to convey an unsophisticated consciousness, but Faulkner continually mediates Lena's thought through a deeply sympathetic narrative voice. Her comic meditations are accompanied by narratorial commentary, sympathetic but patronising, hence the epithet 'sheeplike'. Grace's method is closer to that which Faulkner uses in *The Sound and the Fury* (1929) where the first narrative voice encountered by the reader is that of a simple-minded man. The commenting narrator is not obtrusively present in *Cousins*; the negative associations of Mata's condition are a matter of inflection, surrounding imagery, tone. More importantly, in Faulkner's novels modernism is a means of conveying and controlling the disaster of modernity, but in Grace's novel it is a sign of the problem. Faulkner's modernism is a means of directing a consuming antagonism at modernity; modernism in Grace's novel is meant to reflect lost authenticities and is implicated in their loss.

It would seem, then, that Grace's novel supports the practice in current post-colonial historiography and criticism of emphasising the element of subversive agency in the reponse of indigenous peoples to colonisation. Instead of being passive victims of the colonising powers, the colonised are seen as resourceful, adaptive and adept both at parody of the dominant discourse and at constructing hybrid cultural forms of their own. This applies not only to contemporary writing by indigenous artists but also to the initial responses of indigenous peoples to colonisation. A recent history of colonial New Zealand argues that 'Maori did not passively receive Europe but actively engaged with it. They chose, adjusted and repackaged the new, in many respects into a less culturally damaging form.'[8] However, in advancing this necessary corrective to a binary of coloniser and colonised, it is easy to overstate the degree of agency open to the latter. Maori may, as Belich argues, have anticipated the techniques of trench warfare during the Land Wars of the 1860s and in many instances they effectively resisted British military power, but they were defeated, they lost much of their land, their language and their sovereignty.

In fact, the ability to fit new practices to existing social forms demonstrated the limits as well as the resourcefulness of Maori engagement with the colonising presence. In the early settlement period Maori tribes eagerly used new agricultural technologies to develop traditional gardening methods, selling the surplus produce to the settlers and even exporting to Sydney. But here the technologies could be easily grafted onto long-standing structural patterns of social life, work and economic activity. Maori communal ownership could not so readily be adapted to large-scale farming, in particular to the pastoralism that rapidly transformed and modernised the country in the late nineteenth century. By the late twentieth century the iwi (tribal) structure of traditional Maori life could still be found in the shearing gangs working the large stations (attested in one of the stories in Witi Ihimaera's 1989 collection, *Dear Miss Mansfield*), but ownership had passed inexorably to Pakeha (European New Zealanders) and the growing concentrations of economic power had been overwhelmingly at the expense of Maori. Above all, Maori struggled with mixed success with the central problem Grace rehearses in her novel: how to use new techniques and knowledges without compromising essential cultural values, practices and understandings.

Clifford is interested in the ways in which indigenous peoples have found what he calls 'specific paths through modernity'.[9] My purpose here is to look at the ways in which Maori and Pakeha writers have managed the local adaptations of modernism in their figurings of colonisation, modernity and each other. These configurings and reconfigurings make for an ongoing 'bicultural' dialogue in New Zealand literature, but they also illustrate both the 'impurity' of those local adaptations and the continual misreadings of the other that have characterised ethnic representations since first contact. Clifford argues that 'ethnographic texts are orchestrations of multivocal exchanges occurring in politically charged situations. The subjectivities produced in these often unequal exchanges ... are constructed domains of truth, serious fictions.'[10] This applies to the whole history of racial representation in New Zealand literature. If biculturalism means a process by which each party becomes knowledgeable about and at ease with the cultural understandings of the other so that two mutually respectful cultures come into being, then New Zealand literature, for all its well-intentioned preoccupation with ethnicity, gives little evidence of the achievement of such a condition.

The points from which modernity and empire have been observed are naturally very different for Maori and Pakeha. Nicholas Thomas observes that 'modernity itself can be understood as a colonialist project in the special sense that both the societies internal to Western nations, and those they possessed, administered and reformed elsewhere, were understood as objects to be surveyed, regulated and sanitized.'[11] The process of being 'surveyed, regulated and sanitized' was for Maori precisely the means by which the negative force of empire were most keenly felt, while for Pakeha it was the means by which the country was made available for orderly economic exploitation.[12]

For Maori, modernity and colonisation were from the outset of settlement connected, but they were not synonymous. Maori eagerly chose what they wanted of the former and fiercely resisted the latter once it became clear that land sales were compromising tribal sovereignties. As inventively (although not as extensively) as the Japanese warrior class who chose to use modern Western technologies in order to preserve what they saw as the essence of their cultural traditions, Maori from the earliest periods of contact were quick to take advantage of the technologies of a more developed material culture.[13] These adaptations were not confined to the material sphere. In their workings of Christianity and traditional beliefs into the hybrid religions of the prophet movements, Maori in the nineteenth century extended a process of negotiation and agency that allowed them to resist assimilation by refiguring the terms of the occupiers' discourse.

This practice of asserting sovereignty by smuggling the old discourse into the new one recurs in the literary movement of the 1970s and 1980s known as the Maori Renaissance.

For Pakeha, modernity and empire remained synonymous terms throughout the late colonial period when modernising technologies like refrigerated shipping encouraged national growth yet also reinforced imperial trading relations. Only from the 1930s when an explicit ideology of economic self-sufficiency appeared did these terms begin to come apart. Each strong effort to modernise the local economy signalled a break with imperial nostalgias.[14] For Pakeha writers since the same decade, modernism has been a crucial force in the ongoing efforts to decolonise local European literary forms by establishing an 'indigenous' tradition. Indeed, Pakeha New Zealand writers have adapted imported cultural material to local needs since the middle of the nineteenth century when they began to arrive in significant numbers. Ann Stoler observes that 'the assumption that colonial political agendas are self-evident precludes our examination of the cultural politics of the communities in which the colonizers lived.'[15] The colonisers in this case were not the homogeneous band of transplanted Britishers they are often represented as being, busily remaking the home country in the Antipodes. Colonial culture encompassed significant differences in political attitudes about race, empire and modernity, and among the descriptions of sublime landscape and romantic Maori are works in which unexpected shifts are already occurring in the structures of ideas and apprehensions of the new world and its inhabitants. Nevertheless, most colonial writers were slavishly imitative; the accents of Tennyson and the sentiments of Kipling are inescapable in colonial writing. Moreover, even among the writers most sensitive to the distortions and limitations of colonial constructions of otherness, we also find notable debts to colonial patterns of thought.

In 1907 Kathleen Beauchamp, a nineteen-year-old colonial, the daughter of a prominent businessman and banker in Wellington, back in New Zealand after school in London and anxious to return, went on a camping trip through the Urewera district on the East Coast of the North Island, travelling with companions through rugged country as far as Rotorua. Already she had begun to write stories under the name of Katherine Mansfield. For the moment she keeps a diary recording her impressions as she passes through scenes of recent historical violence.[16] The landscape surrounding the Ureweras has been cleared to make way for setter pastoralism; the visible scars of colonisation are unavoidable on the land. The memories of massacres related to the Land Wars are still fresh. The evidence of the results of settlement and isolation on domestic lives, particularly of women, are carefully noted by Mansfield. She remarks that a group of Maori seem angry, as indeed they were; she has stumbled on a scene of resistance to the government's application of a dog tax, a cause of considerable Maori resentment which still exists today.[17]

Mansfield passes through Te Whaiti where ethnographer Elsdon Best had run a government store some years previously. Best went on to write innumerable monographs which promulgated a romanticised version of the Maori mental world. Mansfield found the Anglicised Maori of Te Whaiti far less interesting than the 'primitive' Tuhoe, the last tribe effectively to resist Pakeha influence and the subject of a monograph by Best which is still in print today.[18] She encounters picturesque Maori, of whom she clearly does approve: 'at the door a beautiful old Maori woman sat cuddling a cat – She wore a white handkerchief round her black hair and wore and green and black cheque [*sic*] rug wrapped round her body.'[19] She passes near the scene of the kidnapping ninety years later of a famous painting done for the Tuhoe people by Colin McCahon, New Zealand's most important modernist painter, an act apparently motivated by continuing Maori political grievances. She passes through a world laid bare for settlement on the English model: 'Everywhere on the hills – great masses of charred logs – looking for all the world like strange fantastic beasts ... and now again the silver tree trunks like a skeleton army invade the hills.'[20]

Modernity, empire, settlement, ravaged and resilient tradition lay all around Mansfield. In her response to these scenes is to be found the source of the method she elaborated in her later fiction, which involved much more than a nostalgic return to the innocence of a colonial childhood and much less than a developed critique of colonial culture. Mansfield did not make herself a modernist by abandoning provincial New Zealand in favour of cosmopolitan Europe. What she needed was a means of distancing herself from the limitations of the colonial world while retaining the sharp focus of the massive collisions it contained. She carried her New Zealand with her to Europe, both the bourgeois New Zealand of her own family who frustrated and supported her and the wild New Zealand which seemed to her of interest because it was unformed, unruly, unsophisticated.

The key to connecting the discrete areas of experience encountered in Karori, the Wellington suburb where she lived in colonial gentility, the backblocks New Zealand of the Urewera trip, and Europe, was her own derivation of modernism which combines opposing tendencies and involves continual shifts in mood and manner. In her mature work modernism signifies not only a body of design-governing strategies – impressionism, a focus on the image, multiple narrative perspectives, musical form – but also a distancing attitude which allows her to confront and manipulate an experience of dislocation and homelessness that is both personal and historical.  The war and the loss of her brother in France merely consolidated what was already presented to Mansfield in the Ureweras in 1907, and the image of the charred hills was to 'haunt her for years'; they figure in her writing as late as 1921.[21] Her status as a 'little colonial' was both the source of intense dissatisfaction (Karori continually 'shout[ed]' against her capacity for 'intellectual reasoning') and the enabling condition of her particular rendition of modernism.[22]

Mansfield in 1907 was confronted by a variety of choices. She might have remained in New Zealand writing stories like 'The Woman at the Store' (1912), which, as Lydia Wevers observes, indicate what 'the writer KM might have been had she stayed in her colonial dress, and resisted appropriation by Europe'.[23] By remaining she would have been in danger of becoming a 'Maoriland' writer, the name used commonly to designate late-colonial New Zealand in Australasia at least until the First World War. It was the term used in the Sydney *Bulletin*, the most important outlet for New Zealand fiction and poetry in this period, where the name Maoriland or 'ML' replaced New Zealand from the early 1890s.[24] The cultural ties between New Zealand and Australia at this time were extensive, in spite of resistance by New Zealand writers to conscription into the 'horse and saddle school' associated with the *Bulletin* and in spite of an Australian perception of New Zealand writing as excessively formal, conservative, genteel – that is, English. In late 1907 Mansfield was publishing vignettes in the *Melbourne Native Companion*, indicating the attractions of Australian publication for an ambitious young New Zealand writer. Significantly, however, the vignettes were decidedly *fin de siècle* in style and tone; for Mansfield at this time the nineties meant Oscar Wilde and the Decadents, not the cultural nationalism and anti-imperial sentiment of the 1890s in Australia.

The term 'Maoriland' signalled the distinctive shape of an incipient New Zealand nationalism; it marked New Zealand's difference from Australia, its emergence from provincial status within Australasia. Significantly, New Zealand's cultural distinctiveness was associated by *Bulletin* commentators with the Maori presence. Arthur Adams, himself a 'Maorilander', reviewing a 1906 anthology of New Zealand verse, argued that it contained 'a distinctive national appeal and high standard' not, as its editors claimed, because of the strength of the landscape school but by virtue of 'the Maorilander's priceless heritage of Maori and South Sea legend, as strangely beautiful, as richly stirring as the mythology of the Greeks'. By way of this heritage New Zealand, according to Adams, will 'find its unique place in the world'.[25] This view conforms with the ethnology (exemplified by Elsdon Best) current in New Zealand at the time. It also anticipates in some respects the predilection among 1920s' writers for using Maori myth as a source of decorative signs of New Zealandness (much despised by a modernising generation of literary nationalists in the 1930s). Nevertheless, it touches on a cultural dispute about the status of the indigenous culture, its place in the formation of a national identity, and the appropriate uses of Maori cultural material in Pakeha writing, that persists (sometimes in surprisingly similar terms) into the post-colonial writing of the 1980s.

At issue here were the particular forms of settler negotiation of the imperial legacy in Australia and New Zealand. Nationalism is perhaps too strong a term to use of New Zealand in the Edwardian period; nevertheless, the literary cultures in the two countries already displayed quite distinct characters. It is in this context that Mansfield's use of the conventions of the *Bulletin* 'horse and saddle' school is significant. Ian Gordon, editor of *The Urewera Notebook*, notes the importance of the diary account as a source of 'The Woman at the Store'.[26] The debt of the story to the diary is extensive and detailed, yet vital sources of the story are not to be found in her observations and experiences during the 1907 excursion. The story is not merely an indirect transcription of experience. Whatever Mansfield's debt to her Urewera experience, the formal properties of the story are already governed by a deliberately literary intelligence. Mansfield is invoking the themes and style of the colonial story popularised by the *Bulletin*, especially the outback genre identified with Henry Lawson with its gothic naturalism and focus on the terror and isolation of outback life for women, as a means of testing a possible allegiance. She is not simply guying a prominent style and a manner of representing colonial experience, 'adapt[ing] colonial dress and then subvert-[ing] it';[27] rather she is experimenting with the style, exploring its limits, taking what she needs and rejecting that which does not suit her purposes. Mansfield's distance from the outback school she here adopts is demonstrated by the venue she chose for publication: the story was published by Murry in *Rhythm*.

Bridget Orr argues that the *Urewera Notebook* reflects the ethnology of colonial travel literature and observes that Mansfield is less the subversive deconstructor of the dominant forms of colonial thought, as W. H. New and Lydia Wevers have argued, than a 'colonial mimic whose participation in advanced metropolitan culture is both ambivalent and constantly under threat'.[28] Orr questions particularly whether Mansfield 'rebelled against racial bias'.[29] The vignettes in the *Notebook* certainly place Maori as part of nature – exotic, archaic, defeated. At times Mansfield seems to confirm the stereotype, as when she describes a Maori woman:

> She sits – silent – utterly motionless – her head thrust back — All the lines of her face are passionate violent – crudely savage – but in her lifted eyes slumbers a tragic illimitable peace – The sky changes – after the calm is all grey mist – the island in heavy shadow – silence broods among the trees … The girl does not move But … very faint and sweet and beautiful – a star twinkles in the sky – She is the very incarnation of evening – and lo – the first star shines in her eyes.[30]

This passage, certainly, is redolent of the dying race topos: the beautiful, doomed savage. There is also, however, a deliberateness in the writing, the conscious invoking of the heightened style of the nineties that modifies the Maoriland theme. A few months later, back in Wellington and soon to depart again for Europe, Mansfield wonders in her notebook 'Does Oscar [Wilde] – and there is a gardenia yet alive beside my bed – does Oscar now keep so firm a stronghold in my soul?' She decides that he does not because she is developing a 'wider vision' that includes, along with Wilde and Symons, Ibsen, Tolstoy, Elizabeth Robins, Shaw, D'Annunzio, Meredith.[31] Realism and aestheticism, satirical caricature and psychological study, a self-conscious style and moral force – all these are necessary to her art. The beginnings of a modernism embracing symbolism, realism and a trenchant sense of social oppressions, especially in respect of women, are here taking shape. Perhaps Mansfield's disputed status as colonial ethnographer or incipiently post-colonial subverter of empire is less important than the considerable uncertainties she displays and her willingness to express the range of those ambivalent attitudes and stylistic preferences.

In 1907 'modernism' was scarcely available to Mansfield, but this was also the case for her contemporaries, James Joyce in Dublin until 1904 or D. H. Lawrence in Nottingham until 1908. Their situations were remarkably similar in respect of the dislocated cultural land-scapes they inhabited: energetically engaged in modernity but able to observe traditional worlds. Lawrence, as Raymond Williams has shown, found himself 'on a kind of frontier, within sight both of industrial and of agricultural England' (although the distance be-tween Eastwood and Haggs Farm was surely not as great as that between London in 1906 and the Ureweras in 1907).[32] Joyce's situ-ation was closer still to Mansfield's. Traditional Ireland in the first decade of this century was mediated by way of the Celtic Twilight movement just as the old world of the Maori was mediated by way of Maoriland and romantic ethnology. Mansfield, like Joyce, in 1907 was working her way through the legacy of the nineties, adopting familiar mannerisms, allowing at times a florid excess of dreamy symbolism to invade her prose but also undercutting the heightened passages with sharply observed, deflating realism and with self-di-rected ironies. As a friend noted on Katherine's return from the Urewera expedition, the 'decadence' was already waning: 'she had come down to earth violently.'[33] Mansfield is not so much caught between stylistic streams as negotiating her way through them to-wards a new synthesis.

Maoriland persisted into the 1920s in the smug patriotism of popular journalism and the habit among 'Kowhai Gold' poets (*Kowhai Gold* was a middle-brow anthology of 1929 which became synony-mous with the vices of 1920s' poetasting) of adding Maori detail to their poetry. In the 1930s a generation of writers appeared in New Zealand eager to depict themselves as offering the serious begin-nings of a national literature; these writers might be described as modernist-nationalists. They rejected colonial verse forms, the decorative use of local flora, and the idea that romanticised Maori myth would provide the basis of a distinctive local culture in favour of a poetic predicated on an attention to the details – geographical, social and linguistic – of the local. They saw themselves as demythologisers of entrenched settler myths: the Edenic myth of God's Own Country and the romantic colourings of colonial ethnology. They disliked the vagueness, the nostalgia, the turning away from the actual of Maoriland. But while Mansfield rejected Maoriland in favour of international modernism, they did so in favour of a fiercely localised modernism.

The oxymoronic term 'modernist-nationalists' is a product of the difficulties of categorising a movement with complex local and international sources and indicates the multiple contradictions in the literary-cultural stance of the 1930s' generation. Contradictions inevitably attend such movements away from their defining moments in the metropolitan centres, but at their most sharply focused make them particular and forceful, not provincial. In the writing of the 1930s' generation we find a strong, morally charged emphasis on realism, a preoccupation with establishing a distinctively national kind of writing, a high modernist valorisation of tradition, a continual indebtedness to contemporary English literary fashion, a concern with defining and promoting a post-colonial consciousness. Like the Australian writers of the 1880s and 1890s they were regional realists, insisting on the need to be faithful to the local shapes of experience, language and landscape, but they were also deeply influenced by both waves of English modernism – Lawrence and Eliot, as well as by Auden and Spender.

These conflicting impulses meet in the stories of Frank Sargeson, who had struggled and failed in the late 1920s to write in the manner of the high modernists (just as George Orwell and Graham Greene had), and set himself, once back in New Zealand, to develop a style commensurate to the world that lay, somewhat disappointingly but inescapably, to hand. The workings of modernism in Sargeson's stories, even the 'classic' stories of the 1930s and 1940s with their unrelievedly colloquial and understated style, is much more complex than has been allowed. His writing is characteristically laminated with the residues of styles he has tried to master, those he admires, those he has vigorously rejected as well as what he has deliberately assimilated and consciously applied to his own writing.[34]

There is a famous passage at the close of Sargeson's 'Sale Day' (1939) in which the story's protagonist, Victor, in an act of indirect sexual threat towards a servant girl, another Elsie, plunges a randy tom cat into the open wood-burner and jams the lid down. The story is a quintessential expression of the masculinist-colloquial-regional style which Sargeson developed out of Hemingway, Sherwood Anderson and Henry Lawson and applied to the material of New Zealand life. There is, however, another possible source of the scene in Faulkner's *The Sound and the Fury* when Jason Compson torments the black boy, Luster, with two tickets to a circus which the latter passionately and hopelessly wishes to attend:

> 'I don't want them,' I says. I came back to the stove. 'I came in here to burn them up. But if you want to buy one for a nickel?' I says, looking at him and opening the stove lid.
>   'I aint got dat much,' he says.
>   'All right,' I says. I dropped one of them in the stove.
>   'You, Jason,' Dilsey says, 'Ain't you shamed?'
>   'Mr Jason,' he says, 'Please, suh, I'll fix dem tyres ev'y day fer a mont.'...
>   'You can have it for a nickel,' I says.
>   'Go on,' Dilsey says. 'He aint got no nickel. Go on. Drop hit in.'
>   'All right,' I says. I dropped it in and Dilsey shut the stove.'[35]

In this case, the power is all on the side of Jason, who controls the emotions of the other. In Sargeson's story the power is more ambiguously disposed. Elsie controls the stove and the chops that are cooking and can manipulate the heat, and by extension Victor's emotional state. For Sargeson, women as the repressive agents of puritanism hold power in a colonial society.

What is important here is the stylistic context. Sargeson's colloquial style and paratactic sentence structure are more obviously aligned with Hemingway than with Faulkner's style of modernism that develops the stream of interior consciousness and runs towards longer, complicated sentences and a focus on sensibility. This is the Joyce–Woolf–Huxley line, which Cyril Connolly calls 'mandarin'.[36] In fact, both colloquial and mandarin tendencies are to be found in Faulkner, as they are in all the major modernists except Woolf, who rarely ventures outside the upper-class world of sensibility. The two streams are certainly present in Mansfield. In Sargeson's story the colloquial-realist line from Hemingway seems dominant, the mandarin line forcefully repressed. Yet he too is struggling to inform reality with richness. His problem is that 'richness' is not immediately available in the social world he wishes to convey, as it was for Woolf in Bloomsbury and was not for Mansfield in colonial Wellington; hence he must indicate it as an absent presence, a something under the surface waiting to be noticed. That 'something' is not merely the inarticulate emotions or baffled sexuality which Sargeson's favoured victims, damaged by women, can express only as violence. It is also the rich, self-conscious style which Sargeson admired but eschewed because it conflicted with the self-restraint necessary, as he saw it, to be a New Zealand writer at mid-century.

Mansfield developed a modernism that involves a debt to symbolism as well as imagism, a concentration on sensibility without the elaborate stream-of-consciousness of Joyce and Woolf, and a ferocious line of social satire that moderates the impressionistic lyricism. Sargeson's fiction, for all its seamless simplicity of manner, is similarly marked by contradictory elements. He follows the Hemingway manner in his penchant for inarticulate male heroes, his spare prose, his interest in the psychic wounds society visits on the individual. But, while abjuring the inwardness of Mansfield's writing, he continually alludes to the uncomprehending forces within the self in the moments of reactive violence that punctuate his texts. Sargeson established himself as a geographer of the New Zealand experience by refusing to follow on from Mansfield. Later he attacked her influence and belittled her writing. The source of this antagonism and belittlement lies in his powerful attraction to the deliberate 'artificiality', the legacy of Wilde and the nineties, which she never wholly expelled from her writing.[37] In a sense Mansfield made Sargeson as a writer because the kind of writer he became was determined by his unconscious recognition of the force of her writing, which he felt obliged so vigorously and self-limitingly to resist. What is interesting in Sargeson's stance is the literary repression, which he projects in his stories onto characters like Victor who are Sargesonian might-have-beens, irreparably damaged by maternal and puritanic repression of the sensual self.

Modernism was never a unified concept or phenomenon, but a varied response to a modernity which arrived in different parts of the world at different historical periods with different intensities, with particular and local penetrations, seductions and disadvantages. The impact of modernity on the Irish Catholic bourgeoisie of Joyce or the colonial commercial bourgeoisie of Mansfield or the Maori prophet movements of the nineteenth century was utterly different. Moreover, the local accommodations of modernism often meant mixing quite different varieties. Distinct interpretations of modernism lie behind the symbolism of the Australian poet Christopher Brennan, the realist fiction of Frank Sargeson, and Mansfield's synthesis of both kinds. The trick is to attend to the particular resonances of local modernities and to negotiate the mixed kinds of modernism that appear at particular historical junctures. For Allen Curnow it was always possible to be both a mandarin and a colloquial poet. For Sargeson, the point was not so much to choose between plain and decorative styles of modernism as to inform his pared contemplations of reality with signs of the depths and possibilities within it yet to be figured in adequate forms.

A further complicating factor is that modernism in New Zealand was partly impelled by a reaction against the dominant forms of religious belief brought by the settlers: high and low Protestantism. For Curnow, the Anglicanism from which he lapsed into poetry was associated with the power of the father and, indirectly, with the nostalgia for an English 'Home' which he came to regard as enervating and corrupting of the settler imagination. In Sargeson's case it was mothers who carried the virus of puritanism which sapped the life force of sons and preserved colonial attitudes. For both Curnow and Sargeson, becoming a writer and losing faith were associated phenomena: both involved difficult breaks with powerful sources of authority, and both involved a particular sense of responsibility towards the reality that was 'local and special'.[38] Modernism here, then, has something in common with the literary nationalism of America in the 1850s: an assertion of the value of the new world that goes with the loosening hold of the puritan imagination. As in the writing of the American Renaissance, the writing of the New Zealand literary nationalists is accompanied by the force of a loss recently experienced, the gothic shapes cast by the rebellious psyche, the sense of the inadequacy of the world now accepted as the unavoidable realm of the real.

These rebellious sons were quick to usurp parental power and establish themselves as fathers. Sargeson begat 'the sons of Sargeson'. He also played an important role in encouraging the young Janet Frame to establish herself as a writer on her release from her years in psychiatric institutions. Frame had to struggle to assert the baroque tendencies of her modernism against Sargeson's austere and nationalistic version. Curnow chose a line of sons, not all of whom remained acceptable or tractable. The Abrahamic power assumed by these figures meant that James K. Baxter, Curnow's chosen poetic son, was able to commit a double disaffiliation by refusing not only Curnow's nationalism but also the strictures of his secularism. Baxter set about remythologising the land where Curnow found 'never a soul at home' by combining the beliefs and symbols of Catholic Christianity and Maori religious forms.[39] In Baxter's poetry and in the paintings of Colin McCahon traditional Christian images are continually forced into new relationships with the spiritual significances latent in the new world so as to explore the place of inherited meanings. Baxter himself, preoccupied as much by the resonances of displaced religious symbols as by the realities for which they once stood, prepared the way for a later effort to make the gods at home in Aotearoa/New Zealand.

The most protracted effort of contesting the secular temper entrenched by Curnow, Sargeson and C. K. Stead has been that associated with the Maori Renaissance, which began to take shape around the time of Baxter's death in 1972. In the fiction of Hulme, Ihimaera and Grace the dead ancestors have a real, sometimes vocal place in the world of the living; supernatural events frequently occur; and myth has a substantive as distinct from a merely decorative function. The gods return in Maori Renaissance fiction but, in spite of echoes of late colonial romantic ethnology, Victorian mediaevalism and Tennysonian plangencies, they are not simply the old gods and myths of Maoriland. Their status is somewhere between the self-consciously metafictional elements in magic-realist texts and the complex reconfigurations of traditional Maori cultural materials in the hybridised religio-cultural systems of the prophet movements. Just as Maori nationalist movements in the nineteenth century reworked Old Testament stories of the chosen people and millenarian aspects of Christianity to make local adaptations capable of advancing political and cultural programmes of the day, a century later Ihimaera's *The Matriarch* (1987) represents Maori life in terms of the Italian Risorgimento as well as the Maori prophet movements for contemporary political purposes.

Ihimaera's *Dear Miss Mansfield*, published in 1989 to mark Mansfield's centenary celebrations of the previous year, coincided with a period of intense national revaluation and reform of long-established economic, political and cultural practices. At the centre of the cultural component of this effort of redirection was the term 'biculturalism': the racial legacy of empire was to be replaced by a new relationship of partnership; Eurocentrism was to be replaced by a consciousness of New Zealand's Pacific location. A Labour government elected in 1984 had set about addressing Maori grievances. The late 1980s saw extensive efforts to reorganise educational and governmental institutions on bicultural lines. A tribunal was established to investigate land claims by Maori dating back to 1840 with the power to recommend restoration and/or compensation. In 1987 Maori was declared an official New Zealand language. The Te Maori exhibition, which toured museums in the United States during 1984–85, returned triumphantly to tour New Zealand. Ihimaera's Maori nationalist epic *The Matriarch* rewrote New Zealand history from a Maori perspective. In 1985 *The Penguin Book of New Zealand Verse*, edited by Ian Wedde and Harvey McQueen, represented New Zealand poetry in bicultural terms and implied that both the Maori and the Pakeha traditions in the book had achieved indigenous status.

Various agendas and ambivalences are to be expected in such a politically charged period and in such politically charged texts. The motives of Pakeha in investing in romantic constructions of the past are in part locatable in the general effort in the 1980s to revise New Zealand's embarrassing colonial past and fashion a new and distinctive national imagery. As with Paul Keating's multicultural Australia or Tony Blair's 'cool' Britain, David Lange's Labour Government's determination to purge the negative associations of the past aimed to project a modernised and updated New Zealand in order to reposition the country (and its products) in a new international order. The motives of Maori in this process of revaluation are both more obvious, having to do with long-standing grievances about loss of economic and cultural power, and more complex, raising unresolved issues among Maori about the relations between modernity and tradition. If *The Penguin Book of New Zealand Verse* represents these conflicts for Pakeha, *Dear Miss Mansfield* does so for Maori. A work written by a Maori nationalist in homage to New Zealand's greatest Pakeha writer, *Dear Miss Mansfield* contains multiple ironies.

These ironies are concentrated in the opening novella in *Dear Miss Mansfield*, 'Maata', which Ihimaera describes as an 'attempt to provide a Maori response' to the question of what might have happened to 'Maata', the novel Mansfield worked on and abandoned. The fictive answer given in the story is that the manuscript was buried with its subject and co-author, Maata Mahupuku, as a mark of respect according to Maori custom, one which countermands Pakeha respect for the product of a person, its separate status. 'It was something which, in Maori tradition, would have been returned at the tangi [funeral].'[40] Ihimaera's 'Maata' is semi-factual, being constructed around the search of the Maori narrator for the manuscript of Mansfield's lost novel.[41] The research method employed by the narrator, a journalist, moves progressively away from the objective 'Pakeha' historical approach to research, following instead the Maori way of proceeding by establishing *whakapapa* (genealogy) and recognising the appropriateness of not revealing culturally privileged knowledge. The mystery of 'Maata' as a person and as a text becomes the centre of the story, displacing Mansfield the cultural icon and rereading her relations with Maori. Maata, as the co-author of the lost novel, is thus the silent but active partner at the heart of New Zealand's literary origins.

In a sense, then, Ihimaera is reinscribing Mansfield's legacy in the bicultural context of the late 1980s. Significantly, Mansfield is described by the narrator of 'Maata' as 'the first, and perhaps the last, of the great New Zealand short story writers'.[42] Sargeson is not mentioned; presumably, for Ihimaera, he is not an important influence, needing to be neither resisted nor acknowledged. Sargeson's struggle is a Pakeha one to come to terms with being in New Zealand without the homesickness of settler culture. Mansfield has greater resonance for Ihimaera, partly because she took a small world and made the larger one take note of it, partly because her stylistic changeableness and the high colours of her prose are sympathetic to Ihimaera. Her lost novel also offers a face of 'Maoriland' that might be renovated, one in which Maori have an active if unacknowledged role in producing New Zealand cultural meanings rather than simply lending a decorative marker to the nation's signifier. Ihimaera thus offers respect to the legacy of Mansfield while subverting its received meanings and associations. Mansfield, who 'has always been associated, in New Zealand, with an orientation towards Europe, and away from [the] indigenous, Maori culture', becomes a means of unsettling the cultural-nationalist project, indeed the whole post-settler legacy.[43]

At the heart of the ironies and conflicts in *Dear Miss Mansfield* is Ihimaera's ambivalent response to the question Clifford raises about the Mashpee Wampanoag Indians, required to prove their identity in a Boston court: 'Were the plaintiffs of 1977 the "same" Indians?'[44] In other words, at what point does the hybridity celebrated by post-colonial critics but regarded with animosity by the defenders of indigenous traditions undermine the culture that is less dominant in the exchange? How much modernity can a traditional culture assimilate to its own purposes without becoming part of the modernity that would assimilate it? Mansfield is, of course, one of the forces of change that separate pre-contact Maori people from Ihimaera. By Maorifying a revered Pakeha icon he indicates that Maori may choose what they will of other cultures without compromising their essential cultural being. His sly tribute to Mansfield announces that nothing that came with colonisation is alien to Maoriness. This suggests not so much a hybridising exercise as one that grandiosely extends the essential Maori self – that is, the mental and cultural world of the Maori as it existed before European contact – to include all that it has encountered since contact. Ihimaera has indicated elsewhere that he regards the whole of modernity as potentially part of the Maori world, even claiming in an interview that the view he saw in New York from his apartment encompassed a Maori world too.[45]

When Clifford asks, 'What are the essential elements or boundaries of a culture?', Ihimaera seems to reply that so long as the central body of meanings of the culture is intact it has no boundaries or, rather, that its boundaries are so large and encompassing that they permit a seemingly infinite process of inclusion.[46] However, Ihimaera's statements on this topic are inconsistent. He has allowed that Maori culture was in vital ways broken by colonisation. The links to past, which he figures by the metaphor of a fraying rope, were damaged by the arrival of Europeans, many irreparably.[47] In what sense, then, is a work 'Maori' when it includes alien elements so explicitly and is written, albeit subversively, in a European literary form? What are the connections between the pure sources of Maori cultural forms and the contemporary versions?

Ostensibly, Ihimaera liberates Maata from Maoriland and claims Mansfield's legacy for Maori as well as Pakeha writing. Yet Maoriland returns in his own text when Elsdon Best (traces of whose ideas may also be discovered in Keri Hulme's *the bone people*) is cited: 'The mentality of the Maori is of an immensely mystical nature.'[48] Best here is referred to in a manner that indicates some ironic distance from his construction of Maori mental life. Nevertheless, Ihimaera's own stories and novels continually stress the spiritual qualities of Maori people. It is precisely at the point where Maori cultural distinctiveness is identified with mysticism or spirituality that the colonising legacy becomes most difficult to avoid because late colonial representations of Maoriness (most fashionable just at the moment when Maori no longer posed a serious military threat to settler expansion) were saturated with the theme. Colonial discourse thus effects a double misprision in which the Maori presence makes New Zealand distinctive as 'Maoriland' while romantic ethnology makes the Maori a tamed and spiritualised other, supplanting the cannibal savage of 'Old New Zealand'. In the 1970s and 1980s the mystical Maori returns, but this time figured in the representations of Maori by Maori. It comes, moreover, at a time when Maori economic claims were being advanced with especial urgency. The claims involved both the return of alienated land and a share of the modernising technologies and 'improvements'. Maori were seeking to preserve their traditions and to have a greater share in the modernity that had compromised those traditions. An ambivalence about the relations between those terms, in particular about the point of their intersection signified by the term 'hybridity', is therefore not surprising.

Hybridity is threatening because it implies that the 'pure' pre-European sources of the culture can never be recaptured in their original forms. To reach those sources a text like *The Matriarch* or *the bone people* must negotiate its way past the colonial and intervening representations of Maori culture. Is it possible, however, to recover what lay before the interposition of the new knowledges, some of which have become indistinguishable from Maori cultural forms with which they were conjoined? In their workings of Christianity and traditional beliefs into the hybrid religions of the prophet movements, Maori in the nineteenth century extended a process of negotiation and agency that allowed them to resist assimilation by refiguring the terms of the occupiers' discourse, and this practice of asserting sovereignty by inserting the old discourses into the new ones is employed by Ihimaera in texts like *The Matriarch* and *Dear Miss Mansfield*.[49] Yet in the process the discourse of the colonisers also insinuates itself into the hybrid forms in ways not always recognised, so that the demarcation between 'authentic' Maori cultural values and adaptations of imposed ones becomes increasingly blurred.

There has been no single Maori position on the issues of tradition, the past and racial essentialism; even the matter of customary fishing rights currently provokes vigorously opposed Maori responses. Ihimaera himself offers several, in some respects contradictory, responses rather than a single coherent one to the term 'sovereignty'. In laying claim to the Maori ghost of Katherine Mansfield, perhaps Ihimaera merely conjures up all the unexorcised feelings of longing and displacement associated with her name and extends them to both cultures. For Ihimaera as much as for contemporary Pakeha writers, Mansfield figures '*not* as a point of origin, nor as the founding term of a national culture, but as a phantasmic and sometimes troubling sign of displacement'.[50] In the context of her centenary and of a moment of bicultural achievement, Ihimaera thus questions while seeming to affirm the cultural-nationalist narrative by which, as Linda Hardy puts it, Mansfield will 'assume a position, in relation to the literature of New Zealand, not unlike Shakespeare's for "English" in general: a position of priority and pre-eminence'.[51] 'New Zealand literature' now includes that produced by the colonised as well as by those seeking to extirpate from themselves the taint of having been colonisers, but the cost of that inclusion is an extension of the unsettling about origins, sources and adaptation.

What was the nature of modernism in New Zealand? Its sources and peculiarities lie in a variegated reaction to the modernity so assiduously and efficiently applied by the settlers in the colonial period to New Zealand agriculture, economy, polity, legal and educational systems – to every area of civil life. Mansfield's modernism was part of a reaction against the modernisation that had made her father rich. It is rebellious, but dependent on the cheques from home. It is self-consciously international, but informed by local shapes, nostalgias and ambivalences. It is contemptuous of the smug provincialism of late-colonial New Zealand, but does not wholly escape Maoriland. Sargeson's modernism attempts to turn away from what he sees as the cosmopolitanism of Mansfield's eminent version of modernism, arriving at a modernism attentive to the New Zealand she abandoned. Cultivating a pared style, Sargeson cannot wholly suppress his attraction to an artificial one. Eschewing Maoriland's romantic valorisation of the Maori, Sargeson instead exoticises (and slyly eroticises) the Pakeha bloke. Ihimaera reaches back behind Sargeson's settler-fixated modernism to a Maori-fixated Mansfield and constructs a bicultural legend at the heart of Pakeha originary mythology. Yet *Dear Miss Mansfield* is caught between the modernist and the colonial in Mansfield. Ihimaera's text is subversive, hybridising, actively engaged in discursive politics, but it too does not wholly escape Maoriland. He finds himself repeating as well as contesting late colonial constructions of otherness.

In all these revisions of the literary past we find a series of engaged readings and misreadings, albeit at times collusive and even creative ones. Maoriland constructions of Maori myth, it has been said, enabled 'a nationalist vision which reinforced, rather than challenged, imperial values'.[52] Pakeha demythologising of Maoriland produced its own myths and blindnesses. It might also might be said that recent Maori redactions of their own myths have reinvoked those Maoriland whisperings. If colonialism is truly, as Nicholas Thomas argues, a cultural process, 'its discoveries and trespasses ... imagined and energized through signs, metaphors and narratives', then the ongoing struggle between the narratives of Maori and Pakeha demonstrates how the early figurings of the other persist long after the colonial moment has passed.[53]

## Notes

1  James Clifford, *The Predicament of Culture: Twentieth-Century Ethnography, Literature, and Art* (Cambridge, Mass., Harvard University Press, 1988), p. 3.
2  *Ibid.*, p. 4.
3  Patricia Grace, *Cousins* (Auckland, Penguin, 1992), p. 235.
4  See, for example, Stephen Slemon, 'Modernism's last post', in Ian Adam and Helen Tiffin (eds), *Past the Last Post: Theorizing Post-Colonialism and Post-Modernism* (Calgary, University of Calgary Press, 1990), pp. 1–11.
5  Clifford, *The Predicament of Culture*, p. 3.
6  William Faulkner, *Light in August* (New York, Vintage, 1972), p. 4.
7  Grace, *Cousins*, p. 12.
8  James Belich, *Making Peoples: A History of the New Zealanders from Polynesian Settlement to the End of the Nineteenth Century* (London and Auckland, Allen Lane/Penguin, 1996), p. 154.
9  Clifford, *The Predicament of Culture*, p. 5.
10  *Ibid.*, p. 10.

11  Nicholas Thomas, *Colonialism's Culture: Anthropology, Travel and Government* (Cambridge, Polity Press, 1994), p. 4.

12  Ian A. Gordon remarks that twelve years prior to Mansfield's Urewera trip in 1907 the Tuhoe people had threatened armed resistance to European road survey parties. Ian A. Gordon, Introduction to Katherine Mansfield, *The Urewera Notebook*, ed. Ian A. Gordon (Wellington, Oxford University Press, 1978), p. 52.

13  The Japanese salaryman, as Hiroshi Yoshioka points out, even today sees himself as the heir of the samurai in spite of the utter distance of his actual life from that of the traditional warrior class. Japanese commercial and popular culture is permeated by imagery of samurai warriors. Soap operas, products, advertising continually invoke the warrior as a quintessential sign of Japaneseness. The samurai ideal is deeply implicated in the desire to preserve cultural essentialism. See Hiroshi Yoshioka, 'Samurai and self-colonization in Japan' in Jan Nederveen Pieterse and Bhiku Parekh (eds), *The Decolonization of Imagination: Culture, Knowledge, and Power* (London and New Jersey, Zed Books, 1995), pp. 99–112. The modern Japanese salaryman who sees himself as a samurai is not that different from contemporary Maori politicians proclaiming themselves 'warriors'.

14  The emergence of an argument in favour of economic self-sufficiency through the protection of local manufactures was not coincidentally related to the emergence of cultural nationalism during the Depression and war years. Both economic self-sufficiency and cultural nationalism were promoted by the first Labour government during these years in the name of modernisation. In the 1980s another Labour government set about 'modernising' the country, its culture and economy, this time by breaking with residual colonial habits and dependencies by opening the country up to international competition, freeing the markets, and encouraging an innovative and aggressive local entrepreneurship in place of the old habits of looking to Britain as both market and protector.

15  Anne Laura Stoler, 'Rethinking colonial categories: European communities and the boundaries of rule', *Comparative Studies in Society and History*, 31:1 (January 1989) 136.

16  The diary was published in 1978 as *The Urewera Notebook*.

17  Mansfield, *The Urewera Notebook*, p. 52.

18  See Gordon's commentary in Mansfield's *Urewera Notebook*, p. 59. Compare the map of Mansfield's journey included in the *Urewera Notebook* (p. 32) with that in the recent reprint of Best's *Tuhoe: The Children of the Mist: a Sketch of the Origin, History, Myths, and Beliefs of the Tuhoe Tribe of the Maori of New Zealand; with some Account of Other Early Tribes of the Bay of Plenty District*, vol. 1 (4th edn; Auckland, Reed, 1996).

19  Mansfield, *The Urewera Notebook*, p. 38.

20  *Ibid.*, p. 34.

21 *Ibid.*, p. 30.
22 Katherine Mansfield, letter to John Middleton Murry, 8 December 1919, quoted in Clare Hanson (ed.), *The Critical Writings of Katherine Mansfield* (London, Macmillan, 1987), p. 1. Mansfield does not simply feel inadequate about '[n]ot being an intellectual'; she is here protesting to Murry that 'intellectual reasoning is never *the whole truth*'.
23 Lydia Wevers, 'How Kathleen Beauchamp was kidnapped', *Women's Studies Journal* 4:2 (December 1988) 6.
24 J. O. C. Phillips, 'Musings in Maoriland – or was there a *Bulletin* school in New Zealand?', *Historical Studies*, 20:81 (October 1983) 527.
25 Arthur H. Adams, 'Parnassus, M. L.', *Bulletin* (24 January 1907) Red Page. See Theresia L. Marshall, 'New Zealand literature in the Sydney "Bulletin", 1880–1930, with a literary index (volume two) of New Zealand authors in the "Bulletin", 1880–1960', Ph.D. Dissertation, University of Auckland, 1995. See also my chapter, 'Literary scholarship, criticism and theory', in *The Oxford History of New Zealand Literature in English*, 2nd edn, ed. Terry Sturm (Auckland, Oxford University Press, 1998), p. 701.
26 Mansfield, *The Urewera Notebook*, p. 27.
27 Wevers, 'How Kathleen Beauchamp was kidnapped', p. 16.
28 W. H. New, *Dreams of Speech and Violence: The Art of the Short Story in Canada and New Zealand* (Toronto, University of Toronto Press, 1987); Wevers, 'How Kathleen Beauchamp was kidnapped'.
29 Bridget Orr, 'The only free people in the empire: gender difference in colonial discourse', in Chris Tiffin and Alan Lawson (eds), *De-Scribing Empire: Post-colonialism and Textuality* (London, New York, Routledge, 1994), p. 165.
30 Mansfield, *The Urewera Notebook*, pp. 84–5.
31 *The Letters and Journals of Katherine Mansfield: A Selection*, ed. C. K. Stead (Allen Lane, London, 1977), p. 35.
32 Raymond Williams, *Culture and Society: 1870–1950* (London, Chatto & Windus, 1967), p. 207.
33 Mansfield, *The Urewera Notebook*, p. 90.
34 See Stuart Murray, *Never a Soul at Home: New Zealand Literary Nationalism and the 1930s* (Wellington, Victoria University Press, 1998), pp. 142 ff.
35 William Faulkner, *The Sound and the Fury* (London, Vintage, 1995), p. 255.
36 Cyril Connolly, *Enemies of Promise* (Rev. Edn; London, Routledge & Kegan Paul, 1949), pp. 45–57.
37 Mansfield once observed in her journal that when New Zealand is more artificial she will 'give birth to an artist who can treat her natural beauties adequately', *The Letters and Journals of Katherine Mansfield*, p. 26.
38 Allen Curnow, Introduction to *The Penguin Book of New Zealand Verse* (1960), in *Look Back Harder: Critical Writings, 1935–1984*, ed. Peter Simpson (Auckland, Auckland University Press, 1987), p. 133.

39 Allen Curnow, 'House and land', in Allen Curnow, *Collected Poems: 1933–1973* (Wellington, A. H. & A. W. Reed, 1974), pp. 91–2.

40 Witi Ihimaera, *Dear Miss Mansfield: A Tribute to Kathleen Mansfield Beauchamp* (Auckland, Viking, 1989), p. 54.

41 A fragment entitled 'Maata' has since been published in *The Katherine Mansfield Notebooks*, vol. 1, ed. Margaret Scott (Wellington, Lincoln University Press/Daphne Brassell, 1997), pp. 237–61. Scott observes in a note that 'Maata is based not on the real life Maata, KM's New Zealand friend, but on herself and the story is largely autobiographical' (p. 237).

42 Ihimaera, *Dear Miss Mansfield*, p.18.

43 Linda Hardy, 'The ghost of Katherine Mansfield', *Landfall*, 43:4 (December 1989) 427.

44 Clifford, *The Predicament of Culture*, p. 8.

45 Witi Ihimaera interviewed by Mark Williams, in Elizabeth Alley and Mark Williams (eds), *In the Same Room: Conversations with New Zealand Writers* (Auckland, Auckland University Press, 1992), p. 223.

46 Clifford, *The Predicament of Culture*, p. 8.

47 Witi Ihimaera, 'And then there's us: a Maori perspective', in 'Multiculturalism South: new cultural perspectives from Oceania', special issue of *Poetica* (Tokyo), ed. Yasunari Takada and Mark Williams, 50 (1998) 198–200.

48 Ihimaera, *Dear Miss Mansfield*, p. 41.

49 Belich argues that Maori constructed 'a new Maori religion of many variants, which converted European Christianity as much as it was converted by it … The conversion of Christianity by Maori was not solely a matter of retaining elements of tradition, but of developing non-European interpretations of Christianity, non-Christian interpretations of the Bible, and new elements that were neither traditional, nor Christian, nor Biblical.' Belich, *Making Peoples*, p. 223.

50 Hardy, 'The Ghost of Katherine Mansfield', p. 420.

51 *Ibid.*, p. 417.

52 Phillips, 'Musings in Maoriland', p. 534.

53 Thomas, *Colonialism's Culture*, p. 2.

# 12

# Settler writing in Kenya: 'Nomenclature is an uncertain science in these wild parts'[1]

## Abdulrazak Gurnah

The term 'settler' as it refers to Africa is now notoriously associated with the slogan of one of apartheid South Africa's most militant opponents, the Pan African Congress: 'One settler one bullet'. The slogan has the swagger of its time, when the apparently precipitate retreat of European colonialism from Africa in the period of de-colonisation in the early 1960s seemed to point to the inevitable defeat of the armed settler societies in the South. With the slogan, the PAC were signalling that they would not make deals with colonial-ism, and however outrageous their position might be made to seem in the duplicitous language of European civility, at least in its deal-ings with non-European people, the PAC was taking up what it saw as a more principled position than the broadly liberal fudge of the African National Congress. The PAC, like other nationalist move-ments which privileged cultural identity in the post-colonial period, may well have talked itself into political suicide as a result of this principled machismo, while the ANC talked itself to power.

Yet even before 'One settler one bullet', the term 'settler' no longer referred to the ambivalently heroic imperial icon of the early part of the century. The settler of that period was both a courageous pioneer and someone driven to such desperate measures by poverty; Christian warrior and religious fanatic; a civiliser taming the wilder-ness with unexpected sympathy but also being made uncouth by the intemperate exercise of power over lesser people. In citing these ambivalent pairings, and there are many others possible, I wish to emphasise the *range* of constructions of the settler in the imperial period rather than their dichotomous nature. These constructions were as much a response to the needs of narratives of self and other (including others found within Europe), as they are fragmented accounts of the meaning of the imperial enterprise itself. In the construction of the settler, the native was a subordinate and indistinct figure, who had to be subdued and, with luck and guile, made to work. In the upheavals in the colonised territories that followed the end of the Second World War in 1945, the 'settler' had increasingly come to seem the figure of imperial shame and indictment even within settler cultures themselves, connected in what at first were ambiguous ways to the notions of 'racial' and cultural difference and hierarchies which had resulted in the obscenities of the war. The war, of course, also politicised and armed the native, most spectacularly in Madagascar, Algeria and Kenya, and so recourse to the ameliorative benefits of European modernity in colonised territories could only be sustained with escalating violence.

But as I have already suggested, the ambivalent construction of the settler figure was present, *even within settler culture itself*, much earlier than the period after the war. In the case of Kenya, which is where my discussion will focus, this is evident in the writing. The starkly self-privileging accounts of European settlements around the turn of the century and over the following two decades were followed by less adamant versions that displace the colonial story into more familiar narrative shapes and that later become self-justifying and defensive. My argument here will suggest that this development was connected to the sustained challenge to the hegemonic discourse of late-nineteenth-century European modernity, which, among manifold outcomes, resulted in modernism. I will not be attempting to make the case that the *writing* practice of Karen Blixen and Elspeth Huxley, for example, shows the same characteristics as the 'high' modernists, but that European settlers in Kenya both gave account of themselves in the terms of established European discourse, and themselves offered challenge to it. They were, in other words, European, and their writing reflects the way that theirs was a subjectivity and culture of the modernist period. Their condition relied and turned on that identification as European, as did the form taken by their justification for the displacement of Africans and the appropriation of African land.

The challenge of modernism was not specifically anti-imperialist in the sense that war, conquest and empire demonstrated courage and daring. The movement can be considered to be pro-imperialist in its lament for the lost wholeness of a more 'classical', more balanced and integrated, period. The imperial narrative privileged the tribe and its difference, which is one reason why 'race science' and anthropology offered such useful rationale to the Victorian desire to legitimise hegemony. The desire could only be fulfilled by diminishing the humanity of the subjected other, which paradoxically provoked cynicism and pessimism about the self, to whom the other was a kind of pre-psyche. The howling savage was European man's true self, as Conrad demonstrates with such dreary assurance in *Heart of Darkness*. With modernism, though, it is the focus on the fragmented self that demonstrates that the idea of the tribe as organic community is fraudulent, is no longer possible, and all that the individual can do is hang on to those bits of the communal ethos and practice that make sense. The ambivalence in settler writing derives from these two sources, the tribal imperatives of the imperialist narrative and the yearning for a wholesome self – which, paradoxically, depends on turning the European into the native.

I will now return to the two senses of the word 'settler' I mentioned earlier: the ambivalent imperial icon and the figure of imperial shame. The second sense of it had intruded into my budding consciousness when I was a child in Zanzibar in the early 1950s, when the Mau Mau Emergency was being vigorously policed in Kenya. It was customary at that long-ago time to bring children to order by threatening them with the Mau Mau, as at other times we were threatened by the askari or the local madman or the snakes and jinns and cyclops that inhabited our stories. None of these figures was like us, most likely they did not wash and go to school and show respect to their parents or the elderly. They were the demonic in our epic of self and other. But why was the Mau Mau demonic, when they were after all only fighting to scare the Europeans off their land? In part the Mau Mau were constructed as demonic by the censored reporting of colonial order, of course, which focused on their brutality, their blood-lust and the degradations they subjected *themselves* to – on their bestial and irrational savagery, in short. But they were none the less recognisable as demonic because nightmare narratives of the barbarism of the interior were still potent in the popular imagination of the coast. For centuries the city-states of the East African coast had lived in fear of the 'interior' and its savage populations, though most of them were not too savage to be ruthlessly exploited at every opportunity through trade and slavery. The imperial construction of the Mau Mau could be comfortably affiliated to the narrative of the 'interior'; to a certain extent it endorsed and exploited the construction, although it was primarily intended for domestic consumption in Britain.

The settler in the meantime (or *setla* in Kiswahili), remained on the margins of recognition, so profoundly other that his condition could only be mythicised. The myth-making was not entirely an attempt to narrate what is incommensurable, but was also prompted by the way the settler was constituted in the colonial narrative of that time and that place: dedicated and implacable, evil when crossed, firmly taking ownership of the lands of the interior from the wild animals and the wild people, and making both pliant to his complicated desires.[2] Whatever the settler was doing up there in the Highlands, it was best to leave him alone.

The Mau Mau were finally defeated and their alleged mastermind Jomo Kenyatta was safely locked away, which left the settler striding across his Highlands again and Zanzibari children no longer troubled by the invocation of the Mau Mau. Into these happy scenes of childhood bliss burst a radio station. It was called 'The Voice of Free Africa', 'Sauti ya Afrika Huru'. Its naming was intended as a parody of 'The Voice of America', which at that time was bending our ears with its incomprehensible paranoia about communism.[3] 'The Voice of Free Africa' was broadcast in Kiswahili from Cairo, which played host to most of the independence movements across Africa, which was still largely colonised. The station must have irritated the colonial authorities, but it was never jammed, so they must have thought it was too crazy and extreme to bother with. There was a daily programme on that station called 'The Voice of the White Dogs', whose subject was colonial vileness. Its tirades were delivered with relish and loathing, the speaker driving himself to a frenzy of anti-colonial invective, and in the pauses between items there were bursts of drumming and martial music. It was on that station that we first heard the settler being publicly indicted as the visible symbol of colonial injustice, and in the process he was drawn near to us. Instead of being something incomprehensible, in the White Dogs narrative he came to seem more like our hidden and rejected selves: greedy, frightened, alien. There were, incidentally, a great many other 'White Dogs' which drove this station into a fury, but the barbarity of the settlers and the imprisonment of Jomo Kenyatta were our daily fare.

Before returning to white settlement in Kenya I want to establish a context for it by looking at the Algerian and South African experience, which were the more usual ones of brutal war and dispossession. Frantz Fanon, writing in the early 1960s and in the same era as 'The Voice of the White Dogs', has this to say about the French settler in Algeria: 'The settler's work is to make even dreams of liberty impossible for the native. The native's work is to imagine all possible methods of destroying the settler ... For the native, life can only spring up again out of the rotting corpse of the settler.'[4] This was also the height of the Algerian war of independence, at which time Fanon had identified himself so much with the FLN that he spoke of himself as Algerian. What he has in mind here in the essay 'Concerning Violence', in *The Wretched of the Earth*, is the conduct and consequences of French settlement in that country, despite the essay's subtitle of 'Violence in the International Context'. The first substantial appearance of the French in Algeria in 1830 was in a comprehensive war, an invasion, 'or rather, in the term of that period: conquest'.[5] In this context Todorov refers in *The Conquest of America* to the period senses of 'war' and 'conquest' in relation to the invasion of Mexico, which I think is relevant to the French incursion into Algeria. It was 'war' but was described as 'conquest'. It was conquest followed by continuous war for decades, with enforced dispersal of the native population to release land for French settlement. That period of 130 years until Fanon's summary of the settler's ideology above was punctuated by grotesque violence by both coloniser and colonised, and ended in the brutal excesses of the French forces in the Algerian War of Independence in the 1950s and early 1960s, and the equally brutal expulsion of the settlers after 1962.

The settler in South Africa was an agent of violent rupture in a similar sense, though the nature of settlement changed dramatically in the aftermath of the industrialisation of mining. It attracted migrants from sources unique to this part of Africa. In the early years of the twentieth century, South Africa was second only to the United States as the destination of choice for Lithuanian, Latvian and Baltic Jews fleeing intensifying persecution in the Russian empire

and the contested Baltic states.[6] In describing European settlement
of South Africa, the Afrikaner is often constructed as crazed by a
land-lust that was somehow sanctified by the shedding of African
blood – something commemorated every year with the celebration
of the Blood River covenant and given state symbolism by the
monumental circle of ox-wagons in Pretoria which was the euphe-
mism for Afrikaner triumph. This elides British involvement in the
brutalities of settlement, which is excluded from popular history.
Settlement of the Eastern Cape involved the British in what they
called the Kaffir Wars, which lasted well into the sixth decade of the
nineteenth century, only ending with the tragedy of the Xhosa slaugh-
ter of their own cattle in 1857. A young Xhosa woman of sixteen,
Nongqwause, saw two 'new men' in a vision. The 'new men' were
the resurrected Xhosa dead from the decades of war with the British.
Their message to the living, conveyed through Nongqwause, was
that they were not to plough or plant their fields, and they were to
kill all their cattle. They were to build new houses and new cattle
pens for the resurrection. When all this was done, there would be
two days of darkness, during which the European invader would be
swept into the sea. On the third morning the sun would rise from
the west, and then the earth would open and the pens would fill with
cattle and the 'new men' would rise. It is estimated that 40,000 people
died of starvation in the disaster, and that 150,000 were displaced
into colonial labour.[7] It is a story of desperation and hope in the face
of despair, and a tragedy whose dimensions are epic, but it is only
*one* of many stories of displacement and dispersal in the history of
European settlement in South Africa.

There are some striking differences between settlement in Kenya
and the two regions I have been discussing, Algeria and South Africa.
Different conceptions and self-conceptions of the settler figure result.
European settlement in Kenya was an entirely twentieth-century
phenomenon, and in the founding myths of the settler narrative
began as almost a kind of game. Hunters and aristocratic adventurers
like Lord Delamare wandered into the landscape, browsing the imperial playground as fancy took them, and found this part of it empty.
So they returned to found estates. This emptyish land had been
acquired not by war and invasion, but by the civilised process of
simply drawing a few lines on a map in 1886 in the aftermath of the
Congress of Berlin, though the claim was backed up by the sweatier

presence of warships and troops in the vicinity. But these were to intimidate fellow Europeans rather to subdue the natives.

At this time the British government was financing the building of the Uganda railway. One reason for this was 'high policy'. The occupation of Uganda was undertaken both to frustrate French advance into the region and to prevent the 'head-waters' of the Nile from falling into the wrong hands and threatening Egypt. The building of the railway was also intended, it was argued, to bring the East African slave trade to an end. In the daily business of building an empire in Africa after the missionary and explorer heroics, it was always a good idea to use the response to the slave trade as a justification. It ensured occupation of the moral high ground while the dirty deeds were done. The railway was completed in 1901, and the events of this heroic feat are immortalised in one of the canonical texts of the Kenya settler narrative, *The Permanent Way* by M. F. Hill,[8] although there were many other reminiscences and accounts, including Colonel Patterson's 1914 text *The Man-Eaters of Tsavo*. There is a powerful suggestiveness in that title, *The Permanent Way*, a celebration of both the permanence of the railway and of possession, and an understated triumphalism of enterprise and technology over ancient chaos, though it is worth remarking that the casualties of this heroism were mostly Indian 'coolies'. The monument to the construction of the railway in Nairobi Station names the Europeans who died, most of them through 'natural causes', but does not mention the Indians. Also, the attached Railway Museum has on display a series of remarkable photographs of the works which show Europeans in a variety of useful activities and only an indistinct melee of natives in the background. Yet the figures, quoted here from a triumphal account of British ingenuity and resourcefulness, tell a starker story: 'The cost in lives was 2,493 Asians and 5 whites. 31,983 coolies were imported from India. Of these 6,454 were invalided back and 16,312 were repatriated or dismissed.'[9] Elspeth Huxley, the main chronicler of Kenya settler experience, and whose text *The Flame Trees of Thika* (1959) I will discuss in more detail later, gives an account of what followed the arrival of the railway:

> Once the railway had been built, some method had to be found to enable it to pay its way. For miles and miles it ran through country either unpeopled altogether, or sparsely and intermittently peopled by nomadic cattlemen. There was nothing for it to carry out, and no cash to pay for

anything it might carry in ... The only answer the British Government could see to this conundrum was to invite in settlers who would cultivate unused land, introduce crops and livestock marketable in other countries ... This was the rationale behind 'white settlement'.[10]

This was not quite how it was, but then, as Todorov again has argued, what is important about statements concerning the subjugation of the other is whether they are accepted by the contemporary public. They are, he argues, 'more revealing for the histories of the ideologies than their production. The notion of "false" is irrelevant here.'[11] Huxley's remarks appeared in 1990, twenty-seven years after the independence of Kenya, in an anthology she edited called *Nine Faces of Kenya* (though it really revealed only one face), whose thinly disguised argument was the celebration of European settlement. It is worth noting that in the passage above the phrase 'white settlement' is put defensively between quotation marks, as if it is a misrepresentation, a misconstruction or even an act of shame. By 1990, settler narratives of dispossession of non-Europeans of their land had acquired a kind of elegiac and self-justifying woundedness about them. From *The Permanent Way* to *Nine Faces of Kenya*, the optimism and assuredness of *A Colony in the Making* (1912) and *White Man's Country* (1935) had given way to the nostalgic and abrasive *We Built a Country* (1961).[12] But, as I shall argue, this unsettledness was there earlier, is related to issues of white subjectivity in the time of modernism, and can be observed in the deconstructive complexity, the ambivalence and the self-irony in the two texts I shall study presently: Huxley's *The Flame Trees of Thika* and Karen Blixen's *Out of Africa* (1937).

A further difference between the settlement of Europeans in Kenya, and Algeria and South Africa, is that Kenya's colonial sponsors specifically targeted the upper middle classes. As Terence Ranger has shown in his 'The Invention of Tradition in Colonial Kenya', the 1890s saw the 'gentrification' of British colonial activity in Africa, which itself was a consequence of overproduction of brand new 'traditions' in Europe:

> While life was being restructured in Britain itself, with the rise of the bureaucracy and of the service traditions in school, army, church and even commerce, most European activity in tropical Africa, whether official or unofficial, had remained tatty, squalid, rough and inefficient. With the coming of formal colonial rule it was urgently necessary to turn the

whites into a convincing ruling class, entitled to hold sway over their subjects not only through force of arms or finance but also through the prescriptive status bestowed by neo-tradition.[13]

To encourage the right kind of settler, a number of financial handicaps were put in place. Even where Europeans who did not belong to this class managed to settle in Kenya, especially in the period between the two world wars when the rigidities of social distinctions were coming under challenge in Europe, they were either part of the 'officer class' or on its margins, and were able to reinvent themselves as part of what Ranger calls the 'new upper middle class' culture.[14]

It was, in any case, a literate and copiously literary community. I will now turn to my two chosen texts from this output in greater detail. They are in important ways representative of the milieu and its narrativisation. Whatever else they do, they give an account of the settler enterprise in ways that the settlers and a European contemporary public found acceptable. But my interest in them is also because they contain ambivalences which betray the larger uncertainties of the period, both at this point in colonial history and in relation to modernism. In a general sense, I have discussed how a narrative and 'history' of settlement in Africa was constructed through a discourse of empire, which in itself depended on tropes of difference and hierarchy. It is within this tradition of empire writing that the particular texts examined in this discussion find their contexts, but the discomfort with which they do so shows their ambivalence. I will look at how Karen Blixen's *Out of Africa* and Elspeth Huxley's *The Flame Trees of Thika* represented Europeans and their relation to African people and to the landscape they occupied. The differences between the two texts will also be explored – they were published at different times and with varying ambitions. I will argue that issues of authority were central to these narratives, in their attempts to construct a 'moral provenance' that justified ownership of the land. But modernist concerns also echo precisely because these texts have not resolved their relation to a discourse of Europe, despite or indeed because of that displacement, and this produces instability – and hence crises of resolution that lead to the placing of those quotation marks around Huxley's 'white settlement'.

Huxley's family were part of the between-the-wars migration, whereas Blixen was of the earlier aristocratic wave of adventurers, as the period furniture, the vintage wines and the crystal glassware that decorate her text indicates. Huxley's rendering of the bourgeoisification of the aristocratic romance of adventure has a familiar satirical ring reminiscent of the modernist horror of entrapment by the concrete and the quotidian:

> They came in quest of adventure, stayed to make a colony, and, in the process destroyed what they came to seek. They brought wives, and wives made homes. An inexorable process began. Patterned chintz replaced the sacking and amerikani spread over packing-cases to be used as tables; curtains went up over unglazed windows; china cups bought at local sales replaced tin mugs. Soon prints of the Midnight Steeplechase hung on mud-block walls, followed by the Laughing Cavalier and Van Gogh's sunflowers on roughly chiselled stone ones; creepers half-concealed corrugated-iron roofs; then came dressed stone bungalows with wide verandas, and tennis courts and stables, herbaceous borders, tea on the lawn. By stealth, civilisation had arrived.[15]

This ambivalence about a satirised civilisation that crushes the spirit, and which is a recurring trope in Blixen's *Out of Africa*, proposes a site of authenticity outside the fragmented self. It suggests a lost self or essence of self, and a wholeness that cannot be retrieved with Western discourses of modernity. It is an ambivalence also to be found in some modernist writing and practice. Hence in *The Waste Land* Eliot looks for an authentic lost essence in Hindu mantras, and Pound finds it in, of all places, the mean imperial delusion of an Italian fascist. Other examples are possible; I cite these two in an attempt to make my meaning clear. In Huxley and Blixen, the landscape and the African, when one is a metonymy of the other, represent both the unknowable and unchanging, that irretrievable universal that I referred to a moment ago, and the exotic, which, as Hayden White suggested, can be made understandable or made familiar tropologically.[16] The move from a metaphorical apprehension of the exotic to a dispersion of its elements is not logical but tropical. No 'civilised' (rational) argument can be put forward for dispossessing the native of land and freedom, but since the native can be represented as a metonymy of the wilderness – therefore in need of ordering and 'taming' – then to that extent he can be made subject to colonial understanding. The African is both part of the landscape, one and the same with it, eternally signifying that which Western discourse has banished through progress, and is also dangerous and disturbing, preferably represented as absent. If we accept Harold Bloom's suggestion that a trope is a defence against literal meaning in discourse, then it is possible to conceive the exotic as at once irretrievable essence and alien other.[17] So the landscape and what it signifies are simultaneously an exiled self whose spirit modernity crushes and a nameless 'other' that must be controlled or expelled.

The landscape is figured as vast and unreadable, or, to use Conrad's word, 'inscrutable'. It is a moment of sublime potential, if we take the sublime to be the failure of the imagination to represent what confronts it in its known order of meaning, and therefore through anxiety and horror arriving at a recognition of transcendence. Coetzee puts it like this in his essay on readings of the South African landscape: 'The very incapacity of the sensuous imagination, occurring together with the realisation that the mind has a standard by which it is capable of measuring that incapacity, is then reconceived as an evidence and a symbol of the relation of the mind to a transcendent order.'[18] But the landscape of Africa in European writing never has this sublime charge. Marlow's 'inscrutable' describes his alienation from the primeval disorder of the night of the first ages. For Olive Schreiner in the opening of *The Story of an African Farm* (1883), the huge emptiness of the Karoo signifies banality and indifference, a vast limbo for the implicitly European spirit whose striving for transcendence (of the Emersonian kind) ends in defeat and resignation. Landscape here signifies colonial aridity and emptiness, the Karoo as site of displacement and exile from Western discourse. Here is Huxley writing on the landscape of 'Africa' in *The Flame Trees of Thika*:

> [U]ntil you actually saw it and travelled on it on foot or on horseback or in a wagon, you could not possibly grasp the enormous vastness of Africa. It seemed to go on for ever and ever; beyond each range of hills lay another far horizon; always it was the same, pale brown grass and bush and thorn-trees, rocky mountains, dark valleys, sunlit plain; there was no break and no order, no road and no town, no places even: just marks on a map which, when you got there, turned out to be merely expanse of bush or plain exactly like the rest of the landscape.[19]

This apparent failure of the imagination to conceive the landscape other than within its own discourse expresses an ambivalence towards it. By the early decades of the century, the desire to claim everything for the Empire by renaming it had been replaced by a desire to know things by their true names. Both strategies express and demonstrate the desire to possess and acquire authority over the things being named. The quotation which forms the subtitle of this paper – 'nomenclature is an uncertain science in these wild parts' – refers to the perplexity and discomfort of not knowing the names of things, and then suggests that it is an African disorder that prevents their being known. The inability to read the landscape is a concession of its alienness and expresses an insecurity about how to represent it within Western discourse, and perhaps also expresses the invalidity of that discourse's authority over the land.

As we have seen, in reading the exotic as universal and prehistoric, the landscape and the African are metonymically linked. Blixen runs the two together constantly and with something of a flourish. The central yearning of *Out of Africa* is to find the true self in the other, and then to expel the other by representing its otherness: 'all the time I felt the silent overshadowed existence of the Natives running parallel with my own, on a different plane. Echoes went from one to the other.'[20] This moment of recognition is followed immediately, in the very next utterance, by the distancing of the native as exotic: 'The Natives were Africa in flesh and blood ... We ourselves ... often jar with the landscape.'[21] But the African also has to be disengaged from the landscape in order to be dispossessed of it, and because the process is tropological the narrative does not arrive at a crisis of contradictions. So Huxley, as with Blixen above, can run the two tropes of African alongside each other without appearing to notice that they cancel each other out:

> The Kikuyu, as a rule, were not much interested in their surroundings. Although they had a name for all the shrubs and trees and birds, they walked about their country without appearing to possess it ... The natives of Africa had accepted what God, or nature, had given them without apparently wishing to improve upon it in any significant way ...
>
> I discovered gradually that a legend existed to fit every bird and beast, but the Kikuyu very seldom told them to Europeans...
>
> The Kikuyu did not reckon time in years, new or old, or in any way cut it up into sections. It flowed on like a stream. They had rainy seasons and dry intervals...[22]

In all three examples, there are internal contradictions. The Kikuyu have no interest in their surroundings, yet they have a name for all the shrubs and trees and birds. The gradual 'discovery' of legends already implies their existence, which comes to light through dedication and the growing trust of the colonised. But in fact the legends were deliberately undisclosed – which is the real discovery that Huxley casually disavows. The Kikuyu (like other natives under European colonialism) made no temporal distinctions, but they knew the difference between the rainy season and the dry season, and presumably when to plant, when to harvest, and other little things of that kind.

Blixen expands this trope of the landscape as signifying essence to include the animals, and by this inclusion can speak of the African and animals interchangeably:

> When you have caught the rhythm of Africa, you find that it is the same in all her music. What I learned of the game of the country was useful to me in my dealings with the native people ...
>
> As for me, from my first weeks in Africa, I had felt a great affection for the Natives. It was a strong feeling that embraced all ages and all sexes. The discovery of the dark races was to me a magnificent enlargement of all my world. If a person with an inborn sympathy for animals had grown up in a milieu where there were no animals, and had come in contact with animals late in life ... their cases might have been similar to mine ...
>
> [Natives] were quick of hearing, and evanescent; if you frightened them they could withdraw into a world of their own, in a second, like the wild animals which at an abrupt movement from you are gone ... [23]

In both texts, in fact, figuring the landscape and the African in it as authentic essence irretrievably lost to Western discourse, and simultaneously representing the African as alien and inferior other, does not bring the self into crisis. If the first of these is an expression of unease characteristic of modernism, the latter affiliates effortlessly with the narrative of the exotic's inferiority. In the examples above we see the way observations by Huxley and Blixen about a group of Kikuyu are expanded to say something about Africa and the Native. These observations widen infinitely into Europe and its other – Africans steal, they have no word for gratitude, they are fatalistic, are resigned to pain, cruel to animals. Here is Blixen again: 'All Natives have in them a strong strain of malice, a shrill delight in things going wrong, which in itself is hurting and revolting to Europeans ... Natives have usually very little feeling for animals';[24] and here is Huxley:

No words for thanking people existed in the Kikuyu's language, and Europeans often accused them of ingratitude ... Perhaps gratitude was simply a habit Africans had never acquired towards each other, and therefore could not display towards Europeans; or perhaps Europeans were looked upon as beings of another order to whom the ordinary rules did not apply; if they wished to help you, they would do so for reasons of their own, and were no more to be thanked than rivers for providing water, or trees for shade.[25]

Far from appearing to be alien malaise to the native, Huxley imagines that Europeans are mistaken for bountifulness itself, whose coming and going is eternally incomprehensible and capricious. She imagines that the Kikuyu were too childish to understand that they had been robbed. My argument here is not that this writing is relentlessly incapable of disengagement from the imperialist discourse, or the opposite position that sees an inversion of that discourse's worldview – an argument identified by Abdul R. JanMohamed in his *Manichean Aesthetics*.[26] At several points in *Out of Africa* Blixen ironises her superiority over the native. For example, she describes transcribing a deposition for an African man, and when she comes to read it back to him to check for accuracy she read his name as it appeared in the text and he gave her 'a great fierce flaming glance' of exuberance and vitality. Blixen's text continues: 'Such a glance did Adam give the Lord when He formed him out of the dust.'[27] I find it hard to imagine that Blixen, a reader of Nietzsche and the writer of *Babbette's Feast*, could have been writing that without irony. My point here is simply to refer to the way the representation of the exotic is able to call on the resources of the narrative of non-European inferiority, while still figuring it as authenticity.

It is interesting to see how the film of *Out of Africa* re-presents this material in a contemporary popular context.[28] It uses additional material from Karen Blixen's life, and makes explicit what Blixen had left allusive or even left out altogether. More importantly, the film makes Denys Finch-Hatton, played by Robert Redford, into the central (male) heroic figure. He is familiar with the landscape and as mysteriously knowledgable about it as the native, although unlike the native he is not part of it. He is sympathetic, even elliptically critical about the imperial enterprise. 'This land does not belong to you', he says to the Karen Blixen figure at one point. It is Finch-Hatton who disciplines Blixen's romanticism, who looks mutely reproachful when she is excessively insistent on 'helping' the natives. To him the natives are their own real selves rather than a metaphor of the self's lost authenticity. It is, in other words, as if he knew all along that the settlement project was doomed precisely because it could not have legitimacy within its own discourse. The film takes Blixen's text out of its time, adds, through Redford's character, what a contemporary reader would have been unlikely to know, and then reworks and recodes the narrative, as Laura Kipnis argues, 'into representations of the past that make sense only as an attitude or necessity of the present'.[29] It does this in order to make itself 'receivable', as Todorov puts it, to its contemporary audience for whom the modernist idea of an unsettled ego and its lost essence no longer has an edge, and for whom the certainties of empire have already been shorn away.

In a discussion of J. M. Coetzee's *White Writing*, Benita Parry remarks of South African writing that it could only see the landscape as ahistorical and unreadable, and Coetzee, she argues, sees this as constituting 'a failure of the historical imagination, its inability to imagine a peopled landscape, thereby perpetuating the fiction of an uninhabited subcontinent and registering the cultural failure that is South Africa'.[30] The same failure is there in settler writing from Kenya, which sought to accommodate the difference of the other without in any way having to change its own world-view. In settler writing of this period, which is characteristically 'liberal', the native is essence at best, an attribute only capable of retrieval by Western discourse and always unstable and in danger of corruption. Yet this fetishised genuine universal could not allow the other to become a self, since it was necessary to dispossess the African in order to turn the landscape into a fallow arena for the self's subjectivity. Such a narrative could exist tropologically but was always in danger of imploding with its own contradictions, especially once the inevitable challenge was made.

## Notes

1 E. A. T. Dutton, *Lillibulero or the Golden Road* (Zanzibar, no publisher, 1944), p. 79.

2 In relation to this I might add that for some bit of cleverness or other, the school prize I was given at the age of eight was a copy of *The Man-Eaters of Tsavo* (1914) by Colonel J. H. Patterson. It was a story of the lions who pestered the construction gangs of the heroic Uganda Railway

(that is, the Indian 'coolies') and of the man who shot them – Colonel J. H. Patterson himself, of course. Somebody had gone to the trouble and expense of translating it into Kiswahili for the benefit of young African schoolchildren.

3 Perhaps also the CIA's 'The Voice of Free Europe' may have been the source, and the inspiration for this parody may have been the Soviet Union's irritation with that station.

4 Frantz Fanon, *The Wretched of the Earth*, trans. Constance Farrington (1961; Harmondsworth, Penguin, 1965), p. 73.

5 Tzvetan Todorov, *The Conquest of America: The Question of the Other*, trans. Richard Howard (New York, Harper & Row, 1984), p. 53.

6 Dan Jacobson, *Heshel's Kingdom* (London, Hamish Hamilton, 1998), p. 59. Lithuanian Jewish descendants came to play a huge part in the politics and culture of of South Africa, among them Joe Slovo, Abie Sachs and Nadine Gordimer. The parents of both Saul Bellow and Norman Mailer migrated to South Africa first and only later went to the United States.

7 Noel Mostert, *Frontiers* (London, Jonathan Cape, 1992), p. 122.

8 M. F. Hill, *The Permanent Way. The Story of the Kenya and Uganda Railway. The Story of the Tanganika Railway. Being the Official History of the Development of the Transport System in Kenya and Uganda*, 2 vols (Nairobi, Kenya Departments of State and Public Institutions, Kenya and Uganda Railways and Harbours Administration, 1950–59).

9 Ronald Hardy, *The Iron Snake* (1965), quoted in Elspeth Huxley (ed.), *Nine Faces of Kenya* (London, Collins Harvill, 1990) p. 51. Around six thousand 'coolies' stayed on in Kenya, to run the railway system, set up in trade, build houses for the Europeans and constitute the core of what were later to become 'East African Asians'.

10 Huxley (ed.), *Nine Faces of Kenya*, p. 69.

11 Todorov, *The Conquest of America*, p. 55.

12 Lord Cranworth, *A Colony in the Making* (London, Macmillan, 1912); Elspeth Huxley, *White Man's Country*, 2 vols (London, Chatto & Windus, 1935); J. F. Lipscomb, *We Built a Country* (London, Faber & Faber, 1961).

13 Terence Ranger, 'The invention of tradition in colonial Kenya', in Eric Hobsbawm and Terence Ranger (eds), *The Invention of Tradition*, ed. (Cambridge, Cambridge University Press, 1983), p. 215.

14 Ranger, 'The invention of tradition in colonial Kenya', p. 219.

15 Elspeth Huxley, *Out in the Midday Sun* (1985), quoted in Huxley (ed.), *Nine Faces of Kenya*, p. 104.

16 Hayden White, *Tropics of Discourse: Essays in Cultural Criticism* (Baltimore, Johns Hopkins University Press, 1978), p. 5.

17 Harold Bloom, *A Map of Misreading* (Oxford, Oxford University Press, 1975), p. 91.

18 J. M.Coetzee, 'The picturesque and the South African landscape', *White*

*Writing* (New Haven, Yale University Press, 1988), p. 54.

19  Elspeth Huxley, *The Flame Trees of Thika: Memories of an African Childhood* (1959; Harmondsworth, Penguin, 1962), p. 28.

20  Karen Blixen (Isak Dinesen), *Out of Africa* (1937; Harmondsworth, Penguin, 1954), p. 28.

21  *Ibid.*

22  Huxley, *The Flame Trees of Thika*, pp. 47, 80, 94.

23  Blixen, *Out of Africa*, pp. 24, 25, 25–6.

24  *Ibid.*, pp. 38, 40.

25  Huxley, *The Flame Trees of Thika*, p. 112.

26  Abdul R. JanMohamed, *Manichean Aesthetics: The Politics of Literature in Colonial Africa* (Amherst, University of Massachusetts Press, 1983).

27  Blixen, *Out of Africa*, p. 110.

28  *Out of Africa*, dir. Sydney Pollack (United States, 1985).

29  Laura Kipnis, 'The phantom twitchings of an amputated limb: sexual spectacle in the post-colonial epic', *Wide Angle: A Film Quarterly of Theory, Criticism and Practice*, 11:4 (October 1989) 44.

30  Benita Parry, Review of J. M. Coetzee, *White Writing*, in *Research in African Literatures*, 22:4 (Winter 1991) 198.

# 13

# Modernism's empire: Australia and the cultural imperialism of style

**Bill Ashcroft and John Salter**

In 1997 a Constitutional Convention was held in Canberra to decide the terms of a referendum on an Australian Republic.[1] Nearly a hundred years after federation it seemed that finally Australia was to become independent. Unresolved at the time of that Convention, however, and still unresolved today, is the status of Aboriginal land. Some years after the Mabo and Wik cases, which overturned the official legitimation of colonial occupation and the alienation of Aboriginal land, the results for indigenous owners have been negligible.[2] More than two centuries after its colonisation Australia remains locked in a peculiarly post-colonial predicament, a predicament revolving around the definition of Australia, the relationship of Australians to place, and the heterogeneous provenance, if not the very identity of Australian culture. This irresolution, encapsulated in the image of a reluctant republic and its reluctant reconciliation, signifies the persistent ambivalence of a white post-colonial culture whose very terms of reference are both unstable and under constant negotiation.

The filiative dynamic of a settler culture ensures that 'imperial' cultural discourse appears seamlessly transported to the colonised society. But that appearance obscures a ceaseless and unresolved struggle over representation. One of the more perennial arguments in post-colonial studies centres on the post-coloniality of settler colonies. The advanced character of their economies and political structures leads to the misapprehension that the cultures are 'first world' and therefore indistinguishable from the European model. However, we find in these cultures the most complex and ambivalent struggles over strategies of cultural self-determination and self-representation.

The problem of place and identity that Australia faces two hundred years after white settlement, is one for which the question of Australian modernity remains a highly indicative example. The unresolved problem of Aboriginal land is not simply a problem of racial and cultural exclusion; it is a failure of inherited discourses of spatiality to conceive adequately the nature of Australian place. This predicament emerges directly from the unreflective use of Eurocentric and imperial discourse to describe and define the energies of a post-colonial culture. Australia was settled at the climax of the Enlightenment; it became a federation when European modernism began to overturn many of the values of that Enlightenment. Yet understanding Australian cultural development in these terms, with reference points firmly embedded in European history, misapprehends the peculiar cultural dynamic generated in a colonised society from the moment of colonisation. The significance of empire in Australian modernism lies less in the historical and cultural influences of this European cultural movement than in the very employment of Eurocentric discourse to understand post-colonial cultural reality. This has seemed uncontroversial to generations of Australians who saw themselves as British. Yet for the heterogeneous and dislocated (as well as invaded) populations of Australian cultural life, such discourse has not only proved unhelpful, but has hindered understanding of how Australian reality could be represented. The lingering assumption that Australian culture is a transported version of the British model has led directly to the political and cultural irresolution which plagues Australia today.

The high-cultural discourse of modernism, with its imposition of a set of largely uncontested parameters upon a non-European cultural reality, may be seen to be metonymic of the operation of imperial domination. Modernity and modernism are rooted in empire. But the dissemination of 'modernism' as a cultural category throughout the dominions, and particularly in Australia during the first half of the century, consolidated the circulation of Eurocentric cultural power. The use of the category 'modernism' in Australia ensured that cultural production in the first decades of the century which used features of the stylistic innovation prevalent in Europe were seen to 'inherit', 'mimic', 'copy' or 'follow' European cultural fashion. On the contrary, however, the imposition of the term 'modernism' effectively submerged the specific energies of the cultural activity occuring at the time. The disparate collection of practices in art, literature and architecture that were regarded as 'modern' were engaged in the project of Australian artists and writers to discover a way of constituting their post-colonial reality, particularly their relationship with place, and to discover a creative articulation of Australian difference.

Modernity and modernism are, of course, very different things. But they are both, in different ways, dominated by historicism. To be 'modern' is to have a certain purchase on history. To be modern is to be 'civilised', ground-breaking, forward-looking. Both modernity and modernism are evidence, both discursively and historically, of the profound cultural power of European civilisation. Modernity is both an epoch and a discourse. As an epoch it coincides with those great shifts in European history, the Renaissance, the Reformation and the discovery of the New World, which heralded the rise of Europe to world cultural and political prominence. Europe constructed itself as 'modern' and constructed the non-European colonised cultures as 'traditional', 'primitive', 'pre-modern'. As a discourse, modernity identifies those major discontinuities separating modern social institutions from traditional social orders, such as the pace of change, the scope of change, and the nature of modern institutions. The advent of various technologies inititated an ever-accelerating pace of change, and the scope of this change came to effect the whole globe.[3] But above all the discourse of modernity gave rise to those strategies which enabled European society to consolidate its position as 'civilised' and culturally dominant.

Modernism, on the other hand, represents the contemporary paradox of modernity. For the rediscovery of the 'primitive', around the turn of the century, in exhibitions of those artefacts plundered from colonised societies, stimulated artists and writers to reject nineteenth-century traditions of naturalism, of consensus between author and reader, to disengage from bourgeois values and adopt complex and difficult styles which both dismantled and critiqued traditional forms of representation. Such 'primitive' images seemed to release European artists and writers from those very principles of Enlightenment rationality and representation which lay at the heart of modernity itself. This recirculation of the primitive representations of the colonised back to the heart of empire – as modernism – is a key paradox of European cultural dominance at the height of imperial power. In Australia, where the 'barbaric' and 'primitive' were precisely what civilisation and culture were designed to resist, this created confusion over the ways in which Australian difference could be represented. But such recirculation shows modernism to be a feature of what Pratt calls 'transculturation'.[4] Modernism is a discourse of the contact zone. In its culturally and politically disruptive dynamic, we see one of the clearest examples of the ambivalent nature of colonial discourse.

This transcultural paradox becomes compounded, however, when high-cultural modernism recirculates back into the Empire as a culturally dominant discourse. Here we discover that the hybridity of the contact zone is traversed by relations of power which cannot be accommodated by notions of cultural heterogeneity. Habermas has pointed out that the term 'modern' arises at historical junctures at which the relationship with the past and with tradition comes under review.[5] 'Modern' describes an epoch's consciousness of its link to the past and a simultaneous difference, or break, or transition from it. The established modern itself becomes, in its turn, the object of renewal and replacement. But replacement is not simply a question of outmoded styles. As T. S. Eliot explains, the placement of the 'really new' work in the tradition may be a 'new planting' that re-orders the existing order of the (metaphorical) garden of culture.[6] The modern never indicates a fixed historical reference point.

'Modernism' is, above all, a way of talking rather than a way of being or doing. This identity as a language-game is of profound significance to post-colonial societies, because it is language, above all, within which representation of all kinds is grounded. Wittgenstein's term 'language-game' is somewhat more useful than the term 'discourse' because language-game suggests the relative unboundedness and interrelatedness of speaking positions and practices involved in 'modernism'.[7] Like any category, 'modernism' is like a rope made up of many overlapping and intertwining speaking practices, but there is no essential thread, no essential quality which is present in all the practices described by the term.

In discursive terms, the range of diverse practices which meet the rules of inclusion into the 'modern' is vast, and modernism itself a huge and baggy monster. Modernism is most often defined in terms of what it is not rather than what it is. As T. S. Eliot wrote, in his 1923 review of *Ulysses*, 'the ordered, stable and inherently meaningful world view of the nineteenth century could not accord with the immense panorama of futility and anarchy which is contemporary history'.[8] In literature the distinctions may become relatively specific. In their attempt to throw off the burden of the realist novel, says Barth, modernist writers adopted 'the radical disruption of linear flow of narrative; the frustration of conventional expectations concerning unity and coherence of plot and character'.[9] However, the tendency for the modernism language game to become a universalist, essentialist, inclusivist and Eurocentric way of talking may be found by any random selection of commentaries of modernism. In *Mapping Literary Modernism*, Ricardo Quinones asserts that, 'Not only in the central consciousness of Modernist works but in the total register of their sensibilities we find a new complexity at work. A whole new range of experience, with new objects, new attitudes and different stylistic levels, is thus able to be presented in Modern literature.'[10] Such assertions, of a 'central consciousness', the existence of a 'total register' of modernist sensibilities, a 'new complexity', are by no means an unusual consequence of the assumption of an ontological specificity in modernist works, an assumption which dissolves under even the most cursory analysis. Although most critics would concede the heterogeneity of modernist practices, the term 'modernism' continually reasserts itself as a monolith in cultural discourse.

## The myth of 'belatedness'

When this universalist and monolithic category is deployed outside Europe the hegemonic character of its use becomes more obvious. The very term 'modernism' categorises cultural production in set and even stereotypical ways. The conventional interpretation of postwar modernism in Australia is dominated by the myth of 'belatedness'. According to this theory, modernism did not really appear in Australia until after the First World War, when modernist styles in painting (and very little modernist literature) were adopted with only a superficial understanding of the political and aesthetic issues at stake in the modern revolution. Australians were isolated and provincial, and 'hardly any Australians, in the first decades of this century, understood what was at stake in modernism, or could conceive the enormous pressure under which immediately pre-war modern art was formed.'[11] Thus modernism was regarded either as an 'incomprehensible aberration' or as 'superficially chic and exciting'. 'This lack of access to the tradition from which the necessity of modern art arose meant that modernism tended to arrive in Australia as a style (in the modern sense) without content. It looked new and clever and it did not really matter that no one knew what it was for.'[12] Consequently 'modernism' was soon popular in interior decoration and in popular culture. 'Anything more substantial was inevitably decades late, so that artists struggled to understand movements that were already worn out and superseded by others.'[13] In short, the modernism of the 1920s and 1930s in Australia arrived late, was a superficial mimicry of the European cultural revolution that spawned it, and was soon cowed and demoralised by a powerful conservative nationalism which preferred the Heidelberg landscape tradition in art and realism and narrative in writing.

A contrary, though similarly historicist, view of Australian modernism offered by Andrew Milner suggests that in fact Australia was modern before modernity, and now postmodern before postmodernity.[14] This is not a modernity characterised by the sophistication of its high culture, its radical or avant-garde intelligentsia. Rather, it is the *absence* of these things, the emphasis on the precultural social environment determined by its nature and landscape which establishes Australia's radical modernity. It is perhaps not too reductive to say that this view defines Australian modernity in terms of the 'primitive' from which European modernism drew its inspiration. Australian modernism is embedded in that primitivism which remains the source energy of modernism's break with bourgeois values and traditional expressive forms.

David Carter, attempting to uncover the prehistory of Milner's claim, is intrigued by the very *excess* of the arguments in cultural commentary which turn 'to metropolitan modernism in order to define Australian distinctiveness'.[15] Rather than a view of Australian belatedness 'in which modernity comes to be associated with an always-lacking cultural maturity: we were not yet quite modern, we had not yet grown up' – the discourse of modernity itself allowed 'the possibility of a radical originality in the peripheral culture in which the very absence of history makes modernity peculiarly its own'.[16] This allows us to reread Marcus Clarke's description of the 'weird melancholy' and 'funereal gloom' of the Australian landscape, for instance, through its appropriation of Edgar Allan Poe, not in terms of Romantic gothic, or settler alienation, but as 'the primeval discovered as the modern, and vice versa, the prehistoric as the unprecedented, "the strange scribblings of nature learning how to write"'.[17]

Consequently, critics such as A. A. Phillips, who coined the term 'cultural cringe' as the quintessential description of belatedness, can be seen to define a progressively modernising realism which 'defines both the original and originary modernity of Australian culture and its *continuing* modernity (its anti-belatedness)'.[18] The generation of New Criticism-trained critics of the 1960s, such as Harry Heseltine, repeat this rejection of belatedness, claiming that the qualities which 'define the very modernity of the modern also define the very "Australianness of Australian writing": that peculiarly modern element in modern literature which … Australian literature so early laid hold on'. From the beginning Australian literature has known nihilism, nothingness, the 'horror of primal experience', 'the terror at the basis of being'; and these are its recurrent concerns, from Marcus Clarke to Lawson to A. D. Hope and Patrick White.[19]

These directly opposed arguments about Australian modernism demonstrate very clearly how a language game can generate conflicting hermeneutic possibilities. For what is absent from either consideration of Australian cultural life is any problematising of the term 'modernism', or even the 'modern' itself. The argument about Australian modernity circulates entirely within a discourse which itself remains unquestioned. The beginning of a deconstruction of the modernist discourse in Australia is the question, 'what does it mean to be modern, to whom is this important?' The Milner argument about Australia's modernity attempts a radical shift in our understanding of cultural dominance and cultural description. The Carter elaboration demonstrates how Milner's argument lies on a trajectory, even a tradition, of Australian cultural commentary. But what is most significant to any view of the link between cultural discourse and imperial power lies precisely in what is left out of these arguments.

These propositions about the pre-modern emergence of Australian modernity are at base arguments about the irrelevance and inapplicability of imported cultural categories to post-colonial practices. This is, of course, a regular point of contention in post-colonial theory, because dominant discourses, from language itself to disciplines and cultural practices of all kinds, may be transformed into culturally relevant tools by a process of appropriation and interpolation. But universalist categories such as modernism have shown themselves to be very resistant to appropriation because they identify sites of social and political controversy as well as modes of cultural practice. The view of modernism as a social phenomenon (despite the limitation of the term to a high-culture debate) sees the idea of the modern as the site of a struggle over the nature of Australian identity itself. 'Modernism' located a hotly contested battle between sides which themselves had no clear idea about what the term entailed. Indeed so strong was the universalising force of the term as a social category that questions about artistic intention or content became virtually irrelevant.

### The 'quarantined' culture

By 1913, the year Stravinsky's *The Rite of Spring* was first performed, the year of the Armory exhibition in New York, a date often taken as a high point of modernist art, there was ample evidence in Australian society of a nation becoming 'modern'. A highly urbanised, coastal and city-dwelling people had an increasing experience of mechanisation and material modernisation. But in terms of modernist artistic and literary developments, we find a country which John Williams has described as effectively 'quarantined'. 'By about 1921 … an improvised, unstated but de facto cultural quarantine existed in Australia. It was propagated by an inchoate grouping of racial supremacists, anti-Semites, anti-bolshevists, protectionists, anti-industrialisers and the leaders of an élitist and conservative art-world establishment.'[20] Australian high culture, 'which by default seems to have become almost synonymous with visual art',[21] existed on a plane of its own, quite divorced from the relatively unselfconsciously modernising urban culture. Even those most virulently opposed to 'modernism' took for granted the changes and benefits of modernisation. This in itself alerts us to the elitist confinement of 'modernist' discourse.

'Modernism' became the focus of a battle over what it meant to be Australian and what it was about Australian culture that might be constituted as separate and different. On the one hand a conservative, imperial nationalism institutionalised the impressionism of the nineties as the indigenous Australian art and villified the modern as 'French', unpatriotic, degenerate, superficial and even Jewish.[22] On the other, according to this thesis, a demoralised, defensive avant-garde in Australian art fought a losing battle to import modernist style into Australia until, like Roy de Maistre, they were driven out to seek refuge in London.

According to Williams, the dominance of the nationalist agrarian school of Australian art coincided with the election of the Bruce Page government in 1923, which 'marked the last inflow of modernish art to Australia until the eve of the second world war'.[23] That the nation was becoming a cultural desert at this time was confirmed, according to Williams, by the 1923 exhibition of Australian paintings held in London, 'whose old-fashioned provincialism was praised as a virtue by Lionel Lindsay – proof for him that Australians had preserved themselves from 'the revolutionary manias of a rotted world'.[24] 'The isolationist thinking that underwrote that exhibition came naturally enough to a nation remote from world centres; one whose most potent visual and verbal images often centred upon notions of the virtue of isolation.'[25]

If we analyse the language of the 'quarantined culture' thesis, we see how comprehensively it recapitulates the language of imperial discourse. Modern art, like modernism itself, was *exported* to a nation which dwelt on the edge of the civilised world, a nation whose agrarian preferences sequestered it from the modern, which was by definition European. Whatever the events of the time – and there is no doubt that a conservative government provided the background for a conservative resistance to modernist art – the language of isolation, marginality, provincialism, backwardness is precisely the way in which the post-colonial society exists in the gaze of empire, what Lacan calls the gaze of the *grande autre*. What transpires in the elaboration of this thesis is a process of othering, and this process is driven by an absence of any examination of the term 'modernism' itself. 'Modern' remains the signifier of European dominance and civilisation, a term of transparent value and desirability. The concept of the modern retains the same imperial function it has had for five centuries – a focus of 'civilisation' and advancement, a shimmering object of desire and longing. The consequence of this cementing of signification into a centre/margin binary is the occlusion of any attempt to understand what other cultural trajectories and projects might have been engaged.

The social controversy surrounding modernism, however, focused on two fronts, the Nietzschian vitalism of the *Vision* school[26] and the institutionalisation of the Heidelberg tradition of landscape painting in the Australian Academy of Art. The Academy – proposed and supported by Robert Menzies, the federal attorney general who was to become Australia's longest serving prime minister – provided government support for the arts at the cost of cultural conformity; it would not only 'set standards for the work' but also 'raise the standards of public taste by directing attention to good work'. In Menzies' opinion, much of modernity 'consisted in doing all the things that Rembrandt would not have done, and to be really original the artist had to paint a face in the form of cabbage and vice versa'. Menzies' comments on modern art point out the extent to which both sides of the argument were deeply embedded in Eurocentric cultural values. Where modernism was widely held to mean the importation of a European paradigm shift, resistance to it in Australia was couched in terms of the timelessness and universalism of moral and artistic values best represented in the European Masters. In a letter to the *Argus* in 1937 Menzies wrote:

> I find nothing but absurdity in much so-called 'modern art', with its evasion of real problems and its cross-eyed drawing … I think that in art beauty is the condition of immortality – a conclusion strengthened by an examination of the works of the great European Masters – and that the language of beauty ought to be understood by reasonably cultivated people who are not themselves artists.[27]

Menzies' Eurocentrism reached the status of a virtual manifesto in his maintenance of Britishness, but the Eurocentrism of the vitalist school represented by Lionel Lindsay was more complex. For Lindsay, Australia's provincialism – an art that Somerset Maugham called 'old fashioned' on seeing the 1923 British Academy exhibition – was something Australia could offer the world. Yet, paradoxically, that 'difference' was something Australia inherited from a long tradition of European art. In his catalogue essay for that exhibition he replied that 'if to be alive is to be one of the Red Army of art that has trampled upon the great tradition we inherit from the Greeks, then

I am thankful for the appellation, and find in Mr Maugham's implication of provincialism a delicate compliment.'[28] Provincialism offered 'escape from all the revolutionary manias of a rotted world' and left Australia 'unaffected by the stunt art that has ravaged the older civilizations'.[29]

The use of the term 'modernism' as the site of a social and cultural controversy in Australia has made it difficult to dislodge from cultural discourse. Although the contest over the social phenomenon of modernism is limited to the domain of high culture, it is nevertheless invested with the often bitterly fought cultural political agendas of the time and epitomises the struggles over Australian identity which preoccupied various cultural elites. The conventional narrative of Australian modernism, its belatedness, its rearguard action fought in the quarantined culture, sees it as principally an issue of the inheritance of European style, in most cases an inheritance devoid of any sophisticated understanding. Australian modernism is usually restricted to a phenomenon of Australian culture between the wars, a discrete and apparently discontinuous period which bore little relation to the dominant concerns of Australian cultural history. Such an assumption has very little to say about the kinds of concerns that 'modernist' artists and writers were exploring in their work, or the cultural basis of the images they were producing. The situation is further complicated by the fact that very often the artists' own sense of their professional identities was confused by the intense pressure to see their work in the context of European models. But when we look at the concerns their work was addressing we see that, far from being a discrete period in Australian cultural life, modernist artists were intimately involved in the struggle to develop a mode of cultural self-representation, a struggle which had dominated the work of artists and writers before them. Indeed it is the very tactic of talking about these concerns in terms of a universalising and chronologically hierarchical discourse which prevents any real understanding of these concerns. Australian 'modernism' was neither less nor more than the European model, neither prior nor belated. It locates a range of cultural practices characterised by a profound difference from that model, a different agenda, a different range of interests, purposes, content and strategies.

From its first appearance modernism offended the vitalist tendencies of Australian culture,[30] the *Vision* group, for example, seeing it as cultural decadence. Modernism is often seen as an outgrowth of the symbolist[31] poetry movement in late-nineteenth-century France, particularly when works draw attention to their form and use forms and language which obscure their subject.[32] This clash of symbolism with vitalism[33] produced decades of anti-modernism in Australia which found its first focus in art – as in the opening lines of Lionel Lindsay's book *Addled Art* (1942): 'Modernism in art is a freak, not a natural, evolutional growth. Its causes lie in the spirit of the age that separates this century from all others.'[34] Anti-modernism did not really turn its attention to literature in Australia until after modernism found a focal point in the *Angry Penguins* movement. In art Australian modernism has its origins in the very early decades of this century, but concerned mainly the works of women artists.[35] The mainstream tradition was impressionist landscape[36] as painted by (male) artists such as Tom Roberts, Elioth Gruner and Arthur Streeton, a nationalist tradition loosely referred to as the Heidelberg School, after a camp where its major exponents briefly resided in the 1880s.[37] But by the time of the Second World War 'modern' artists had combined with 'modern' writers in the *Angry Penguins*, an Adelaide journal which ran from 1940 to 1946.[38] And the full wrath of the powerful anti-modernist tradition came down upon it.

The *Angry Penguins* movement declined rapidly after the Ern Malley hoax.[39] Founder Max Harris attributed the movement's rise to the environment of the Second World War and its disappearance to the 'dispersal of forces' that followed the Malley fiasco.[40] But modernism in Australian literature (and art) outlived anti-modernism.[41] As recently as 1991 John Tranter and Philip Mead included some of the work of hoax poet Ern Malley in *The Penguin Book of Modern Australian Poetry*, describing him as a 'ghostly presence'. They also locate the Ern Malley nadir as the origins of literary modernism in Australia,[42] whereas *Angry Penguins* founder, Max Harris, described the process of the survival of modernism in Australia in terms of changing politico-cultural agendas of the academy and the commodification of literature.

Today the pendulum has swung and many Australian writers and works are thought of *unquestioningly* as 'modern'.[43] Eleanor Dark's *The Little Company* (1945), for example, has been termed modern no doubt because of its concern with the city.[44] But Dark's *Prelude to Christopher* (1934) is also seen as modern because of the way it can be read as an allegory of mid-twentieth-century Australian society, which was itself modernising.[45] And Christina Stead's *For Love Alone* (1944) is modern because, it seems, the protagonist's escape from Australia to England may be read as a rite of passage that parallels the kind of escape from constriction that characterises modernism itself.[46] Among the many other examples which have had the mantle of modernism thrust unquestioningly upon them are Patrick White, Kenneth Slessor, Marjory Barnard, Elizabeth Harrower and Elizabeth Jolley, to name but a few.[47]

## Modernism and the discourse of place

The feature of modernist practice that has been submerged beneath the focus on modernism as a cultural controversy, as a watershed of innovation, is the concern with place. Place does not merely denote landscape but refers to the process of representation itself; it refers to the struggle of a displaced society trying to find the words and the images with which it might constitute a reality that was separate, marked by difference rather than diversity. The impressionism of the Heidelberg School had established a way of seeing that place which struck a chord in those seeking an original representation. The revolutionary nature of this representation, however, ossified very quickly into a tradition. By the end of the First World War, according to conventional history, artists rebelling against this tradition sought new inspiration in the modernist styles of Europe.

The venue for modernist departures in Australia was the conservative Julian Ashton Art School in Sydney. From 1898 the more open spirit was fostered in classes run by Anthony Dattilo Rubbo, whose students included Norah Simpson, Roland Wakelin, Grace Cossington Smith and Roy de Maistre.[48] Cossington Smith's *The Sock Knitter* (1915) and Wakelin's *Down the Hill to Berry's Bay* (1916) are two of the earliest modernist paintings.[49] Though hardly revolutionary, they demonstrate how concerns about the ways in which the subject is located in place persisted into modernist painting despite the gradual development in style. 'In an art world that still held naturalism to be axiomatic', says Allen, 'the conceptual reversal entailed by such a stylistic shift had something of the copernican.'[50]

The dominant tendency of modernist discourse, and that of art history as well, is to see the revolution in style as an end in itself.

But with all the innovative directions and exploratory interests of modern artists (for instance, Wakelin and de Maistre became interested in the use of colour to treat mental disorders, and investigated the link between colour and music), a continuing issue for artists between the wars was 'what does it mean to be alive in this place?' The experiments with colour and form, the move to abstraction and surrealism, the political battles which surrounded the concept of the modern at this time, did not lessen the impact of this question. That view of the landscape painting of the time as lacking 'deeply founded conviction',[51] or as producing images that seemed 'to exist somewhat ambivalently to their time and place, in spite of all attempts at topical references, local scenery or flora, and even indigenous style', misapprehends the struggle necessarily engaged in order to find a form of representation not dominated by received Eurocentric, and particularly Anglocentric, conceptions.

To some extent, of course, the reconception of place involved an increasingly higher profile for urban space, which seemed to embody the values and effects of modernisation, mechanisation and technology. The photography of Max Dupain, for instance, represents the fascination with the angles and surfaces of the industrialised city. This concern for urban space glided very easily into politically committed views of urban work and poverty in the painting of Yosl Bergner's *Aborigines at Fitzroy* (1941), Albert Tucker's *Spring in Fitzroy* (1941) or *Futile City* (1940), or his *Images of Modern Evil* series (1943–46), and Noel Counihan's *At the Meeting 1932* (1944).[52] The theme of work as a focus of the 'subject in place' is just as important as it was for the Heidelberg painters of the 1890s. But now the idealisation of human struggle with rural space, the individual's encounter with the land, is replaced by a view of work 'as the basis for human community',[53] and in particular its absence as a cause of social injustice and dislocation.

## Re-visioning place: Sidney Nolan and Arthur Boyd

The analysis of Australian cultural activity as a palimpsest of interactive responses to the problems of post-colonial place, and particularly of the post-colonial subject in place, disrupts the conventional historicist view of a discrete period of Australian modernism. Thus we can see that the era of the *Angry Penguins*, the era dominated by

Arthur Boyd, Sidney Nolan and Russell Drysdale, rather than a 're-discovery of the landscape', is built upon concerns that had persisted since the mid-nineteenth century. Nolan's comment that 'I gradually forgot all about Picasso, Klee and Paris … and became attached to light'[54] demonstrates how crucial it was for these artists to liberate their professional identities as well as their techniques.

Nolan's best known 'rediscovery' is the figure of Ned Kelly, the 'most important metaphor of an Australian relationship with the land since the Heidelberg settler'.[55] Although Kelly is an unambiguous mythic hero in Australian cultural life, Nolan 'preserves and enhances the ambivalence of the bushranger. He remains the antithesis of the settler: he does not work and he does not settle.'[56] Possibly the most powerful expression of this ambivalence is *Ned Kelly* (1946) (Plate 3) in which the view of the sky through the helmet remains a potent metonym of post-colonial displacement, an ambivalent combination of harmony and alienation, of location and dislocation. In some respects the subject of this painting is representation itself, the sense of an ambivalence exacerbated by the inheritance of forms of representation which are 'out of place' in post-colonial space. The painting appropriates the myth and displaces it, appropriates 'modern' forms of representation and disrupts them.

With Arthur Boyd we see even more clearly the process of appropriation. Many of his early paintings were strange transitional pictures which appropriated European or religious myths and concerns to an Australian setting. In *The Mockers* (1945) the Crucifixion in the background is dominated by the figure of an old king. Pictures such as this and *Melbourne Burning* (1946) are reminiscent of Brueghel in their massed figures and restless movement. But in *The Expulsion* (1947), which depicts Adam and Eve being expelled from a Garden of Eden in the Australian bush, we see a more concentrated example of the process of appropriation. Here the importation of the myth into the Australian bush is less an example of a colonial re-enactment than it is a post-colonial assertion of displacement and ambivalence. In the curious sense of displacement which the picture engenders we find an examination of the whole question of the appropriateness of European discourse in post-colonial space.

This is even more obvious in Boyd's rose paintings. In the late 1970s Boyd produced a series of four paintings[57] which share the symbols of the river and (with one exception) the rose, usually brightly

**Plate 3**   Sidney Nolan, *Ned Kelly* (1946)

coloured and suspended in the sky above the landscape. The four works obviously form a set, yet two of the four (*Crucifixion, Shoalhaven* and *Crucifixion and Rose*) have been separated from the set and read as 'religious' art.[58] This separation means that two of the works now function entirely within a separate discourse, a genre which includes some of Boyd's early works such as *The Mining Town* (1946–47), some works by Leonard French, Eric Smith and many other well-known Australian artists. This reorganisation of Boyd's oeuvre is indicative of what we might call the 'imperial' operation of Eurocentric cultural categories, reorganising Australian culture to confirm its links with the long tradition of Anglo-European religious art – a 'thematic category … as ancient as art itself'.[59] Not only does this reorganisation of Boyd's set of paintings obscure the themes they share; it also obscures the specific cultural relevance they bear to the experience of everyday life in Australia. A corollary to this lies in the inclusion of a selection of 'Aboriginal' works in the same category of 'religious art'.[60] An inclusion of this kind in a European cultural category 'as ancient as art itself' clearly suggests that the reorganisation and appropriation of Australian culture is a continuous process. The main problem with this is that the category 'religious art' cannot account for either Boyd's or the Aboriginal works. It cannot explain, for instance, why the crucifixions depicted by Boyd are *in* the river or why one of the figures on the cross is female, or why the rose should be floating in the river.[61] Yet these things require little explanation once universalist European cultural categories are dropped and the works related more directly to Australian experience. A rereading should begin with the obvious: the rose, icon of England, simply does not fit in the context of the Australian place.

In the earliest of these four paintings, *River in Flood with Carcass and Rose* (1974–75) (Plate 4), two disparate symbols, the rose and the carcass, are simply juxtaposed. But the work does more than 'contrast' the symbols. It interrogates them. Boyd wrote about this painting: 'The rose symbolises imposition and the cultural arrogance of the English as they tried to make 'a little England' in Australia. I was trying to show the fragility of transporting this culture into such a harsh environment. The rose and carcass are contrasting symbols.'[62] The rose looks as though it has been simply added to the background of the sky in this painting, or perhaps suspended over the landscape. But these are symbols of two different *orders*. They are not related but, rather, *forced* together and held by the frame of the painting.

This theme of incompatibility is enlarged in *Shoalhaven River with Rose, Burning Book and Aeroplane* (1976) (Plate 5), which contains a much more complex iconography of the landscape. The rose again appears suspended, but this time in a much smaller sky where it seems to hover. Boyd has pointed to the incompatibility between the rose and the landscape in this painting: 'The rose represents the desperate attempts of the Europeans to impose their civilisation and culture on an essentially primitive landscape. It always floats because it cannot take root. If it does, it destroys, like lantana.'[63] Thus *Shoalhaven River with Rose, Burning Book and Aeroplane* may be recognised as a portrayal of the impossibility of a symbiotic relationship between this place and a simple transplantation of the culture of England/Europe. The icon of the floating rose, rather than the rose firmly attached to the soil, and the fact that it has been floating in this way for two centuries, further illustrates this impossibility.

**Plate 4** Arthur Boyd, *River in Flood with Carcass and Rose* (1974–5)

The final two of these four paintings are the most enigmatic. They not only reveal the falsity of colonial assumption of place (of an England transported) but also attempt to imagine or reconceive the place *without* the metaphoric rose: as a sort of direct, or unmediated (by the cultural assumptions of England/Europe), link between white Australia and the earth of this place. A (white) Australia of this sort has never yet existed. In *Crucifixion and Rose* the crucified figure has none of the 'grace' or 'beauty' or 'modesty' of his Renaissance counterparts. These are the kinds of things the rose symbolises, and they are absent. Thus the rose is floating, half submerged in the river.

But this is not simply the portrayal of the death of (European) 'beauty'; it is the portrayal of the death of a particular (European) conception of 'reality'. The river seems benign in this painting, but this is the same river that threw up the carcass in *River in Flood with Carcass and Rose* (1974–5), causing such havoc and loss. *Crucifixion and Rose* is the portrayal of 'European Man', stripped of all artifice and veneer. The rose, having failed to take root, has itself perished in this place. In the naked figure of *Crucifixion and Rose* is the resolution; the bringing together of the two disparate icons of *River in Flood with Carcass and Rose*. This is a death, but there is a companion painting, *Crucifixion, Shoalhaven*, which mitigates the death. In this painting, the figure is a woman. Boyd remarked that one critic referred to these two paintings as 'his' and 'her' crucifixions.[64] The two texts may be read together, but not to the exclusion of the other two.

The two significant points of the 'her' crucifixion is the absence of the rose and the fact that the figure is now female. This is not a portrayal of death, but of birth or rebirth, as in a resurrection. The texts of these four paintings together suggests that the new will be born out of the destruction of the old. Transposing this notion to questions of Australian identity suggest, further, that the new will have an authenticity linked with this place that the old (symbolised by the hovering rose) could never attain.

The category 'modernism' is irrelevant to these readings, but, more importantly, having 'found' new meanings, for one set of works, outside, or placed tangentially to, the orthodox cultural categories, the way is left open for others. The further point is that many of these extra-category meanings tend to intersect and overlap because the works are now circulating within other language-games. Such an

**Plate 5**   Arthur Boyd, *Shoalhaven River with Rose,
Burning Book and Aeroplane* (1976)

affinity is shared by the Boyd 'rose' paintings and Sidney Nolan's *Ned Kelly* paintings.[65] Rather than a figure in the landscape, that black geometrical representation of Kelly suggests a piece cut out, or missing, from it. This is an ontologically ambiguous representation. And in those Kelly paintings which do not have eyes in the eye slit, where one can see the landscape through the eye slit, there is a clear sense of seeing the place as it might appear from within the mask. But what is this mask of armour which separates being from the place, if not the limitations of Anglo-European perception?

Both Nolan's Ned Kelly and Boyd's roses suggest relationships with place other than those conceptualised within the Anglo-European tradition. And this theme is to be found everywhere in Australian art and literature. With those categories a jump from 'art' to 'literature' is usually only accomplished by showing one illustrating the other. But the theme of the-ambiguous-figure-in-an-alien-place is actually enhanced by that art/literature jump. An example of this occurs in David Malouf's *Harland's Half Acre*. The protagonist Frank Harland, modelled broadly on Australian artist Ian Fairweather, discovers that to represent the place (and the subject-in-place) in art, he must begin from a black or uncoloured page (premiss) rather than the uninscribed 'white' page.[66]

These works illustrate the continuity and reciprocity between various formations of Australian cultural production. They also illustrate how categories such as 'modernism' really only serve to reorganise works, disturb existing relationships, and create a space for Anglo-European cultural preference. A complex example occurs in the works of Patrick White, who quite early in his career was seen as 'modern'. In most cases this simply meant that an author did not write in the realist mode. For example, when White's novel *Voss* (1957) first appeared, realist writer Katharine Prichard saw it, compared it with Vance Palmer's *Seedtime* (which appeared in the same year), and said it was 'anaemic and completely out of tune with an Australian atmosphere and environment'.[67] But *Voss* was always a 'difficult' novel.[68] It became even more 'difficult' when Richard Meale (1988) turned it into an opera with a libretto written by David Malouf.

Malouf's *Voss* offended the expectations of the Eurocentric category of opera. It failed because it did 'not add up to credible operatic language'.[69] And for those who thought it succeeded, it did so because it conformed to the (universalist) expectations of opera.[70]

Yet here again, the categories of Anglo-European culture not only provide an exceptionally narrow understanding of *Voss* the opera but also serve to conceal the network of themes the work shares with other Australian cultural works and themes. The point is that when the text is taken out of the language-game of (European) culture and allowed to circulate within other contexts – such as Boyd's roses or Nolan's Ned Kellys or any of the Malouf works – new meanings emerge. Ultimately, these all echo the concerns of those works cited earlier of ambiguities in the relationship between the subject and place of existence. They are all attempts to *re-imagine* a new subject and a new place. And this is eloquently portrayed in *Voss* the opera. The opera is in two acts. The first act is set in Sydney in the 1830s – the known world. The second act is set in the unknown world – the bush where Voss and the party are to go on their fateful expedition. The known is the world of Mr Bonner and his family: England-transported to the antipodes. Metaphorically it is the perceptual 'armour' depicted in Nolan's *Ned Kelly*. Its preferences and formality and glitter obscure the other world: the one Voss plans to 'discover'. It is also, to use Boyd's metaphor, the rose that strangles all other perceptions of place.

## Women and modernism

The most fascinating aspect of the modernist reconception of place between the wars is the fact that it was the women artists and writers who made the most innovative advances. This is significant because they tended to be greatly underrepresented in exhibitions and in commentary about the period, yet in Sydney particularly it was women who seemed best to appropriate the modern style. But the style is less important than the content of these paintings, which pivots on a complex interrelation of work, place and the body. Dorrit Black's *The Olive Plantation* (1946), which imposes a stylised art-deco aesthetic on the landscape, demonstrates the ways in which industrial technology could be appropriated to the task of reconceiving a place in which the location of the human subject is a matter of constant negotiation. The element of process and becoming is metonymised in Jessie Traill's and Cossington Smith's systematic documentation of the stages of the Sydney Harbour Bridge's construction. Certainly the bridge was a potent symbol of national achievement at the time;

yet in the depictions of its construction there is something much more, because much less than the finished bridge, for it was only during its construction that the bridge attracted such attention. The paintings made a statement of affirmation of the human work involved, but also articulated the process of occupying place, of reconstructing place, which itself lay at the core of the problems of its representation.

In contrast to the dominantly male style of impressionist landscape, which had ossified by this time into a nationalist tradition, the landscapes by Cossington Smith in works such as *Eastern Road, Turrumurra* (1926) and *Landscape at Pentecost* (1929) painted a picture of unsettled, almost liminal space, of 'farmland turning into suburbia, clusters of houses encroaching on fields, telegraph poles stretching half-way down the hill like scarecrows and then stopping for no reason'.[71] The inter-war period, in which the innovativeness of Wakelin and de Maistre seems ultimately to have retreated before the conservative onslaught, saw women artists and women writers providing the most powerful images, the most concerted exploration of the question of place itself.

It is in this activity that we find an uncanny fusion of the interests of feminist discourse and post-coloniality. For Proctor, Traill, Black, Preston, Cossington-Smith and many other women at the time were operating at the very juncture at which 'writing the body' and 'writing place' merge. The persistent need in post-colonial culture is to reconceive the lived space in which difference is focused. This need to write out of a sense of place is remarkably germane to the exhortations of *écriture feminine* for women to 'write the body'. Hélène Cixous says:

> Woman must write herself: must write about women and bring women to writing, from which they have been driven away as violently as from their bodies – for the same reasons, by the same law, with the same fatal goal. Woman must put herself into the text – as into the world and into history – by her own movement.[72]

If we see 'writing' as a metaphor for representation we can see that a complex fusion of processes occurs in the work of women 'modernists' in Australia. For the body can be written in various ways, yet it seems that in post-colonial settler cultures the problems of writing the body and writing place merge most formidably. Women

**Plate 6** Margaret Preston, *Aboriginal Landscape* (1941)

must write their bodies by reconceiving the body as a site of difference. There is no primordial self, no original place to be recovered; rather, these must be reinvented in the creation of some 'original relationship with the universe'.[73] Hence the fascination of female modernists for images of process, for in process it seemed lay the secrets of representing this original relation. This is because the 'original relation' is not a 'return' to European origins. The relation between the people and the land is new, as is that between the imported language and the land, so the 'original' relationship, like the language, must be created anew. Women must re-create their own original relationship with the excluded and negated subjectivity located in their bodies. This explains something of the element of ambivalence, transition and process characterising the depictions of the building of the harbour bridge or of streets that are neither rural nor yet quite urban. It also explains why women artists and writers in Australia, at the same time as they are making stylistic advances, are the ones wrestling most urgently with questions of location and subjectivity.

It is at this point that the merging of women's attempts to write the body with their attempts to 'write place' – to conceive in the metaphor of process a way of reconceiving, re-creating an originary relationship with the universe – overlaps with the incorporation of indigenous images and forms. It is not only women in the 1930s and 1940s who appropriated aboriginality in the task of 'constructing indigeneity', but it is certainly women, particularly Margaret Preston who created the most striking images of post-colonial hybridity in these decades. Of course this appropriation, whatever its intentions, has been recognised as deeply ambiguous, since the attempt to reconceive post-colonial place and subjectivity within a hybridised aesthetic runs the risk of submerging aboriginal identity. But it is significant in its depiction of the broader strategy of constructing indigeneity in settler colonies.

The Aborigine, even as a subject, had been eclipsed from the time of Heidelberg, and the idea of drawing inspiration from their art was a radical departure from notions of cultural essentialism. Margaret Preston, who 'discovered' Aboriginal art in the 1930s, reflected the interests of the Jindyworobaks in believing that here was the key to an original Australian art.[74] Her painting *Aboriginal Landscape* (1941) (Plate 6) is in many respects, like the paintings of the construction of the Harbour Bridge, a representation of a cultural process and a signification of social possibility. In one sense a depiction of the kind of primitivism which underlay ideas about Australia's precocious modernism, the painting is remarkable for what it cannot say, as much as for the image of possibility it represents. As a painting, it has nowhere to go, no school, no tradition to initiate. But as a representation of the land as 'place', an inhabited space in which peoples of various origins must reach some way of constituting their own reality, their own post-colonial 'originality' freed of the weight of tradition, it is striking. The very inability of the painting to foreshadow a counter-tradition is a gesture towards the possibility of a process of representation that at least believes it can shake itself free of tradition. This remarkable confluence of *jouissance*, place and indigeneity is a far more interesting and productive than the discourse of 'modernism' can suggest. It is the very excess, the constant surplus of such cultural representation, which categories such as modernism serve to obscure in their incorporation of post-colonial reality into a universalist aesthetic.

The concept of modernism has been such a battleground for social and class interests in Australia that, whether conceived as the site of social controversy or as an innovative aesthetic, its 'imperial' function of confirming the myth of colonial marginality and backwardness has entered the Australian psyche. If there is a 'heart' to Australian modernism it lies in its most provisional and heterogeneous expression: the efforts of those women artists and writers who strove to write the body, write place to construct their indigeneity through the appropriation of images of process and discovery. The struggle to conceive ways of representing Australian place and the subject in place has always been a struggle against imperial forms of reality construction. Whatever the modern means in Australia, it is ultimately in the excess of self-representation and the horizontality of place that the 'modernity' of its construction of reality can come into being. This is the surplus which continually resists the cultural imperialism of style.

## Notes

1 One of the best sources for information on the issues and background of the Australian republican debate is to be found at http://www.edfac. usyd.edu.au/staff/souters/republic.html. For the party politics that lay behind the Convention, see Innes Wilcox, 'Elections 96', *Age* (22 February 1996) 12, also at http://www.theage.com.au/republic96/elect96. html.

2 A comprehensive coverage of the Australian Native Title debate will be found at http://headlines.yahoo.com/Full_Coverage/aunz/native_title. A synopsis will be found at http://www.smh.com.au/daily/content/ features/features/970503/features4.html. And for an insight into the party politics associated with Native Title that influence the Australian Republican debate, see Margo Kingston, 'Canadian Apology "Irrelevant"', *Sydney Morning Herald*, 9 January 1998. Also at http://www.smh. com.au/daily/content/980109/pageone/pageone1.html.

3 Anthony Giddens, *The Consequences of Modernity* (Cambridge, Polity Press, 1990), p. 6.

4 Mary Louise Pratt, *Imperial Eyes: Travel Writing and Transculturation* (London, Routledge, 1992), p. 228.

5 Jürgen Habermas, 'Modernity – an incomplete project', in Hal Foster

    (ed.), *Postmodern Culture* (Sydney, Pluto, 1983).

6  T. S. Eliot, 'Tradition and the individual talent', (1919), in Frank Kermode
    (ed.), *Selected Prose of T. S. Eliot* (London, Faber & Faber, 1975) pp. 37–
    44.

7  Wittgenstein describes language-games in *Philosophical Investigations*
    (Oxford, Blackwell, 1963). See especially Numbers 65–67.

8  T. S. Eliot, review of James Joyce's *Ulysses*, *The Dial*, November 1923.

9  John Barth, *The Literature of Exhaustion and the Literature of Replenishment*
    (Northridge, Lord John Press, 1982), p. 68.

10  Ricardo Quinones, *Mapping Literary Modernism* (Princeton, Princeton
    University Press, 1985), p. 121.

11  Christopher Allen, *Art in Australia: From Colonization to Postmodernism*
    (London, Thames & Hudson, 1998), p.98.

12  *Ibid.*

13  *Ibid.*

14  Andrew Milner, 'Postmodernism and popular culture', in S. Alomes and
    D. den Hartog, *Post Pop: Popular Culture, Nationalism and Postmodernism*
    (Footscray, Victoria, Footprint, 1991), pp. 46–57.

15  David Carter, 'Modernity and belatedness in Australian cultural dis-
    course', *Southerly*, 54:4 (1994–5) 9.

16  *Ibid.*

17  *Ibid.*, p. 8.

18  *Ibid.*, pp. 12–13.

19  *Ibid.*, p. 14.

20  John Williams, *Quarantined Culture: Australian Reactions to Modernism, 1913–
    1939* (Cambridge, Cambridge University Press 1995), p. 5.

21  *Ibid.*, p. 6.

22  In 1927, Lionel Lindsay was 'honoured to propose the toast on etching'
    at the Royal Academy and proceeded to villify modernism, behind which
    he said lurked the spectre of the Jew, as the corruption responsible for
    all the ills of British society. 'What is wrong with your public and the
    times? You all know the reason – this malady of modern art. And who
    is to blame for the continental infection?- the press and a people that
    England has so long welcomed, the Jews. I am no Anti-Semite ... but
    I am decidely hostile to the dealers who bribe a corrupt press.' Lionel
    Lindsay, *Comedy of Life: An Autobiography* (Sydney, Angus & Robertson,
    1967), p. 259. The alliance of futurism with Judaic bolshevism was 'well
    established' says Williams, 'the standard inter-war critiques of modernist
    art were already evident in March 1919: it was a fad that would soon go
    away; it was made by rootless, urban cosmopolitans with foreign sound-
    ing names, people who set themselves apart from the world of true
    beauty that lay in the countryside; its value was inflated out of all pro-
    portion by a few dealers, who often, like [Picasso's dealer] Kahnweiler,
    were of Jewish origin' (*Quarantined Culture*, p. 161).

23  Williams, *Quarantined Culture*, p. 29.

24  *Ibid.*, p. 7.

25  *Ibid.*

26  *Vision* was a Sydney periodical edited by Jack Lindsay, Kenneth Slessor and Frank Johnson. It published only four issues in 1923–24 but was very influential. It was both anti-modernist and anti-nationalist. Major contributors were the editors, Norman Lindsay, Hugh McCrae, R. D. Fitzgerald and others. This group of artists and writers had no liking for Australian cultural life and their method of injecting doses of Nietzschian 'Dionysian' vitalism into Australian life was to paint pictures of fauns and satyrs prancing through the Australian bush.

27  Robert Menzies, reply to letter from Norman McGeorge, *Argus* (3 May 1937). *Herald* (Melbourne) (4 May 1937); *Argus* (28 April 1937); *Age* (28 April 1937); *Argus* (3 May 1937).

28  Lionel Lindsay, 'Australian Art', *The Exhibition of Australian Art in London 1923: A Record of the Exhibition Held at the Royal Academy and Organised by the Society of Artists, Sydney* (Sydney, 1923), p. 168.

29  *Ibid.*

30  See further: 'Modernism in Europe was a response to the authoritarian and materialist beliefs of the nineteenth century but in Australia it was also a reaction against the widespread acceptance of vitalism and deterministic Darwinism.' Julian Croft, 'Responses to modernism, 1925–1965', in L. Hergenhan (ed.), *The Penguin New Literary History of Australia* (Ringwood, Victoria, Penguin, 1988), p. 412.

31  See Edmund Wilson, *Axel's Castle: A Study in the Imaginative Literature of 1870–1930* (1931; New York, Scribner, 1959). Irving Howe cited the ambitions of the Symbolists as: 'a) to create an autotelic realm of experience in their poetry, with a minimum of references back or correspondence to the external world, and with an effort to establish the effect of formal coherence through an epiphany of impression; b) to abandon for the most part logical structures and to create a revelation of insight as a substitute for orderly and formal resolutions; c) to depend heavily on the associations of images, sometimes on kinesthesia and dissonance of images; d) and thereby make the writing of the poem itself into the dominant matter of the poem', 'Introduction, the idea of modernism', in Irving Howe (ed.), *Literary Modernism* (New York, Fawcett, 1967), p. 29.

32  See further: 'Formal experiment may frequently be a consequence or corollary of modernism, but its presence is not a sufficient condition for seeing a writer or work as modernist.' Howe, 'Introduction', p. 22.

33  Modernism in Australia has also been thought of as a synonym for vitalism. Michael Roe, for example, referred to the period 1890 to 1914 as 'an era of extraordinary ferment for European culture and intellect – a ferment perhaps best labelled 'the onslaught of vitalism' (although

'modernism' would do well enough)', Michael Roe, *Nine Australian Progressives, Vitalism in Bourgois Social Thought 1890–1960* (St Lucia, Queensland, University of Queensland Press, 1984), p. 1.

34 Lionel Lindsay, *Addled Art* (Sydney, Angus & Robertson, 1942), p. 1.

35 See Janine Burke, *Australian Women Artists, 1840–1940* (Collingwood, Victoria, Greenhouse Publications, 1980).

36 See further: 'Conservatism is inevitably a rearguard action, and the fight, in the face of change, became more and more desparate ... What ought to have been clear was that the old establishment was in its death throes and a new one was being born', Richard Haese, *Rebels and Precursors, The Revolutionary Years of Australian Art* (Ringwood, Victoria, Penguin, 1981), p. 4. See also Humphrey McQueen, *The Black Swan of Trespass: The Emergence of Modernist Painting in Australia to 1944* (Sydney, Alternative Publishing, 1979).

37 For Roberts's work, see Virgina Spate, *Tom Roberts* (revised edn; East Melbourne, Lansdowne, 1978). For Gruner, see Barry Pearce, *Elioth Gruner 1882–1939* (Sydney, Art Gallery of New South Wales, 1983). For Streeton, see Ann Galbally, *Arthur Streeton* (East Melbourne, Lansdowne, 1979).

38 *Angry Penguins* was initially sponsored by the Adelaide University Arts Association but was soon taken over entirely by Max Harris and John Reed and published from Melbourne. The journal declared itself anti-political and was wide-ranging. Its articles dealt with art, literature, jazz, cinema and the visual arts. Among its contributors were Sidney Nolan, Albert Tucker, Arthur Boyd, Geoffrey Dutton and Peter Cowan. The journal ceased in the wake of the Ern Malley hoax.

39 In 1944 academics James McAuley and Harold Stewart sent poems to *Angry Penguins* under the pretence that they were the work of a recently deceased insurance salesman and mechanic, Ern Malley. The accompanying letter was supposedly from Malley's sister. The editors of *Angry Penguins* published the poems, believing them to be genuine and of great literary merit. The hoax was discovered by the press and the perpetrators publicly confessed that they had simply 'opened books at random, choosing a word or phrase haphazardly. We made lists of these and wove them into nonsensical sentences. We misquoted and made false allusions.' The purpose of the hoax was not particularly to embarrass Max Harris but to redress a 'literary fashion' (i.e. modernism) whose distinctive feature was, in the hoaxers' words, 'that it rendered its devotees insensible of absurdity and incapable of ordinary discrimination'. M. Harris and J. Murray-Smith, *Ern Malley* (Sydney, Allen & Unwin, 1988) p. 6.

40 London literature and art critic Herbert Read became involved when he supported the Ern Malley poems. Also Harris was prosecuted by the South Australian police, and eventually fined, for publishing indecent

material. Some of the farcical testimony of Detective Vogelsang is recorded in Harris and Murray-Smith, *Ern Malley*, pp. 12–13.

41 Harris distinguished between the demise of *Angry Penguins* and the future of Australian modernism. 'Australia was now part of the ebb and
flow of modernism ... The concept of modernism was being validated
day by day despite McAuley and the others. The galleries were buying
modernist paintings, *New Directions* and other foreign publications wanted
the poems that were being written, including my own ... Australian
modernism was taking off.' Harris and Murray-Smith, *Ern Malley*, pp.
44–5.

42 Tranter and Mead, in fact, locate the origins of modern Australian poetry
in the work of Kenneth Slessor. Slessor's last two books were published
in 1939 and 1944. The latter, as they also point out, is the same year of
the Ern Malley hoax. J. Tranter and P. Mead (eds), *The Penguin Book of
Modern Australian Poetry* (Ringwood, Victoria, Penguin, 1991).

43 Joseph Furphy's *Such Is Life* (1903) has been read as a postmodern novel.
See Anastasia Anderson, 'The postmodern position: a reading of Furphy's
*Such Is Life*', *Imago: New Writings*, 9:2 (1997) 65–75.

44 Croft, 'Responses to modernism', p. 422. This is also the reason Slessor
is often thought of as modern. Cf.: '[Slessor's poetry] for the first time
in Australian poetry is a voice like some of those we hear around us
from day to day ... The neon-lit urban streets filled with busy traffic
and anonymous crowds, the mournful sounds of the city harbour at
night – these are the modern landscapes of discontinuity and doubt.'
Tranter and Mead (eds), *Modern Australian Poetry*, p. xxviii.

45 See further: '[T]he novels of Eleanor Dark show clearly the acclimati-
sation of this mode [modernism] in Australia ... Dark in this novel and
*The Little Company* (1945) showed that the modernist tradition in the
novel was as much at home in Katoomba where she lives.' Croft, 'Responses to Modernism', p. 422.

46 See further: 'Teresa Hawkins ... escapes first from the constriction of
her family and then from an emotionally parasitic lover to find freedom.
In this novel Stead celebrates the notion of a rite of passage – to somewhere out of the parental (or more specifically, paternal) Australia – and
like Eleanor Dark conveys both the social oppression and natural freedom of the Australian environment.' Croft, 'Responses to Modernism',
p. 423.

47 For Patrick White, see for example A. Chaman, 'Modernism in Patrick
White's plays – an exercise in synthesis', *Literary Half-Yearly*, 11:4 (1975);
or V. Brady, 'Making things appear: Patrick White and the politics of
modernism', *Island*, 52 (Spring 1992). For Kenneth Slessor, see A. Taylor,
*Reading Australian Poetry* (St Lucia, Queensland, University of Queensland Press 1987); or V. Smith, 'Australian modernism: the case of Kenneth Slessor', in Margaret Harris and Elizabeth Webby (eds), *Reconnoitres:*

*Essays in Australian Literature* (South Melbourne, Victoria, Sydney University Press and Oxford University Press, 1992). For Marjory Barnard, see Croft, 'Responses to modernism', p. 423. For Elizabeth Harrower, see N. Mansfield, '"The only Russian in Sydney": modernism and realism in *The Watch Tower*', *Australian Literary Studies* 15:3 (1992). And for Elizabeth Jolley, see for example J. Kirkby, 'The nights belong to Elizabeth Jolley, modernism and the Sappho-erotic imagination of *Miss Peabody's Inheritance*', *Meanjin*, 43:4 (1984).

48  See Heather Johnson, *Roy de Maistre: The Australian Years* (Melbourne, Craftsman House, 1988). For Nora Simpson, see Burke, *Australian Women Artists*.

49  See Bruce James, *Grace Cossington Smith* (Melbourne, Craftsman House, 1984). See also Lloyd Rees, 'Roland Wakelin's "Down the Hills to Berry bay"', *Art and Australia* (17 March 1980).

50  Allen, *Art in Australia*, p. 99.

51  *Ibid.*, p. 113.

52  For Tucker's works see James Mollison, *Albert Tucker* (Sydney, Macmillan, 1982). For Counihan, see Bernard Smith, *Noel Counihan – Artist and Revolutionary* (Melbourne, Oxford University Press, 1983). For Bergner, see Cecil Roth, *Jewish Art* (London, W. H. Allen, 1961).

53  Allen, *Art in Australia*, p. 118.

54  *Ibid.*, p. 125.

55  *Ibid.*, pp. 125–6.

56  *Ibid.*, p. 126.

57  *River in Flood with Carcass* (1974–75); *Shoalhaven River with Rose, Burning Book and Aeroplane* (1976); *Crucifixion, Shoalhaven* (1979–80); and *Crucifixion and Rose* (1979–80).

58  R. Crumlin, *Images of Religion in Australian Art* (Sydney, Bay Books, 1988).

59  M. Manion, 'Foreword' (1988) in *Ibid.*

60  These include *A Bush Tucker Story* (Johnny Warrangula Tjupurrula, 1973); *Rock Wallaby Dreaming* (Tim Leura Tjapaltjarri, 1982); *Moon Dreaming* (Tommy Lowry Tjapaltjarri, 1987); *Wagilag Ceremony* (Mathaman, 1963); and *Yarla Jukurrpa (Bush Potato Dreaming)* (Paddy Jupurrula Nelson and Larry Jungarrayi Spencer, 1986); *The Thunderman, Djambuwal* (Mitinari, 1951); *Old Man's Dreaming on Death or Destiny* (Old Mick Tjakamara, 1971); *Tngari Dreaming at Wilkinkarra* (Anatjari Tjampitjinpa, 1986); *Tingari Dreaming at Marra-pintinya* (Yala Yala Gibbs Tjungurrayi, 1982); and *Yarumayi Jukurrpa* (Jeannie Nungarrayi Egan, 1987).

61  See, for example, Sandra McGrath, *The Artist and the River: Arthur Boyd and the Shoalhaven* (Sydney, Bay Books, 1982). McGrath quoted Boyd on how the rose 'destroys like lantana'. But when he said this he was in fact referring to *Shoalhaven River with Rose, Burning Book and Aeroplane*, which was *not* one of the 'religious' works.

62  McGrath, *The Artist*, p. 262.

63 *Ibid.*, p. 272.

64 *Ibid.*, p. 254.

65 A selection of Nolan's 'Ned Kelly' series is available at http://www. netspace.net.au/~bradwebb/kelly5.html

66 David Malouf, *Harland's Half Acre* (Ringwood, Victoria, Penguin, 1985); see for example pp. 14, 114–27 and 175–8.

67 Katharine Susannah Prichard, 'Comment on *Voss* and *Seedtime*', *Overland* (Spring 1958) 14.

68 See, for example, James McAuley, 'The gothic splendors: Patrick White's *Voss*', *Southerly*, 25:1 (1965); G. A. Wilkes, 'A reading of Patrick White's *Voss*', *Southerly*, 27:3 (1967); Ingmar Björksten, *Patrick White: A General Introduction* (St Lucia, Queensland, University of Queensland Press, 1976); D. Tacey, *Patrick White, Fiction and the Unconscious* (Melbourne, Oxford University Press, 1988).

69 See, for example, Tom Suttcliffe, 'Lost in a great Australian desert', *Guardian Weekly* (26 April 1987) 18.

70 See, for example, B. Beresford, '*Voss*: the opera', *Quadrant* 30:5 (1986) 68–69; R. Covell, 'Exploring changes in *Voss*', *Sydney Morning Herald* (31 May 1986) 48; J. Koehne, 'Interiors/exteriors', *Age Monthly Review* (2 March 1987) 12–13; M. Ewans, '*Voss*: White, Malouf, Meale', *Meanjin*, 48:3 (1989) 513–25. Australian opera commentator and writer John Cargher once claimed (even after the production of *Voss*) that 'there is no such thing as "Australian music"', let alone "Australian opera", and there never will be'. J. Cargher, *Bravo! Two Hundred Years of Opera in Australia* (Sydney, Macmillan, 1988), p. 233.

71 Allen, *Art in Australia*, p. 105.

72 Hélène Cixous, 'The laugh of the Medusa', in Elaine Marks and Isabelle de Courtivron (eds), *New French Feminisms* (Brighton: Harvester, 1980), p. 245.

73 Ralph Waldo Emerson, 'Nature' (1836) in *Selections from Ralph Waldo Emerson*, ed., Stephen E. Whicher (Boston, Mass., Houghton Mifflin, 1956), p. 21.

74 The Jindyworobaks were an Australian nationalist cultural movement of the late 1930s–1950s. It was begun as a club in Adelaide by Rex Ingamells. In 1938 he published an essay entitled *Conditional Culture* which set out the aims and ambitions of the group. It advocated Aboriginal culture as the true source of Australian culture and saw the traditional language forms of imported Anglo-European literature as artificial and non-representative.

# Index

Note: Page references in *italics* indicate illustrations and figures; 'n' after a page reference indicates a note number on that page.